Delusion, and Detection

LANGUAGE AND LANGUAGE BEHAVIORS SERIES

Howard Giles

SERIES EDITOR

Department of Communication
University of California, Santa Barbara

This series is unique in its sociopsychological orientation to "language and language behaviors" and their communicative and miscommunicative consequences. Books in the series not only examine how biological, cognitive, emotional, and societal forces shape the use of language, but the ways in which language behaviors can create and continually revise understandings of our bodily states, the situations in which we find ourselves, and our identities within the social groups and events around us. Methodologically and ideologically eclectic, the edited and authored volumes are written to be accessible for advanced students in the social, linguistic, and communication sciences as well as to serve as valuable resources for seasoned researchers in these fields.

Volumes in this series

Volumes previously published by Multilingual Matters in the series Monographs in the Social Psychology of Language and in the series Intercommunication may be obtained through Multilingual at 8A Hill Road, Clevedon, Avon BS21 7 HH, England.

Editorial Advisory Board

Deceit, Delusion, and Detection

W. Peter Robinson

LANGUAGE AND LANGUAGE BEHAVIORS
Volume 6

SAGE Publications
International Educational and Professional Publisher
Thousand Oaks London New Delhi

For information address:

 SAGE Publications, Inc.
2455 Teller Road
Thousand Oaks, California 91320
E-mail: order@sagepub.com

SAGE Publications Ltd.
6 Bonhill Street
London EC2A 4PU
United Kingdom

SAGE Publications India Pvt. Ltd.
M-32 Market
Greater Kailash I
New Delhi 110 048 India

Printed in the United States of America

Library of Congress Cataloging-in-Publication Data

Robinson, W. P. (William Peter)
    Deceit, delusion, and detection / by W. P. Robinson.
        p. cm. — (Language and language behaviors; v. 6)
    Includes bibliographical references and index.
    ISBN 0-8039-5260-0 (alk. paper). — ISBN 0-8039-5261-9 (pbk.:
alk. paper)
        1. Communication—Moral and ethical aspects. 2. Truthfulness and
Falsehood. 3. Interpersonal communication. 4. Mass media.
    I. Title. II. Series.
    P94.R55 1996
    177′.3—dc20   95-41791

This book is printed on acid-free paper.

96 97 98 99 10 9 8 7 6 5 4 3 2 1

Sage Production Editor: Astrid Virding
Sage Typesetter: Janelle LeMaster

For Carol, Clare, and Katherine

Contents

Acknowledgments

The insightful comments of Howard Giles led to extensive revision across the whole manuscript, and Elizabeth Robinson substantially reduced the errors and improved the precision of Chapter 2. Jacqueline Goldberg helped considerably with the literature base.

My own empirical work was assisted by the research initiative fund of the Vice Chancellor of the University of Bristol, to whom I am pleased to express my thanks.

I am similarly grateful to the Oxford Department of Experimental Psychology and the President and Fellow of Wolfson College, Oxford, for providing the ambience in the summer of 1994 that enabled me to establish the structure and gain the momentum for the writing of the manuscript.

I am also grateful to the following for permission to reproduce their work: Judee Burgoon and David Buller for 18 propositions of their interpersonal deception theory, Paul Ekman for his checklists relevant to lie detection, Pamela Kalbfleisch for her interrogation strategies, and Robert Mitchell for Table 2.1.

Catherine Harvey, Carol Marks, and Mary Pope have been excellent word processors and I thank them for their typing and for the cheerful patience with which they have tolerated amendments.

Prologue

When do people tell the truth and when do they tell lies and why? These challenges can be unpacked into a myriad of questions. The specific and general inquiries can be decomposed to an agenda that could encompass the whole of human history along with its realizations for the billions of people currently alive and the thousands of languages and cultures currently extant. Principles of selection had to be applied to yield a finite text.

Being truthful is the primary theme, the contrast with lying and untrue utterances being the main counterpoint. For all but one function of language, the question of true or false does not arise. It can be posed only about statements that claim to represent some truth about reality. In English, such statements are made most transparently using the declarative form of the structure known as a sentence. It will be proposed in Chapter 1 that lies are a subset of false representations. Whether the distinction between true and false has more than heuristic value has been contested. It will be necessary to resolve that issue and comment on the criteria that may be used to discriminate between them. Two deeper commitments will be necessary to defend that position, one to a form of realism and the other to rationality. *Realism* will not be defined as presupposing that all experience is veridical, that the categories human beings use for talking and thinking necessarily have some existence independent of people, that people act on objective rather than subjective reality, or that today's well-founded beliefs will remain well founded in the future. The realism to which there needs to be a commitment is the view that criteria can be established and evidence brought forward to show that some beliefs are untenable and that it would be perverse not to treat some others as valid pro tem.

The commitment to rationality is used to mean that some inferences can be shown to be invalid; the human mind appears to be designed so that it can be empowered to distinguish between valid and invalid arguments but has no freedom to choose which shall be which. This dual commitment is necessary if the idea of a sensible contrast between true and false statements is to be sustained.

It will be evident by the end of Chapter 1 that questions about truth telling versus lying are not going to be easy to formulate, investigate, or answer, and to facilitate the maintenance of as much coherence as possible, theory and empirical evidence are introduced from a developmental perspective in Chapter 2. There it is suggested that children are born as extreme realists. They have to learn to differentiate between appearance and reality and come to realize that appearances provide only cues to reality and that these have to be interpreted. In the developing mastery of language, the use of statements to communicate facts is a late function to emerge and in the first instance is probably best treated analytically as simply relaying truths but without any contrastive category of false statements. After the true-false differentiation is achieved, the further isolation of lies from other kinds of false statement has to be made. Both of these achievements require an appreciation that other people have minds, that oneself has a mind, that the contents of other minds are not transparent to self but can be inferred, and that what is in one's own mind can be concealed from others and misrepresented.

The rapidly growing literature on children's incremental development of understanding about these mental matters has included an interest in lying from its earliest experiments. The theoretical framework to date has been one of isolating the sequence and underpinning competencies of intellectual development associated with the appreciation of lying. Progress with the topic, however, has been complicated by the propensity of caretakers to disapprove of lies, thereby overlaying the cognitive issues with affective and moral repercussions. Although the verbal disapproval is seemingly extended to all lies, the maturing child has to learn that this is not so. Sometimes lies are tolerated, sometimes they are expected, and sometimes they are required. There do not seem to be studies of children's development or their perception of when they should be telling the truth and when not. The sociocognitive factors facilitating or otherwise affecting the relevant changes have not been detailed, and hence there are as yet no interactive studies comparable to those with adults reported in Chapter 4.

Prior to that, some broader questions about deception in the world of adults are posed, mainly at the level of the individual person (Chapter 3). There are people who live double lives and others who exhibit a variety of faces in different contexts with different people. Some of these people can be classified as chronic liars and therefore of immediate relevance. These issues are discussed under headings such as The Presentation of Self, Impression Management, and Facework and Individual Differences in Lying. Moving to more incidental lying, there are the beginnings of an ecology investigating who reports lying to whom about what in both informal and formal interpersonal situations. These studies tend to be descriptive and taxonomic but can be judged to be wholly appropriate for exploratory endeavors. The chapter moves from a beginning that centers on persons to an ending that shifts to include a situational perspective. Toward the end of Chapter 4, there is also a second switch of perspective from using lies to detecting lies by others. In what situations should people be wary and of what kinds of persuasory lies that are exploited by would-be deceivers?

This background of standing features is succeeded by a consideration of what is viewed as the mainstream of work on interpersonal deception—the experimental studies concerned with deception and detection in face-to-face interaction (Chapter 4). There have been impressive empirical and theoretical developments in this area that are heavily dependent on a detailed analysis of nonverbal behavior and the cues emitted that may be indicative of lying (e.g., Ekman, 1985/1992). The point of departure for Buller and Burgoon (in press) is the communicative situation involving interpersonal exchanges in real time. This view facilitates a reconstruction of the interplay of the factors increasing or decreasing the probabilities of deception or detection being successful. Combining Buller and Burgoon's interpersonal deception theory with Ekman's checklist of questions related to the interplay and Kalbfleisch's (1994) list of interrogation strategies, the triangulated contributions provide a succinct integration of what has been learned so far and point to testable hypotheses for the future. The final section of Chapter 4 serves as a reminder that nonverbal leakage is not the only source of information about truthfulness and lying; statements themselves have value for diagnosis both directly and indirectly. Claims about facts can be shown to be incompatible with what is known from other sources. The research techniques themselves, however, do not aspire to go further than the probabilistic judgments now accepted as a realistic goal for analyses of nonverbal behavior. With court transcripts, it is desirable to achieve the highest possible probabilities of correct diagnosis, of course, and the work using the polygraph with appropriate interrogation items reflects the difficulties in achieving this aim (Chapter 5).

Chapters 2-5 have few cross-references to each other and fewer than might be expected within them. In the future, there will need to be more articulation and integration. For example, work with the polygraph can be seen as a special situation in which to apply interpersonal deception theory (Chapter 4). Are the Machiavellians, supersalespeople, poker players, and other putative experts in simulation of Chapter 3 actually more proficient in their knowledge about and use of deception and detective competence? How do childhood experiences relate to future skills and evaluations? There are also more macro perspectives relevant to the interpersonal activities, however, and an appreciation of these will be increasingly necessary for an understanding of who does not tell the truth to whom and why not.

Chapter 6 makes this qualitative leap in perspective from the immediate communicative situation to that from society as whole. The social structure, with its values, norms, and institutions, sets frames of reference that have dramatic consequences for truth telling. For example, a strong truth bias and trust would be a disastrous recipe for people trying to live in a totalitarian state. Even in a quasi-democratic country, there are asymmetries in rules about lying that allow more to be passed down the status hierarchies than up them. Etzioni-Halevy (1989) offers some interesting theses about the sociological conditions that are likely to lead to increases in corruption and subsequent denials around those activities that become exposed. Her thesis of lying arising more strongly when theoretically and structurally independent social orders become interdependent is illustrated through the misrepresentations of reality to be found in the media (Chapter 7) and other social orders (Chapter 8). Among the latter, special attention is drawn to the peculiar characteristics within certain social orders that reduce the priority of truth telling, for example, procedural rules in law courts.

In both of these chapters, general sociological explanations associated with the pursuit and maintenance of power, wealth, and status run alongside social psychological explanations for the particular misrepresentations selected for public consumption. The self-serving-other-denigrating biases of attributions are combined with ideas of in-group-out-group discriminations. The resultant irrational statements can be reconstrued as "rational" when their social functions are made clear. In addition to attributions being asymmetric, simple counterfactual claims are made for the same self-serving purposes. In the more macro contexts, the proactive falsifications are typically motivated by concerns for personal or group advancement, and the reactive falsifications are more likely to be defensive denials or justifications once accusations have been laid. In both cases, winning is accorded a clear priority over truth telling. Both strands will need to be articulated eventually with the interpersonal work reported in Chapters 3 and 4, but with both of these, the significant determining factors seem to lie above the levels of interpersonal communication. It would not be difficult to argue a case that gaining personal advantage through lying is often a cause for admiration rather than censure in the United Kingdom and the United States, particularly among the in-groups of the elites and if the lies are addressed to members of out-groups.

Chapter 9 questions what the public believes and thinks about lies told by elites. A national U.K. survey shows that there is a strong moral condemnation of such lies and that this is now associated with a strong distrust of many of society's authorities. At the same time, the adult population of the United Kingdom seems to prefer to use its moral condemnation mainly for rhetorical purposes in communion with like-minded others rather than as a public political platform for demanding reforms. Given the incidence of people's own capacities for lying to organizations for personal gain, it will be interesting in the future to find out more about the reasoning that condemns politicians for taking bribes but permits their fraudulent claims to the tax authorities. Morality might also be raised as an issue with respect to the subsequent careers of whistle-blowers (Chapter 10). According the truth priority over alternative courses of action is typically a lonely marathon for those who adopt it by exposing the truth about public hazards.

The simplest message from Chapters 6-10 would be that, in matters of importance, truth is an early casualty of vested interest. Winning and not losing take precedence over truth for many people when the truth will be costly or lying will be advantageous; pragmatism takes precedence over virtue.

That this is nothing new is taken up in Chapters 11 and 12. Throughout the text, references are made to the ideational ancestry of European culture and its relevance to truth telling and lying. In Chapter 11, it is proposed that, like children, our distant forebears will have used language primarily for its social functions of regulating encounters, marking personal and social identity, defining and negotiating role relationships, influencing the states and behavior of self and others, and expressing themselves. When "facts" defining the nature of the world and the human place in it were first proposed, they may well have attained the status of truths without contrastive possibilities of alternatives or falsehoods. The contexts in which untrue utterances and lies emerged will remain unknown. The idea of the possibility of statements being false is likely to have arisen in everyday specifics; the extension to lying as a verbal form of deception perhaps in competitive conflicts. Even in the preclassical Greek language, to say was to mean and appearance was not dissociated from reality. True and false as contrasts, unintentional false and intentional false seem to have arisen among the pre-Socratic philosophers. Prior to this explosion of the creative imaginations in ancient Greek philosophy, the received truths of religion and received notions of duty and virtue in preceding civilizations were not open to debate, and even in the classical era, philosophers were careful to keep their philosophical analyses separated from the stories of the gods and the heroic myths. These latter were not subjected to critical analysis and alternative hypothesizing but left in their separate domains. Their functions were social not representational; they served to inspire and warn and to instruct and socialize.

Leaving the issues of the pantheon and heroic legends to one side, the role of truth in human affairs had become a key question and, by the time of Socrates, a polarization was clear. In the *Gorgias* (Plato, 1971), his antagonists assert the importance of speech as a means of winning arguments and defeating opponents. Socrates asserts its primacy for inquiring after truths about the world, presupposing its capacity for representing possible and actual realities. For the idealized Socrates, arguments should be won because the conclusions are based on rational derivations from premises that can be accepted as true.

In Chapter 12, illustrations are offered to suggest that Socratic principles have been crucial to the growth of human knowledge in the fields in which it has developed most: logics, science, and technology. In contrast, where successive elites have had vested interests in the maintenance of general ignorance or false beliefs, much less progress has been made, and that which has been made at the ideational level has not been translated into policies and practice. Continuing concealment and misrepresentation of truths are probably inherent in societies that are either individualistic and competitive or strongly hierarchical and consensual—in short, any societies in which those with privileges wish to maintain them.

Like Topsy, this text around the topic of truthfulness and lying, just grew. For the author at least, the putting together of the components has been a fascinating and profound experience. It is quite impossible to argue that the topic has no ethical implications. It has, and perhaps in the not too distant future, more societies will begin to establish cultural foundations for their development that insist on a fundamental commitment to realism, rationality and trust with a watchful wariness. Until what is true is consistently accorded priority over winning, there cannot be any sustained "vision of the good" that can be translated into better human communities.

CHAPTER ONE

Representations of Realities

Socrates (Plato, 1971) posed questions about truth, goodness, and justice over 2,000 years ago. That they have yet to be answered and translated into actions that enable most human beings to lead virtuous and just lives in the light of true beliefs could mean that the questions are impossible to answer. It could also mean that, despite the invention and discovery of rational and reasonable criteria for distinguishing the true from the false, the virtuous from the vicious, and the just from the unjust, too many of those people who have had the power or capacity to inform and influence other members of their societies have been unable to do so or have chosen to enhance or sustain their own positions of privilege at the expense of the vast majority of their fellow human beings. Certainly, many individuals and social movements have tried to evangelize, particularly through education, and have been oppressed, repressed, and suppressed.

Of course, human history is more complicated than can be summarized in a pair of generalizations. For most of history, most people have been trapped in struggles for survival, coping with famine and pestilence or fending off attackers, having neither opportunities nor resources for exploring answers to questions about the meaning of life. Probably the majority of people currently alive are still strapped to what they see as a struggle to survive, although for an increasing number, survival is being redefined as retaining a competitive advantage over others.

In addition to the absence of opportunities and resources, the simple ignorance of the human species has been a factor. The progressive decrease in ignorance through time, however, has not been accompanied by governing elites rushing to afford the governed the educational opportunities and resources to decide for themselves

1

what is true and what is false, especially on matters of social justice and policy.

The idea that governing groups exercise power to control rather than to serve the governed and that keeping the governed ill equipped to inform themselves of better alternatives is a very ancient hypothesis. Much of the empirical evidence presented in later chapters could be interpreted to show that vested interests remain pervasive reasons for the rarity of the awareness of possible solutions to age-old problems.

In totalitarian states, those who ask whether the state is good and just are likely to find out the answers quickly and finally. In nontotalitarian states, those who ask such questions too persistently are likely to be either ignored or persecuted by the authorities. Winning the competitive struggles, or at least not losing them too drastically, continues to be a concern that dominates over inquiring after truth so as the better to pursue virtue. One of the themes of this book is the competition between the disposition to tell the truth and the temptation to try to win and not lose, regardless of what the truth of the matter is. Unfortunately, it is not possible to plunge straight into the social psychology of truth telling and lying. There are linguistic, philosophical, and definitional problems to examine before the plunge.

First, it has to be noted that questions of truth or falsity arise for only one of the functions and one of the core sentence structures of language. Whatever classificatory system of the functions of language is adopted, for all languages it will include the referential or representational function. What the precise relationships may be between the linguistic representation and what is being represented may torture some philosophical minds, but that some such function exists is not doubted. In English, it is achieved explicitly and most simply through statements (propositions), most frequently in the form of declarative sentences. Not all statements serve the representational function, and not all sentences function as statements. Other functions of language are served by statements, questions, and commands. These issues are the first to be treated; it is helpful to remember that language is used for much more than recording the truth. Second, some of the issues set out in the agenda of philosophers concerning whether truth is an epiphenomenon, a construction that has no value, or an invention that is defensible and valuable are discussed. This last position is asserted and defended, but it is noted that the criteria for evaluating whether a statement is true or false will vary with the type of knowledge and claim made. At that point, it is feasible to proceed with the problem of defining what a lie might sensibly be defined to be. The issues are rehearsed, and the scene is then set for representing the current state of knowledge and belief about telling the truth and telling lies.

Representation and Other Functions of Language

What is truth? Certainly, the question is ancient, and almost certainly and regrettably, different answers will continue to be given to it until the end of human experience. The question is too comprehensive, too deep, and too abstract to be answered without hesitation or equivocation in the opening paragraphs to the volume. Some constituent aspects of it, however, have to be confronted from the beginning, if only to set the frame of reference within which a text can be developed.

In offering his analysis of the principles underpinning cooperative conversation and, by extension, all communication, Grice (1975/1989) employs the category of *quality* under which he offers a super-maxim, "Try to make your contribution one that is true." (p. 27). He adds two more specific maxims:

1. "Do not say what you believe to be false" (p. 27).
2. "Do not say that for which you lack adequate evidence" (p. 27).

These instructions are in plain English and may serve as an easier springboard from which to dive into the contesting currents than would an undignified sprint or a heavy marathon through the history of philosophical treatments of the issues. The position to be adopted here is that at some point(s) in human history the invention of the ideas of truth and falsity was an essential contrast to devise if human beings were to be able to communicate with each other, nonverbally and verbally. Had our species not invented the idea of deception and if it had preserved implicitly the maxim, "Say what you mean and mean what you say," life could have been simpler than it is. If we could have constrained our communicative acts within Grice's (1975/1989) maxims, life would also have been more plain. Breaking out of those constraints in ways that have achieved negotiated significance has enabled the species to develop its particular cultures—but at a price. For example, there is a sense in which Brown and Levinson's (1987) examination of politeness could be construed as an exercise in demonstrating how the flouting of the Gricean maxims enables people to express consideration, sympathy, amiability, and deference, with degrees of differentiation well beyond the use of simple statements, such as "I like you" or "I submit to your superior status." The exercise of the creative imagination through which questions and statements can be generated that are superficially silly, nonsensical, or untrue, also serves for the production of poetry, prose, and scientific theory. The libraries of the world as well as the encyclopedic contents of every human head could not have been generated, considered, and tested if there had been no contrast between truth and various forms of deviation from it. De Saussure (1925/1959) emphasized the basic point that all units and structures of language gain meaning and significance contrastively. Identities and categories depend on specifications of similarities and differences. The semantics of statements require contrasts with "true," if true itself is to have meaning.

Why and how human beings developed their communication systems in the ways they did is well beyond this book, as is any enquiry into the stage at which the adoption of the representational or truth-stating function of statements was followed by deceitful exploitation. Some useful points to be made can be illustrated, however, by describing the route by which one well-documented child came to use language.

Halliday (1975) charted the early phases of his son Nigel's vocalizations and verbalizations with a richer range of observed activity than has been the common practice. He demonstrated that the description and explanation of the beginnings of mastery of communication through language have to be embedded in its full interactional context and are best viewed, initially, as a functional-structural dynamic, with units and structures being predominantly but not entirely subservient to functions (pragmatics).

Halliday (1975) found that social functions of vocalizations were paramount from 9 to 18 months of age and that instrumental (getting things for self), regulatory (making others do things), interactional (encounter regulation), and personal (reactions to events or states) units were the first to appear. Among these were nã (give me that), bø (give me my bird), ã (do that again), do (nice to see you), and nŋ (that tastes nice). This child began to talk, it seems, because verbal interaction with others was pleasurable; it was not because he was hungry or in pain. The design of the baby includes an impetus to interact with people, an impetus to interact with other features of the environment, and an impetus to develop the schemes of interaction. If one wishes to say that the reasons why babies begin to talk are biological, then they are sociobiological—that is, they participate in joint action with caretakers. As Halliday illustrates, Nigel later expanded his functional range to include the heuristic (finding out) and imaginative (let's pretend) functions, and he increased the number of communicative acts associated with each of these until, by the age of 16 months, he had over 50 in his repertoire.

About the time Nigel reached his 50 meanings, he also ceased to rely solely on inventing his own units (mainly un-English in form and actually heavily reliant on tone). Two important changes occurred. First, Nigel interpolated a third level of linguistic structure, the lexicogrammatical, between soundings and meanings. Individual sounds ceased to be expressive of individual meanings. Combinations of sounds were used to form "words," and words and tones were sequenced to create "meanings." Thus the tristratal essence of language became established. (At some later point in time, the child also has to learn to distinguish between the semantic and pragmatic levels; different forms can serve the same general functions, and the same form can serve different functions. The appropriate choice requires knowledge of the cultural norms of the society.) Second, Nigel's speech began to distinguish between using language and learning language. He deliberately solicited from his caretakers "names" of objects, attributes, and actions, and he practiced combinations and alterations in both monologue and dialogue.

It was not until Nigel was 22 months old that he began to use language for what Halliday (1975) calls the *informative function* (more commonly called the referential or *representational* function)—that is, to tell someone something he or she might not already know. As Halliday points out, although this idea of language being used to represent a reality for the listener or reader is predominant in adult thinking about language—and philosophical analyses in particular

—it is but one function and it is a sophisticated function that emerges late (p. 21).

This somewhat extended description and commentary has a three-fold purpose. First, it hints at the amount and quality of practice and experience that is part of early language mastery. Second, it serves as a reminder that reference per se begins with nonverbal pointings, moving to vocalizations that focus on here-and-now objects and actions and only much later to making statements about what is not present. Third, it implies how the possibility of coming to be able to knowingly make false statements that may mislead other people is likely to be a protracted and muddled achievement (see Chapter 2), just as are other early achievements.

The developmental sequence is not surprising. Phonological and psychological identification of particular entities or experience is a logical precursor to any conjunction of actions with objects, events with experiences, or expressions of feelings. Being able to refer to objects and actions with units is a necessary condition of being able to combine units into structures and to utter them to some effect, be it expressive, regulatory, or instrumental. Getting things done via noisemaking is a very useful competence to acquire. Why should infants wish to make statements about the cat being on the mat in the kitchen, unless the statements be in answer to a question or a need?

It is probably not totally fortuitous that Nigel's early regulatory demands and expressions correspond to Wittgenstein's (1951/1967) opening paragraphs about the moving of "slabs" "here" and "there" that served to enable him to argue his way into his analysis of language games, of which but one enables speakers to make statements that are true or otherwise.

In addition to the data and accounts supplied by Halliday (1975), both the ideas of Vygotsky (1961), about the primacy of the social functions of language over the representational, and Austin's (1962) essays on performative utterances have served to remind those working in the relevant areas that a functional-structural approach to language use and language development is more fruitful and realistic (Robinson, 1972, 1981) than either the purely functional or the heavily structural perspective that came to characterize the activities of many linguists and others in the 1960s and 1970s. Grammar without semantics would have no raison d'être, but neither would grammar and semantics without pragmatics. The functions do not serve structures; the structures do serve functions. The simplest model of the linkage can yield matches between form and function at the level of sentence. If there was a tight match, in English it would be very strange if that matching did not take on the pairing of declaratives with (making) statements, interrogatives with (asking) questions, and imperatives with (issuing) commands. Today, in situations in which misunderstandings are to be avoided at all costs, those pairings might well be recommended to minimize risks. In appropriate circumstances in current usage, however, the pairings can be crisscrossed so that all but one combination occurs in English: The imperative form cannot be used to ask a question. All others are possible and are used.

Influence via Representation

If the primary function of the declarative form is to make statements, it would be perverse to suggest that it would be used to make false rather than true statements. The essence of the utterance of a statement is that it takes a topic and makes a comment about it. The topic is shared between speaker and listener, the comment tells the listener something presumed to be new and hitherto unknown. The idea that false statements might be made is necessarily parasitic on the presumption that most statements are true; the parasitism could not be reversed.

Such would be the version of the story told by those who wish to assert a *correspondence theory* of the relation between truths about the world and the means by which language can represent (or refer to) these truths. The meaning of "correspondence" has more than exercised the minds of philosophers, with at least one positive climax to such thinking emerging from the activities of Wittgenstein (1922/ 1974) and Popper (1972). Popper's analyses include, but extend well beyond, the mundane and particular propositions exchanged in everyday discourse to the philosophy of the physical, biological, and social sciences with his claim that empirically relevant propositions that are not falsifiable are likely to be meaningless (Popper, 1972). Popper's position is frequently misrepresented, and it is important to remember that he was never a logical positivist and neither has he ever claimed that we are in touch with an assured account of any objective reality. What he has argued is that, at least as far as the nonsocial sciences are concerned, human beings have to behave as if there is an objective reality and that scientific specialists have to generate descriptions and explanations of dispassionately processed data, which remain falsifiable in principle, to make way, if necessary, for better descriptions and explanations in the future. His form of rational realism remains open and provisional. At the same time, the probabilities that many imaginable but seldom uttered statements are true is close to zero, and they are best treated as false. The transformations to the world as a result of human activity are founded on what people assume is rational realism. The stores of "believing that" and "knowing how" in minds, artifacts, and archives around the world represent the achievements predicated on such assumptions.

Influence via Inspiration

Alternative stories are conceivable. If the idea that the representational function of language has some kind of superior status is dropped and if a paramount status is given to the functions of the regulation of the states and behavior of others and to the development, maintenance, and dissolution of social relations of various kinds, then the truth of any statement can be made subservient to these, and precedence can be given to those statements that please, amuse, frighten, defer to, or dominate appropriate others. Later in this book, it is suggested that truth is quickly sacrificed to such social functions as a value once issues of victory and defeat become important. Over 2,000 years before Senator Hyram Johnson proclaimed that "Truth is the first casualty of war," the opening paragraphs of Thucydides's (1971) "History of the Peloponnesian War" had recorded that at the outset of hostilities words change their meanings and peacetime virtues become weaknesses. He noted also that truth is subsequently defined by victors. In Plato's (1971) *Gorgias*, Socrates argues for an indissoluble link between truth and goodness and can find no justification for ever falsifying facts. In contrast, Gorgias and his succeeding protagonists argue initially that the art of the rhetorician is to be able to make the weaker argument sound the stronger and the stronger the weaker. Since that time, St. Augustine and Kant have supported the Socratic case, and Aristotle, Cicero, and St. Thomas Aquinas have supported versions of Gorgias's case. In today's sophisticated world of action, it might be suggested that the Socratic view is championed mainly by observers and losers; the Gorgias view prevails among the practices of participants and winners. In the world of dispassionate enquiry about the nature of particular or general events, the Socratic view prevails.

One of the difficulties faced by research into truth and falsity is the confusion of description and explanation on the one hand and moral evaluation on the other. People seem to go to great pains to avoid and deny accusations of lying, whereas they are fairly relaxed about forms of deception that are just as effective but that do not finally require statements that can be shown to misrepresent reality. A lie by any other name seems to smell much better.

Here an attempt will be made to tread a dangerously narrow path from which any slippage will probably show a personal bias toward a Kantian position: Other things being equal, true statements are better than false statements. Also, as an abstract principle, false statements are always wrong per se. This prescription, however, is not the only moral principle relevant to human conduct, and as soon as more than one principle is involved, it is logically necessary and empirically inevitable that in particular situations principles will be in conflict. Real people in real situations who subscribe to moral principles cannot avoid offending against them; they have to choose which are more or less important in any given situation. Using this model, living cannot be free of wrongdoing; wrongdoing can only be minimized. Lying can be less wrong than the consequences will be if the truth is told. I think this is Kant's (1785/1964) position, which is, however, occasionally reported as an absolute imperative, "Thou shalt not lie—ever." Kant was a realist as well as an idealist. Just as some of those who oppose Kant's position misrepresent him, so the position I should like to adopt here will probably be a victim of accentuation contrast (Sherif & Hovland, 1961) or outgroup differentiation and denigration (Tajfel, 1981) in the minds of some readers.

Certainly, some radical social constructionists will be disposed to deny both that there can be lies and that if they did exist, they would be wrong. Their position has more than a kernel of truth to it as a point of departure for asking questions about particular assumptions about reality but only for some claims about reality on some occasions. It provides a valuable weapon for contesting claims about certain aspects of reality, but if used to excess, it commits suicide in solipsism.

One of the strengths of a social constructionist approach is to challenge received wisdom. For example, historically, today, and in the future, the banner of truth has been and will be used to justify the creation and maintenance of differentials in power, wealth, and status and to defend social injustice in societies. Claims that large social groups of human beings are inferior biologically to other groups have been one device used by ruling elites and their beneficiaries to hold on to their power, wealth, and status. Perhaps Plato himself best exemplified this contrast. What he wrote about the men of gold restricted not only theoretical duties but also de facto privileges to a few males in Athenian society; he also wrote off all non-Greeks as fit for slavery. At its peak, what has been labeled as Athenian democracy was confined to a very limited in-group. So it has always been and remains. The concentration of power and privilege to less than 1% of the population of a sovereign state, and sometimes to no more than a few families, characterizes most of the signatories of the United Nations' declaration of human rights. Justifications that the dispossessed are more primitive and animal like, have smaller brains, have lower intelligence, are feckless, and are prone to criminality and immorality are part of the documented record that some of the descendants of erstwhile entrepreneurial spirits and contemporary financial wizards have used typically to increase and retain their privileges. The stability of oligarchical regimes rests very heavily on populations not asking potentially revolutionary questions about social injustice or answering them but not acting in the light of those answers. Differentiated societies are justified by myths that are left unanalyzed (or "undeconstructed" in the jargon).

To the extent that this story is true, the case for the general primacy of the social functions of language being dominant over the representational is strengthened. This is further enhanced when the statements made in the representational mode are actually false but are used to justify institutionalized discrimination, such as slavery and its modern equivalents. This line of argument must, however, presuppose objective realities against which claims about the relevance of smaller brain size of certain human groups can be contested. At various times and in various places, the fact that women have smaller brains on average than men has been used by men to justify differential rights. Although women can argue for parity with men as human beings and can point to a history of institutionalized and informal discrimination against them, the argument of the case collapses if it is also accepted that the facts about brain size and any definition of social justice are simply social constructions: An unanswerable case trickles away into arguments without premises or foundations and is converted into a rationally unresolvable struggle for dominance.

That those in pursuit of power and those exercising it exploit false statements is not an argument against the imperative of a distinction between truth and falsity. (Neither is lying confined to such people, of course.) It is a warning, however, that care will have to be exercised in weighing evidence that appears to justify privileges for the protagonists of any evidence. To deliberately make false statements against one's own interests is not viewed as problematic to the same extent as is lying.

What logical objections are there to a proposal that a criterion of correspondence between reality and statement could be appropriate for distinguishing between true and false statements? If an idealized version of "the whole truth" is posited, even though it cannot be imagined, then anything less may be argued to be less than true. What is gained by this way of defining "true" is not evident. It certainly does not help in any effort to distinguish between truth and falsity, and if all meanings have to be considered in terms of contrasts, then nothing is gained. The argument is simply reiterating the point that more might be stated than has been stated.

More cogent philosophical arguments would focus on the subjective nature of experience, necessarily circumscribed by space and time and hence question the epistemological status of any statement uttered. Perhaps one person's description or explanation of an event is necessarily significantly different from that of others. Perhaps today's descriptions or explanations will be seen to be mistaken. There can be no decontextualized objections to the first criticism, although for any particular statement in a particular context or situation, many candidates could be ruled out as being untrue by an appeal to noncorrespondence with any defendable version of reality. There can be no logical objection to the second criticism. In extremis, all our beliefs are bets about reality and could be wrong. At any point in space and time, however, it should be easier to show that some are more likely to be wrong than others, in that there is less or no evidence to support them. Just as perception is transactional and cannot be better than more or less sensible constructions of realities, so conception cannot transcend comparable limitations.

Arguments along these lines are inevitable, given the tendency of human intellects to explore the limits of ideas. They are useful to the extent that they may expose presuppositions and presumptions of which people were previously unaware. They are also potentially dangerous. In the mouths of the descendants of Gorgias, they can be used to make the weaker argument seem the stronger. Not everyone distinguishes between logical possibility and empirical probability. Sometimes, some university students reach a stage where they are able to generate a massive battery of logically appropriate objections to any empirical claim but are not able to proceed to reflect on the possibility that the very same set of objections could be extended to everything that they believe to be true. Played on occasions as an intellectual game, the strategy has potential for probing the status of claims to knowledge; as a recipe for living it is impossible.

No matter how solipsist, skeptical, anarchic, nihilistic, or even social constructionist some people are when playing their academic roles, none extend these same doubts into the whole of the rest of their experience. In all their other roles, people draw distinctions between what they believe to be true and what they believe to be false, between what they are fairly certain about and very unsure of, and between what they know they do not know and what they are sure they do know. They separate what they believe to be social constructions from what they decide to treat as objective reality. There is something both absurd and insane if professional concerns become uncoupled from daily life and practice. Clearly, there is currently a risk in Western social science of just such a crisis developing with social constructionism, especially in its postmodernist, poststructural, and postcolonial realizations. Born as these concerns have been in real moral and epistemological concerns about human injustice, their perspectives are prone to undermine the promotion of the very causes they espouse once they go beyond a position that retains the validity of the distinction between true and false statements.

For example, the previously mentioned similarities and differences between males and females qua biological facts are as marked today as they have been since the origins of our species. Through time, the interpretations of what could and should be made of those similarities and differences has varied from culture to culture and from subculture to subculture. Likewise, the justifications of those interpretations have varied.

It is a fact that in the great majority of small communities and in all the large complexes underpinned by the major religions or philosophical belief systems, females have consistently been treated as having different and lesser rights than males. This is particularly surprising in cultures whose mores are supposedly based on the teachings of some of the major religious belief systems. Some of these systems of belief have included profound moral principles seemingly universal in their intended application to human beings, but then, as I have already noted with Plato, principles can be abruptly restricted in application to some in-group, usually to adult male members of the ruling group. This is true of Confucianism, Buddhism, and Islam, as well as of Christianity and Judaism. Voices that have been raised to assert ideas of equal rights and responsibilities and social justice for members of groups other than those in contemporary control have usually had their objections or questions answered initially with opposing ideas or actions that could justify or enforce the status quo.

Worldwide, there has been a continuing intermittent erosion of legally enshrined discriminations against women, but not until the second half of the 20th century did real social emancipation of women begin to make significant progress, and that it is confined to a small number of the richer countries. The text in the Charter of the United Nations about females and males has yet to be translated into the legislation of even one of its member states, let alone the implementation of that legislation. At the present time, the social representations associated with being "female" rather than "male" are arguably the basis of the single most widespread social injustice affecting the greatest number of human beings. The beliefs that have been used to justify the discrimination and to slow down the reformation of societies are very widely distributed, not only in the minds of people but also in the artifacts of the cultures, not least in the languages themselves, if they have categories whose use is presumptive of male dominance. The literatures, the history texts, the philosophical and religious texts, the arts, and technology typically have been and can be used to reinforce the status quo.

To the extent that this account refers to and isolates a few features from what could be an encyclopedia of male-female discrimination that is based on false beliefs sustained by false evidence, the human species has deceived itself on a massive scale. This is at least in part because its members have failed to ask and answer pertinent questions. Earlier adoptions of a social constructionist approach to the social representations of men and women might have exposed the presumptions and assumptions that have sustained gender discrimination.

In extremis, however, they could not have answered the questions in terms of any moral philosophy founded on notions of synthetic a priori truths (Kant, 1781/1934). They could have suggested that women (and male allies) argue the case for equal rights and social justice, but the protagonists would not have had a more principled and defensible case than those who argued for discrimination—unless there are some objective, empirical realities and some moral truths.

Just as Thales observed correctly that there was much water in the world but was wrong if he believed it to be the basic substance, and just as his immediate successors are reputed to have made similar mistakes with earth, fire, and air, so, too, social constructionism asks appropriate questions, using defensible methods for opening up inquiries. Subsequently, it runs the risk of offering wrong or no answers to some questions about some phenomena if its advocates try to push constructionist claims too far. It is not uncommon for ideas to be pushed beyond their defensible limits, and normally, this leads to a subsequent backlash in which future generations discard more of the originally provocative ideas than they should.

Excessive claims are also particularly prone to be caricatured by those who are in real life most likely to lose out if the more moderate and defensible claims are met. The vested interests of any unfairly conservative opposition are most readily served by protagonists who overstate their cases for reform.

Philosophical Approaches: Ancient and Modern

As mentioned in the opening paragraph, questions and answers about truth have long provided philosophers with difficulties, problems, and puzzles. The questions have taken many forms, as have the answers. Questions have been rejected as improper or meaningless, as have answers. How much progress has been made is not obvious. There are peaks of apparent success offering at least temporary clarification. One peak in the classical tradition was Kant. Truths in logic were held to be matters of the validity or otherwise of inferences within a system whose premises were analytically true, meaning that they were simply matters of definition. Although truths in morals could not be treated as analytically true, they did not require empirical evidence to support their status. Conceding that they were synthetic, Kant proposed them to be a priori true; they were a special category of self-evident truths derivable from tests of universifiability and conceptual necessity. Descriptive and explanatory statements about the empirical world remained contingent, waiting for the 20th century principle of verification to be offered as a criterion of evaluation to stimulate further controversy. Meanwhile, the romantic revolt of Nietzsche (1886/1958) that viewed truth as a communal consensus and the historicist arguments of Hegel (1914/1956) for truth being related to time, place and culture were believed to be undermining of the Kantian position.

Through the logical positivists (e.g., Ayer, 1936) or the changing views of Wittgenstein (1951/1967, 1922/1974), the differing accounts of what can and cannot be argued to be true have ebbed and flowed. Post-1945, the argument has been made most strongly in forms of pragmatism in the United States and in the writings of European individuals whom it is difficult to label other than with their names, for example, Habermas (1979, 1984), Foucault (see Rabinow, 1984) and Derrida (1984). Popper (1972) exemplifies the rational realist approach that represents a main line still heavily committed to the idea that human beings invent concepts and construct them into propositions whose truth and falsity can be usefully evaluated.

A Popperian Line of Rational Realism. The rationality consists of a commitment to traditional distinctions between valid and invalid rules of inference and reasoning within logical systems. There is also an acceptance of a world out there, both physical and social, and a faith in the capacities of human intelligence to devise and evaluate descriptions and explanations of that world; there are criteria that help to discriminate better from worse explanations. There are universifiable principles of morality and justice best implemented in practice, not through idealized goals but through carefully evaluated piecemeal reforms of what is agreed to be wrong in contemporary society. Checks and balances to excessive power have to be a public responsibility; the price of freedom is eternal vigilance. Within this framework the pursuit of truth is integral to the pursuit of the good and the just—or to be more precise, the better and the fairer.

A Pragmatic Line of All But the Truth: Antirepresentational Views. It has been suggested that Davidson (1984) has done for language what Ryle (1949) did for the mind. Ryle was concerned that the duality version of the mind-body problem neither described human experience more accurately nor explained it better by invoking the presence of a "ghost in the machine." People can use mentalistic concepts in their thinking, and these may offer useful mutually comprehensible ways of facilitating the tasks of living. They should let matters rest there. Once mentalistic concepts are invoked to explain events or actions, questions arise that are improper; for example, how can a nonphysical entity provoke physical action? Knowing how to do things is knowing how to do them. Knowing that something is the case stands in its own right. "Knowing" contrasts with "believing" and "guessing" and "not knowing"; usage defines the similarities and differences without further need of what does the knowing or believing or how it knows it is guessing. Mentalistic concepts derive their meanings contrastively, and we can manage to live satisfactorily as long as we do not ask what they represent.

Davidson (1984, 1986) argues a similar case for language. Just as mentalistic concepts give rise to improper questions if they are seen as mediating links between persons and their worlds, so language does not have a mediating role between the world and the human beings. Statements can be made, but they do not represent reality. Some statements are more useful than others, and some are true and others false, but if we try to argue that the difference between true and false statements lies in their correspondence or noncorrespondence with what they denote, nothing is gained. Coherence with each other is what is important. The word *true* is a useful description, but it is not an explanation.

In combination, these two theses seek to eliminate many of the hoary and horny dilemmas that have dogged philosophical inquiry over the centuries; the cost is the removal of answers to testable questions about the true and the false, the good and the bad, if there are any such questions. We know that being cruel is wrong, and that is that; we cannot, but also do not need to, justify the claim. If someone asks which day it is, the reply names a day but gains nothing by appending "and that is the truth."

In one extension of this thesis, Rorty (1989, 1991) offers his reasoning. Knowledge is not a matter of getting reality right, "but rather [is] a matter of acquiring habits of action for coping with reality" (1991, p. 1). Rorty (1989) uses the word *vocabularies* to summarize the coherence of ways of talking within universes of discourse. He does not refer to Sapir (1921) or Whorf (1956), but it is difficult to imagine that he would dissent from thinking that social groups develop constellations of concepts organized into ideas that are talked about within their finite worlds; the concepts constrain the wordings, the words constrain the concepts. Both define the limits of the propriety of questions and the acceptability of answers. Human groups break out of such paradigms when their members become converted to a "better" set of ideas and wordings.

All people are members of more than one social group: A person can be a human being, a man, a European, an Englishman, and a social psychologist and have a whole catalog of political, religious, familial, and other identities, any one or more of which can become salient in particular contexts (Turner, Hogg, Oakes, Reicher, & Wetherell, 1987). Modes of thinking and communicating vary with contexts. The notion of a dominating, stable, and uniform personal identity that is invariant across situations is now seen to be a myth for members of complex modern societies. P × S (personality × situation), where either S or P could be dominant, is now taken as a more useful frame for initiating inquiries. What is more, P has a range of possibilities, from personal identity through any of a person's contextually relevant social identities.

Viewed from an extraterrestrial perspective that focuses on activities and discourses rather than on their individual carriers, an observer would indeed see a variety of discourses and practices competing for supremacy in many subworlds of arts, crafts, religions, political parties, and pure and applied sciences. In subworlds of medicine, for example, any notions that scientific medicine legitimated by institutionalized authorities is paramount would be difficult to explain considering the many old bottles and boxes found in pharmacies, let alone the variety of alternative medicines in the societies where scientific medicine is practiced. Worldwide, alternative varieties of medicine are many. The struggles among them may be expected to continue. Some may disappear because people become disillusioned with the inefficiency of alternative medicines in providing cures and immunity. Others may disappear because their adherents are slaughtered and their ideas extinguished. Outcomes remain unpredictable.

What is true of struggles between subcultures in medicine is equally true of all other "fields." There is a continuing competition to capture people's minds. Which views win is and will remain indeterminate. Such ideas would be readily accepted when applied to religion or politics or those entities organized as states but less readily perhaps for all the other sets of scientifically founded views with and within which we function. It is absurd, however, to pretend that dark ages may not return, in forms envisaged in Orwell's (1949) *1984*, Wyndham's *Day of the Triffids*, or terminally in Shute's human reduction in *On the Beach*.

The faith of liberal progressives is ill founded. Rational realism is not guaranteed to win. "The truth will prevail" is as empty a slogan as a belief in the inevitability of progress. *1984*, *Brave New World*, and *On the Beach* are equally plausible futures. More likely, on current trends, the prospects are for the emergence of weakly democratic states in which real power is exercised by small groups of continuing family-based power elites and criminally related fraternities acting in uneasy symbiosis with multinational companies. It should not be very difficult for organizations such as the Yakusa, the Mafia, and the Triads to increase their power bases in international companies dedicated to profits and struggles for supremacy and in states where political power is increasingly centralized and checks and balances are eroded and reduced to well spaced-out elections.

If Rorty (1989, 1991) is right, then appeals to what is truly the case or what it is rational to do should be but weak reasons, which are readily defeated in the world of action. The evidence that follows in this text is possibly more consistent with Rorty's views than with those of a rational realist.

Rorty (1989, 1991) speculates also on psychology more generally. Is he right when he claims that good people are seen as dull? Is he right in claiming that people currently prefer exciting or charming rogues in the tradition of Achilles and Odysseus over the family-loving but dutiful Hectors. John F. Kennedy remains a hero, and although Brecht's *Mother Courage* may continue to pity countries that need heroes, it seems the populations want their heroes and reward them; they do not, however, want the deaths and suffering that normally accompany heroics. Is Rorty right in claiming that people are more likely to be influenced by insightful plays or novels than by philosophers, psychologists, or sociologists? One of the extraordinary features of the past 15 years in the capitalist West has been the political indifference to rationality and to empirical evidence from any outside source. This is not the point at which to develop the idea, but governments have passed laws and instituted policies in the conviction that they would have certain effects. The convictions are their own; they have not consulted evidence or experts and have then appeared to have been surprised that their ideas have not worked. H. L. Menken prayed for protection from the "certainties of the ill-informed." That prayer has not protected the citizens of most of the capitalist West during the past decade and a half. The creative artists, all varieties of scientists, and senior religious leaders have been equally ignored by their political masters and mistresses and by the voters.

Such philosophy is refreshingly concerned to have applications to the problems of living. Its message has to be disquieting for most people. Its approach to notions of the truth is far from Socratic. Arguments that something is untrue or wrong can be and are countered with shrugs and bullets, but that has also been so.

In a different vein and writing in a more traditional style in which the logic appears to be impeccable but one's ability to recall what one has just read is sorely tested, Stich (1990) examines the case against there being a "best form of reasoning" whose justification lies in its leading to discrimination between true and other statements. The argument settles for the wisdom of allowing for what Stich calls "normative cognitive pluralism." Insofar as individuals can and do pursue different instrumental and intrinsic values and insofar as these are best achieved through more than one kind of reasoning, matters of truth and falsity become unimportant in comparison with matters of effectiveness.

I hesitate to criticize what I find difficult to understand. What is worrying is that although one of the stimuli for the considerations is the reasoning exhibited by persons in experiments by Johnson-Laird and Wason (1977) and by Nisbett and Ross (1980), the examples of the "bad" reasoning are never justified as not being bad by Stich (1990). Typically, in such logical puzzles, experimenters assume that "correct" answers are derived by following the rules of the logical system in which the puzzle is set and "incorrect" answers require explanation. Once explanations of their particular errors become available, learners can be given opportunities to learn how to avoid them and this may mean avoiding the intrusion of premises or presuppositions appropriate to other logics or learning rules or skills not previously mastered.

Although the pursuit of definitions and realizations of how true statements differ from false ones can lead to metaphors of correspondence or mapping that are mutually parasitic on what is being mapped, and although what is, in fact, an empirical, and not a philosophical claim that "people" do not value what is true may be defensible, it is so only if one argues that people are deceiving themselves in what they say when they say they do distinguish between the true and the false and, other things being equal, value the true, that the validity of their position can be questioned. Why do they have "to say anything coherent about what it is for a belief to be true and thus [would] be unable to explain what it is that they value"? (Stich, 1990, p. 22). They are under no obligation to explain either and, if so inclined, could just say they find life works more easily if they hold these positions. Exit the developments of formal logics as developed since Aristotle as the rationality of problem solving.

Pragmatism and Social Constructionism

It will be many years before many people are likely to become acquainted with the arguments of Stich (1990), and the implications for individuals living in societies have yet to be elaborated. A combination of radical social constructionism and Rorty (1989, 1991), however, are both very much a part of normative social science in World 3, and both have their weaknesses. The more valid they are the greater the threat but for different reasons. "Deconstruction" without reconstruction is a recipe for anarchy, intellectual as well as social. If the world can be reconstrued as competing discourses and conceptions whose power lies eventually in the armed forces of their respective servants, then there can be no complaints about social injustice, cruelty, or dishonesty. As mentioned previously, radical social constructionism is an idea too extreme; what we have to ask is what might be false about the constructs we have and the justifications offered for differentiations between individuals and categories of individuals and for beliefs logical, metaphysical, scientific, aesthetic, and moral. A Popperian stance of being careful with the social fabric to check that likely interventions will ameliorate rather than exacerbate wrongs is less likely to be socially and morally regressive. Intellectually, extreme social constructionism precludes all academic activity. Any attempt to state anything can be met with skeptical questions that can continue in infinitely regressive chains. With no criteria for evaluating better from worse, what begins as entirely appropriate wonderings degenerates into solipsism.

Rorty's (1989) syntheses are intellectually challenging and socially exciting. We can still draw distinctions between true and false statements; we can pass moral evaluations, and we can aim for community and individual progress. We must not, however, become too analytic, pushing words and concepts beyond their negotiated significance. We must not burden them with possibilities that convert them into masters rather than servants. Ideas and languages are like nuclear energy, money, earthmoving equipment, and microscopes. They have potential for power. They permit the amplification of human powers: sensory, motor, intellectual, and social. They can be used for good or evil, but they can also come to dominate us. The truth cannot save humanity from either evil or domination by our own inventions. It is our responsibility to prevent this.

If these arguments are valid, social psychological analyses based on distinctions between true and false statements or ideas can proceed. Analyses must attend to definitions and somehow cope with the variety of definitions extant. Once empirical work gets under way, it has to concern itself with the implications of social constructionist approaches at all levels, from individual perspectives through social groupings to languages and cultures. Likewise, it has to be careful to disentangle the moral from the empirical. Its protagonists are still likely to be ignored or eliminated if their ideas challenge and threaten the power structure within which they live. If truth is a lost cause that must still be served, how are examples of its expression to be distinguished from false statements?

Types of Knowledge:
Criteria for Evaluating the Truth
of Statements Within Its Branches

When I heard Ayer (1936) propose that all claims to knowledge that could not meet the criteria relevant to the assessment of truths in logics were meaningless nonsense, I thought at first that he was embarking on an extended insightful joke. Later, I thought that I had missed some subtle point. When, after several seminars, I discovered he was sincere in this conviction, I could appreciate why his version of logical positivism was in trouble. It seemed to be self-evident that claims to different kinds of knowledge would need to be evaluated against different criteria. Ayer's argument was entirely appropriate for checking the validity of deductions from analytic statements defining the primitive concepts basic to a particular branch of logic. It was also reasonable to expect that theoretically founded derivations in any other branch of logic would not have arguments in which conclusions were inconsistent with the premises of their arguments. To presuppose, however, that there was just one kind of knowledge was an extraordinary assumption.

To require that claims about what is good or bad, what is beautiful or ugly, what is empirically true or false should meet the same criteria looked to be what Ryle (1949) had called "a category mistake." To check whether or not I have locked the front door as I left home, I may rerun the sequence of departure mentally and be satisfied. I may retrace my steps and check empirically. To check whether it makes sense to believe that water is composed of hydrogen and oxygen, I have to learn to do experiments in chemistry. To check whether there is life after death, I have to wait and see. To find out what moral principles are true, if any, I shall ask and listen to other people's arguments, perhaps read Kant (see Körner, 1955, for an overview), Kohlberg (1984), and others to decide some answers. Likewise, for what is beautiful and ugly, I shall need experience of entities and events that might be aesthetically evaluated, along with the insights from the advice and opinions of others.

Of course, many people can probably live their lives without reflecting on these issues, except in particular instances. People may change the criteria they use to evaluate what is true and what is false at more than one point in their lives. People can change the categories into which they separate branches of knowledge. The division adopted here into logical, empirical everyday, empirical scientific, (empirical) religious, moral, and aesthetic is no more (and no less) than the one in whose defense I believe I can be most rational. I also argue that each can be accorded its own criteria of evaluation against which to assess claims to truth made within it, and although it would be both arrogant and pointless to argue for assured eternal verities, it would be correspondingly absurd and insane to deny having reasonable measures of confidence in the truth of a very large number of statements that can be retrieved from my head. The same is true for all the other heads in the world. These heads also offer an awareness of an infinity of ignorance, an immediate willingness to agree that beliefs are held with degrees of assurance ranging from near zero to near certainty, and a conviction that many of the beliefs held will not be held by those who come hereafter. It remains true, however, that it is eventually maladaptive to prefer false beliefs to true beliefs and that people will therefore remember their best bets about reality rather than false bets. It is inconceivable that drivers would deliberately construct false maps of the areas in which they drive. It would be irrational to have a mixture of false and true. That drivers fail to learn maps and that they forget and misremember them can be explained, but in the absence of cases of drivers deliberately and knowingly learning wrong maps, their existence does not need data to be explained.

For none of the branches of knowledge mentioned is there extensive universal consensus on content or criteria. This is not surprising. First, the beliefs of human beings die with them, and members of each new generation have to acquire their own. Second, the size, distribution, and busyness of the human population diminishes the possibility or necessity of consensus. When needs for consensus between different views in some branches arise, these have typically resulted in conflicts that are seldom resolved in the ways that developing children resolve contradictory intellectual beliefs that they find they have—that is, finding a higher-order principle that "explains" both sets of beliefs.

There probably is almost universal consensus on many facts about food and drink, safety and danger, and simple pain and pleasure. Much mathematics is universally accepted by those who are familiar with its workings. Much scientific belief is not controversial, although some is. Fields of science differ from each other in the criteria of evaluation used to weigh ideas and evidence, and the way scientists in the different fields of science talk about their work reveal more than one strategic strand (Mulkay, 1985). Although it may be that the "truth will out device" (Potter & Wetherell, 1987, p. 153) is as much an incantation as an article of faith, the growth of agreed knowledge and its status in all branches of the sciences has been prodigious in recent centuries. That some "observations" have to be revised and that many "interpretations" at lower and higher levels are contestable and contested does not diminish the size or quality of the growing encyclopedia or the principles and procedure for evaluating the claims made. In contrast, religious beliefs remain a major source of human diversity and conflict, both within and between groups. Given the kind and seriousness of questions posed, the difficulties of rendering the application of the criteria of evaluation communicable and testable by others, and the institutionalized power structures within which individuals live, religious beliefs are likely to be as slow to achieve a consensus as will universal commitments to particular political systems. For both some quite different and other similar reasons, consensus about aesthetics is another prospect receding into infinity. Unless human beings change, consensual aesthetics is not that important for survival; neither interindividual nor intergroup disagreements are the causes of fights or wars. So although political or religious conformity or both are integral to the cohesiveness and strength of a group, aesthetic preferences and judgments are not. (That is not to say that conformity will not be used as a marker of what kind of person someone is and whether he or she is a suitable group member [Bourdieu, 1977]. This may be very important, but to learn and conform to in aesthetics is less likely to provoke cognitive dissonance than is being insincere in public chanting about the nature of God.) The similarity with religious beliefs lies in the difficulty of elucidating criteria that can command agreement. This difficulty predates and has remained since Aristotle's (1926) assertion of "*De gustibus non disputandum est*" was first rendered into Latin.

Intermediate between aesthetics and religion are morals. Again, criteria of evaluation are not readily agreed on, but there does appear to be a continuing consensus in the rhetoric of the Great Thinkers and the statements that get written into the constitutions of states. Philosophers continue to worry about and contest issues in ethics, with periodic enthusiasm for arguments supporting pluralistic, relativistic, pragmatic, and other causes. These are persuasive in the contextual realizations of principles but do not appear to pose serious threats to the truth status of some basic principles. Reference has already been made to the fact that as soon as more than one principle is endorsed, it becomes inevitable that in practice principles will be in conflict with each other and choices about which to break have to be made. In the world of action we cannot escape inevitable tensions between individuals and between individuals and society in terms of rights and obligations, between freedoms to and freedoms from, and between encouraging individual responsibility and providing state support.

How much inequality in which spheres is it proper to permit? What should the principles of social justice be? What kind of society is best or better and how is movement in that direction to be achieved? Some of these issues may remain theoretically and practically intractable for the foreseeable future, but it is important to note that the United Nations was able to agree to a charter.

Individuals killing other individuals to settle disputes is universally illegal. Theft is illegal; its definition varies considerably from culture to culture, but the notion of individuals simply taking what is not theirs is a universal crime. Cruelty is wrong.

Because legal frameworks and moral codes define both the permissible and the desirable, their qualities are crucial determinants of how we live to an extent that aesthetics do not. What are either matured or indoctrinated minds seem to find Kant's (1781/1934) ideas about the possibility of certain moral principles having the status of synthetic a priori truths inescapable; they have to be true because it is impossible to conceive of a society in which they were not true! Although the relative priorities to be accorded to these may remain unagreed and the ways they are realized in different cultures may remain diverse, both the content of some moral principles and their criteria for evaluation seem to have prospects for consensus.

False Beliefs

The immediate temptation to suggest that what is false is defined by being beyond the boundaries of the true has to be resisted. All branches of knowledge have penumbra of that which is as yet not believed to be either true or false and that which may never be treated as either. The history of the human species, however, is littered with false beliefs from past ages. Many metaphysical monsters now exist only in texts, as do countless stories and myths. The great variety of beliefs about the origins and nature of the world and universe has narrowed through time, and there are an infinite number of propositions that could achieve near consensus as being false among those who have had opportunities to contemplate and examine them. These propositions span all the branches of knowledge referred to.

An application of the criteria for evaluation leads to rejections of their truthfulness: No invented logic yields the answer 13.3 for 2 + 2, no one claims that Stalin was ever Queen of England, hedgehogs do not transform themselves into witches, God is not hiding in Mount Vesuvius, catching and eating other people is no longer defended as acceptable conduct, a cherry blossom is not ugly.

How then might false statements link to lies?

Lies: Introduction

To lie is "to utter a falsehood with an intention to deceive; to give a false impression" (Schwarz, Davidson, Seaton, & Tebbit, 1988). The difference between the two halves of the entry captures two of the defining criteria about which people disagree. The first links lying to language use only and includes an intention to deceive. The second permits harmless creatures "to tell lies" if their appearance or other characteristics appear to imply that they are dangerous; the Australian tarantula is a liar on that definition—he looks dangerous but is not. More extreme views can be found among academics. It is possible to find those who defend the idea that all attempts to make true statements are "lies," because verbal activities can never capture the "whole truth" about their reference. Others claim that no utterances are lies because there are only phenomenological worlds composed of the subjective realities of individuals, and so there is no objective reality about which it is possible to deceive people. There may be obscure purposes for which these last two positions may be defensible, but neither will feature strongly in what is to follow. What they share is a double misunderstanding about language and how it works. All units and structures in a language can be defined contrastively. In this case, "telling a lie" contrasts with "telling the truth." To accept that this contrast has neither semantic nor pragmatic value would simply render much language activity meaningless and useless. If any particular contrast is useful to language users, then presumably they are free to use the contrast until they have reasons to abandon it. The contrast between true and false statements is probably a universal feature of all languages.

More seriously, however, the contrast between truth and falsity is the crucial distinction for the utility of the representational function of language. This function exists to convey new information from one head to another and presupposes that its users are generally following the maxim "Be truthful." Although some people might not want to live in a world where no one ever told lies, we cannot actually conceive of a world where everyone always told them. The old Greek paradox of what we are to make of the statement, "I am a Cretan," if we have previously believed that "All Cretans are liars" rests on more than one false presupposition. The false premise of relevance here is that the generalization is empirically absurd and it is impossible to conceive of all Cretans lying each time they make a statement.

To be able to avoid being impaled on either of these mythical horns does not help to resolve the definitional difficulties that are exemplified in the two offerings of the dictionary. The meanings and uses of words are matters of conventions among language users. Dictionary makers know that their attempts to describe such uses are oversimplifications and that any intention they might have to be prescriptive will meet with less than a universal and eternal consensus. As Popper (1976) pointed out, definitions are no more (and no less) than recommendations about meanings and usage, and as Rosch and Mervis (1975) noted, everyday concepts cover more or less fuzzy categories. What empirical evidence exists is consistent with a weakened form of Rosch's hypothesis. Coleman and Kay (1981) found that with their limited sample of people's judgments about possible lies, the major differentiating criteria were false or true, intention to deceive or no intention, and success or failure of deception. Only verbal forms of deception were investigated, and for these the modal requirements of participants were that the lie teller intended to have the victim believe a false statement to be true. Some respondents, however, required this intention to be successful in its deception for the utterance to be a lie. Others did not require the false belief to be based on a deliberate attempt to deceive. In brief, people differed in the way they defined a lie.

Fortunately, this lack of unanimity will not create insurmountable difficulties because the bases for the variations can be investigated and might even be a potential field for study in their own right. The ways people choose to use particular words can be indicative of their psychology. In this instance, it does seem that some people find it difficult to view lies dispassionately; to tell a lie is to do something wrong, and one device for not assigning blame is to limit the definition of the word lie or to modify the untruth into white lies.

It may then be sensible to begin with a conceptual analysis of the range of attributes that can be considered relevant to the act of lying. Either language or deception might be used as an initial point of departure. Deception will figure strongly throughout the text, and questions will be asked about deceptive behavior both in animals other than human beings and in growing humans in the hope that the phylogenetic and ontogenic roots of deceptive behavior generally are informative about lying itself. Presently, it may be better to lead in from language.

Five Approaches to Definitions of a Lie

Any hope that there might be consensus about the definition of the word lie must be abandoned quickly, although what follows helps to elucidate the issues about which the variability of opinion and preference turns. In one respect, a consensual definition may become unimportant. If propositions can be classified in terms of underlying characteristics relevant to lying, empirical work can exploit these directly for its tasks. In another respect, however, this is inconvenient. *Lie* is a brief lexical item, easily inserted into materials and procedures in ways that are more familiar to respondents than labels of underlying characteristics. For particular studies, there may need to be an assessment of the advantages and disadvantages of using the word *lie* or any of its cognate terms against using less familiar but more analytically precise terms or particular examples based on these. To move the enquiry into the difficulties, what are the varieties of statements among which lies might emerge as a category?

True Statements and Deviations From Them

Although their chapter title includes the clause "speakers lie to hearers" and the meaning of *lying* is posed as an issue in the first paragraph, Bradac, Friedman, and Giles (1986) do not actually isolate lying from other forms of deception or evasion in their analysis. Their point of departure is the event of stating of beliefs in propositional communication—that is, when a speaker explicitly or implicitly says to hearer, "I believe that X is Y." With four ex cathedra axioms, which might be called presuppositions about speaker states, comments are offered about these four: intention, accuracy, relevance, and accountability. *Intention* relates to willingness to cooperate with a demand of a hearer for a response. *Accuracy* refers not to the relation between utterance and its reference but to the sincerity of the speaker. Likewise, *relevance* is defined in terms of speaker's beliefs, as is *accountability*. These definitions focus clearly on what is happening in the speaker's head, at the expense of relations between utterance and its reference. Each of these is treated as having binary values of + or –, and hence 12 kinds of proposition are generated that are grouped into three families. The "truth-telling" family has truth telling itself as the + + + + member. The "falsehood" family includes + – + + as falsehood, and the "evasion" family has simple evasion + (±) – + (see Figure 1.1).

Essentially, this analysis is based on logical elaborations of selected premises, which are subsequently backed with illustrations of the semantics of possible exemplars of the categories. Whether the four categories are exhaustive is not immediately relevant. Neither is the question as to whether criterial attributes are defined by all or none rather than by graduated values. What is relevant is that the analysis shows that even if the focus is restricted to the speaker's mind, the options open to a speaker in context are considerable.

Although the word lie does not gain a definition from this analysis, the range of possibilities with which it might contrast begins to emerge.

Words of Deception

Grounded on group discussions, sortings by 180 students, and ratings by an additional 41, Hopper and Bell (1984) focused directly on English words cognate with deception. They began with a thesaurus and listed the entries under deception. From this source and

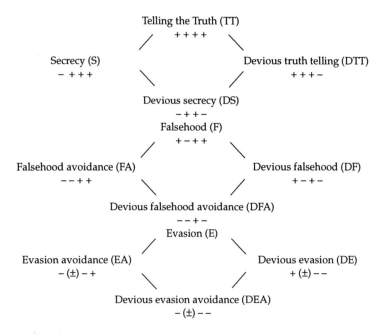

Figure 1.1. Families of belief states for propositional communication.

NOTE: Order of +s and –s: intention to utter, accuracy, relevance, and accountability (– = "not").

others, they compiled a list of 120 items, which by subsequent selection in group discussions was reduced to 46. These were subjected to two empirical studies probing the similarities among them. The statistical analyses yielded six forms of deception:

1. *Fictions*—words such as *exaggeration, myth,* and *white lie* reported as emphasizing structural properties
2. *Playings*—amusements at least as far as intentions are concerned (e.g., *joke, hoax,* and *tease*)
3. *Lies*—false verbal statements communicated with the intention to deceive (*lie, untruth, dishonesty, fib,* and *cheating*)
4. *Crimes*—acts proscribed by law (*spy, forgery,* and *disguise*)
5. *Masks*—activities that mask another person's view of the truth (e.g., *hypocrisy, two-faced,* and *evasion*)

6. *Un-lies*—deception through implication (e.g., *distortion* and *misrepresentation*)

Deception itself emerged last from the hierarchical cluster analysis, presumably as the superordinate concept. Lies were marked off by being restricted to language and their social unacceptability. The procedure adopted was a systematized approach to an activity instigated by Austin (1962), whose own conceptual analyses were fed in part by views of participants in (enjoyable) informal seminars.

What emerges is not unproblematic. What does one do with the responses that are wrong? Ignoring a small human error component that enters into any such task, is all the remaining diversity acceptable? In extremis, it cannot be. Respondents are not free to invent their own meanings for the word *lie*. Anyone who used it to mean a "promise" or a "fable" would be assumed to be ignorant; he or she has simply not learned what the word means in the language community. Yet others will have some idea but less than a complete one. Although, on the one hand, this is not to claim that there is a precise set of criteria discriminating lies from all other acts, on the other hand, it is to claim that the concept has to have either semantic features or protypicality or some other form of circumscription to function in a language system. The degree to which Hopper and Bell's (1984) sample yields a consensus that would extend to all other "competent" users of the English language is unknown.

One strange omission from the rating scales was the contrasts of truth-falsity and speaker's beliefs about the truth or falsity of the language-referent relationship. This means that two of the characteristics commonly cited as prototypical or criterial for a lie were not available for judgment and subsequent emergence.

Hopper and Bell's (1984) analysis exposes the association between the word *lie* and disapproval that is a chronic hazard in empirical work on the subject. On the ratings scale, it ranks tenth of the 46 deception words on good or bad and eighth on both social unacceptability and immorality. (*Fabrication* and *untruth* are ranked just lower, *whopper* and *fib* considerably lower, and *white lie* lower again, especially on the goodness scale.) The words were being rated out of context so that the ratings are a kind of default or resting meaning that could change considerably when given a context. For example, *equivocation* emerges as good in some of the contexts used by Bavelas, Black, Chovill, and Mullet (1990), even though its nearest equivalents in the Hopper and Bell (1984) study of *evasion* and *indirectness* are rated negatively on the evaluative scales.

With Bradac et al. (1986) emphasizing varieties of characteristics of potentially deceiving statements and Hopper and Bell (1984) demonstrating some of the difficulties of being precise in circumscribing *lie*, it may be instructive to examine the results of a directly focused empirical study.

Prototypical Lies

Coleman and Kay (1981) used the word *lie* to illustrate that word meanings could be based on prototypes rather than on distinctive features. Previous demonstrations that some words can have their meanings defined in terms of sets of attributes present or absent (see Brown, 1965; Chomsky, 1965, p. 214) can be contrasted with Wittgenstein's (1951/1967) worry that many words had referents that did not share any distinctive set of characteristics; he invoked the idea of "family resemblances" to cope with the fact that there were no criterial attributes that were either sufficient or necessary for a game to be a game. Berlin and Kay (1969) introduced the idea of the applicability of color terms being matters of more or less rather than Yes or No. Rosch and Mervis (1975) expanded the theme to describe categorization more generally as commonly being a human imposition of sharper boundaries than can be observed in nature. Rosch and Mervis added the useful distinctions between exemplars of a category that were marginal, typical, and par excellence. As such, penguins, ostriches, and especially archeopteryx are marginal birds in different respects. For many people, a chicken is not as typical as a robin, itself a bird par excellence. This approach, realized in formal logic with "fuzzy" sets, seems to be an essential component of any framework designed to cope with human categorization; it avoids the forced absurdities of the kind that arise when British Rail has to define a tortoise as a dog, cat, bird, or insect to arrive at its ticket cost (insect was the preferred category in at least one case).

The prototype schema offered for the word *lie* by Coleman and Kay (1981) comprised the following:

1. It must have a finite list of properties.
2. The schema must include the possibility that the properties themselves would be matters of quantitative rather than qualitative variation.

3. Category membership of *lie* must be a matter of quantitative variation.
4. Having more properties on the list contributes to the category membership overall.
5. Properties may have differential weights.
6. The ideas of necessary or sufficient conditions are too abrupt to apply.

The protypical, fully fledged lie is then defined as a proposition (P) asserted by S (sender) to an addressee (A) such that (1) P is false, (2) S believes P to be false, and (3) in uttering P, S intends that A shall come to believe P.

Coleman and Kay (1981) constructed eight stories and had respondents judge whether a marked utterance in the story was a lie, not a lie, or undeterminable. Participants also estimated how sure they were that other people would agree with them. They were invited to comment on their answers. A 7-point scale was devised with *very sure not a lie* at one extreme and *very sure a lie* at the other. In all stories, the speaker was selfishly motivated. An opportunity sample of mainly students and faculty completed the questionnaire. There was a clear rank ordering, and it was also evident that the elements differed in importance, with 2 the *most important* and 1 the *least important*.

Complications were noted. As with the Hopper and Bell (1984) data, moral judgments obtruded, and respondents referred to the speaker's inferred motivation as an additional element influencing their judgments. Should *lie* include an element of blameworthiness in its definition; for some people it did and for others it did not. (Not surprisingly, perhaps, psychologists and linguists prefer not to include blameworthiness as a defining element, but dictionaries, for example, do not necessarily follow this line.) Seriousness of consequences was also mentioned not just as making a lie worse but as part of the definition. A range of other methodologically contentious issues are rehearsed, reflecting in part the uncertainties surrounding appropriateness of rules of evidence across the linguistics-psychology boundary.

A Wide-Range Approach

Such qualms are less evident in the writing of Ekman (1985/1992) who quotes the Compact Oxford English Dictionary (1971) as stating that "in modern use, the word lie is normally a violent expression of moral reprobation, which in polite conversation tends to be avoided, the synonyms false and untruth being often substituted as relatively euphemistic" (p. 26). Ekman himself insists that free will is also criterial—"a liar can choose not to lie"—as is intention, "misleading the victim is deliberate." He excludes paranoids who have assumed false identities and what he terms pathological liars. He excludes actors because their audience has been given notice that they are not who they appear to be; liars do not inform their victims of their pretense.

Ekman (1985/1992) proceeds to include concealment as well as falsification, nonverbal deception as well as verbal. He adds other means:

> misdirecting, acknowledging an emotion, but misidentifying what caused it; telling the truth falsely, or admitting the truth but with such exaggeration and humor that target remains uninformed or misled; half-concealment, or admitting only part of what is true . . . ; and the incorrect inference dodge, or telling the truth but in a way that implies the opposite of what is said. (pp. 41-42)

A Philosophical Stance

In contrast, Bok (1978), as a self-confessed practically focused philosopher, is careful to weigh arguments for and against the variety of possible uses. She notes that ideas of *the whole truth* are literally impossible extensions of what may be a defensible core idea. She states that the opposition of lying to truth telling is a contrast absent in pre-Socratic philosophy and points out the necessity to maintain a distinction between "the moral domain of truthfulness and deception, and the much vaster domain of truth and falsity in general" (p. 6). Ethics have to be separated from epistemology and from its issues of how we can be sure of any knowledge and the variety of errors we can make in trying to ascertain what it is most reasonable to believe is true. Eventually Bok chooses to use *deception* to refer to acts intended to make others believe what we ourselves do not believe. She then confines *lies* to deceptions that are stated either in language or in some other semiotic system. As she correctly observes, historically, lying has been more circumscribely defined, particularly by religious thinkers who had some doctrinal need to justify the morality of uttering false statements in certain situations (see Zagorin, 1990). Not telling the truth to would-be murderers and thieves was one example, but false confessions with explicit mental reservations were also permitted. Zagorin (1990) offers an extended account of the conditions under which, and the means by which, various kinds of false statement could be nullified as lies. Just as these issues became and become matters of life and death for those being interrogated, so in various legal systems and other settings, issues of what was in fact true—what S believed to be true, what S intended by any action performed, and what the consequences of any actions were—severally became critical points affecting judgments on individuals.

Summary: Definitions

What the five approaches show is that there is a lack of unanimity. Statements do not fall neatly into categories of true, false, and either or neither. People claim to be able to locate degrees of lying, where the co-occurrence of the three criteria (P is false, S believes P to be false, and S intends A to believe P) led to 66 of 67 respondents judging that a lie was being told. The findings of Coleman and Kay (1981) coincide with the preference of the philosopher Bok (1978). The three characteristics appear in the work of the developmental psychologists reported in Chapter 2. In fact, Ekman (1985/1992) has subscribed to a comparable operational definition in most of his empirical work, even if his brief conceptual comments are wider and stretch the word *lie* beyond the general consensus.

Bok (1978), Coleman and Kay (1981), and Hopper and Bell (1984) point to the common insistence on attaching blame to liars not as an independent judgment but as a component of the definition. Likewise, those who wish to exclude altruistic lies or white lies from the category are treating consideration for others as a justification for lying as well as part of its meaning. Outcomes do not seem to have been incorporated into definitions per se, although the seriousness of the positive or negative outcomes feature in the strength of the mitigation or condemnation.

Figure 1.2 is intended to clarify both the definitional issues and some of the questions that have been linked to the evaluation of the

Agency
  Premeditated versus impulsive
  Proactive versus reactive

Motivation
  Whose benefit?
  Self/addressee/others
    Kind of benefit
      Escape-avoid negative
      outcomes
      Achieve positive outcomes

Lies
1. **P is false.**
2. **S believes P to be false.**
3. **S intends A to believe P**

Experiential correlates
  None
  Fear
  Excitement
  Guilt, etc.

Consequences
  Trivial versus serious
  Unintended versus intended
  Gains versus losses for
    self/others
  Short versus long term

Reactions of others
  Indifference
  Amusement
  Approval
  Disapproval
  Anger, etc.

Figure 1.2. Lies: defining characteristics, agency, motivation, experiential correlates, reactions of others, and consequences.

wrongness of lies. Given that the sample of Coleman and Kay (1981) can be taken to be competent in the use of the word *lie*, the prototypicality model has to be preferred to any other model that would tighten the definition to have criterial attributes. If their definition is combined with Grice's (1975/1989) model of cooperative conversation, the kinds of worry that some authors have expressed about the status of white lies, nonsequiturs, and various other indirect or superficially counterfactual modes of communicating disappear. The addressee has the burden of interpretation. If A assumes that S is not being misleading, A has to work out why S has not followed the maxim of truthfulness. Perhaps S has given precedence to a maxim, "Be polite." Perhaps S is not being relevant because any answer will lead to negative consequences. Those who understand the culture will be able to discern what is being implicated rather than being said.

As Bradac et al. (1986) and Hopper and Bell (1984) show, there are many ways of not revealing the relevant informative truth without producing counterfactual statements. Equivocation and concealment are perhaps the most common of the evasive strategies. In one of Bavelas et al.'s (1990) studies, equivocation was rated as more truthful than a true alternative; how that came about has yet to be explained. Equivocation need not involve any of the characteristics of a lie specified in Figure 1.2 and is probably best treated as a category of utterance of interest in its own right. Concealment of relevant information, including emotions, is treated by Ekman (1985/1992) as lying, although Burgoon et al. (1994) found that in patient-doctor communication it covaried more closely with equivocation than with lie telling. Ekman is right in that evidence of concealment of emotion may have been a cue that deception was being attempted. Concealment of facts relevant to the topic is not normally treated as lying per se, although its motivational reasons and consequences may be identical or very similar. The phrase, "the whole truth," in legal oaths is intended to prevent concealment, but a common rebuttal to a discovered concealment is that the accused claims that the information was deemed not to be relevant. Although both equivocation and concealment are cognate with counterfactuals, they are not included as foci in the main text. By confining the core frame of reference to truthfulness, on the one hand, and counterfactuals intended to deceive, on the other hand, much of the cleverness of human communication and miscommunication is omitted, but at least the extremes are considered.

Because almost no empirical studies have checked whether the three characteristics of Coleman and Kay (1981) were present, it is difficult to know when to use the word *counterfactual* and when to use *lie*. This difficulty is compounded in those studies in which participants were instructed to lie; there is a sense in which S may intend A to believe P in such circumstances and the motivation may be sincere, but it is acting out an imposed role rather than being oneself.

The surrounding quintet are some of the questions posed about lies and lying in succeeding chapters.

Conclusions

During the tutorials that inducted me into the debating ways of philosophers, I could glance periodically at an embroidery above the fireplace that spelled out the advice, "Beware lest any man tempt you with philosophy," and it is a salutary warning. Philosophy is prone to develop a paralysis through analysis, and its practitioners are liable to forget the ultimate importance of synthesis, decision making, and action. To serve as a basis for action, philosophy has to be articulated with linguistics, psychology, and sociology. For many people, it has to be articulated with their religious beliefs.

Here, several main issues have been addressed. First, it was necessary to point to the variety of functions language serves. Attempts to describe and explain particular and general phenomena in the world require the use of the representational function. Well-founded (and other) beliefs are expressed using statements. Well-founded beliefs are those for which a person believes there is sufficient appropriate evidence for them to be the current best estimate of what is true. To decide what is most likely to be true, human beings have invented ideas of rationality and realism, which in combination with devised rules of evidence, provide coherent sets of beliefs that are more adaptive than other ideas for leading pragmatically successful lives.

As far as human action is concerned, however, people act in the light of their subjective experience; their interpretations guide their actions. These social representations and constructions may or may not correspond to objective reality, and this contrast is an essential distinction for the human sciences. Although it is valuable to pare away the false beliefs that may have accrued to social representations, however, such an analysis does not provide a basis for deciding what to do with the results. For that, decisions about what is true need to be confronted and brought into plans for action.

The need to decide what is true, good, and just does not appear to have figured very strongly in human affairs in the 2,000 years since Socrates both set down the challenge and proposed some strategies for apprehending solutions. Human activity has been more heavily invested in a Darwinian contest for survival. The avoidance of premature death and suffering and the pursuit and maintenance of power, wealth, and status have figured prominently as mainsprings of human action. Individuals who have been most successful at gaining and maintaining power have typically relegated telling the truth to a lower priority than defeating competitors and warding off threats to their positions. The primary function of their language use has been to exercise dominance and to regulate the actions and experience of others. In addition to issuing orders and inspiring people's support by whatever rhetorical means that have been available, such authorities have typically attempted to prevent others from acquiring the intelligence necessary for making up their own minds about issues of truth and falsity, especially on issues of relevance to religious beliefs and beliefs about the ethical principles that should underpin the functioning and structuring of societies. The adoption of a societal perspective is deferred until Chapter 6. The origin of lying by children is a more appropriate beginning, and that is introduced with some comments about deception in other species (Chapter 2), which leads into lying face to face in informal situations, with Chapter 3 concentrating on the static features and Chapter 4 on the dynamics of deception and detection.

CHAPTER TWO

Children Learning to Lie

Preamble

If the question posed is how and when does lying emerge and develop as a controlled competence in children, then no matter how *lying* is defined, the question cannot be answered at the present time.

Eventually, the following questions will need to be answered for both production and perception of lies within each of the various kinds of knowledge: everyday empirical, scientific empirical, logical, religious, moral, and aesthetic. What are the necessary, sufficient, facilitatory, and inhibitory conditions for the emergence of

1. each category of counterfactual verbal statements (CVSs),
2. a category of CVSs that the child believes to be false, and
3. a category of CVSs that the child believes to be false but intends the target to believe.

The analyses of the conditions relevant will specify the features in the child and his or her environment relevant to development. What role do role models play? Can children learn from discoveries that what adults say to them is not true? What can they learn from listening to others talking about lies? What can they learn from the reception of their own false statements? The questions will be much more detailed than these, and the answers will be embedded in the much more complex charts that have yet to be produced in detail for intellectual development more generally.

Translated into simple English, these abstract prescriptions are intended as a warning against people asking for and receiving simplistic answers. It is probably as misguided to think of a child's first lie as it is to think of a first *word*, for example. It is quite common for people to watch out for and announce a particular noise as a first word. This is hailed as a milestone. As Chapter 1 has implied, however, language mastery is a long, complicated process that is never completed. There is always more to learn about language and how it works. This is also true with falsification and the lying variant of it.

It may be that one of the earliest contexts for false denials by infants is a reactive denial of "No" to an adult accusation that the infant has performed some reprehensible action. If the No is accepted and trouble avoided, the infant should be more likely to use it on the next comparable occasion. Instrumental conditioning would suffice to explain the incorporation of such a reaction. This is not a first lie, however. It meets criterion 1 described previously but is unlikely to meet the other two. The habits, the skills, and the capacity for reflective understanding will be accumulated. Data from own experience, observations of others, and instructions from others will become available for processing, interpretation, and application. In 20 years' time, the descriptions and explanations of the development of the capacity to lie and deceive will probably compose a fat volume in its own right. Initially, it may be helpful to question what biologists' work on deception says about such activities in the rest of the animal kingdom.

Nonhuman Deception

Definitions are recommendations to use words with specifiable meanings. A good definition is one that combines conceptual clarity with eventual universal adoption. It will only achieve the latter if it is useful to the universes of discourse of those who need to use it. The advantages and disadvantages of different circumscriptions of the application of the word *lie* have been elaborated in Chapter 1. There are disadvantages to each degree of restriction, which is also true with deception.

To exclude cases of plant growers using artificial light to "deceive" their plants or contingency learning whereby rewarding or punishment-avoiding effects are achieved via instrumental conditioning, Russow (1986) follows Dennett's (1978, pp. 273-274) proposal that to intend X, the agent must be able to have beliefs and desires about X. Incorporating this leads to "an agent's behaviour is deceptive if and only if the agent intends that, because of its behaviour, another organism will come to have (and perhaps act on) a false belief" (p. 48). This restriction may commend itself to philosophers and other human beings who are primarily concerned with analyzing the nature of human deception; it is not very helpful for biologists who might be interested in questions about the evolution of deception or developmental psychologists concerned with explaining how the human infant achieves the status apposite to Russow's definition. Because that is part of the current brief, it may be helpful to revert to Chapter 1 of the same book (Mitchell, 1986) and examine Mitchell's approach, which is summarized in Table 2.1.

Mitchell's (1986) subdivision has immediate appeal in that the levels appear to differ in the "openness" of any genetic programming and the complexity of the items needed to regulate the deception. The orchids that look sufficiently like certain insects to attract males of the same species into copulation and thereby achieve pollination are genetically instructed to grow as they do. Similarly, better camouflaged creatures avoid detection by predators, except that in this case one can additionally see how variation within a species might be acted on selectively to change the chances of survival of particular variants. As Mitchell points out, the "deceiver" and "deceived" will not always operate at the same level. The blue jays that avoid eating tasty specimens because they look like unpalatable Monarch butterflies are operating at Level 3 but in response to a Level 1 deception. In contrast, fly-fishing people use Level 4 intelligence to design a Level 1 device to catch trout operating at Level 2.

For using this framework, Mitchell (1986) recommends that Lloyd-Morgan's (1894) canon of parsimony be applied: "In no case may we interpret an action as the outcome of the exercise of a higher psychical faculty, if it can be interpreted as the outcome of one which stands lower on the psychological scale" (p. 53). Pushing down actions to the lowest level runs the risk of requiring too much specificity in genetic programming or placing too heavy a burden on classical or instrumental conditioning or both, too much emphasis on each of which has slowed down progress by seducing psychologists into ignoring the complexities of both animal and human behavior, especially concerning its social realizations. Paradoxically, excessive overendowment of a species with capacities can also lead to an

Table 2.1 A Summary of the Levels of Deception, With Examples After Mitchell (1986)

Level	Deception Is Affected By	Program	Examples of Deceiver	Examples of Deceived
1	Appearance	"Always do p"	Batesian mimics; butterflies with falsehead; plants that mimic	Not possible
2	Coordination of perception and action	"Do p given that q is so"	Firefly femmes fatales; birds that feign injury; angler-fish that darts lure	Males that respond to femmes fatales fireflies
3	Learning	"Do any p given that p resulted in q in your past"	Birds of Beau Geste hypothesis; dog that fakes a broken leg	Blue jays that respond to Batesian mimicry of butterfly; foxes that respond to injury feigning of birds
4	Planning	Self-programmed	Chimp that misleads about location of food; humans who lie	Humans deceived by verbal lie

SOURCE: Reprinted from *Deception: Perspectives on Human and Nonhuman Deceit* by R. W. Mitchell & N. S. Thompson by permission of the State University of New York Press. Copyright © 1986.

overemphasis on genetic programing. Chomsky's (1965) unsubstantiated claims about the powers of the language acquisition device, which he invented for all human children, distracted attention from the learning processes and the significance of the role of caretakers for nearly two decades (e.g., see Bruner, 1983; Robinson, 1984). Humanizing animals and plants can also lead to a dottier and romantic anthropomorphizing, designed to increase sales of books rather than to enhance public or professional understanding. (Why anyone dissents from Lloyd-Morgan's canon, I cannot understand; adherence to it makes it more likely that we search exhaustively and analytically for necessary and sufficient conditions of events and changes.)

The four levels form a hierarchy that leads to an expectation that understanding how each higher level is achieved will require understanding of lower levels—and something more. To anticipate: It may be that it is only when children achieve an intelligence equivalent to Level 4 and can bring that to bear on data acquired through processes at Levels 2 and 3 that they become competent to plan deceptions.

The very idea of levels has a heuristic advantage. It does not matter if the four levels change or eventually increase to five or six. What is important at this stage is that a differentiation of levels can be linked to different kinds of effectance and programs along with differentiated examples of deceivers and deceived. This satisfies the old adage that what is critical is the invention of a taxonomy that has a plausible rationale. Once that is available, then appropriate imaginative empirical testing and probing of the various features through cases will serve as secure a foundation as is possible for future revision or rejection.

Here, the definition of deception will follow Mitchell (1986):

1. An organism R registers (or believes) something Y from some organism S, where S can be described as benefiting when (or desiring that)
2. R acts appropriately toward Y, because
   a. Y means X; and
3. it is untrue that X is the case. (p. 21)

Human beings seem to be perennially fascinated by ideas of differences between and similarities to themselves and other creatures. Mitchell (1986) suggests that the observations of Russell of an arctic fox, of Munn with sentinel birds in mixed flocks that uttered warning cries that resulted in their being able to retrieve food from distracted companions, and of Morris with elephants using a free shower lure to protect themselves from attack severally imply Level-3 deception. Whether the great apes can manage Level 4 remains contentious. A decade ago, it appeared that apes could learn elementary sign languages to a level consistent with Level 4 deception. This is now contested because the critical demonstrating incidents are being treated as possible artifacts of large data banks. De Waal (1986) has collected observations of semicaptive chimpanzees that encourage him to believe that they can engage in "non-ritualized, intelligent forms of deception" (p. 221) that "suggest, but cannot prove, the existence of intentional deception" (p. 221). He notes that his own observations extended over 6,000 hours and that instances of possible Level 4 deception are rare. Classifying actions into (a) camouflage, (b) feigning interest, (c) feigning a mood, (d) signal correction, and (e) falsification, De Waal argues for instances of Mitchell's Levels 3 and 4 in each. The strongest illustrations are impressive and improbable products of Level 3; it is not necessary, however, to record a verdict either way. Perhaps it is worth noting that the rarity may itself be informative; chimpanzees that achieve a tactical deception are not sufficiently insightful to realize the implications of deception as a general strategy for gaining individual benefits within the group. Perhaps they are at the margin; accidental or coincidental combinations of circumstances provide occasions that permit the realization of a Level 4 deception, but they cannot learn and generalize from this opportunity.

Child Development

The Beginnings of Human Deception

Unfortunately, none of the work with nonhuman species has looked at deception longitudinally from a developmental perspective within individuals. Mitchell's (1986) analysis does not indicate how progression from Levels 2 to 3 to 4 or beyond might be achieved.

Equally unfortunate, none of the work with human creatures has indicated how the progression from nonverbal to verbal deception is achieved, if indeed that is the direction of development. How children move into a mastery of language as a communication system was referred to in Chapter 1; the argument was based on a functional-structural approach that emphasized a little-by-little accumulation of increasingly differentiated units that could become modified and resynthesized to conform to the phonological, grammatical, and semantic units and structures conventional to the adult language but driven by pragmatics.

No model of the learner was offered. Perhaps a position on such a model needs to be articulated as a framework. One complication is that any model of the child offered will have to include a succession of increasingly complex systems and subsystems. For example, classical and instrumental conditioning are generally viewed as learning mechanisms beyond the victim's control; they occur and human beings do not escape their implications. This is especially true of babies, infants, and young children. Mature adults, however, can choose to enter programs of conditioning that may train them to escape from features of their cultural heritage or personal experience; they can learn to endure pain far in excess of the normal, or they can learn to inflict pain on others, again far in excess of contemporary norms. The earlier mechanical contingencies remain in force but can subsequently be exploited by conscious agents wishing to control themselves.

To continue the discussion, I make the following assumptions:

1. Both classical and instrumental conditioning experiences are major determinants of the probabilities of acts selected for future performance, the intensity with which they are enacted, and the persistence with which they are pursued. They underpin much learning.

2. Observational learning may be a separable category; whether or not it is eventually incorporated as a subtype of some other variety remains to be seen.

3. Babies are problem solvers from a very early age. In addition to being "victims" of conditioning, they are also "agents" who behave as though they are developing hypotheses that they test.

4. Caregivers can structure both the physical and the social environments to optimize the quality and quantity of learning. They can do so through a combination of Assumptions 1 and 2 (and also through direct instruction).

5. Babies experience emotions, needs, and drives, the latter include dispositions to explore and play, to imitate, and to interact happily with other human beings, especially primary caregivers. Activities will be

motivated by needs for contact, comfort, food and drink, and pain escape. How many more motives are listed depends on one's choice of author.

6. Two of Vygotsky's (1978) principles may be particularly apposite for the emergence of capacities to describe and to lie.

   a. He refers to particular actions appearing twice in the developing repertoire. On the first set of occasions they are accidental and involuntary but have observable consequences. Subsequently, they can be controlled to bring about the observed consequences. (This idea fits the possibility that what is learned involuntarily under Assumptions 1, 2, or 3 or all three can subsequently be redeployed consciously and deliberately in circumstances of one's own choosing.)

   b. What can be done initially only in very small measure and only with maximal help from others can be "scaffolded" into a complex and flexible self-directed script. For example, in learning games such as Peek-a-boo, parents will initially conduct the whole ritual with the child as participant observer, but piece by piece they will entice the child into participation as actor, with the child eventually taking over the parental role and creating new variants of the game (Bruner, 1983). Vygotsky (1978) called the scope of these possibilities "the zone of proximal development."

7. Piaget (1970) and many others have demonstrated in some detail some of the achievements of children in the first 2 years of life. It is now possible to write an encyclopedic volume on those facets that have received attention. By the age of 2, children have already established different kinds of what has traditionally been called *knowledge*. *Belief* would be a better word because some of the knowledge is incorrect, but it is also a worse word because English requires that beliefs are propositional rather than procedural. (It sounds odd to assert that skills are based on beliefs, for example.) Knowledge will have to serve. Exemplar kinds are these:

   a. Procedural knowledge—(know-how). Two-year-olds can coordinate eye and hand to pick up an object and put it in their mouth. They can also ask for objects beyond their reach. "Know-how" includes knowing how to be effective verbally.

   b. Procedural knowledge of contingencies (knowing when to use know how). Many associations will be based on classical conditioning: alarm cries related to pain and fear escape and avoidance. Many will be based on shaped routes to rewards. Others will be based on combinations: routes indoors to escape from frightening experiences outside—for example, barking dogs. Again, verbal

knowings are part of the repertoire: knowing who to address in
what manner with what words when and where.

c. Propositional knowledge that cannot be verbalized (knowing that).
   What is believed to be true requires some form of realizable representation to have significance, but there is no reason why this has
   to be encoded in symbolic form: Iconic representations are a form
   of knowing that. (As a complication, it can be noted that just
   because they are encoded in language does not mean that the user
   has them represented symbolically. They can be equivalent to en-
   active [sensory motor] schemes that happen to use language forms.
   They can be iconic [images].)

d. Propositional knowledge that can be verbalized. Languages are
   only one potentially symbolic system among an array that includes
   logics, algebras, and others, but they are the vehicle for realized
   representations of most everyday particular and much elementary
   more specialized knowledge.

Piaget (1970) saw representations as staged, with sensory motor
preceding preoperational and concrete operational thinking, in
which images were the basis of coding with a final flowering of
formal operational capacities realized in what Piaget called sign
systems (abstract and general). Bruner (1966) used the words *enac-
tive, iconic,* and *symbolic,* and argued for their interactive possibilities,
the latter two having early beginnings and growing out of and reliant
on what was already represented for much of their data.

This attempt to provide a frame of reference is a necessary prelude
to any discussion of the emergence of deception and lying. Even so,
what has been offered is mainly in terms of processes, structures, and
opportunities, with almost no content. What can be learned at any
point in time, however, is necessarily limited by the contents of the
contemporary knowledge and experience of the child as the capacities and dispositions. It is perhaps not surprising that any review of
what is currently believed will not be very well ordered, especially
because relevant research is accumulating rapidly on this currently
popular topic.

Fifteen years ago, the study of language development was beginning to escape from (and build on) the obsession with transforma-
tional grammar and was beginning to answer questions about the
growth in the speaking and listening competence and performance
of real children developing in real contexts, the characteristics and

determinants of the sequences, and the relevance of the interactions with other people. Fifteen years ago, deception and lying in children were dead areas. Recent standard texts either make no mention (e.g., Meadows, 1986; Mussen, 1970) or brief mention (Smith & Cowie, 1991) of the topics. If it is the case that nonverbal deceptions precede and then co-occur with false statements, there are various candidate activities of self and others that might provide data for eventual discriminations.

Play itself may defy consensual definition, but it is not impossible to differentiate between playful and serious behavior in young children. One category includes fantasy. Piaget (1970) documented instances of his children pretending that objects were other objects from approximately their first birthdays. Fenson and Schnell (1986) distinguish three concurrent trends of development: increasing decentration as the child shifts the roles from self to doll to doll as appropriate agent, increasing decontextualization from real to less real to imagined objects, and increasing integration from single actions to scripts. By age 2, miniature plays are being performed. Language play was well documented by Weir's (1962) recordings of her 2-year-old's bedtime soliloquies.

To play is not to deceive, but it does require that appearance ceases to be reality and it does require the child to make a discrimination between the real world and the pretend world. Although some children some of the time seem to get carried away by their fantasy activities, most of the time most children can separate the worlds. For how many might this serve as a springboard for the idea that deception is a possibility? If a child pretends to have a pain or injury, does the caregiver occasionally signal alarm rather than connive at the illusion (Harris, 1989)? Does the child notice that the caregiver cannot tell whether the pain is real or not? Similarly with language play? Do children notice that speech does not have to correspond to reality? Anything can be said? Does this possibility serve as data for subsequent motivated falsifications?

Some kinds of nonverbal and verbal play encourage deceit. Even such games as Peek-a-boo, where surprise is entertaining, can base the surprise on setting up false expectations. Hide and search games involving objects may include the laying of misleading clues. Adult deception is made available for young children to copy and learn. These forms of deception, if successful, increase the probability of

ception and lying. By 1993, arguments about the earliest age by which conscious deception could be practiced by children have led to claims as low as 3 years old for some measure of apposite knowledge. Ruffman, Olson, Ash, and Keenan (1993) were worried by two issues in the literature. Are the deceptive acts of 2- and 3-year-olds observed and reported by Dunn (1988) simply learned responses acquired by conditioning or observational learning or did these children believe that their behavior could implant a belief in the mind of others that the children know to be false? Perner (1991) had noted that Piaget's (1932) Jacqueline examples could be at Mitchell's (1986) Level 3 (forms of contingency learning based on conditioning or observations) as could Stern and Stern's (1909) "Did you hurt your brother?" evoking a "No." The "No" could have meant "Don't remind me," for example. Perner extended his skepticism to the 11 of 29 2.9- to 3.1-year-old children of Lewis, Stanger, and Sullivan (1989) who had peeped at a toy within a 5-minute forbidden period of wait- ing for an experimenter to return and then denied doing so. Perhaps they had simply learned that denial avoids reproach. Ruffman et al. reviewed evidence that 3 year olds have or do not have such beliefs and then they set out to test whether or not previous failures to find understanding about false beliefs in 3-year-olds may have arisen from cognitive overloading in the particular tasks given rather than from conceptual limitations. They did not, however, find deception as a means of inducing a false belief easier than the standard false belief task in either 3- or 4-year-olds. In a second test, active participant deceivers did not differ from observers, and it seemed that difficulties experienced by observers were conceptual. A final study failed to show that task complexity or pragmatic problems were limiting factors; it was conceptual limitations that were shown to be limiting factors. This does not reconcile the differences between the four empirical studies and seven theorizing papers that they cite as consistent with their results on the one hand, and the existence of five positively discrepant papers that claim that 3-year-olds do "know" that beliefs can be false (e.g., Chandler, Fritz, & Hala, 1989; Sodian, 1991). Russell, Jarrold, and Potel (1994) have raised the question of underestimation of what 3-year-olds know about deception because estimates rely on an additional executive load. Progress is being made with an articulation.

In a chapter that predates work on theory of mind, Freeman, Sinha, and Condliffe (1981) drew attention to the hazards of conducting experiments with young children, and the children they described certainly came alive as little people rather than as information processing systems. Similarly, in Freeman's 1994 account of why 3-year-olds may not be able to comment accurately in answer to questions about events and other people's beliefs about those events he suggests that 3-year-olds focus on action and perception, on seeing and doing, rather than on cognition: believing and thinking. He suggests that tasks and situations intended to display green shoots of a competence should capitalize on the natural strengths, knowledge, and biases of young children; they should also exploit familiar situations. Freeman is clearly worried about experimenters running a procedure, obtaining data, averaging their results, and interpreting what children say at face value. The same article claims to illustrate how failed false belief children would act out a search procedure that seemed to take into account the false belief, at least with direction of gaze. Changing the question from "think" to "will look" enhanced performance (Lewis, Freeman, Hagestadt, & Douglas, 1992). One of the conditions in one of the studies of Ruffman et al. (1993) included the following "information":

> Now that Sally is in the playground and she can't see us or hear us, Green Boy is going to go and take all the Smarties. He'll wander over to the Smarties pile and eat all the Smarties. Then he'll leave a crayon behind and then he'll go back to where he was before. (p. 79)

These are long sentences, as are others in the game. In fact, the narratives are acted out with characters in context and check questions are inserted into the procedure. One can still question, however, whether the procedures are ahead of children's intellectual powers and experience to an extent that some of them are reduced to ritualized responding to some point that they latch on to. Freeman (1994) argues for and cites evidence (Mitchell & Lacohée, 1991) consistent with the view that the provision of iconic tracers or support can enhance children's performance, and that is exactly what one would expect if Vygotsky's (1978) zone of proximal development and Bruner's (1983) scaffolding concepts have any validity—both notions imply that an incremental addition of units of competence or understanding are optimal for developing mastery.

Clements and Perner (1993) are offering the basis of a constructive synthesis. Using a standard false belief test modified only so that children's direction of gaze could be registered, especially just prior to the posing of the question, "Where will Sam look for the cheese?" 10 children looked at the right place and pointed to the wrong one; 2 looked at the wrong place first but then gave the right answer. This result was replicated in a second study. Particularly interesting in the second, more complex study, was the relationship between understanding and age. If eye movements are used as indicators of implicit understanding, the dramatic increase is across the third birthday, but for explicit understanding indexed by action prediction, the corresponding competence level is reached a year later at 4. Again, this is not surprising, any more so than much earlier findings that giving good reasons for conserving judgments lagged behind getting the answers right that lagged behind nonverbal action-based indicators of mastery (Donaldson, 1978; Peill, 1975).

Comment

The research concerned with exposing children's developing beliefs about their own and other minds could be at risk of following a parallel course to that followed by the disputatious Piagetian enthusiasts of the 1960s and 1970s. In that earlier enterprise, ideas about and techniques of testing concepts such as egocentrism, conservations, or seriation escalated into a plethora of disputed definitions. Investigations became procedurally more complex and occasionally oversimplified so that the original focus of intellectual development became lost in methodological quarrels. The arguments about earliness of initial competence seemed to take precedence over the detailed description and explanation of the intellectual development of children. How children came to change their thinking and what particular changes occurred in what order should have remained the prime concern. On a smaller scale in a more limited area, a similar story could be set to be reenacted with the theory of mind research.

There are investigators who follow Lloyd-Morgan's (1894) canon of parsimony. There are others apparently anxious to endow children as young as possible with as much as possible. To credit any child beliefs with the glamorous and grandiose title of "A Theory of Mind" may be good for marketing, but it distracts from the scientifically exciting possibilities of describing and explaining the details of differentiation and integration (analysis and synthesis), the kinds and levels of procedural and propositional "beliefs," and the factors that facilitate, retard, distort, or prevent learning and development. The range of issues this contrast raises is explored in-depth and detailed by Chandler (1988).

To date, the studies referred to here on the child's increasing powers to cope with a correct diagnosis of what should be believed by someone else generally appear to be progressing in a more cooperative spirit than marked the 1960s and perhaps the research will avoid being sucked into a whirlpool of quixotic fencing. The attempts to reconcile divergent findings described with similar terminology are leading to further results that simultaneously advance knowledge and refine terminology. The length of the lag between what Clements and Perner (1993) call "implicit" and "explicit" is a quarter of a lifetime for the 4-year-olds. Intuitively, this seems to be a long time to make the upgrading, but it is necessary to remember that the children's priorities do not dictate that they develop this particular understanding as fast as possible. There are ice creams to be eaten, stories to be told, and games to be played.

In developmental psychology, there are difficulties in explaining any change or upgrading, but eventually, explanations also have to be consistent with the particular rate of development shown. Knowing that others can have false beliefs is but one necessary condition of becoming a successful liar. What happens later has not been investigated. Above age 5, investigators have relied almost entirely on children's comments about the word *lie*.

Development of Deception From Age 5

Peskin (1992) gave children a task in which they wanted to obtain an "X sticker," but had to cope with two puppets, one that never wanted the X sticker and one that always did. On each trial, the puppet chose before the child. The 3- to 4- and 4- to 5-year-olds pointed truthfully and then found the puppet took the X sticker. The 5- to 6-year-olds were not fooled by the dishonesty of the puppet. Over six trials, the 3- 4-year-olds showed no change, and the 4- to 5-year-olds learned quickly not to point at their preferred choice for the deceiving puppet but continued to do so for the honest puppet that did not want the prized sticker. Perner (1991) argued that this could be fast learning of a contingency rule. This is less likely to be the case with the studies of Russell, Mauthner, Sharpe, and Tidswell (1991) and Sodian (1991). Sodian noted that the ability to point deceptively correlated highly with telling a nasty puppet that a reward was in a box that was locked when it was actually unlocked. That older children succeeded on the first trial in a novel task reduces the likelihood of their behavior being informed by learned contingencies. In a comparative analysis of autistic, mentally retarded, and normal children, Sodian and Frith (1992) have shown that normal children were better at a false belief task than they were at two deception tasks. Performance on false belief predicted performance of deceptive pointing and being untruthful. Preventing wolf from getting the Smarties by locking the relevant box appears to have been the easiest of the tasks given, but this was not tested for significance against the deceptive strategies. Children were also given a final demonstration of deceptive pointing and being untruthful by a female doll and were asked, "Why did she do or say this?" Overall for the sample as a whole, distinctions appeared between effects on behavior and the actor's belief; typically, the reasons given were pragmatic and consequential rather than preventively rational, "so that the wolf doesn't get the sweet." Of the successfully deceiving normal children, 50%, however, did refer to the beliefs of the actor "because the wolf thinks there's no sweet in the box." The text is not quite clear, but it seems safe to infer that performance is more likely to be in advance of verbal state of belief explanations than the reverse.

In a different genre, in work related to levels of social understanding, Selman (1980) included a checkerboard game in which two players had to discriminate among six unmarked pieces of the opponent to work out which two were the "carriers." The winner was the person moving his or her own carriers to the end of the board first. Children aged 5 to 13 played and were allowed to say what they like. The youngest, most naive children just played and did not bother to win. Level 1 children would identify their pieces falsely, apparently expecting that the other child would believe them and not realizing that in this context if Cretans always lie, the truth is inferrable. Neither did they think the other child would lie. At Level 2, reciprocity of expectation appears (ages 7-12). At Level 3, tactics became mixed and contingent with double bluffs. Selman's is one of the few studies that examines deception developmentally with a concern for establishing a sequence. Given the ubiquity of such tactical games and their popularity, it is surprising that more colleagues have not taken up the challenge to develop the model. There are almost certainly more taxonomic details to be discovered and the dynamics of transitions need investigation. Perhaps too it is in such games that Ekman's (1985/1992) "duping delight" first manifests itself; the excitement and tension of potentially successful deception can be learned in games without risk of the penalties to be incurred in real-life contexts.

Conceptions About Lies

What are lies? As Chapter 1 showed, adults show diversity in their definitions. Strangely, developmental psychologists (Morton, 1988; Perner, 1991) are fairly uniform in a criterial rather than prototypical or family resemblance definition—citing an intention to mislead as a necessary condition. None mention a moral component, although the intersect of lying and wickedness has confounded work with adults, both empirically and conceptually. That intersect has tempted some to define the word lie in a way that makes all lies bad, whereas others subdivide lies by reason for their occurrence or intended outcomes so that some lies become "good" (Bok, 1978). As will be seen later, there are apparently strong reactions of disapproval by young children to counterfactual statements, especially if the label *lie* can be made to stick to them. Interestingly, this kind of issue does not seem to have arisen in studies of children's behavior with respect to deceptions and lies but only in their commentaries. Could this be because the studies are all in "game" situations, where deception and lying are typically either neutral or part of the game? In contrast, in real life, parents and others have presumably been commenting on the evils of children lying from before the time when children could grasp the category. Piaget's (1932) early work implied that "wrongness" incorporated lies, some verbal mistakes, and swear words. These all formed an undifferentiated category of disapproved of utterances. Piaget's conclusion is supported by six examples of answers to an interrogatory that opened with "What is a lie?" but the little sequences that follow would not pass as sufficient evidence for the conclusion today (Piaget, 1932, pp. 136-137). At the same time, Piaget asserts that "the child [is] perfectly acquainted with a lie when he meets one" (p. 136) and "knows perfectly well that lying consists in not speaking the truth" (p. 138). He also claims that children aged 5 to 7 know the difference between an intentional act and an involuntary mistake but do not use it to define *lie*. Again, the succeeding text suffers from the same difficulties of inferences drawn from the earlier interrogatories. Piaget does appear to have "led the witness" too much. The comments of children about wrongness defined it as equivalent to that which is punished, and in today's frameworks this would be located in Kohlberg's (1984) Stage 1 of moral understanding.

Piaget's (1932) idea of "moral realism" was applied to accidental damage as well as lying, but although the first has an intensive history of examination, the latter has been relatively neglected. Piaget's evidence suggested to him that until the age of 9 or so, a lie was defined by truth or falsity alone with the speaker's intention being irrelevant. As suggested previously, the initial evidence was weak. In the moral dilemma stories that followed with a further sample, Piaget asked who was naughtier of two characters—one whose statement was a long way from the truth but had no intention to deceive or one whose statement was slightly untrue but was intended to deceive. By age 10, the deceptive intentions were judged to be naughtier; at age 6 to 7, the size of the lie was the determinant. This often replicated finding has been criticized methodologically. Wimmer, Gruber, and Perner (1984) attempted to retest the hypothesis with a tighter, carefully controlled design. Across a variety of kinds of fibs and across four studies, when children were asked whether or not a character in a story had told a fib and whether this merited a gold star or a black point, the results confirmed the Piaget result that intention was not used as a relevant criterion by children below age 6. These investigators, however, also included questions about intention (the German equivalent of "on purpose"), and when this was used, the results fell into an interesting pattern. On the one hand, a majority of both 4.5- and 6-year-olds discriminated between false statements made on purpose and those which were not; on the other hand, 19 of these children still called an unintended false statement a fib, whereas none of them showed the reverse pattern. Because all 19 also solved the "false belief" test, the evidence for their "realist definition of lying" (p. 17) is impressive. In a contrast between cases in which the speaker's counterfactual statement arises from situational changes rather than a deliberate attempt to prevent a third party from finding the object, but where the speaker is an "innocent" intermediary in a chain, half of the 8- and 10.5-year-olds continued to talk of the second being a lie whereas the first was not. The series of studies yielded results that were consistently indicative of Piaget's diagnoses of "moral realism" about lying by 5-year-olds and older as being overestimates arising out of methodological weaknesses in his designs and interrogatories and especially in the failures to check that children could understand and remember what it was they were supposed to be doing.

In a final study that highlights the need to be scrupulously careful in any experimental design that includes a sequence of questions, Wimmer et al. (1984) replicated their earlier finding with 4- and 5-year-olds: The children recommended rewarding a protagonist who intended to tell the truth but then said this statement was a lie if it was factually incorrect. When the sequence was reversed, no such paradoxical conjunction appeared: Unintended mistakes were judged to be lies and were then stated to merit punishment. This is interpreted to mean that action-based knowledge can be shown to be more advanced than verbally formable knowledge but that the moral associations of the word *lying* can override this. It is also proposed that the existence of this conflict may, when realized and reflected on, serve as the data for a resolution that brings the child to a combination of falsity and intention to deceive as the defining properties of a lie. Ironically, this neat demonstration of 1985 resolves some of the paradoxes that appeared in Piaget's (1932) account of over half a century before.

Peterson, Peterson, and Seeto (1983) used samples of forty 5-, 8-, 9-, and 11-year-olds as well as 33-year-olds in obtaining data from about 10 video events that included two guesses (one with no consequences for the victim and the other guess resulted in the person taking the wrong direction to a destination), an "exaggeration," a swearing, a white lie, an altruistic lie, a practical joke, and three self-protective lies with different outcomes. Respondents had to say whether or not each was a lie and rate each act for badness or goodness. A general interview asked three further questions. The results of a 10×5 analysis of variance (ANOVA) are too extensive to report. All three self-protective lies were seen as lies by virtually 100% of all respondents; the white and altruistic lies attracted similar categorizations by over 90% of the sample. Swearing was the lowest, with only 38% of 5-year-olds seeing it as lying. The practical joke and the guess with an inconvenient outcome were both seen as lies by over half the children and by 50 and 30% of adults, respectively. The gradual decline with increasing age was most marked with the joke and both guesses. No analysis was made of the relationships between items so that no sequential linkages can be isolated. Asked whether they ever told lies, the answer "never" was given by 75% of the youngest and by 42%, 35%, and 0% of the increasingly older age groups. Lies were seen as always wrong by 92%, 88%, 78%, and 28%. Punishment as a consequence was mentioned by similar declining percentages. Loss of trustworthiness rose as a consequence. Experience of guilt was mentioned by 22% of 10-year-olds. The somewhat overwhelming mass of results offer descriptions without explanations. What is the status of the answers that they never lie given by 60 children? How do these children differ from others in other respects and why? By focusing almost exclusively on age trends, what-goes-with-what questions are generally neglected. Certainly, the 10 categories were differentially appraised, and the self-protective lies were seen as the worst, with no differentiation between them. The data do reinforce the continuing commitment to some nonlies being lies, even among 11-year-olds.

Also, using Australian children, Bussey (1992) reported a comparable mapping study of definitions of, wrongness and rightness of, and evaluative reactions to both lies and truthful statements, as a function of statement truth value, type of content, acceptedness of statement, and whether there was punishment following. With four age groups (ranging from 4.9 to 11.0), there were many means for planned comparisons. With 12 vignettes and 8 or more questions to answer about each, each child appears to have been asked 96 questions across two sessions. Both the number of comparisons made and the number of questions asked give cause for concern: the first because false positive results will be mixed with true positives and the second because one wonders how confused the children may have become in such extended interrogations. The youngest group of children did much better than chance in discriminating between lies and truthful statements; other groups were almost perfect. It is suggested that speaker's belief, punishment, and the involvement of a misdeed were irrelevant. Children evaluated lies as worse than misdeeds, but their evaluation of truthful statements in relation to misdeeds was less discriminating. Generally, lies linked more strongly with other variables than did truthful statements. Punishment had its customary relevance, being confused with lying in younger children. For both lies and truthful utterances, there were significant developmental changes, with internal evaluations rising at the expense of punishment.

Burton and Stricharz (1992) focused directly on the three potential criterial characteristics that are most commonly cited as defining a lie and asked how the presence of these affected children's judgments of whether these are lies. Suspecting that a prototypical approach might be more appropriate, the three elements were (a) the speaker's belief in the falsity of the proposition, (b) the speaker's intention to deceive the listener, and (c) the objective falsity of the proposition. Following Coleman and Kay's (1981) ranking of these from most to least important (in the order given) gave an eight-cell manifold. With four child age groups and an adult group, judgments were elicited about a statement made in each of eight puppet plays. Was the puppet telling a lie, the truth, or something else? Participants were asked why they answered as they did, with follow-up probes to exhaust their reasons. The resultant multiple analysis of variance (MANOVA) is best reduced here to salient results. As with the Coleman and Kay's sample, adults were unanimous in their judgments if all three elements were either present or absent: In their judgments as to whether a statement was a lie, they gave most weight to the speaker's belief that the proposition was false; the other two elements varied in importance as a function of the characteristics of the other element. Preschoolers and first graders used factuality only. Fifth graders were transitional, with belief system being more important than intention. The study is particularly important because it does separate belief state of speaker from intention, a separation that has been omitted from many studies. The results do not illuminate sequences or processes, but like Bussey (1992) and Peterson et al. (1983), they provide a descriptive frame of reference within which changes and the reasons for their occurrence might be more sited. These changes should be best detectable by experimental manipulations of the kind used by Wimmer et al. (1984). Given the order effects shown by Wimmer et al., it looks as though further clarification of the relevant issues will have to rely on individual children being given simpler interrogatories with shorter series of tasks. Much of the work illustrates a paradox. Younger children may well give consistent answers to a particular question, but variations in the context in which any question is posed are likely to be associated with variations in the answers. Reference has already been made to a modern eye being able to discern how Piaget's (1932) interrogatories may have affected answers and led to wrong interpretations. Likewise, the temptation to assume that randomizing or controlling order effects will wash out their relevance may result in the disappearance of significant data. This must be especially so when children are not really understanding questions or are struggling to do so. If they were sure of the point of each question, they would already have mastered the problems at issue. One of the challenges of experimenting at these early ages is to find the precise contexts and tasks that will pinpoint where children are in their development. What *early* means is necessarily vague, but it is intended to cover anything up to the age at which the child is able and willing to tell an experimenter that he or she does not understand the task or does not know the answer. If the tasks are too far advanced, children are likely to cooperate but base their reactions on unknown factors (see Robinson & Robinson, 1981, for example) using rules such as "when asked, do something," or "when in doubt guess."

Lies Versus Other Speech Acts

Mistakes, jokes, and lies are three categories of counterfactual statements. It has been suggested that these differ only in the speaker's intentions, a premature and possibly mistaken claim. Contextually and formally, they are likely to differ. Wimmer et al. (1984) found concordance between being able to identify another's belief as false and registering a mistake in 4-year-olds. Children, however, have been making mistakes with language almost from their first verbal utterances. Overgeneralizing, undergeneralizing, and identifying are all common parts of performance and learning. Sometimes wrong words or structure appear to be used deliberately to solve whatever communication problem the child has; the child "knows" the words are wrong, but they are the best available, and if used, a helpful respondent may supply the correct word. Mistakes are often registered with smiles and laughter; these reactions imply a realization of the amusement to be derived from calling an elephant an ant.

Leekam (1991) employed a "Look mum, I painted that picture" story, followed by two denouements: one in which mother discovers for herself another signature on the picture and another in which the son himself points to the other signature. There were two questions: one about the mother's belief about the painter's identity and one about which boy was naughtier. For a second story, a third question about which boy was just joking was added. The belief question was answered correctly by over 90% of the children aged 6 to 9. The joking answers were not better than random at age 6 but were differentiated by most of the children of age 7 and older. The differentiation for the moral question was similar. Children were not asked anything about lying. This study points to the kind of gap encountered in the previous section: 2- and 3-year-olds laughing at false references but not identifying the kind of joke Leekam used until they are 6 years old. Sullivan, Winner, and Hopfield (1995) have compared the kinds of knowledge a liar or a joker presumes in the other person. Comparing their differential competence, children who cannot work out what a listener does not know fail to distinguish between lies and jokes. Being able to work out what precisely a listener does know was not related. Task analysis in terms of constituent competences tested against the order in which compound competences emerge in combination with empirically discovered contingencies is an ideal method for working out how lies per se and different kinds of lies relate developmentally both to other speech acts and to underlying items of knowledge.

Conceptual and Experimental
Approaches to Children's Lies

Conceptual Concerns

If someone is to utter a statement that he or she believes to be false but intends the target to believe, it might be constructive to ask what prerequisite intellectual feats are necessary for this act to have a reasonable chance of success as well as to ask about the competence and attitude of the listeners.

Following the original analytic approach of Flavell, Botkin, Fry, Wright, and Jarvis (1968) to the problem of referential communication, it might be argued that the following have to be true for a lie to succeed:

1. What L believes or knows can be different from what S believes or knows the facts are, for example.
2. In this instance, L does not know what S has said or done, and neither does anyone else who might tell L.
3. S has to be able to construct an account of events that is compatible with the facts and dissociates S from those.

4. S has to deliver that account with "normal" speech and nonverbal behavior.

5. S has to remember the false account and maintain it if the topic is broached on subsequent occasions.

These steps are not so much successive stages as nested necessary conditions. Step 5 may occasionally be achieved before Step 1 at the level of successful deception per se, but all five steps are necessary for planned lies founded on an intellectual analysis.

In this section, reference has been made to the form in which knowledge is coded and the experimental studies show that the child does not master Step 1 at all levels immediately. Typically, it might be expected that each development will be phased.

Discovering how children come to differentiate lying from other kinds of speech acts will clearly be an extended enterprise. Many speech acts simply require an intellectual understanding and a set of associated skills to be used successfully. The conceptual mastery of lying is probably confounded by what adults say and do. The first confusion seems to be an extended categorization of speech acts that are punished or condemned by adults. The pragmatic imperatives to avoid punishment might be expected to delay differentiation of the precise categories of act meeting such reactions. At this stage, children are unlikely to be required to tell white lies. A later confusion, however, may arise from the subsequent subdivision of lies into the socially desirable, socially acceptable, and socially unacceptable. It may be this differentiation that brings the question of the motivational component of the liar into salience. On a sociocognitive conflict model of development, children have to work out why lies are disapproved of on some occasions and true statements are disapproved of on others. The resolution of that set of superficial contradictions is related to differential consequences of truth and falsity for others and a realization that "society" may expect its members to sacrifice truth to consideration for others. This requires reflective inquiry into one's own motivation and the strategies appropriate to social consideration, which begins to take on characteristics of formal operational thinking. It is possibly the intellectual demands of considered altruistic conduct that delay the use of intention as a factor in the evaluation of lies.

Perhaps it is appropriate to introduce into the commentary a general model of phased development that seemed to provide useful guidance for describing and explaining the child's developing competence to avoid ambiguity when speaking about specific referents (Robinson, 1984). For the case in hand, let X be *lie*.

Phase I. Children are mainly victims of X. Their capacity for being an agent with control over X is limited by their ignorance of the character of X and how it functions in language in communication. They achieve a measure of mastery of X in use (know-how). However, partly as a result of associative learning in both its classical and its instrumental conditioning guises; they may also learn about X in use through observation and imitation. In addition, they are agents, however, and can purposefully use X, relying on corrective or explanatory feedback from others for the development of context-bound rules of use. These various processes acting separately and in combination may lead to children using X successfully much of the time. Limitations of intellectual capacity and an absence of opportunities or capacities or both for reflecting on the workings of X, however, will be manifested when their rules for using X fail. They will not be able to diagnose the reasons for failure and will not be able to formulate a diagnosis and act effectively on it.

Phase 2. Either through their own reflective efforts or as a result of scaffolded teaching by competent others or others simply telling them about the workings of X or as a result of sociocognitive conflicts with others, they will come to realize how (and perhaps why) X works as it does. As a result of contemporary reflective analysis in particular new situations or through a consideration of past events or through imaginative rehearsing of situations involving X, they will consciously develop and organize their understanding about X. We might expect an associated period of learning practice in which the use of X is tried frequently with care and awareness. Children (or adults) have become reflecting agents in respect of X, organizing their "believing that"—and perhaps they become temporarily less efficient in their know-how. Their competence has been raised to a higher level of understanding (programming) with greatly enhanced potential for efficient use of X.

Phase 3. Once the principles relating to X have been understood, the use of X will probably and gradually become reduced to a routinized reaction, except for situations in which for various reasons it might be important not to make mistakes with X and for situations in which trouble in using X occurs. In the face of anticipated or present trouble, the problem can be raised to a conscious reflective analysis, diagnoses made, and corrective action taken—other things being equal. The know-how is greater than that at the transition from Phase 1 to Phase 2 and is in a potential dialectic relation to a believing that of understanding.

As mentioned previously, this model was proposed originally for the development of the child's control of ambiguity in verbal referential communication, but it could apply to other units of experience and behavior. Within the orbit of language in communication, these could include learning the meanings of words, rules of spelling in the written language, rules of pronunciation in the oral, rules of grammar, rules for varying forcefulness and politeness of requests, rules of etiquette more generally, rules for taking the listener into account, rules for telling jokes well, and rules for persuading an audience. Learning to lie and learning about lying can be accommodated equally well.

Discussion

Although it may be premature to attempt to generate a comprehensive model of the development of children's lying, at least there are more than the beginnings of guidelines as to the likely features of such a model. The age range to be covered by the model may well range from infancy to adolescence and perhaps later. The earliest component, counterfactual verbal statement (CVS), probably occurs initially in play and in infancy. Including a criterion that the CVS must be believed to be false in their definition of a lie is not considered criterial by all 10-year-olds. Including an intention to deceive seems to arise at an even later age, if at all. More than one study has shown a lack of consensus among adults.

A minor issue is what to call these various CVSs. There is something odd about an insistence that the word *lie* be reserved for statements that meet all three criteria. On the other hand, there is something odd about leaving the definition to children who change their criteria as they develop.

Methodologically, it has been necessary to note that not all words for the concept are equivalent; neither is a true statement a perfect complement to a lie. The questions that follow are not psychologically equivalent for all children: "Was that true?" "Was that truthful?" "Was it a fib?" "Was it a lie?" Piaget's (1932) original published examples hint at the problems of the relevance of sequential effects of questions to answers obtained, especially with younger children. Wimmer et al. (1984) demonstrated the significance and risks quite dramatically. Nevertheless, some studies continue to ask many questions of the same child, possibly contaminating what might be clearer patterns in simpler settings. Freeman (1994) and Perner (1991) both demonstrated how contextual variations in aids supplied to facilitate task understanding can affect answers, presumably especially during periods of growth of understanding. Fortunately, more psychologists are now aware of the importance of distinguishing between conditions that facilitate the appearance of the beginnings of competence and those that test the firmness of a belief in the face of seductive evidence that it might be invalid: Bruner's (1983) distinction between "first within competence" and "finally in performance." More psychologists now see superficial differences in results as potentially informative information about the child's degree and state of understanding rather than as an occasion for terminological arguments between investigators.

The appearance of careful experiments whose results are parsimoniously interpreted has to be an important advance on any tendencies to overinterpret or misinterpret. Two kinds of study are noticeably rarer than is desirable for optimal progress: training experiments and field studies. The systematic investigation of means of advancing performance, understanding, or both is an important next step. Demonstrating which techniques can advance children, especially when the various techniques are based on different models, is one of the tightest methods for discovering how change and development can occur. Careful field studies are likely to show how developments do in fact occur (Robinson & Robinson, 1981). There must also be corpuses of child—other interaction extant other than Dunn's (1991) work that would begin to show which kinds of experience facilitate or inhibit the mastery of the steps that have to be taken by children to manage what they eventually can manage.

In several areas in this chapter, mention has been made of different processes that might be responsible for development. The three-phase model is eclectic and includes several varieties of learning but assigns different roles to them. Associative and observational learning can introduce and maintain particular behavioral scripts in the repertoire; they are pragmatically and procedurally controlled. It is only with imaginative reflection that a semantic basis for the success or otherwise of the procedural repertoires becomes understood and the knowledge can move to a hypothetico-deductive mode of operation—if and when this is required.

Perner (1991) has emphasized what is referred to here as the semantic base—the propositional knowledge with its constituent concepts and their relationships. Based on a belief-desire model of representation, their questions have centered about the emergence or construction of particular beliefs. In both Piagetian and Brunerian models of development, early propositionally based beliefs are founded on and grow out of procedural routines and contingency rules. In Piaget (1932), action schemas are incorporated into and coexist with symbolic schemas, that, in turn, are incorporated into and coexist with sign-based schemas. For Bruner (1983), knowledge is progressively and concurrently represented enactively, iconically, and symbolically. (In a more recent application of Lloyd-Morgan's [1894] canon, Harris, 1992, has offered a very carefully sustained and persuasive account of how such developments may be heavily based on the simulation process, illustrating how experiments in the theory of mind area have, perhaps unwittingly, been designed to minimize the extent to which simulation strategies might be used to solve the problems posed. How this might apply to the act of lying has yet to be determined.)

Socialization Into Truthfulness and Lying

The previous section was coherent in parts, but overall, the descriptions and explanation of growing competence and understanding of time and false statements were fragmented at best. There was no work on truth and truthfulness per se. Lying had been approached as a subset of other concerns in two cases, namely as a component of the theory of mind work and as an aspect of moral development in Piaget's (1932) inquiries. Only the studies seeking to probe the differentiation of lies from other utterances and the changes in definitions with age were directly concerned with lying. None of the studies were set in contexts that questioned what other persons in the child's environment were doing that might provide information for children to learn. Apart from the original case studies, only Dunn's (1988) has involved observations of interactions with other children or adults.

If there is but little work exploring the output side of what children can manage with lying or say about it, however, there is still less on the input side of socialization. Mussen's (1970) Handbook had no references to lying or deception in the index and the situation has not changed. Hints from personal observation and experience were offered in the previous section that current Western practices and commentaries to children are probably confused and confusing.

Probably, most parents and other adults in authority over young children are clear in their condemnation of lying, especially when the lies are addressed to adults. Discovered lies are likely to be the occasion of punishments and minilectures about the wrongness of lying. Probably, all deliberate counterfactuals are included in the single category, *lie*, as far as the parental rhetoric is concerned. It is possible that this commandment is never explicitly countermanded or elaborated. What is a clear compartment for adults may not be so for children.

Reality, Play, and Dreams

Reference has already been made to the various forms of pretense that are socially acceptable and encouraged. Children play games with objects that substitute for other objects. They create characters out of dolls and toy animals. Children are told stories the world over. Many of these are fictional and are not intended to misinform. The prime conscious intention may be to entertain, but some also have informative and moral content. Values will be explicitly or implicitly endorsed within the stories, much of the content will be about the events and actions of living creatures, and some of these will be either true or false. Animals do not wear clothes or hold conversations, but when Mother Hare has her children clean their teeth to ensure that they do not go bad, both a putative practical fact and a value are available for learning. The torn and dirty clothes and the fears and tears of naughty Peter Rabbit contrast with the lovely tea enjoyed by his better-behaved obedient sisters.

To sort out what is true and useful and what is false and possibly dangerous is a great challenge. Children have killed themselves imitating fictional characters that jump off cliffs and fly. The issue of children and adults modeling violence toward others from TV programs is but a modern controversy that is older than Homer's *Iliad*. Stories have been told from time immemorial for children and adults to model themselves on heroes and saints, but, typically, stories have evil villains as well as virtuous citizens, and the risk is that these can also become models. It is, of course, logically possible to imagine a society that kept its entertainment and its implicit socialization held to the world as it is, and perhaps a clearly marked off better (or worse) world in the future as well, but this is not current practice. The task confronting children is to sort out when statements can be counterfactual and when they cannot. They can be in fantasy but not in reality. They can be in play but not in real life.

The problem is confounded further by young children's incapacity to distinguish between dreams and reality (Piaget, 1951), what is remembered, and what has been constructed. That this is a far from trivial issue is illustrated by the current controversies about child abuse, perhaps particularly with respect to what are known as satanic rites. Children have been removed from parental custody because they have reported taking part in unspecified rituals with their parents. Subsequently, charges have been dropped and children returned home. What has been true and what has been false has remained undetermined. One crucial feature has been that children's memories may be that much more suggestible than those of most adults. (Adults do, of course, suffer from the same reconstructions, especially if they are subjected to powerful interrogations as prisoners.)

A further source of potential confusion will be the behavior of parents or teachers. They will make false statements unintentionally (that younger children may diagnose as lies) and they will tell lies. It is likely that children will occasionally hear parents tell each other or other adults about lies they have told. Children may decide that there is one rule for adults and another for children, but that is only one of several explanations that they might entertain.

Tales My Parents Told Me

Parental discipline tactics themselves may be a further source of puzzlement. One particular parental tactic in child rearing that some of us will recall is threats—future punishments for current or recent misdeeds. Three kinds of these could be classified as two-edged:

1. Physical debilities
2. Abduction and punishment by natural or supernatural agents
3. Postdeath hells

Telling lies was open to punishment by variations on a theme of Pinocchio, a character whose nose grew longer every time he told a lie. Pimples on the tongue were supposed to be one consequence of having told lies. A whole range of actions disapproved of by parents could give rise to physical deformities—for example, masturbation leading to members falling off, hairy palms, and a variety of other symptoms. One inference that could be drawn from these nonconsequences was that parents lied to control children's behavior.

Abduction by natural agents or supernatural agents for offenses was another kind of threat issued. Various social groups qualified as abductors: gypsies, tinkers, the devil, and wolves. The police were a preferred authority cited by working class mothers of 5-year-olds in Britain (Cook-Gumperz, 1973; Newson & Newson, 1976). Their intervention was invoked for disobedience, temper tantrums, and any other issue. "You wait 'till your father gets home!" was another common tactic. Because fathers were often not informed about the misdemeanors and the police were never informed, a logically adept child could reach one or more of at least two conclusions. Whether any children so threatened developed a disrespect for the police as a result of their nonappearance has not been studied.

When Not to Tell the Truth

If it is true that parents condemn lying by their children, then once these children have understood the implications of this proscription, they will have to begin to learn about the circumstances when lying and deceit are required or expected. For example, children may be expected to be loyal to the family and not to tell outsiders what really happens within their home. If mother and father have secrets from each other, children may learn not to pass on such secrets as they become privy to them. Among siblings, there may be rules that prevent them from informing on each other's misdeeds—that is, grassing, telling on; likewise, among classmates at school. In brief, there will be loyalties to individuals and groups that override requirements to tell the truth in the same way that captured spies and prisoners are not expected to betray their colleagues or country.

Politeness will be invoked as a reason for telling white lies about disliked birthday and Christmas presents and children have to learn how to dissimulate emotions and sentiments.

Children will learn to play their different roles as offspring, sibling, friend, pupil, and team member; insofar as these role requirements have private worlds, their contents will not be divulged across the boundaries.

Very little of this learning will be facilitated through the specification of explicit rules: secret societies and gangs being exceptions. Rather, children will learn by breaking the rules and being reprimanded or punished. As roles proliferate toward and following maturity, the same considerations will apply, although the likelihood is that the myth of truthfulness as a virtue will be preserved.

Conclusions

Although many questions remain to be answered with respect to those that have to be asked about the various areas of significance for the development of lying and deception in children, there are very clear signs of progress in the theoretical frameworks, suitable methodologies, and charting of sequences. With the exception of Dunn's work (1988, 1991) no recent naturalistic studies of the very young have been brought into complementarity with the experimental work on deception in the relevant variations of false belief paradigm; likewise for the slightly older age groups. The relations to teasing and joking are beginning to be clarified, and experimental games of deceptive choices have been used to provide relevant evidence, but such results have not been calibrated against the competencies children display in games with peers. Which kinds of deliberate falsifications emerge, in what sequence, and why, have yet to be observed. There are interesting paradoxes. It seems that children can discriminate behaviorally between lies and other speech acts, while still giving relatively confused accounts, but this is only a new exemplification of an older problem of discrepancies between earlier and later phases of mastery. If it is the case that progress will be mainly a matter of filling out the details within the frameworks, these achievements are limited to single acts of deception and falsification. Work has yet to be launched on how the single falsifications and lies of children become woven into communication in real situations. At present, there are no linking studies that lead into adolescence and adulthood. Hence, Chapter 3 is a direct leap to adults. Within the world of adults, no sequential or developmental perspective is represented so that the so-christened standing features are also static.

CHAPTER THREE

Lying Face to Face: Standing Features

Barnes (1994) confessed to having a jackdaw-like approach to his integration of work on lying, but it is difficult not to have such an approach. Relevant work appears in a wide variety of fields under a wide variety of headings. In part, the reasons for this are methodological. Social scientists rely heavily on the speech and writing of people for their data. The professional lives of psychologists would be so much easier if people knew the truth about themselves and revealed it to us. They don't, they can't, and they won't, however. Mao Tse-tung invited 100 flowers to blossom in what had been an oppressive totalitarian regime. Many did so and had their heads chopped off. As will be discussed in Chapter 6 and as history repeatedly records, revealing what one thinks is a hazardous venture if these thoughts offend the power structure within which one hopes to survive; similarly for the social networks of which one is a member. All social relationships have idealized norms against which we all fail. Social positions have idealized norms too, and we all fail to meet these also. Some hide these failures from themselves. Some hide them from others. Some hide them from both. Lies are one means of constructing and maintaining preferable versions of reality.

Both misperception and deliberate falsification are likely to contaminate the data analyzed by psychologists, especially social and personality psychologists. The chapter opens with three sets of topics in which lifestyle is treated as a construction by the individual. To effect change and development, human beings may well create discrepancies between what is inside the head and what is done. This has been a dilemma since time immemorial. If change is desired should the focus be on behavior or thinking? Whichever is changed first, charges of insincerity or hypocrisy can be leveled against the individual. Facework is much older than Goffman (1959), but his writings have been the major point of departure for such work in this century; self-presentation and impression management are taken to represent two related developments from Goffman. Although developmentally, discrepancies treated as aspirations and acknowledged discrepancies may be acceptable, concealed characteristics are a difficulty for psychologists.

Efficient facework by patients and respondents has been a hazard for clinical and personality psychologists, in particular bedeviling interpretations of questionnaire data. One solution was to include lie scales in these, items to which there should be universal assent or dissent. Any substantial deviation would be treated as indicative of lying and would require further investigation in clinical settings and would be discarded in survey work. Subsequently, high scorers on the lie scale became of substantive interest as well. The disposition of respondents to give "socially desirable" answers was a second source of concern for questionnaire users. Neither of these lines of inquiry have linked up with other work on lying. Neither has Machiavellianism, even though one of the techniques for obtaining real lies derives from this area. The succeeding two sections look at how often people report they lie to whom about what. With opportunity samples of students being the major source of information for work on lying in informal encounters, the studies serve mainly to define likely terms of reference for the future and point to the arduous and probably impossible task of obtaining ecologically valid databases. These difficulties are less apparent in the study of formal interpersonal encounters. How consumers and bargain hunters can be misled has been charted, how they might be inoculated against deception has not. Studies of lying in professional consultations seem to be limited to two analyses of doctor-patient communication.

The Presentation of Self, Impression Management, and Facework

Are these three fields or one? If they are really three in one, is this because colleagues are failing to specify the similarities to and differences from the writings of their predecessors simply to capture the market for their own ideas? Or are the overlaps not so great as might appear at first sight? Goffman (1959, 1969) is normally cited as the inspiration for modern work in the general area, and certainly he published an appealing array of terms along with a wealth of insightful observations. For Goffman, face wants were conceived as the social value someone would like to claim from others, a due measure of respect and consideration. People take both preventive and corrective measures to preserve or enhance face. The illustrations cited by Goffman show the tactical operations used by people to exploit these ends, the emphasis being on what people can do and actually do in particular situations. Staying close to situational contingencies, Goffman avoided questions about discrepancies between appearance and reality or between an inner self and a phenomenal self, although his dramaturgical model certainly presents what is shown as a continuing stage performance where life is but a stage.

Brown and Levinson (1987) likewise confine their questions to surface considerations. In their theory of the speech acts associated with the pursuit of politeness and efficiency in interpersonal encounters, they stress the functions of preserving their own and others' positive and negative faces with people conniving cooperatively with others to their mutual satisfaction. By remaining at the level of speech acts, this analysis avoids any exploration of a duality of true self and reality but presumes its existence.

With self-presentation theory (Jones & Pittman, 1982; Schneider, 1981), the idea of an inner and an outer self emerges explicitly. Beginning with a notion that people wish to claim a likable and pleasant identity and therefore present such an image to others, the principle came to be extended to other wishes: to be seen as dominant, dependent, or competent, and subsequently whatever other characteristics someone might wish to claim. As with ideas of impression management (Hogan, 1983; Schlenker, 1980) or self-monitoring (Snyder, 1987), these conceptual analyses make a necessary dissociation between a planning homunculus and an apparent persona. For some writers, these issues are situation specific; for others, they are endemic, but there is in fact no necessary conflict between the two positions. Some people may become drawn into occupations or activities that pull them toward more and more generalized role playing activities, which may or may not be mutually "inconsistent." One's whole life can become determined by the need to maintain the consequences of earlier choices. The extent to which people can hold on to a simple expression of what they think they are must be heavily affected by sociopolitical situations. Those who have survived in semiefficient totalitarian states for any part of their lives have to be particularly careful in what they say and what they do, even when they are with those they may wish to treat as their nearest and dearest. If close kin are told that it is their duty to denounce family members to the Gestapo, the KGB (or NKVD or OGPU), or any of the many other secret polices that still operate in many countries of the world, impression management has to be total and continuous. Both before and since 1989, Eastern and Central Europe have provided an extraordinary set of living conditions. A great many leopards have now changed their spots. Doubtless, many of these who have disavowed their markings are genuine; for them, it would have been simply suicidal to have proclaimed their true selves earlier. They were successful in their deceptions. Some among them, however, are doubtless still spotted leopards who are now deceiving their fellow citizens with their enthusiastic adoption of the trappings of Western capitalism. Some of the prominent politicians who have proclaimed they were cupboard liberals all along stretch the credibility of even the most trusting. Of the Eastern Europeans one meets, the Bulgarians, Rumanians, and Ukrainians seem to have particular difficulty in knowing which of their leaders are sheep that pretended to be wolves and which were really wolves but are now pretending to be sheep.

Impression management and self-presentation studies in the West are themselves presented as issues particularly relevant to success in business negotiations and now figure very strongly in politics. The Kennedy and the Nixon presented to the public were not the figures portrayed subsequently in their biographies. TV recordings of Margaret Thatcher throughout her decade as prime minister show clear signs of the training provided by the image makers. Companies specializing in the image making of persons, organizations, and institutions have enjoyed a boom in their business in the past 20 years as more and more organizations have realized that it is cheaper and easier to create images than reality. It may be no accident that over a similar period the credibility of the main political and economic institutions of the United States and the United Kingdom has dropped to an all-time low (see p. 253). In part, senior politicians have only themselves to blame; too many have been shown to have deceived too many of the people too much of the time. Some of the deceptions could be argued to have been "in the national interest" and as matters of private morality, but Watergate and Irangate must have rendered many trusting Americans skeptical of the integrity of presidents, just as the cupidity of ex-cabinet ministers of Britain in securing enormous salaries in industries they helped to privatize, and the financial scandals involving some politicians in France, Italy, and Spain have persuaded much of the populace of these countries that the cynics were indeed realists. Greece? Japan? South America? Africa? The Philippines?

The images of truthfulness and honesty projected by the media and by high authorities via the media have accentuated the discrepancies between the preaching and the practices. In short, too much impression management arouses suspicion, with the consequence that the image making backfires into fewer people being fooled for less of the time. Although these considerations are at the level of activities in the public arena, the same principles may be operating at interpersonal levels. Certainly, in business, subordinates in the United States rank the trustworthiness of the boss as their primary concern (Hogan, 1983), and in domestic relations, the reported incidences of infidelities may well be rendering relations between spouses more untrusting than in earlier times. Whether younger generations are now more suspicious and cynical than their elders were about other people is unknown. What they hear on the media and their personal experience probably offer more opportunities for observing and learning about differences between appearance and reality, but there do not seem to be any data about their orientations toward trust in interpersonal relations.

Certainly, the charming rogue is not an entirely mythical beast. Typically, the stereotype is presented for the male sex only. Someone with schemes and plots for making money and who is a big spender himself lives in "the fast lane" in all respects. Perhaps a series of women will imagine they can socialize him into a lifestyle in which all the adventures are with her. All but the last fail! Males have a variety of ways of creating false impressions with females, just as females have their masks. Who is hunting for partners and who is being hunted is not for debate or decision here. Suffice it to say that the processes can be fraught with misunderstandings and deceptions, with either sex being able to exploit the other until whatever game is being played can come to be an end in itself for the exploiter of dangerous liaisons.

The human capacity for simulation should not be underestimated. The capacity for feigned innocence of vicious crimes is but one of a whole range of performances to which ordinary people are susceptible. Fortunately, most people are not so obsessional in their exploitative ambitions that they learn how to subvert and mislead others in their daily encounters.

Before leaving impression management, there is a cognate issue that needs to be mentioned. Both children and changing adults need to develop themselves. If this learning is concerned with role performances, then practice with knowledge of results will have to be a major learning strategy. If someone who is learning mathematics or how to play tennis is not a deceiver or hypocrite, why might it be said that someone learning to appear self-confident is a hypocrite? Learning to control emotions that will interfere with role performances applies to training for many occupations. Hiding fear and suppressing anger are commonly held up as positive social virtues. The idea that it is only through practice with knowledge of results that one can acquire skills is an ancient hypothesis and has long been a part of established wisdom. Character training by similar means is just as ancient, and it is possibly only a post-Enlightenment oddity that has given rise to the notion of a true self that needs to actualize itself, an idea that reaches its paradoxical apogee with existentialism.

Societally based programs for the training of character would now be held up as indoctrination by some people: a symptom of totalitarianism or an infringement of individual rights. An opposed view would point to evidence that it is only through systematic and efficient experienced-based procedures that societies can promote the practice rather than just the rhetoric of the virtues required for civilized communal living.

In society at large, the words used to discuss such problems are not purely descriptive. Neither are they simply susceptible to the evaluative biases arising from a personal or group concern to have right on one's own side. The problem is deeper than that and goes beyond to beliefs about the fundamental nature of human beings. The Rogerian (Rogers, 1970) variant of the Rousseau position about the intrinsic goodness of human beings and the value of individuality and free choice has to argue that any imposition by others is likely to be a diminishing infringement of self-actualization, a suppression of the real person; to that extent people are victims of their socialization and are not their true selves. In one type of contrast, the adoption of an existential rather than an essentialist position can lead to a similar position, in this case the socialization has precluded free choice rather than distorted the emergence of the true self.

Both views contrast with an eclectic view that recognizes that the preservation and development of cultures and societies requires training of character and skills and an education in which an optimistic bias trusts that most of the people will use their capacities for self-regulation and self-presentation skills for good rather than evil. When these skills are used for improper personal benefit or to avoid just deserts, they are labeled as lies, deceit, and hypocrisy. When used for the good of others of one's own group, they are given more positive accolades. Our espionage agents are heroic, theirs are traitorous or villainous. If people succeed in growing into their preferred roles and these roles are positively valued, then their enactors are accepted. If they fail to become the roles they aspired to, they are judged as inadequate or deceivers.

These wider and deeper problems cannot be properly aired in the present context, but it would be misleading not to mention them. At some time in the future, the study of lying and deception will have to be properly anchored in rationally and empirically defensible constructions of human nature that embrace more than psychological perspectives. Meanwhile, it can be questioned what progress psychologists have made in their examinations of lying and deception as a matter of individual differences. Are there enduring differential dispositions to tell lies, and if so, with which characteristics do these co-occur?

Individual Differences in Lying

One of the many reasons why it is difficult to integrate work on lying results from the independence of the strands of research. Even within psychology whether lies can be detected and, if so, how, has been primarily associated with research on nonverbal communication and emotion. Recently, the same questions have been approached from a communication perspective. Posing general questions of detection in interpersonal situations has given rise quite naturally to complementary questions about dispositions to deception. These fields, however, have remained separated from concerns with definitions and any developmental perspective. The questions of who actually lies to whom about what have been left to other more anthropological-minded colleagues.

Each of these has remained distant from the perspectives of personality and individual differences and from the sociocultural and historical. Finally, it is not possible to separate the sociological approach from that of personality but for analytic purposes it may be useful as a preliminary.

Hartshorne and May (1928) deserve to be quoted and, better still, read, for their pioneering studies into the generality of honesty and deceit among children. They are usually reported as emphasizing the role of situational variables as determinants of both the frequency and the participants who chose to be dishonest. There were correlations across situations; the matrix was positive, but the coefficients were generally around .3. The data have been reanalyzed and a claim has been made that Hartshorne and May and those who cited them had underestimated the variance attributable to persons. Subsequently, personality theorists have been interested in the lying component of deceit and dishonesty mainly for two reasons.

In the first place, they have had a methodological concern about the validity of self-reporting questionnaires and interviews. If some people lie more than others, then their answers to the substantive questions of relevance could be invalid. The psychologists' answer to this threat was to devise lie scales. If a respondent could be diagnosed as a liar on a special subset of items, then this could alert the psychologist to the possibility of lies on other scales. (That a clever respondent would restrict lying to the matters he or she would wish to conceal is also an issue.) Lie scales arose separately from the question of the possibility that some respondents were prone to give socially desirable answers, replies that would be acceptable to the interviewer or author. Whether these should be classed as self-deception rather than lying per se has not been answered satisfactorily as yet, and personality questionnaires still treat the issues of lying and giving socially desirable answers as distinct problems. Conceptually, the two are distinguishable but in practice they can become blurred. Lie scale items typically refer to acts that everyone has performed at some time in their lives, and whether respondents admit to this behavior is the index of truth telling. The object of the lie scale is to check on the probability of replies to other items being dishonest. The most common use is therefore in the field of clinical psychology, and the major personality inventories incorporate such a scale—for example, CPI, EPI, MMPI. Paulhus (1991) proposed that two factors underlie the scales, a self-deception factor through which judgments about the self are biased in favorable directions and an impression management factor through which people ingratiate themselves with an audience. He adds that the label "impression management" is preferable to "lying," which is an "overly harsh and sweeping indictment." "After all, such individuals may misrepresent themselves only to avoid social disapproval" (Paulhus, 1991, p. 21). Whether this quotation is itself an instance of self-deception or impression management could be questioned, but the distinction between lying to others and lying to oneself may indeed be analytically helpful.

The oxymoronic qualities of the argument are accentuated by the subsequent suggestion that the distinction helps to explain the positive correlations between self-deception and measurements of adjustment. The self-deception component of social desirability, of which Edwards's (1957) social desirability scale appears to be a relatively pure measure, has been found to correlate positively with adjustment (Taylor & Brown, 1988), mental health (Linden, Paulhus, & Dobson, 1986), and self-esteem (Winters & Neale, 1985). Taylor (1989) has argued very persuasively that if self-deception is maintained in a positive direction, this can save people from facing up to the unpleasant realities of life more generally and not just to their own position in it; conversely, realism results in depression. If Taylor is right (and I suspect he may well be), then he has perhaps diagnosed a major reason why social progress is so difficult to achieve: Too many people are happy with the way they believe things to be. They are happy with their false beliefs, adult victims of Freud's wish fulfillment principle rather than honest confronters of reality. Postmodernism could be a sophisticated version of this phenomenon. To assert that all human dealings with what are commonly presumed to be external realities are simply social constructions could itself simply be a current way of escaping from facing up to finding out what is true and what is false.

In contrast, deliberate impression management to influence others is more clearly measured by the EPI lie scale (Eysenck & Eysenck, 1964). People who score high on this scale are those who at job interviews will promise actions geared to improve efficiency, for example. They will promise much and deliver either little or less. In times of change and uncertainty, however, they are likely to be successful applicants; interviewing panels will be fooled. One reason why it is dangerous to separate the sociological from the psychological perspective here is that in times of uncertainty groups are very likely to put their trust in such promises of assertive leaders. This gives a bridge to Machiavellianism (Christie & Geis, 1970).

Although it could be true that institutions and societies wishing to appoint effective leaders might succeed in appointing powerfully honest persons, they can also find that they have appointed ambitious power seekers who have taken Machiavelli's (1514/1961) advice to heart. The concept embraces at least two components: (a) an individual drive to achieve and maintain personal power, status, or wealth or all three and (b) an indifference to the means of securing the ends. A logical consequence of such an approach is that truth and falsity are irrelevant criteria on which to select actions. Presumed effectiveness is the sole criterion, and if lies and deceit are the best strategic or tactical means, so be it. The various Mach(iavellian) scales are heavily loaded with items admitting a readiness to lie and deceive. (It is slightly odd that serious respondents would admit to employing such tactics, because their efficacy turns on others believing the lies they are told.)

That the wrong means can be used to justify the achievement of good ends has been a sincere defense of many people who have pretended to virtue throughout history. Cicero (1971) saw dishonest rhetoric as a necessary, if eventually unsuccessful, means of protecting the Republic of Rome from the imperial ambitions of Julius Caesar, and he posed the problem of the virtuous person (man) attempting to work for good in an evil world. It is irrational and stupid to trust and tell the truth to people who are intent on evil of some kind. Such arguments can be advanced, however, with equal plausibility by those whose deceptions have not been in the service of good ends.

Whether truth telling is sensible might therefore be judged to be contingent on the societal circumstances. In turn, the societal conditions may be seen by people to be a product of human nature, conceived as an enduring and inevitable set of qualities genetically transmitted. Perhaps most often these characteristics are represented as being the vicious ones of territoriality (Ardrey, 1969), aggressiveness (Dart & Craig, 1959; Lorenz, 1966), genetic competitiveness (Dawkins, 1976), and the will to dominate (Nietzsche, 1886/1958), especially by leaders with a totalitarian credo. Telling lies is but one powerful instrumental tactic to achieve tactic for persuasion and manipulation on the path to greater power. It is noteworthy that some of the most ruthless demagogues of the 20th century have founded their initial campaigns on lies about their opponents, for example, Franco, Hitler, and Stalin. Also, Nixon began his political career as a colleague of McCarthy prosecuting in the Alger Hiss case.

Just as the profile of the authoritarian personality can be conceptualized at various levels of abstraction from characteristics of basic psychological processes of perception, motivation, and reason through ideology, values, to attitudes and specific behavioral dispositions, so one might argue for a related set of characteristics defining an ideal type of Machiavellian. The major difference would seem to be in the will to power being dominant over the need for order and structure.

People can also be prolific liars for non-Machiavellian reasons. Elsewhere, reference has been made to confidence tricksters who rely on charm and charisma to separate the trusting and gullible from their money. For them, deceit could be just a lifestyle and might not be part of an ideology. For Machiavellians, however, a dark view of human nature is probably an essential framework that both justifies their own behavior and helps to explain why they are wiser than their more trusting fellow creatures.

The tendency of personality theorists to look for correlations among questionnaires is myopic if it does not ultimately result in validity checks beyond self-reports, but as a technique for building up patterns of personality characteristics, it has great value, as Adorno, Frenkel-Brunswik, Levinson, and Sanford (1950) demonstrated with authoritarianism. Machiavellianism has not enjoyed the same dramatic development, but its inception did not follow in the aftermath of the ethnic slaughters of Jews, Slavs and Gypsies by the

Nazis. The Zeitgeist of the 1970s was not one of fear that the Machiavellians were taking over societies. Certainly, the extent of recently exposed corruption in high places in the United Kingdom and the United States could be taken to imply that social conditions have encouraged the promotion of Machiavellians to positions of power and influence during the past 15 years. Wrightsman (1991) suggests that Machiavellians thrive under conditions of social change and uncertainty, both of which have characterized the United Kingdom and the United States in the immediate past.

Although there does not seem to be any behavioral evidence that high Machs are better at hiding simulated lies than low Machs (Christie & Geis, 1970), external validation of their (successful) competitive characteristics has been shown to be highlighted in situations in which they are interacting face to face on tasks that have possibilities for improvisation and the display of irrelevant emotion. Geis and Christie (1970) extracted this generalization from a review of 38 of their experimental studies.

As suggested in the opening paragraphs of the section, the personality or individual or both differences perspective has not been exploited for the elucidation of interpersonal processes or vice versa. Neither have they been linked to the societal level of analysis. If popular stereotypes are valid one might expect certain occupations to attract and create Machiavellians: politics, journalism, and drug running. One might expect crooked solicitors and convicted fraudsters to be high scorers. Whether such groups would fill in questionnaires honestly is another matter. Christie and Geis (1970) may have endeavored to reduce response biases, but by definition their propositions have to refer to duplicity and exploitation. If someone is a strong Machiavellian, it should also be true (by definition) that he or she would not admit this to others. (Of the heavily ambitious Machiavellians I have encountered, none has presented himself or herself as anything other than a servant to the community, regardless of the context or state of intimacy of any conversation.) Impression management is not a part-time exercise for those who are serious players. Whether spouses who share the ambitions discuss these or whether they connive without words is a puzzle; my own suspicion is that the understandings are normally implicit and that any joint plotting is discussed in socially acceptable terms. One of the extraordinary oddities of court appearances is the truth bias that white well-educated, middle-class fraudsters seem to evoke through their self-presentations. Judges, juries, and the public find it hard to believe that Peregrine Falcon could have been a predator. He denies the charges so convincingly. Top people stand as character witnesses. Surely, they cannot all be dupes or fellow conspirators. The family protests at the persecution of such a stalwart citizen. Symptoms of stress and ill health appear. Without prejudice to particular cases, this is exactly what one would expect of a successful well-practiced Machiavellian.

One reason why they survive is the gullibility of those charged with trying them. Another is that it looks bad for their in-groups if a member is discredited. A third is that members of the family may well lose their wealth and status, and they act out sympathetic denials. A fourth is that they may well start leaking damning information about their colleagues if they do not act to prevent a verdict of guilty. In this century in Britain, Horatio Bottomley (Anonymous, 1923) played the role to the full. He was a member of Parliament (MP) twice. He owned national magazines that served to raise war bonds and lottery money. He floated companies on the stock exchange, mainly mining ventures in Australia. He lived opulently and when declared bankrupt moved his string of race horses to Belgium. He bankrupted wealthy but trusting elderly people as well as rich youths. He embezzled both lottery and bond money on a grand scale. None of his 400 companies yielded stable returns for the investors while they were in his care. He appeared in over 600 court cases and even succeeded in gaining libel verdicts against some of those he swindled. He was a great patriot. He was a staunch supporter of Britain as manifested through his John Bull magazine. He was cheerful and amiable, even during his many court appearances. The example is mentioned as a reminder that these careers can be successfully prolonged at the highest levels in society. The performance does fool enough of the significant people for long enough. Why people imagine that today is peculiarly different from yesterday is hard to understand. Tomorrow, too, will have such characters who will cause much suffering to the few and some suffering to the many and will then survive into a prosperous old age. They will not score high on self-report measures, however.

Sociologically, it is those who approach the "ideal type" of the concept who are important in accounting for variance. Any variance in Mach scores within an undergraduate population may relate somewhat to variance in other activities. These may be relevant to social relationships formed and lifestyles adopted, but their impact on society will be trivial compared with that of today's Horatio Bottomleys, whose financial or political ambitions lead to disasters and disillusionment for the many.

Just as with organized crime or wealth, power and status, it is the elites versus the rest that has most of the impact for the society as a whole, so with Machiavellianism. Self-report measures will not capture this variance. How valid this same point is for other measures of philosophies of life will presumably depend on whether those philosophies are socially acceptable. Western societies tolerate a wide range of beliefs about human nature. No sanctions are imposed on those who believe human beings are biological amoral or good. Proscriptions are introduced at the lower level of beliefs about the right frameworks within which individuals and societies should conduct themselves. At that level, lies in the service of criminal actions become culpable, not because they are lies but because of what they were intended to and did achieve. At this level, self-report measures could be expected to become invalid.

Discussion

Gilbert, Krull, and Malone (1990) have extracted a neat hypothesis from Spinoza (1982) that information is first processed as being true but may then be evaluated as false. It is a neat idea because a little reflection leads easily to a conclusion that any other default position would be inefficient for at least two main reasons. One is that if a proposition is true, its meaning, if not its pragmatic significance, is transparent and therefore its decoding is at its simplest. Because there are many ways in which it might be false, both the semantics and the pragmatics would be more complex to decode; there would be more variants that one has to interpret and from which one then has to select. The information processing load would be such that whatever the human capacities for distributed parallel processes turn out to be, neither brains nor minds could function to hold simple conversations. Even the simplest implications from the flaunting of Gricean (Grice, 1975/1989) maxims in cooperative conversations can be difficult to decode. In competitive or conflict situations, they could be overwhelming. A second would be that most of what one is told in everyday life is likely to be true. Again, in the interests of efficiency, a truth bias set under such conditions may lead to decoders failing to spot lies when they should have rather than underestimating the incidence of truthful statements (Gigerenzer, 1991; Kahnemann, Slovic, & Tversky, 1982), but effort is saved. Both assumptions are consistent with Zipf's (1949) principle of least effort.

Given true and false propositions to decode, the participants in the experiment of Gilbert et al. (1990) were required to judge their truth value, but on some trials, their information processing was interrupted, which increased the probability that false propositions would be judged as being true but not vice versa. This was so even when the truth value was portrayed prior to the proposition being presented. In a final experiment, presentation and checked comprehension of a false statement increased the probability that it would subsequently be recalled as true.

Perhaps this study will become a classic, as demonstrating phenomena of application well beyond the field of lie detection and trust but of particular relevance to this field. Elsewhere, reference is made to the truth bias in interpersonal relations and encounters (Chapter 4), in children's assumptions about authority figures (Chapter 2), and how too great a collapse of trust in authority (Chapter 7) should lead to an alienation and anarchy in societies. Cognitively, trust is a truth bias. Socially, human beings who trust others are therefore vulnerable to exploitation by those who trade on this predisposition. Machiavellians are therefore a particularly virulent form of parasite. The more they succeed, the greater the loss of trust in any society until, if they are not checked and reduced in number, the community collapses to a collection of paranoid individuals, to what Hobbes (1651/1914) saw as a state of nature.

Not surprisingly, Machiavelli's (1514/1961) own adopted prince consigned him to exile for most of his life. Machiavelli was an astute observer of the recipes for success in the city princedoms of medieval Italy and the ruthlessness with which both church and secular princes operated. Efficient modern totalitarian states are typically run by Machiavellians par excellence, and lies and deception are endemic to the workings of all relationships within such states. The groundwork for discussing how lies and deception function in these and quasi democracies is set down in Chapter 6, but having raised questions about who is likely to lie more or less, it is sensible to first consider under what conditions people lie, what about, and why.

Lies in Informal Interpersonal Encounters

Field Studies: To Whom, About What, and Why

The twofold limitations of field studies deriving from sampling problems and the specific topic are particularly evident in the data currently available. Any estimates of the frequencies with which certain kinds of lies are told will vary with the kinds of persons sampled, their conscientiousness and understanding of what exactly they are to be recording, and the perceived dangers of self-exposure. Primary school children at term time in a rural area are unlikely to yield a similar pattern to actresses auditioning in Hollywood. Respondents cannot interrupt conversations to note lies as they tell them. One cannot imagine an entry, "The police interviewed me about the bank job I did last week. I told them I was watching *Sesame Street* at the time." Sadly, most of the data are confined to well-educated young adult Americans, particularly students in communication courses. What the studies have in common is that the deceptions reported are naturally occurring acts in everyday interpersonal situations.

The self-reported, two-person single conversations of 130 unspecified persons (students) collected by Turner, Edgley, and Olmstead (1975) were analyzed to reveal that 61.5% of conversations included some form of deception. These were more common if the other participants were not intimates. The five reasons for deception extracted were saving face of self and others, guiding the interaction, avoiding tension or conflict, influencing social relations, and achieving power over others. Although respondents were asked to write out an "important" conversation, the mean length of the exchanges seems to have been just over five utterances, and with no control for participants or contexts, it is difficult to base any conclusions about behavior on the study. Camden, Mothey, and Wilson (1984) extended the classification of reasons but confined their collection to white lies. Hample (1980) asked respondents to recall one recent lie and then interviewed 13 out of the 39 students who had participated. A further 314 students were surveyed on the phone or in person, but what they were asked is not stated. Hample arrived at an estimate of a frequency rate of 13.03 lies per person per week and noted that most were defensive reactions to minimize trouble in situations in which the lying was virtually automatic. Lippard's (1988) subsequent diary study comprised 940 examples of acts of deception of which 81.2% were lies. In contrast to the result of Turner et al., most were directed to intimates (21.1% to close friends, 11.9% to cross-sex partners, 26.1% to friends, and 14.9% to parents). Lippard expanded the motivation categories to a basic eight but with 16 subcategories. Conflict avoidance accounted for 29.2%, protecting others 18%, and protecting self-image 16.5%. Cross-tabulations showed motivation-recipient interactions so that the most common lies were told to avoid trouble with parents; mainly, these were about what the respondent was doing when not at home. Excuses to professors accounted for 5.9%. Overall, 273 of the 940 lies were addressed to higher-status and only 13 to lower-status persons. Lippard notes that most lies were responsive not initiating, thereby echoing the reports of Hample and of Knapp and Comadena (1979).

O'Hair and Cody (1993) did not code the motives their student respondents gave for lying against any categorical framework, and on average, these students registered only negative effects of lying, although the authors mustered 25 such consequences overall: 16% referred to loss of trust and 13% to the need for more lies to cover up and nearly 13% mentioned guilt. For the consequences of being caught, loss of trust or respect was mentioned by 25% and losing friends by 18.5%. Despite its recency, this inquiry is no more than exploratory, but it serves as a reminder of the elementary questions that have yet to be answered about peoples' beliefs about lying.

What do these studies tell us? First, they show variety as a function of instructions. None have offered checks of either reliability or validity, and the details typically required by psychological journals are not given. With diary studies, it is notoriously difficult to calibrate the relation between what a person chooses to record and what actually happens, and if estimates are to be made of the incidence of lying, future studies will have to use more than one technique to cross-check the data. Students are only one small section of the population. "Excuses to professors" would not figure as a category of lie for most people. Likewise, who the recipients are will vary. The idea that most lies are responsive needs elaboration. If calling persons to account for what they have been doing and who with is a prerogative of those with higher status in situations for matters considered relevant to the context, then higher-status participants will be using fewer responsive lies. Professors do not ask students, "Who were you with last night, out in the pale moonlight?" Parents may claim wider jurisdiction but are unlikely to ask why an essay has not been written. Role relationships normally carry specific rights and obligations and they certainly carry expectations. Explanations for deviations are likely to be sought, and when true explanations are unlikely to be acceptable, the respondent is on the horns of a dilemma, an avoidance-avoidance conflict. As Lippard (1988) notes, the incidence and types of these dilemmas will change as a function of a large number of variables, including, of course, the extent to which a person's possible conduct is unacceptable to one or more of the significant others.

The generalization that most lies are in fact reactive rather than proactive might prove to be a robust finding, and such lies are likely to be linked to motives of conflict avoidance and protection of self and others and to be addressed to higher-status persons. Proactive lies, on the other hand, will probably be found to be as strategies adopted in a lifestyle designed for the positive pursuit of power, wealth, and status (see the first section of this chapter and Chapter 6). They may well be addressed up, across, and down a status hierarchy. They are the lies that can have very serious consequences for very large numbers of people. Examples of these are many, but perhaps the most frightening exemplification of the idea is in George Orwell's (1948) *1984*, in which the power of the state becomes nearly total through its fabrications. Orwell was right to choose the possible future rather than a fictitious past as the setting. The present global TV village with a few individuals having the power to eliminate millions of people at the press of a button is ripe for exploitation by Big Brother or Big Sister.

Role Relationships

Metts (1989) has pioneered a focus on the kinds of and reasons for deception as a function of the type of close relationship and as an explorer has run the risk of being subject to charges of relying on a weak methodology that gave rise to sampling errors of unknown significance. A sample of 300 modal-age and 90 adult reentry undergraduates enrolled in economics and communication courses replied anonymously to requests, first for a detailed description of a situation in which the respondent had not been completely truthful with a target person defined by the participant as currently very important to them, and second for an account of the reasons why the participant behaved in that way. Participants also specified the type and duration of the relationship, and from the range reported, marriage looked to be heavily confounded with age, and engagement somewhat so. Coding frames were developed to yield reasonable reliabilities of scoring. Metts noted that the instructions may have biased recall toward falsifications (47%) rather than what she classified as concealments (32%) and distortions (21%). In the results, falsifications were more likely to be reactive than proactive, with omissions showing the reverse pattern. The same two forms reversed their probabilities of occurrence in marriages, as contrasted with relationships of friendship, dating, or engagement. Reasons also displayed interactive effects, with friendships protecting self more, relative to other relationships, and dating relatively fewer. Married partners were proportionately more concerned to save partner's face. There were no associations between the kind of deception and the three qualities of the relationships: commitment in each direction, closeness, and satisfaction. From the other perspective, however, those who gave the partner focused reasons rated partner commitment, closeness, and satisfaction higher.

In discussing the results, Metts (1989) suggested that the relative frequencies of reasons for deception reported might be a function of the dominant underlying characteristics of the types of social relationship—friendships often being directed toward utility functions based on a social exchange model and dating being based more on romantic closeness and exclusivity demands, with the face preservation of partner being a (necessary?) condition of satisfying stable relationships. The longevity of marriage is likewise facilitated if partners do not interrogate the other and evoke falsifications that may eventually be exposed; hence, concealment and the lack of questioning. This will contrast with the uncertainties of dating and engaged couples, in which people may be potentially jealous and insecure.

Metts (1989) draws attention to the fact that her opportunity sample seems to have selected positive close social relationships and that distressed relationships could be expected to have quite different patterns—if deceptions in these can be ascertained. Anticipating the message from interpersonal deception theory (Chapter 4), Metts did distinguish falsifications from other forms of deception, such as concealment. Whether "distortions" as underestimations or overestimations are not lies is contestable. Because they are accurate in a quantitative rather than a qualitative manner, they may have other peculiar characteristics, but that is a matter for future research.

Miller, Mongeau, and Sleight (1986) had cohabiting student couples separately fill out questionnaires about the role of deceptive communication in close relationships. When asked to estimate how much deception occurs generally, they suggested that it occurred to some extent. In their own relationships, they thought there was hardly any deception. Although pairs believed their partners were not deceitful, they believed they would be able to detect any deceit that did occur. What deceit was believed to be practiced was hiding "bad" personal habits. Individuals were concerned about the impact discovered deceit would have on their relationship.

One long-standing presumption is that if departures from the normal are indicators of attempted deceptive behavior, then the greater the familiarity between deceiver and detector, the greater the likely accuracy of detection (Brandt, Miller, & Hocking, 1980). This idea stems partially from the more general idea that a knowledge of a person's normal behavior when being truthful can serve both to prevent false positives and to secure accuracy with polygraphs (see Chapter 10). Although the latter may be true, it does not mean that increasing lie detection accuracy will be monotonically related to increasing intimacy. McCornack and Parks (1986) have argued for a complicated set of processes. Increasing involvement will lead to increased confidence that partner deception could be detected and that the partner will never lie to them. In consequence, partners will become less able to detect each other's attempted deceptions without practice or knowledge of results and the ability should be attenuated. In their most recent path analysis of the claims of 90 couples, this sequence was found to fit the data. Other sequences did not. In the study, instructions differentially alerted the judging partner to three degrees of suspicion that answers given to interview questions could or did include some lies. This did not affect the results of the path analysis. The conclusion was that although being suspicious might be related to each of the three variables of interest, it did not affect the relationships between them. The study did place the judging partner in an observing role, there was no interactive dimension, and the lies told were to six items on the Machiavellian scale (Christie & Geis, 1970). This is also a thematic ambiguity about confidence; what was measured was confidence in the accuracy of judgments. This is not the same as confidence in the relationship itself, but presumably, the two could have been confounded in the study itself. To have thought hypothetically of a partner, "I'm sure I would know if he or she was lying to me," might have encouraged respondents to assert that they could detect lies when in fact they had no experience on which to base their judgments. Perhaps the judgments of confidence and truth bias were in fact two indices of general trust rather than indices of a presumed ability and a disposition. As Levine and McCornack (1992) point out, there is a need for modeling of the kind they have conducted, and logical possibilities have to be checked against empirical realities.

Commentary

Are assays into a limited ethology of lies worthwhile? Both the limitations and contingent qualities of the results obtained so far are considerable. A beginning had to be made, however, and that beginning must by definition be exploratory. There are now some fragile estimates of what some American undergraduates are willing to report to their teachers. It is unfortunate that the articles available do not list their methodological weaknesses; contemporary norms of publication, however, differ by discipline. Linguistics, communication studies, and anthropology follow rules that are only partially common to social psychology. On the positive side, it can be noted that prior to the conduct of the studies, some colleagues had claimed that lies were endemic but could not cite any evidence at all. Some social myths upheld and continue to uphold the idea that lies are rare and wicked. Whether they are seen as wicked remains to be evaluated (see Peoples' Lies to Social Organizations in Chapter 9), but certainly they are not rare. There is reassurance that the diary method yields some kind of result, at least with literate and willing adults. There is no technological reason why this cannot be improved on. In language studies, persons have been "wired" for speech samples, which have then been played back to them with interview questions relevant to the purposes of the research. Such a procedure would overcome the fallibility and selectivity of written recollections. Participants could be asked about instances of lying, equivocation, and other forms of concealing the truth. The demands on participants and analysts would be considerable, but the amount of time and effort invested in research should be a function of the problems being studied rather than the convenience and preferences of investigators.

Clearly too, the difficulties of investigating lying in role relationships are daunting. Real secrets are carried to the graves if possible. Fitzpatrick (1990) points to the joint importance of openness and positive statements in the success of marriages. Argyle and Henderson (1985) cite trust as the top rule governing both close friendships and marriages. Discoveries of serious deceit often deal a double blow to close relationships, first through the acts hidden and second from the fact that lies were told to hide them. If friends or partners discover that a trusted intimate has been lying over a period of time, they have no reason to believe they will not be deceived again. There does not appear to be a feasible method for collecting information about the incidence and distribution of serious lies within close relationships.

Only when appropriate technology and methodology are brought to bear will it be possible to map out the ecology of lying—if that is a feasible and sensible enterprise. Would there be any point in having such data, stratified by age, sex, and other demographic variables? If the job of social psychology is to describe and explain the types and incidence of social behavior and experience, the answer has to be positive. Only when such naturally occurring distributions can be examined will social psychologists know what has to be explained. How do types of lies differentiate as children develop? How do men and women differ in their lying and why? Is the practice of some occupations heavily associated with deceiving speech, and if so, what effects does this have for the domestic and leisure lives of such people? A long list of other questions could be added.

Lies in Formal Interpersonal Encounters

In Chapter 2, the account of development of lying ignored individually or socially based differences among children, and in Chapter 3, people have been treated as people in general or as differing in personality. The relevance of their role relationships, however, began to become apparent once it could be observed, for example, that parents and professors would be the most common recipients of lies of university students, itself a special category of persons. Similarly, role relationships of friendship, courtship, marriage, and estrangement have been shown to be relevant to the quantity and quality of both deceptive and detective behavior. Data in these areas are scarce, as they are for role relationships outside the domestic and social spheres. People also tell lies at work. They can tell lies in their dealings with any of the persons with whom they interact. In the absence of a systematic principled framework for interpersonal lying in face-to-face situations involving other than personal role relationships, the best that can be done is to note the array and report on some of the role relationships that have attracted attention.

Historically, the face-to-face exchange of money for goods and services has grown to be a dominating activity of modern consumer society, and although much of this business is heavily regulated to prevent or punish false descriptions, there is still a need for buyers to beware. Sellers are primarily interested in selling rather than in meeting people's needs. Advertising and the issue of falsification of information coming from company headquarters are treated in Chapters 7 and 8. Here the focus remains on the face to face: how the sales staff persuade customers and what misleading tactics might be used to increase sales. The only other relationship considered is that of doctor-patient. This has distinctive qualities. Doctors can tell patients they need treatment when they do not, as can all manner of professionals, but two other components of patient-doctor interaction are unique. The first is that doctors may lie to patients to protect them from immediate suffering . They can underestimate the risks of operations or the chances of recovering from illnesses. They can reassure patients that there is nothing wrong when they know there is. Whether this is right or wrong, humane or arrogant, is discussed by Bok (1978) as a special case of the considerate lie, a class identified by St. Augustine but yet to be systematically studied. Only one study can be reported on—whether and in what circumstances doctors think it right to conceal the truth—and only one can be cited—about patients lying to doctors and the circumstances of these deceptions. Lying to a professional is unusual. The patient goes to the doctor for help but can then lie about the symptoms. Doctors can lie to patients. The question of why is discussed in the second section. The general discussion takes up some of the relationships yet to be explored.

Consumer Focus: Caveat Emptor

Consistent with the newspeak spirit of modern times, the customers who used to buy from shop assistants are now consumers purchasing goods and services from sales executives supported by marketers and advertisers. The idea of a person being assisted in a store to buy what they think they need or want is an echo of a myth of an earlier age, bourgeois Vienna at the turn of the century perhaps. In such times, with relatively static populations and customer loyalty being a high priority, it was important for long-term success in business to have stable relations of mutual satisfaction—and trust.

Such an ambience was not universal. Doubtless many of the itinerants operating through street markets and from door to door were viewed as untrustworthy. Ineffectual medicines were sold and shares in El Dorado companies were not uncommon (Anonymous, 1923).

Whether there are now more or fewer rogues relying on deceptions about their wares is not of immediate concern. Whether there has been a shift in power away from the customer to the seller and whether sellers have become more indifferent to anything but their profits is a socially and sociologically very important question, but it is beyond the current purview. At the level of society, a population that treats with skepticism the utterances of the various authorities with vested interests in maintaining high levels of consumer activity is incompatible with such a society's having a dynamic competitive consumer economy—one of the tensions or contradictions of capitalism. Banks may encourage people to borrow when interest rates are low, but this is problematic if people believe that rates will soon rise. Investing in stock exchange-linked pensions and insurance is dangerous if markets could be low when the time comes to cash the policies. Buying anything if you think you could be the victim of a swindle is likely to discourage buying. Insofar as people have become wiser and warier about the boom and recession patterns of economies, they are likely to resist the advertising of political and financial institutions. On the other hand, they have to place their savings somewhere. A pendulum effect through time is a likely pattern. Too much falsification results in too few sales, greater honesty becomes more profitable, and then there is a return to more exaggeration and falsification. The current level of skepticism about authorities seems to have spread to the appraisal of a wide range of advertisements and sales talk and linked up with the previous suspicion with which door-to-door salespeople and secondhand car dealers have traditionally been greeted. Perhaps the markets have created an emptor who now has a predisposition toward caveats in many purchases.

Elsewhere (Chapter 9), issues of the credibility of authorities are treated, and the facts reported are consistent with the suggestions entertained here that on both sides of the Atlantic, the truth bias referred to earlier in this chapter for interpersonal interactions may no longer be valid in many consumer-seller contexts.

The thrust of this possibility should not be underestimated or overestimated. Many goods that people buy in shops correspond very precisely to the descriptions on the packet in quality and quantity. Short measure must now be very rare. Coffee arabica will be arabica. A cotton vest will be made of cotton. Goods, white and brown, do conform to their specifications and function with much greater durability than even 20 years ago. What might be called everyday shopping has probably never been easier, at least in terms of not having to worry about the qualities of what one is buying. Those who buy cheap expensive watches and solid gold rings on street corners or find extraordinary bargains through dark markets are the stereotypical victims of their own greed. Confidence tricksters have traditionally caught their fishes by baiting hooks with inducements that implicate their fishes as probable beneficiaries of criminal activities—and they still do.

So what is there of social psychological interest in buying-selling face to face? At least two sets of problems become writ large in the buyer-seller relationship. One operates at the microlevel of the confidence trickster, sharp salesperson, and advertiser and is discussed in this chapter; another functions at the macrolevel of governmental and commercial financial institutions, which is dealt with in Chapter 7. Both are concerned with persuasion and what changes a person from not having or doing a particular X to one acquiring or doing X. Analytically, it can be useful to distinguish between a person becoming aware that X exists and then the wanting and acquiring an X, although the two may well be mixed together in a single incident.

Interpersonal Tricks

The "rules" of marketing and selling are a particular example of the earlier work on attitude change and persuasion arising from the classical studies of Hovland, Lumsdaine, and Sheffield (1949) and Hovland, Janis, and Kelley (1953). In this field, it has been necessary to abandon the optimistic hopes of psychologists that there would be generalizations that would encompass a simple listing of the effective factors that would contribute to credibility of source and the credibility of messages, independent of the characteristics of the receiver, the topic, and the context. Current models of such influences are both more modest and more complex; they recognize that factors are interactive and that the totality of possible influences determines the outcomes.

Cialdini (1985) has assembled evidence relevant to the three selling strategies that he has christened foot in the door, door in the face, and the low-ball effect. All are deceptive in that the initial requests or statements do not reflect the ultimate outcome desired. Only the last involves clear lies. In the first, a small request is used to gain compliance so that the desired compliance with a larger request will be more difficult to deny. The first request is not predicated on a lie, but the cultural expectation is that only one request will be made. In the second, the anticipated rejection of an unreasonable request is used as a precursor to gaining assent to a much smaller subsequent one. Again, the first request is predicated on a deception but not a lie per se. In the low-ball situation, the seller strikes a bargain that is then "reneged on" by higher authority in the expectation that the victim will still proceed with the deal at a higher price. This is both a deception and a lie.

These are but three strategies of many, some more deceptive than others. The tactical presentation of these can also be tailored to the prospective buyer. Marwell and Schmitt (1967a, 1967b) listed 16 verbal compliance gaining tactics (see Table 3.1) subsequently investigated and evaluated by Miller, Boster, Roloff, and Seibold (1987). Burgoon and Miller (1985) provide further comment on the workings.

P. DePaulo (1988) expands on the variety of ways in which false impressions might be conveyed without actual lies being told. These have been documented as conveying more than they say. He mentions the incomplete comparison (where the inferior product is never mentioned) and the play on false positive associations (if it is natural it is healthier and purer), but he could have added the contiguity of enjoyable stimuli (relaxing, romantic music and small furry animals), metaphoric extension (a tiger in the petrol tank is preferable to a snail or a tortoise), and snob and expert appeal (top people drink Chateau Plonk, and scientists in white coats use Massacre toilet cleaner). The list could be extended.

With professional actors using well-rehearsed edited scripts that may have been scrutinized by social psychologists, it is not surpris-

Table 3.1 Typology of Compliance-Gaining Strategies

Strategy	
Promise	If you will comply, I will reward you.
Threat	If you do not comply, I will punish you.
Expertise (positive)	If you comply, you will be rewarded because of "the nature of things."
Expertise (negative)	If you do not comply, you will be punished because of "the nature of things."
Liking	Actor is friendly and helpful to get target in a "good frame of mind" so that he will comply with the request.
Pregiving	Actor rewards target before requesting compliance.
Aversive stimulation	Actor continuously punishes target, making stimulation cessation contingent on compliance.
Debt	You owe me compliance because of past favors.
Moral appeal	You are immoral if you do not comply.
Self-feeling (positive)	You will feel better about yourself if you comply.
Self-feeling (negative)	You will feel worse about yourself if you do not comply.
Altercasting (positive)	A person with "good" qualities would comply.
Altercasting (negative)	Only a person with "bad" qualities would not comply.
Altruism	I need your compliance very badly, so do it for me.
Esteem (positive)	People you value will think better of you if you comply.
Esteem (negative)	People you value will think worse of you if you do not comply.

SOURCE: Marwell & Schmitt (1967a).

ing that the performances recorded in studios do not manifest cues of deceit in the final advertisements. If they did, the recordings would not be used. To the extent that actors and salespeople either believe in or distance themselves from their performances, any signs of guilt or shame will be attenuated. Again, it would be odd for an organization to continue to employ someone who was unconvincing as a salesperson. It would be odd for someone who found the work hypocritical to continue in that mode as a career.

Among other studies, P. DePaulo (1988) cites his own study (De-Paulo & DePaulo, 1989), which used videotapes of retail salespersons and car buyers who had bargained over their last purchase. The former had to try to sell liked and disliked products, the latter had to trade in liked and disliked cars. Judges could not discriminate between the honest and dishonest performances, but this was not surprising because subsequent detailed objective analyses of the tapes conducted by the experimenters could not find any evidence of actual verbal or nonverbal discriminators. The performers were skilled dissemblers. The judges' differentiations were found to be related to three factors—more postural shifts, more speech hesitations, and a slower speech rate—but these are three of the invalid presumptions commonly found in alerted lay judgments (Ekman, 1985/1992).

As more people become familiar with the likely moves made in any of these sales scripts, there should be a drift toward ritualized routines. My last car purchase began much too promisingly, with a heavy discount and a high trade-in price. The standard moves then followed. First, the mechanics inspector noted the high mileage, which had already been written down by the salesman. The trade-in price was slashed. Over a cup of coffee and some hums and hahs, the price crept back to halve the gap up to the salesman's "discretionary limit." Then, a visit to the sales manager's office became necessary. During the next 15 minutes, I read and presumably they talked about some topic. The salesman returned with the special-favor-to-an-old-customer story. Eventually, the original trade-in was reestablished. Until one has played the game more than once, anxiety and worry may well encourage an early closure by the customer, but when they know that you know. . . . (In my last class in which Cialdini's (1985) work was discussed, three students had been thrown a low ball, but only one caught it—and will not do so again.) Such scripts have not been common practice in Western societies outside certain specialist lines, such as car sales and antiques, but it has been the accepted mode of conducting purchases across much of the South and East from time immemorial. Within Indian society, it would be improper to buy a carpet without extended discussion and bargaining over tea, as the conversation moves to a predictable agreed price; a social occasion cannot be foregone with a rapid exchange. To call the moves deceptive or to call the false statements lies would be to misinterpret the situation—unless you are an outsider or a naive purchaser. In a

1. The most satisfactory factor analytic solutions yielded three factors accounting for 43% of the variance: concealment-equivocation (23.6%), falsification (10.0%), and total truthfulness (9.7%).

2. (a) Concealment and equivocation were covarying actions, apparently geared to fear of disapproval, face needs, and maintenance of social relations; (b) falsification was prevalent for achieving personal benefits; and (c) truthfulness was made up of items about which patients claimed they always told the truth.

3. Distributions by age, race, education, and gender for the three factors yielded significant three- and four-way interactions, thereby precluding simple generalizations but noting profiles of complex overrepresentations.

4. For falsifications, lower-educated, ethnic minority males below age 55 were significantly higher scorers, and the least likely subgroup to falsify were those older than 54, unless they were lower-educated minority females.

5. Overall, 85.3% of respondents admitted to equivocation-concealment, 34.2% admitted to at least one falsification. Those scoring a maximum on truthfulness and a minimum composed 3.1% of the sample.

One of the interesting discriminations is the differential linkages of concealment-equivocation and falsification. With fears and anxieties of various kinds, it is not surprising that patients revert to minimization but not falsifying tactics. If Miller's (1959) approach-avoidance gradients are relevant, it is easy to imagine the approach needs carrying a patient into the surgery. Once arrived, avoidance tendencies should become stronger and in the actual consultation might well lead to understatements from which doctors may have to draw out the truth. Patients fearing the worst are likely to be ambivalent about their original decision to seek medical comment; the direction of ambivalence may well reverse once in conversation with a doctor, but concealment-equivocation would serve as a basis for further probing in a way in which clear falsification would not. To find out whether this functional analysis is valid would require sequential analyses of dialogue in which equivocation-concealment is an opening move.

If a patient is to get time off from work or financial benefits or both, equivocation-concealment would probably be counterproductive: overstatement and exaggeration (especially about the difficult to verify) have to be the direction of any departure from the truth. Five of the 11 loading items referred to this kind of gain; the other 6 were a different kind of insurance, directed toward securing special treatments that might be withheld if the mere truth were told.

As with other real-life problems involving lying, the stakes become high if researchers move from anonymous field studies to observations of real interactions followed by interrogation. The sampling frame chosen by Burgoon et al. (1994) shows shrewd originality, but it will have been short of persons with the experience of consulting a doctor about a possible terminal condition. Patients with diagnosed cancers will be underrepresented in jury rooms. Any study, however, designed to catch such people for interviews after they have just consulted a doctor is fraught with humanitarian issues. A study designed to check on falsifications that were intended to obtain disability pensions would face other perils and difficulties. Large insurance claims may well be at stake in such cases, and insurers do retain investigators to check out the subsequent behavior of some successful claimants. Mental disturbance and stress, supported by medical evidence, are now well-known devices for arguing for mitigation in criminal and civil cases.

Following Burgoon's (1994) precedent, Shepherd (1995) compared the ratings of doctors and patients on their agreement or disagreement with a doctor telling the truth considerately, equivocating, or lying considerately to a variety of patients with illness of varying severity. It was expected that doctors who had faced these dilemmas would be more likely to judge equivocation and lying as acceptable than junior doctors or patients. Overall, lying was most strongly disagreed with across all 12 cases. Equivocation was acceptable in 7 of 12. Truthfulness was acceptable across all 12. For the patient types, the rejection of deception was strongest for elderly, then ordinary adults, then those who might harm others or themselves, and it was least objectionable for young children who would not be able to understand. Deception was least rejected for terminally ill patients, then temporary serious, and finally permanent difficulties. Contrary to hypotheses, patients were less against deception than were doctors, and older doctors were more disposed to accept lying than younger ones. All measures were based on questionnaire answers, and the questions placed respondents in the role of observers rather than participants.

Clearly, the issues merit further exploration. Bok (1978) discusses some of the ethical issues, but there is no empirical evidence on the preferences and moral judgments of those actually involved in making decisions. How many terminally ill patients are pleased at being told the truth and how many wish they had not been and what are the differences between the two sets? Although it can be argued that it is patronizing not to tell the truth, it can also be viewed as considerate. Similarly, there can be ways of conveying the truth without rendering it explicit, and presumably, that could be a preferred option. At the present time, societies do not have policies on these issues, and doctors are left with individual responsibility for what they say in individual cases.

Discussion

The selection of sales people falsifying or concealing information for customers, and doctors and patients doing the same to each other are no more than illustrations of an infinite variety of formal role relationships in which deception can occur.

Deceptions by employees to employers can occur at every phase of the relationship: falsified curricula vitae with invented referees and experiences, lies at interviews or on personality tests used for selection, lies at work to minimize debits and maximize credits for personal reputations, lies about expenses and reasons for absence, and lying about employer's responsibilities for illness precipitating early retirement. Reciprocally, superiors can lie to employees about prospects, can pass false information about them up the organization, can issue false threats, and can display false accounts. Both sets of actions seem to be endemic. The first set is a mixture of the rare and the normative. Exaggeration and a measure of falsification seem to be generally viewed as improper on applications, just as feigned injuries are, but within limits, both are seen as normative at interviews or in accounting for absences. Expenses are a no-man's land. Some false claiming seems to be expected in some circumstances, but occasionally, people are picked out and dismissed for making false claims. TV documentaries cite continuing senior UN officials as making grotesque claims, whereas a British vice chancellor can feel obliged to resign his job for reorganizing his first-class air tickets into cheaper ones for his family's benefit. If everyone in the United Nations Organizations or the European Unions who had made money on travel expenses were to resign their jobs as a matter of principle, one suspects there could be many vacancies. Perhaps it is a case of the more senior the position, the greater the presumed freedom to exploit such supplements; only if an outsider challenges is there a risk of retrenchment. Also, as Hogan (1983) has shown, the trustworthiness of superiors and bosses is the issue of most importance to employees in his inquiries. The dangers of challenging superiors with whistle-blowing are demonstrated in Chapter 10. To accuse any superior of deception is risky, especially if the charge is valid. The gossip is that in most corporate organizations deception down the hierarchy is standard practice but that attempts to challenge the right of superiors to lie will invoke charges of dis-loyalty and reduce prospects of continuing successful employment with the organization. Even little emperors retain the right to lie about their clothes.

Any social psychologist who ventures into such fields of inquiry may regret the decision. First, gaining access to information will be fraught with difficulties. The financial cost to any organization of allowing any study will be great. The potential cost to individuals of telling the truth is great, in revealing both who they think is deceiving them about what and who they are deceiving about what. With the potential price of exposed lies about offenses being redundancy or criminal proceedings or both, the idea of data collection for scientific purposes is naive. This discussion raises interesting problems beyond those about deception in the buyer-seller role relationship, and the prospects of informative studies are remote.

Some of the features of doctor-patient communication can also be elaborated. Little was made of doctors lying to patients about treatments. Even when the treatment is at public rather than personal expense and professionals are salaried, those responsible for recommendations have a doubly vested interest. First, in conditions of uncertainty, a failure to recommend treatment when it is necessary is more likely to evoke criticism and litigation than a positive recommendation that turns out to have been unnecessary. Second, treatment provides work for one's fellow professionals and boosts the societal importance of one's occupational group. In the past 100 years, the medical profession has transformed its power, wealth, and status upward, whether functioning as a public or a private sector group. This principle applies to other groups for which the state pays bills; legal aid cases for lawyers and inspection services for health, safety, or educational standards.

Once the transaction is doubly commercial as a personal charge to the client and an individual profit to the professional, the two vested interests in recommending (expensive) treatment are rendered even more transparent. In a country that has changed its rules for fees of professionals in the past 15 years, such as Britain, the medical elite with private sector specializations have raised their prices far beyond the rates of inflation, and excessive billing against private insurance has become a source of complaint. The same has been true of lawyers and accountants and those other highly qualified groups whose services have to be employed and who are sufficiently well organized to ration their numbers; in addition, they may be tempted to create work when it is in their interests to do so (Perkin, 1989). What is true of the self-employed professions is equally true of those technicians and skilled tradespeople whose services are in demand and who can ration their numbers. Unnecessary work, replacements rather than repairs, previously repaired components being billed as new, and undone work charged for are several standard forms of falsification that have shown up in surveys of consumer protection groups. Confrontations in such situations may well evoke lies as reactions.

As a final example of lying in formal face-to-face encounters between peers, lying in car accidents is perhaps the most notorious. Very frequently, clearly incompatible accounts of the reasons for crashes emerge, and without witnesses, the truthfulness of the disputing parties may be impossible to adjudge.

Who Lies When and Why

The circumstances of lying in formal role relationship encounters seem to be most heavily influenced by perceived cost-benefit analyses. The smaller the likely costs of detection and the greater the likely benefits of successful deception, the more likely it is that deception will be tried. In the case of car accidents, telling the truth may invalidate one's insurance cover, lead to increases in insurance premiums, and result in court appearances and sentencing, whereas a simple lie whose character is known only to the other participants eliminates all those costs. The other participant may seek vengeance, and the liar has to live with the lie, but in practice, vengeance seems to be rare, and living with lies told is not a very overwhelming deterrent for many.

Again, much of the motivational variance would appear to be taken up with the variables of income and wealth. Some of this will be driven by needs to survive, but much more of it appears to be based on a maxim of maximizing financial returns for energy expended. In the examples selected, proactive lies are more common in sellers, whether it be goods, services, or self that are being sold. As in children and other face-to-face encounters, reactive lies in formal relationships are likely to be first-line defenses against accusations of lying or other offenses; in certain circumstances, they can be protective of others. Some of the proactive lies have the ambiguous status of being simultaneously normative practice and condemnable if exposed. Perquisites of the workplace and the job more generally enjoy this ambivalence. Blue collar pilfering of goods has its equivalent in white collar "freebies" and the use of phones and post. The free phone calls of salaried staff have more than their equivalents in those exchanges of cash for goods or services of the self-employed that do not appear in the business accounts. There appear to be norms governing tolerated degrees of fraudulent expense claims; occasionally, there is a public exposure of someone who exceeds the ill-defined norms of lining one's own pockets. For example, the U.S. vice president, Spiro Agnew, complained when forced from office that no one had told him that the rules had changed.

To fail to mention cultural diversity as a source of variance would be to fail to mention most of the variance, but this will be developed in Chapter 11 in which an attempt is made to integrate the face to face with lies in public.

To fail to mention the moral and the legal would be to fail to mention the rhetorical parameters of threats to curtail or control. As with the socialization of children, so it is with face to face in formal encounters. Children are told not to lie. They are punished for lying. Their problem is to work out when which kinds of falsification are required, when they are expected, and when they are tolerated. Each of these will have fuzzy and variable borders. These considerations apply to adults also. Occasionally, in particular circumstances individuals are exposed, called to account and perhaps punished. Meanwhile, the universal ideal of "lying is wrong" is left as an ideal to be invoked against particular lies. As to where the borders are between tolerance and intolerance, tolerance and expectation, and expectation and requirement is a set of research problems that has not yet been addressed. Neither have systematic attempts been made to find out what the determinants are of the changes in the rules that afflicted Spiro Agnew.

If much of the content of the chapter has served to document what people already believed to be the case, then this is an example of everyday experience being in line with the collected empirical evidence. The most worrying feature for would-be researchers is the methodological hurdles. People will disclose what they believe about lying by other people (see also Chapter 9), and those in stable positive social relationships will offer comments about themselves and their partners. If relationships are seriously deceitful, however, or if a salesperson is chronically consigned to lying or if someone is Machiavellian and ambitious, there is every reason to extend the deceit to research questions. The deception is too important and the risks of disclosure and exposure too great to be honest with researchers. It is alleged that well-established persons in higher-status positions of organizations that are internally competitive need to be minimal disclosers just in case what they really believe can be used against them by rivals. Perhaps an index of equivocation competence might be used to gain inverse estimates of likely willingness to be honest and open.

In Chapter 3, the focus has been on who is likely to lie about what in what situations and why. In Chapter 4, the switch is to the dynamics of how to lie without being detected.

CHAPTER FOUR

Lying Face to Face: General Dynamics

Shakespeare was not the first author to comment on the complications arising from the human capacity and propensity to deceive, but he did issue a salutary warning: "Oh, what a tangled web we weave, when first we practice to deceive!" If the contents of Chapter 2 are essentially correct, the child has been well prepared and well rehearsed in deceptive behavior as adulthood is entered. If the contents of Chapter 3 are valid pointers, then lying is currently an integral component of everyday living in the United Kingdom and the United States, more so for some than others.

It was noted in the opening paragraphs of this book that living would have been simpler had deception not become included in the repertoire of human abilities, and social psychologists would have been spared from analyzing the consequential set of difficulties. The role of deception and lying in everyday encounters is particularly problematic because it is a superordinate game, parasitic on the whole of the rest of social living. There is a sense in which social psychologists need to be able to describe and explain everything else of significance within their discipline before they can cope with a superimposition of deception and lying. The possibilities of describing and explaining lying and deception are inevitably constrained if there are no adequate ways of accounting for undeceptive behavior.

In addition, deceptions themselves are not confined to a single layer of activity. The world of espionage and counterespionage exemplifies the extravagances to which supergames can be taken. Agents become double agents who, to disguise their true allegiance, have to continue to act as simple agents on some matters and move into being double agents only on others. Of course, an apparent double agent may really be faithful to the original allegiance or have been selling out to a third party. These levels of capacity clearly exist beyond spy-thriller novels. At least one play dramatizes through soliloquy the confusions of identity that can take over the life of a double agent. Logically, it must be true that spies can cease to know which side they are ultimately serving, especially if they begin to suspect that their controllers are deceiving them so that they become solely dependent on themselves to define both objective and subjective reality.

Spy catching is one of the societal needs that has given impetus to the growth of interest in the detection of deception by psychologists. A comparable pressure has come from legal institutions. How are the police, juries, and judges to know who is lying and who is telling the truth? Medieval tests for exposing the crime of witchcraft were mostly cruel, bizarre, and unevaluated. Throwing a witch into a lake and concluding guilt from flying away and innocence from drowning recorded no instances of witches escaping. If physical torture ever had extraction of the truth as one of its goals, it too could give rise to false positives.

Perhaps amateurs lying in interpersonal encounters in open societies can be shown to be less complicated than successful professional spying requires? Although it may be true that none of us displays the same open attitudes and behaviors across all situations to all those we interact with, very few of us are leading two lives simultaneously and essentially insulated from each other. On the other hand, many citizens are engaged in criminal or other secret activities that are kept concealed from potentially opposing forces, rivals, and unreliable associates. All people trim the truth for one reason or another, some more frequently than others, and the claims made by psychologists that lying is endemic to everyday encounters would be difficult to refute.

So what are the research questions about interpersonal lies and deceptions and how might they be answered? As is so often the case, there is an initial difficulty in defining a frame of reference. We have looked at the issue of "face," which is as old as Chinese civilization; pretending to appropriate patterns of respect and deference is an ancient practice. In more recent times, these questions have been elaborated in concepts of impression management, self-presentation, and facework. Should these be included as part of the falsification story? This was the first topic raised in the last chapter and the decision to confine the focus to verbal falsification per use was no more than a pragmatic need to contain the coverage. Literature has grown relatively independently of the more dynamic succession of experiments on deception and detection. Under what conditions can who lie about what without being detectable? Under what conditions are liars detectable, and what gives them away? As will be seen, hopes of isolating simple main effects of infallible individual cues rapidly gave way to suggestions for probabilistic profiles, and the empirical evidence for those has yet to include the kinds of consideration introduced in the concluding section on the more ecologically realistic interpersonal detection theory constructed by Buller and Burgoon (in press). In everyday encounters, liars may not know whether or not they are suspected. Normally, it is participants and not observers who are making judgments and they are doing so on-line, in real time, and their judgments are consequential if they reveal them, whether or not they are right.

I will begin at the beginning, however.

Experimental Studies of Verbal Falsification: Performance and Detection

The few field studies of the incidence, varieties, targets, and motivation of lies and other forms of verbal deception have been pursued relatively independently of experimental studies, which have themselves appeared in more than one tradition and with less cross-referencing than might have been expected. The various approaches did begin to come together in the 1980s.

In what is usually cited as the first experimental study, Fay and Middleton (1941) had three men and three women answer questions with complete sentences over a loudspeaker system. As each question was asked, the interviewees were instructed to answer with either a true or a false statement. Listeners were required to judge whether or not answers were truthful. True statements were identified on 50% of occasions and lies on 60%. Male speakers were judged somewhat more accurately, but females were somewhat better judges. Against today's standards, this investigation would not have served as more than a pilot study. Interviewees were not lying; they were pretending to tell lies to order. Listeners were alerted to the existence of lies and, seemingly, to their likely incidence. The judgments of truth were clearly at chance level, and no statistical analyses were conducted to justify any of the three claims made about lies, speakers, or judges.

Unfortunately, as mentioned at the beginning of this chapter, this form of investigation seems to have served as a precedent for the design of many future studies. Kraut (1978) filmed five male students answering interview questions with a 50% lie rate. Other students passed judgments of lie or truth and gave rationales for their judgments. Analyses of the films were also made. Objective analyses suggested lying answers were shorter in length and more improbable in content. Their response latencies were longer. The five interviewees differed from each other but were relatively consistent in their own proficiency. The judges both differed from each other and fluctuated within a particular target. The cues they used were postural shifts, gaze avoidance, and amount of smiling; response latency, fundamental frequency, and answer length; and consistency, plausibility, and social desirability of answer. This study compounds the weaknesses of the Fay and Middleton (1941) design. Interviewees found themselves in some additional trouble with the procedure because questions were semantically linked to each other and theoretically obliged respondents to give mutually inconsistent answers. "Have you ever played soccer?" might have required a lying "Yes." This could be followed by a question requiring a truthful answer about when the interviewee had last played a game. By subsequently eliciting ideas about cues used by judges, Kraut obtained ex post facto rationalizations, which may or may not have represented the original determinants of judgments about differences between lies and truthful statements.

A number of similar experiments seem to have sacrificed criteria of validity for those of convenience, and unfortunately, what can be said to justify laboratory simulations for many areas of social psychology cannot be used for lying. The techniques described are reminiscent of the joke about the person looking for money lost on a dark night under a street lamp; the money may have been lost some distance away, but it was easier to search where it was lighter. Pretend lies are easy to collect, but no evidence has been brought forward as yet to show that their features share any similarities with real lies, other than their falsity. They have been motiveless lies in more than one sense. The speaker has had no reason to lie in the situation. Neither were there particular actions to cover up. Typically, the lies have had to be invented almost without warning and without any sense of what is to be concealed. One argument might be that at least the lies have revealed their authors' beliefs about what has to be concealed when lying, but even that is not true. Their beliefs may not have been matched by their competence. In contrast, the judges were possibly showing what they believed to be distinctive about lies, but they might have been able to volunteer their theories more comprehensively and simply in other circumstances, for example, in interviews.

It may be that there are no significant research questions about the real dynamics of deceiving that can be answered via laboratory-based simulations of deceptions, at least at this point in time. Certainly, ordering students to invent lies in monologues in situ does not appear to have any virtues. To begin to have utility, any participants should have a reason for lying that they have accepted as a sufficient reason. They should be doing so in a context of some situational familiarity and sense, and they should feel potentially accountable for any lies they have told. "I was asked to do so by the experimenter" has no such quality.

If it could be shown that simulations give comparable data to real situations, then such experiments could have a role to play (see DePaulo, 1988). What appears to have occurred in this field is in the opposite sequence to that which should have been followed. Recordings of persons telling real lies and telling the truth should have been used first. Discriminating cues emerging from objective analyses of these recordings could then have been compared with identical analyses of actors pretending to lie. If these two sets of results were indistinguishable, then investigators could have exploited the cheaper, easier simulations as materials for subsequent experiments, with occasional recalibrating checks. In fact, such comparisons have yet to be made. As a result, the general tendency has been to write off the "pretend" studies rather than to check out whether they were getting valid answers despite their artificiality.

How good people are at detecting lies is a separable question, and it is regrettable that the first studies incorporated the double hazard of pretend lies being judged by amateurs who were not required to identify the bases of their judgments. Had this been done the idea of people using the wrong cues might have emerged earlier. It could also have emerged that judgments were heavily determined by task requirements. People might have been more obliged to express uncertainty rather than be misleadingly cooperative. Uncertainty has now become a dominant theme, and Ekman (1985/1992) in particular stresses the contingency of his lists of cues (see Tables 4.1, 4.2, & 4.3). This may have been overdone. Some lies by some people in some situations are detectable with certainty by a majority of ordinary adults and by all trained lie detectors. Some lies by some people in some situations remain undetectable, even by trained detectors working with the latest technological aids. For example, the allegations of Anita Hill that she had been sexually harassed by the now Supreme Court Justice Clarence Thomas did not appear to be based just on misunderstandings. The allegations seemed to extend beyond two possible interpretations of the same events. Lie detectors were used and their results invoked at hearings but not accepted. Perhaps Clarence Thomas and Anita Hill know the truth about the allegations but no one else does! Likewise, some approximation to the truth must be known in all serious criminal trials; the accused knows whether he or she killed or robbed the victim. The expertise of the lie detectors has not significantly altered the balance of forces between prosecutor and defense, or so it would seem.

Fortunately, there is now work with either naturally occurring lies or lies in situations contrived to have sufficiently plausible verisimilitude to enable some charting of what features serve as possible indicators, who knows how to use these, and who is using the wrong ones.

From the statements of laypeople, it is possible to extract what they believe are the features indicative of truth telling and falsification, and one of the points made by Ekman (1985/1992) and others (e.g., Friedman & Tucker, 1990) is that people display a measure of consensus about cues to deceit, but of these, some are valid, others are invalid, and yet others that have a degree of validity are not cited. What are to be the standards of calibration? These have come from the painstaking observations of the scientists running and rerunning videos watching for possible discriminators with two kinds of comparisons: within individuals lying and not lying and between individuals lying and not lying. For these, researchers have preferred to use "genuine" rather than enacted lies.

Miller and colleagues (1987) (see Miller & Stiff, 1993, for a review) have approached deception from the perspective of communication science rather than social psychology and more particularly from the idea of deception being one mode of persuasion—that is, inducing (false) beliefs in another. Adopting such a line, there are as many reasons for lying as there are goals for inducing beliefs in others by other persuasive means; lies differ from the other tactics because they are untrue. Classifications of lies by motive of author would correspond to whatever classification is eventually adopted for reasons for uttering truthful propositions, with the single exception of the truth-falsity distinction.

Miller and Stiff (1993) devised nine criteria against which relevant research should be evaluated, the first two of which go to the core of the most common concern of critics—whether the participants are sufficiently motivated to deceive and to detect deception. Miller et al. (1987) are unenthusiastic about simulations of deception, and most of their own contributions use what they dub the Exline (Exline, Thibaut, Hickey, & Gumpert, 1970) procedure. This involves someone cheating and then being interviewed. Typically, a stooge and a real participant are given a joint task to perform, the experimenter leaves the room for a phone call, and the real participant looks up or is tempted to look up "the answers" left behind by the experimenter. The returning experimenter runs the remaining trials, calculates the results, compliments the pair on the quality of their performance, and then asks how they managed to do so well, interviewing the real participant first and separately. Typically, cheats do not confess. Controls are typically truthful participants who had no cheating opportunity. Variations can be constructed, by having tasks that include rewards, for example. According to Stiff and Miller (1986, p. 27), the procedure cannot be used more than once with the same participant, but manipulations can be imagined in which some less than perfectly matched repeat trials might be enacted—different time, different laboratory, different experimenter, different task, and different interrogatory. Given the difficulty of devising ethically acceptable procedures in the area, some experimentation along these lines would be worth exploring further.

The procedure is restrictive. Lying to an experimenter about looking up answers is not potentially destructive of trust between husband and wife, and the objective costs of being caught out could not be dire. The lies are reactive not proactive. At least, however, they are real. (They could also be compared with simulated lies by the same person in another context, a contrast that 50 years of research has yet to make.)

Using the idea of Cody and O'Hair (1983) that constructing lies involves greater cognitive effort that telling the truth, Stiff and Miller (1986) have examined the verbal content of truthful and lying statements, with the latter in fact having more self-references, acceptances of personal responsibility, and fewer words. They point out that these particular differences may be task specific. They add that students judging the videos for veracity relied more on their judgments on four specific kinds of utterances only one of which overlapped with a real difference—that is, number of words. Their findings on actual and perceived nonverbal indicators accord with the literature more generally.

Stiff and Miller (1986) also noted how the interviewer's behavior was relevant to the verbal and nonverbal behavior of participants where questions or other forms of probes were negative, defined as requesting further information but conveying "a degree of skepticism" about earlier replies. Blinking, smiling, and latency of reply were reduced and hand gestures were increased. None of these were related to actual veracity. Statements of personal responsibility and self-references were higher with negative probes and with veracity, but modifiers related only to probes and not veracity. In brief, Stiff and Miller produced the strange array of relations all too frequently found in the area: truthfulness of messages, probe negativity, and independent judgments of truthfulness showing a variety of relationships to verbal and nonverbal activities. Ekman (1985/1992) and his colleagues have had the advantage of a long-standing history of working in the separable but intersecting areas of nonverbal communication and emotion (see Ekman & Friesen, 1975), and because his was the most active laboratory in the mid-1980s, it is sensible to summarize his approach (Ekman, 1985/1992).

Ekman (1985/1992) has relied on a variety of sources for his analyses. Fiction, faction, and personal observations are combined with results from systematic studies to build up a story about success and failure in the ongoing struggle between liars and lie catchers. What liars can fail to do and thereby expose themselves to detection falls into two categories: leakage and deception cues. Leakage refers to cues that indicate that deception may be occurring and what the truth may be. Deception cues are indicative that something is being concealed but do not provide information about what or why. For his systematic data, Ekman relies heavily on a study he conducted with nurses, and he is correct in claiming that the verisimilitude of this investigation to real life gives its results a plausibility not shared by many others.

In a pilot study, student nurses were told that they would see some gruesome medical films but were asked to suppress any signs of feeling while they watched. This context was powerful enough to evoke feelings but did not result in sufficient suppression until supported by stronger instructions. To achieve this, Ekman (1985/ 1992) explained to them that as nurses they would encounter gory and distressing situations in which they would have to control themselves to remain efficient and considerate to the victims. Watching gory films and being able to lie convincingly about their contents to an interviewer would provide practice for the exercise of such control in the presence of patients and their carers. With this additional justification, the task combined a plausible context with a vocationally relevant and apparently acceptable justification for deception and lying.

Ekman (1985/1992) found considerable variance in the main sample's ability to hide their feelings; subsequent interviews led to the suggestion of relatively stable individual differences in a more general competence to lie and deceive. Participants' comments about themselves corresponded to their observed behavior. In contrast, none of a number of psychometric tests discriminated between the incompetent and the adept. The adept were simply skilled at lying; they were not psychopathic, and according to their accounts, they did not exploit their proficiency for their own benefit. The incompetent knew of their incompetence and were apprehensive, a condition that Ekman suggests increases detectability. This will be particularly so if the interrogator is believed to be percipient. Ekman proceeded to argue his way to a list of factors that may contribute to lies failing:

The potential interrogator being suspicious and presumed to be skilled, the liar being unpracticed, with a biography of failed lies and frightened of being caught

The stakes of being caught being high, in terms of rewards and punishments (especially punishments), the punishment for either the lie or its referent being heavy, the interrogator being neither a beneficiary nor a victim of the lie

Strangely, in the section discussing guilt about deception, Ekman (1985/1992) lists factors increasing the likelihood and strength of guilt but does not explicitly state that greater guilt implies increased chances of detection, although these factors reappear as probabilistic indicators in the appendices. To complete the trio, he adds "duping delight," the thrill that some people derive from lying and deception. Sometimes, this is a public display to impress those who know. Sometimes, it seems to be a challenge to the other participants: "Call me a liar if you dare!" Whether this kind of behavior correlates with risk-taking pleasures in other social or physical situations has not been pursued, but the delight in duplicity certainly characterizes at least some of the people one encounters in contemporary Western society.

Although apprehension about detection and guilt about the deception (and its reference) are general states that increase the probability of detectability, these have to be realized in observable features, and people have beliefs about the signs that may give them away. They can therefore act to suppress them and reduce the chances of detection.

At this point, the story becomes doubly complicated. Possibly, almost all people have beliefs about indicators of lying and deception. Insofar as they have to distinguish between truth telling and lying, they need to know which values of which variables serve as reliable and valid discriminators. Few, however, are trained as lie catchers. Indeed, for most people any competence acquired is fortuitous. People are left to find out from their own experience, as observers and as participants, both as agents and as victims. They have to build up their own databases and theories. The relationship between these and reality may well be wrong. If this is so, then as liars trying to avoid detection, they will suppress the wrong indicators, but they are wrong, of course, only if the lie detectors are using different cues. If they are using the same ones then there is a folie-à-deux or more. Theoretically, in these circumstances, the professional lie catcher should be able to detect those who are concealing the wrong cues, until such time as knowledge spreads about the reality.

These complications do not affect investigations in which the lie catchers are counting and otherwise measuring possible cues rather than passing judgments about who is lying and when. In the study of the nurses, a control group of truth-telling nurses offered one kind of comparison between aroused liars and nonliars where the liars did not stand to be punished for either lying or an offense that might now be exposed. Ekman (1985/1992) has relied on these objective data to build up the checks reproduced in Table 4.1.

The 38 questions are not a magical set and, in the future, its numbers may expand rather than contract. At least these questions point to the characteristics of the lie, the reality, the liar, and the lie catcher and the interdependence of the four as determinants of the ease or difficulty of both deception and detection. The cues are those that are available without the aid of technology or institutionalized interrogatory contexts. Arrested suspects are likely to be subjected to stronger tactics and may well find themselves attached to machinery that registers indicators of arousal. To date, however, there is no publicly available evidence that such facilities increase detection rates without increasing false positives as well. With his experience in emotions, it is not surprising that Ekman (1985/1992) has shown special interest in the significance of emotions in deceptive communication, but it is difficult to know what to make of the fact that two of the most prominent contributors to the field seldom refer to each other's work (Ekman and DePaulo).

Lies About Emotions

Table 4.2 lists Ekman's (1985/1992) indicators of concealed information about concealed emotions and Table 4.3 lists the signs that an emotion displayed is not being felt. In his highly readable account, Ekman wisely does not commit himself to assessments of how many people are proficient in disguising emotions in which situations but perhaps implies that most of us are not that adept at falsifying emotional states.

B. DePaulo (1992) emphasizes the distinction between faking emotions per se and the wider questions of lying and deception. She notes near unanimity in demonstrations that "people can successfully convey [to] the others the impression that they are experiencing something they are not." Their performances tend to exaggerate the indicator of particular emotions but not so as to render their impressions incredible. Torris and DePaulo (1984) found that interviewers could not discriminate between genuine and feigned introversion

(text continues on page 126)

Table 4.1 Ekman's Checklist for Lie Catchers

Questions About Lie	Ease of Detection	
	Hard	*Easy*
Can the liar anticipate exactly when he or she will lie?	Yes: Line prepared	No: Line not prepared
Does the lie involve concealment only without any need to falsify?	Yes	No
Does the lie involve emotions felt at the moment?	No	Yes: Especially difficult if A. Negative emotions such as anger, fear, or distress must be concealed or falsified B. Liar must appear emotionless and cannot use other emotions that have to be concealed
Would there be amnesty if liar confesses to lying?	No: Enhances liar's motive to succeed	Yes: Chance to induce confession
Are the stakes in terms of either rewards or punishments very high?	Difficult to predict: Although high stakes may increase detection apprehension, it should also motivate the liar to try hard	
Are there severe punishments for being caught lying?	No: Low detection apprehension; but may produce carelessness	Yes: Enhances detection apprehension, but may also fear being disbelieved, producing false-positive errors
Are there severe punishments for the very act of having lied, apart from the losses incurred from the deceit failing?	No	Yes: Enhances detection apprenehsion; person may be dissuaded from embarking on lie if she or he knows that punishment for attempting to lie will be worse than the loss incurred by not lying

Does the target suffer no loss, or even benefit, from the lie? Is the lie altruistic not benefiting the liar?	Yes: Less deception guilt if liar believes to be so No: Increases deception guilt
Is it a situation in which the target is likely to trust the liar, not suspecting that he or she may be misled?	Yes No
Has liar successfully deceived the target before?	Yes: Decreases detection apprehension, and if target would be ashamed or otherwise suffer by having to acknowledge having been fooled, she or he may become a willing victim No
Do liar and target share values?	No: Decreases deception guilt Yes: Increases deception guilt
Is the lie authorized?	Yes: Decreases deception guilt No: Increases deception guilt
Is the target anonymous?	Yes: Decreases deception guilt No
Are target and liar personally acquainted?	No Yes: Lie catcher will be more able to avoid errors due to individual differences
Must lie catcher conceal his or her suspicions from the liar?	Yes: Lie catcher may become enmeshed in his or her own need to conceal and fail to be as alert to liar's behavior No
Does lie catcher have information that only a guilty and not an innocent person would also have?	No Yes: Can try to use the guilty knowledge test if the suspect can be interrogated
Is there an audience who knows or suspects that the target is being deceived?	No No Yes: May enhance duping delight, detection apprehension, or deception guilt

(continued)

123

Table 4.1 Continued

| | Ease of Detection | |
	Hard	Easy
Questions About Lie		
Do liar and lie catcher come from similar language, national, or cultural backgrounds?	No: More errors in judging clues to deceit	Yes: Better able to interpret clues to deceit
Is the liar practiced in lying?	Yes: Especially if practiced in this type of lie	No
Is the liar inventive and clever in fabricating?	Yes	No
Does the liar have a good memory?	Yes	No
Is the liar a smooth talker with a convincing manner?	Yes	No
Does the liar use the reliable facial muscles as conversational emphasizers?	Yes: Better able to conceal or falsify facial expressions	No
Is the liar skilled as an actor—able to use the Stanislavski method?	Yes	No
Is the liar likely to convince himself of his lie believing that what he says is true?	Yes	No
Is she or he a "natural liar" or psychopath?	Yes	No
Does liar's personality make liar vulnerable to fear, guilt, or duping delight?	No	Yes
Is liar ashamed of what liar is concealing?	Difficult to predict: Although shame works to prevent confession, leakage of that shame may betray the lie	

Question		
Might suspected liars feel fear, guilt, shame, or duping delight even if suspect is innocent and not lying or lying about something else?	Yes: Cannot interpret emotional clues	No: Signs of these emotions are clues to deceit
Does the lie catcher have a reputation of being tough to mislead?	No: Especially if liar has in the past been successful in fooling the lie catcher	Yes: Increases detection apprehension; may also increase duping delight
Does the lie catcher have a reputation		Difficult to predict: Such a reputation might decrease deception guilt, it may also increase detection apprehension
Does the lie catcher have a reputation of being fair minded?	No: Liar less likely to feel guilty about deceiving the lie catcher	Yes: Increases deception guilt
Is the lie catcher a denier, who avoids problems, and tends to always think the best of people?	Yes: Probably will overlook clues to deceit and vulnerable to false-negative errors	No
Is lie catcher unusually able to accurately interpret expressive behaviors?	No	Yes
Does the lie catcher have preconceptions that bias the lie catcher against the liar?	No	Yes: Although lie catcher will be alert to clues to deceit, he will be liable to false-positive errors
Does the lie catcher obtain any benefits from not detecting the lie?	Yes: Lie catcher will ignore, deliberately or unwittingly, clues to deceit	No
Is lie catcher seized by an emotional wildfire?	No	Yes: Liars will be caught, but innocents will be judged to be lying (false-positive error)

SOURCE: From *Telling Lies: Clues to Deceit in the Marketplace, Politics, and Marriage* by Paul Ekman. Copyright © 1992, 1985 by Paul Ekman. Reprinted by permission of W. W. Norton & Company, Inc.

Table 4.2 Ekman's Types of Information Concealed With Clues

Type of Information	Behavioral Clue
Verbal line not prepared	Indirect speech, pauses, speech errors, illustrators decrease
Nonemotional information (e.g., facts, plans, fantasies)	Slip of the tongue, tirade, emblem
Emotions (e.g., happiness, surprise, distress)	Slip of the tongue, tirade, micro expression, squelched expression
Fear	Indirect speech, pauses, speech errors, voice pitch raised, louder and faster speech, reliable facial muscles, facial blanching
Anger	Voice pitch raised, louder and faster speech, facial reddening, facial blanching
Sadness (maybe guilt and shame)	Voice pitch lowered, slower and softer speech, reliable facial muscles, tears, gaze down, blushing
Embarrassment	Blushing, gaze down or away
Excitement	Increased illustrators, voice pitch raised, louder and faster speech
Boredom	Decreased illustrators, slower and softer speech
Negative emotion	Indirect speech, pauses, speech errors, voice pitch raised, voice pitch lowered, manipulators increased
The arousal of any emotion	Changed breathing, sweating, swallowing, squelched expression, increased blinking, pupil dilation

and extroversion, a wider remit than the recognition of particular emotions.

Assuming these are valid conclusions, how does it come about that feigned emotions are not detected? A number of reasons might be advanced. First, cultures have at least two kinds of rules about the expression of emotions, relating respectively to those that should not be expressed when they are experienced and those that should be

Table 4.3 The Betrayal of Concealed Information, Organized by
Behavioral Clues

Clue to Deceit	Information Revealed
Slips of the tongue	May be emotion specific; may leak information unrelated to emotion
Tirades	May be emotion specific; may leak information unrelated to emotion
Indirect speech	Verbal line not prepared; or negative emotions, most likely fear
Pauses and speech errors	Verbal line not prepared; or negative emotions, most likely fear
Voice pitch raised	Negative emotion, probably anger or fear or both
Voice pitch lowered	Negative emotion, probably sadness
Louder, faster speech	Probably anger, fear or excitement or both
Slower, softer speech	Probably sadness or boredom or both
Emblems	May be emotion specific; may leak information unrelated to emotion
Illustrators decrease	Boredom; line not prepared; or weighing each word
Manipulators increase	Negative emotion
Fast or shallow breathing	Emotion, not specific
Sweating	Emotion, not specific
Frequent swallowing	Emotion, not specific
Micro expressions	Any of the specific emotions
Squelched expressions	Specific emotion; or may only show that some emotion was interrupted but not which one
Reliable facial muscles	Fear or sadness
Increased blinking	Emotion, not specific
Pupil dilation	Emotion, not specific
Tears	Sadness, distress, uncontrolled laughter
Facial reddening	Embarrassment, shame, or anger; maybe guilt
Facial blanching	Fear or anger

SOURCE: After Ekman (1985/1992).

expressed when they are not being felt. Of the first set, anger is the prime example of a state that all societies require that members control on some occasions; it is illegal to attack others physically. Even when lives are devastated by crimes against those closest to a person, anger may be excused but will not gain credit if expressed nonverbally. Typically, control of anger is heavily practiced, both to diminish its evocation and to conceal its experience. So is the expression of other strong emotions (e.g., fear and happiness), with the exception of grief, which is a permitted ritualized (and hence dignified) expression, in context. Hence, adults will have extended experience of exercising control, attenuating or eliminating the experience of emotions, especially negative ones. In the reverse direction, people have to learn to meet the face wants of others: appearing to pay attention or to be interested when bored, giving the appearance of amiability when indifferent (or hostile), playing humble and deferent when feeling superior and disquieted, feigning belief when an unbeliever, and politely accepting what is said when knowing it is a pack of lies. Such acting does not just involve positive emotions. Certain roles may require the simulation of anger. Parents and teachers, and others in charge of children, may simulate or exaggerate annoyance deliberately to achieve states and actions in the other.

The feigning of emotional states is therefore a set of skills that is endorsed as appropriate or even required. When feigning is normative and when it is judged to be improper is situationally determined. Hence, any well-rehearsed feigner who wishes to deceive others has only to learn to apply the simulations in improper situations. Such a faker does not learn the competencies themselves. The throwing of a switch for this kind of deception contrasts with the potential complexities of lying with false verbal statements, which is likely to require the suppression and concealment of one set of events and the invention of another set. This exercise in creative imagination has to be enacted in situ, squared with others subsequently, and maintained indefinitely.

These two sets of reasons would seem to be sufficient grounds for making empirical distinctions between feigning emotions and creating false verbal realities, without invoking the trusting bias that is relevant to the acceptance of verbal falsifications. Normative feigned emotions may come into the same category as the white lies of politeness or the conniving lies in which no one wishes to render the truth verbally explicit. As DePaulo (1992) herself notes, successful lying is associated with prior practice and greater confidence in personal competence at lying, as well as a lack of guilt in the particular situations.

It is certainly possible to argue for the positions of DePaulo (1992) and Ekman (1985/1992) being parallel. Neither, however, brings out fully the role of culture in its likely encouragement and discouragement of different kinds of deception, and this could be an important point of departure for separating generally proficient from generally detectable deception.

If the culture encourages its members to control, conceal, and feign emotions, then it may be relatively easy to transfer this competence from appropriate to manipulative contexts. Likewise, the deceptions encouraged in competitive games or negotiations may be easily transferred to situations in which cooperation is supposed to be normative. The good poker player may find that the relevant capacities work for deceiving spouses as well.

Commentary

Ekman (1985/1992) will probably prove to be correct in both his strategic and his tactical approaches to lie detection. First, he accepts the contingent and probabilistic nature of the relationships between indicators and lying. Second, he emphasizes the importance of a multivariate and microscopic approach to detection. *Multivariate* is intended to mean the whole range of possible cues within levels and spheres of analysis as brought out by careful interrogation in suitable contexts. *Microscopic* is meant to be detailed analyses of physiologically based measures. To date, these are infuriatingly variable and unpredictable. There are many measures that can be taken with apparent accuracy: electromyographs (EMGs), electrocardiographs (ECGs), electroencephalograms (EEGs), pressures, electric conductivity, and more. Unfortunately, these measures do not form coherent patterns within or across individuals, despite considerable mathematical and physiological expertise having been devoted to the possible scales and relationships that might be expected to exist among them. Neither do the measures link to reported emotional states or moods in systematic ways, and the physiologically based measures used for lie detection remain anchored to indicators of general arousal, which can arise from many sources other than genuine fear of valid exposure and may not arise at all in those whose lies are not associated with any physiological reactivity. There is no option, however, but to pursue such lines of approach and there is no a priori reason why genuine detection rates might not improve without an increase in false positives as the mysteries of the minutiae of reactions are unraveled (see Chapter 5).

In parallel with the researches of Ekman (1985/1992) and DePaulo (1992), an extended program in Arizona has been gathering considerable momentum. This work has currently culminated in both a strong definition of the state of the art and a theoretical framework integrating the past and pointing to the future.

Interpersonal Deception Theory and Its Future

Burgoon (1994) and Buller and Burgoon (in press) render a secondary reviewer's task doubly difficult. Burgoon's general review of nonverbal signaling is finalized with a immaculate summary of its role and relevance to interpersonal deception. The extended theoretical synthesis of work on interpersonal deception in face-to-face (FtF) communication by Buller and Burgoon is coherent and comprehensive. Any reader would be well-advised to consult these sources; treatment here is confined to a summary of the assumptions and propositions of their integrating account. They offer 18 propositions about interpersonal deception, setting them within a wider framework of 25 assumptions about FtF interactions. They bite the bullet of the complexities of FtF interactions and do not shrink from spelling out the details. Interpersonal communication is multifunctional, multimodal, and multidimensional, with simultaneous and continuous activity by both participants. That many adults have reduced much of their conversation to semiautomatic scripts and perceive the underlying competences in simple terms is psychologically understandable but scientifically wrong headed, just as lay theories of physiology hopelessly underestimate the complexities of catching balls, eating, and the circulation of the blood.

The amounts of information processed in any conversation are high: constructing messages, monitoring their production and reception, interpreting messages and monitoring one's reactions, observing the other, and attending to whatever needs attention. People have intentions and goals that they may or may not wish to reveal. They bring to conversations identities and previous reputations that relate to their credibility in terms of competence, character, composure, sociability, and dynamism. Depending on what is being done, adjustments have to be made in situ. Problems and difficulties that arise cannot be deferred but have to be coped with in the here and now.

It is with the next set of assumptions that issues might become contentious. Citing eight specific references and making a plausible appeal to philosophers and social scientists down the ages, Buller and Burgoon (in press) suggest that "both communicators and their messages are presumed to be truthful" (p. 5). Kellermann (1984) goes further and posits a general positive bias toward an expectation of others also being pleasant and decent. Unfortunately, these presumptions may well be artifacts of the particular communication situations studied and their particular cultural contexts. There are good grounds for members of societies subscribing to such a myth: Analytically, it offers a defensible presumptive position for observing social scientists, and for participants in cooperative interactions, it is almost certainly an intelligent default position. For competitive interactions, any such assumption may be more frequently associated with losing rather than winning, and insofar as living is more competitive than cooperative, those who trust invariably in the truthfulness of others may be less "fit" in terms of survival chances. It is in the particular interests of those with the power in societies to have others subscribe to the myth. Either a cursory or an extended examination of the history of conquests shows that invaders were prone to break agreements and treaties with trusting indigenous peoples until the latter were reduced in all imaginable ways, including extermination. In today's societies, whistle-blowing upward remains a hazardous enterprise (see Chapter 10); those with power, wealth, and status hang on to and fight for their privileges, and if lies are desirable, they are told and maintained. The mighty do not fall when exposed, unless other mighty people let them do so, as can be witnessed in the scandals of corruption afflicting the governments of a number of Western democracies and the extent to which the personal political networks cover, protect, and eventually reinstate their delinquent colleagues. (It may be that the study of lying infects the student of the subject. Certainly, I have become much more conscious of the high incidence of lying and other forms of deception in and beyond FtF interaction since I began studying the topic; most of it has occurred in the pursuit of socially unacceptable goals in socially unacceptable ways.) Buller and Burgoon and their cited authors may have been studying comparatively nice people in relatively cooperative situations.

If this concern is warranted, it does no more than change an emphasis in the model.

Its validity certainly does not detract from the importance of the shift in perspective that Buller and Burgoon (in press) set out to achieve. Drawing attention to the complexities of FtF interaction is a major theme, but it is not the crucial switch. What Buller and Burgoon point out is that such FtF lies as occur take place in communicative situations. They arise in and out of interactions. As mentioned previously in this chapter, they do not arise as simulated acts dispersed among true statements in recorded monologues. In many experiments, observers and not participants have been primed to try to discriminate truthful from untrue statements. The untrue statements have been uttered by actors at the request of experimenters. These features of alertness, acting, and artificiality certainly render many studies of limited and potentially misleading value, but the core criticism of Buller and Burgoon is the noninteractive quality. The "liars" have not had to maintain or defend their fictions. The detectors have not had to make replies that continued the conversations. Immediately, the context becomes interactional in real time, all the complications correctly cited by Buller and Burgoon come into play, defining a context whose tasks demands threaten to overload participants, even without lies and suspicions of lies being present. Perhaps one of the reasons that people choose a default assumption of truthfulness is that attempts to carry open options would render participants exhausted rather quickly.

Buller and Burgoon (in press) move to a definition of a deceptive message as one "knowingly transmitted by a sender to foster a false conclusion by the receiver." (They omit the feature that the message should itself be false, but that is presumably because "deceptive messages" has a wider range than lies and includes equivocation and true but misleading statements.) A further seven assumptions about deception set down the variety of components, goals, functions, and features of deceptive messages, both cognitive and emotional. The complex issues of would-be deceivers deciding when and how to try to mislead the other and of would-be detectors becoming alert to and testing the possibility that they are being deceived have then to be embedded in what has already become a very complicated situation.

Citing numerous references to the empirical evidence in support of them, 18 empirical propositions are presented in a mixture of descriptive and explanatory statements:

P1. As the communication context increases in (a) immediacy, (b) full channel access, (c) conversational demands, (d) spontaneity, and (e) relational engagement, sender and receiver cognitions and behaviors during deceptive encounters change.

P2. As relationships vary in (a) relational familiarity (including informational and behavioral familiarity) and (b) relational valence, sender and receiver cognitions and behaviors during deceptive encounters change.

The first two propositions set the scene for what the determinants of change will be and how their particular characteristics will affect what happens through time.

P3. Sender and receiver expectations for honesty are positively related to degree of context interactivity and positivity of relationship between sender and receiver.

P4. When sender's goal is to deceive, initial detection apprehension is inversely related to conversational expectations for honesty.

As noted in Chapter 3, a truth bias operates, and this is particularly so in positive close relationships to the extent that partners will simply accept what they are told.

P5. Receiver initial suspicion is inversely related to degree of context interactivity and relationship positively.

Also in Chapter 3, it was noted that people are wary of salespeople and have a weaker or no truth bias.

P6. Compared to noninteractive deception, interactive deception results in (a) greater strategic activity (information, behavior, and image management) and (b) reduced nonstrategic leakage (arousal, negative and dampened affect, noninvolvement, and performance decrements) over time.

Telling a simple lie to a tape recorder is much less arduous than inventing a story compatible with what the listener knows and is likely to know and telling this story without giving anything away. To rare and amateur liars, the prospect of trying to cope with the cognitive load while simultaneously suppressing leakage must be frightening. As Ekman's (1985/1992) nurses showed, however, some people have become accomplished liars and those who have developed the constituent skills can manage. Such a competence contrasts with the findings of the Arizona team that deceivers controlled information but left it "incomplete, non-veridical, indirect, vague, uncertain, hesitant, brief and dissociated." They became more formal and disengaged and they assumed greater pleasantness and relaxation, while leaking signs of nervousness, arousal, and negative affect. In short, their deceptions were transparent in many respects.

P7.   Communication goals and motivations affect strategic and nonstrategic behavior.
  P7a.   Senders deceiving for self-gain exhibit more strategic activity and nonstrategic leakage than senders deceiving for other-benefit.
  P7b.   Receivers' initial behavior patterns are a function of their priorities between instrumental, relational, and identity objectives and of their initial intent to uncover deceit.

As Buller and Burgoon (in press) point out, P7a has not been tested. Its thrust is entirely consistent with much of the work reported in Chapters 6 through 8. Proactive lying (strategic activity) is more likely to be a practiced art, even a way of life, as it is for confidence tricksters and other swindlers. High motivation as a main effect is reported as leading to overcontrolled nonverbal behavior by De-Paulo and Kirkendol (1989) but not by Burgoon, Buller, and Guerrero (in press; see also Buller & Burgoon, in press). Main effects are less likely to be found than interactions, and professional proactive liars are less likely to suffer from nonstrategic leakage than amateur reactive ones. Sampling of persons, payoff of detection, and other factors will act as moderators too as P8 implies.

P8. As receivers' informational, behavioral, and relational familiarity increase, deceivers exhibit more strategic information, behavior, and image management but also more nonstrategic leakage behavior.

Riggio (1993) has specialized in the study of communicative competence to encode and control the expression of emotions. From an individual differences perspective, he has shown that high scorers can achieve higher credibility both when telling truth and when lying.

P9. Skilled senders better convey a truthful demeanor than unskilled ones.

P10. Initial and ongoing receiver judgments of sender credibility are positively related to (a) receiver truth biases, (b) context interactivity, and (c) sender encoding skills; they are inversely related to (d) deviations of sender communication from expected patterns.

P11. Initial and ongoing receiver detection accuracies are inversely related to (a) receiver truth biases, (b) context interactivity, and (c) sender encoding skills; they are positively related to (d) informational and behavioral familiarity, (e) receiver decoding skills, and (f) deviations of sender communication from expected patterns.

P10 and P11 have been well supported across the range of laboratories.

P12. Receiver suspicion is manifested through a combination of strategic and nonstrategic behavior.

P13. Senders perceive suspicion when it is present.

P13a. Deviations from expected receiver behavior increase perceptions of suspicion.

P13b. Receiver behavior signaling disbelief, uncertainty, or the need for additional information increases sender perceptions of suspicion.

P14. Suspicion (perceived or actual) alters sender behavior.

Suspicion is a relatively new entry into interactive studies, most of which have been conducted in Arizona and the details of its influence have yet to be explored in-depth.

P15. Deception and suspicion display change over time.

P16. Reciprocity is the predominant interaction adaptation pattern between senders and receivers during interpersonal deception.

P17. Receiver detection accuracy, bias, and judgments of sender credibility following an interaction are a function of (a) terminal receiver cognitions (suspicion, truth biases), (b) receiver decoding skill, and (c) terminal sender behavioral displays.

P18. Sender-perceived deception success is a function of (a) terminal sender cognitions (perceived suspicion) and (b) terminal receiver behavioral displays.

Again, it is post-1990 work from Arizona that dominates the investigation of these propositions. It would be premature to assess the empirical status of the relatively untested propositions linked to the interactive model.

To date, it would offend current copyright laws to reproduce in full the writing of Buller and Burgoon (in press) that is used to justify or comment on the 18 propositions. It might be flattering to them to rework and represent their text, but what was and is admired in Chaucer and Shakespeare becomes plagiarism in the academic world! Suffice it to say that what is written is empirically consistent with the propositions. Because the propositions were designed and tailored to fit the facts as conceived at present, this is not surprising; the achievement lies in the constructed synthesis. Those who wish to read the considerable extent of the empirical base can pursue the reference cited (Burgoon & Buller, in press).

For present purposes, several questions arise. Are there ideas in the model that invite immediate criticisms that can be answered? Are there worrying features in the model? Is the frame of reference sound? Where next?

Comments: Details

Some of the propositions might disappoint those who idealize precision and quantification. For example, what kind of a prediction is it that affirms solely that something will change (P1)? The answer could be that the fact of change is as informative as the proposition can be at this time. If whatever it is can either increase or decrease and in the current state of knowledge the direction is not predictable, then "change" is the right word. It may be that the immediate impetus when lying is for a would-be deceiver to increase the rate of speaking. With a little more experience, however, there can be a switch to a compensatory slowing down, but this may well be overdone. With further experience, it may be that speech rate becomes normal again and no longer indicative of deception. The word *change* may capture most of the contemporary population most of the time, in that only the most proficient deceivers will have practiced their lying speech rate sufficiently to render it indistinguishable from its truthful counterpart. For the amateurs, some will talk faster than normal, others slower; the skilled practitioners will not make either mistake.

In fact, this is the likely sequence for any developing competence involving a skilled performance. In the first phase, ignorance of the existence of the "cue" will mean that it is blatantly available as information for the lie catcher. Once a liar becomes aware of either a valid giveaway or a cue presumed to be valid by any significant other, he or she can practice control over its characteristics. Overcompensation or undercompensation are the two kinds of errors possible, with overcompensation probably but not invariably being the more common prime direction of error. Rehearsal with self-observed knowledge of results may bring the leakage under fine-tuned control eventually. Such ideas are consistent with a more general model of the child's development of mastery of the units and structures of verbal and nonverbal communication that has found some empirical support with other communicative acts (Karmiloff-Smith, 1992; Robinson, 1981): an "involuntary" phase of unconscious effectiveness but with errors that gives way to reflective analysis of the reasons for the lapses, which, if successful, leads to a consciously controlled eradication of errors. In turn, this leads into a phase of unconscious effectiveness that differs from the developmental point of departure by having a facility for reflecting on diagnosing and correcting for lapses in performance.

To the extent that skills of lying follow a succession of such sequences as potential cues are uncovered and then covered, so a more comprehensive control will eventuate. Because each fresh lie is novel in certain respects, however, the skills can never be guaranteed to have been perfected. Similarly, the ways in which individuals master the subskills are likely to be variable in sequence and success so that any model that pretends to a detailed specification of particularities is likely to be wrong. Although it is scientifically sensible to push for precision and quantification, it is pointless to try to carry that pursuit beyond the variability and uncertainties in the realities of the phenomena. Which of the apparently imprecise propositions of Buller and Burgoon (in press) are already at the empirical limits of detail remain to be decided, but already some probably go about as far as they can go.

There is, of course, another set of reasons why some specifications of the model will have a limited shelf life.

The Shifting Battle

Just as it is with the unstable equilibria of the battles between insecticides and insects or between medical treatments and diseases, so it is with human sciences. As liars advance in competence, so can lie catchers; the relations of relative advantage between successful concealments of cues and exposure can change. At the present time, the well-prepared liar probably has the advantage, at least according to the published evidence and provided that there are acceptable constructions available for interpreting the events about which lies may have been told. If this is so, for improved detection rates without false positives, Ekman's (1985/1992) line of attack will need to be combined with interpersonal deception theory for progress to be made. To regain an advantage, lie catchers will have to conduct detailed analyses of minute features of the relatively uncontrollable (e.g., minimal muscle) movements captured on video. Physiological indices more sensitive and interpretable than those currently used in lie detectors may become available. When these can be used to discriminate between the lies and truthful statements from individuals who are known to be proficient liars, the advantages may switch.

Given the expense of the technology that would underpin such advances, the discussion has to be focused on high-level deceptions for which individuals have been professionally trained—namely, spies, rather than everyday FtF interactions. The military technology of today, however, filters down to the rich criminals of tomorrow and may work its way through to the ordinary members of society eventually. If Ekman (1985/1992) is right that profile analyses of many microscopic details may become available to increase detection rates without increasing false-positive identifications, the criminal courts, for example, may begin to find it easier to discount false testimony, but then as soon as the relevant knowledge becomes public, those who need to lie will be able to practice their control over the leaking cues, converting nonstrategic into strategic information.

Such probabilities of raising the stakes serve as a reminder that today's situation is empirically contingent. The actual distribution of successful and unsuccessful acts of deception is contingent. It depends on the whole manifold of the sociocultural history of particular subcultures. Had any particular subculture been more anti-lying in its norms and more effective in their inculcation, in that culture lying might have been rarer and perhaps more proficient. Conversely, insofar as cultures tolerate or encourage lying its incidence should increase. This much is obvious. What is perhaps not quite so evident is that the distinction between strategic and nonstrategic cues will also vary as a function of the knowledge and norms about lying in any particular subculture.

There also can be profound shifts in credibility. In the public domain, the Michigan surveys of the past 20 years and successive Gallup polls in Britain show a similar decline in the credibility of authorities. Such figures as are available imply that the default position may now be one of a general distrust and cynicism, and this may well extend beyond politics to the military and to business. TV, for example, has brought interviews with public and private figures into living rooms so that what needs to be or can be hidden requires more or at least different tactics.

Although there may be no sign of strong forces building up to reduce the truth bias in interpersonal encounters, historically, individuals in societies such as the old Soviet Union would have had to be much less trusting to survive than their contemporary age peers in the capitalist West.

What is, is. The strength of the truth bias, however, must already vary as a function of individual differences, situational variations, subcultures, cultures, and societies. Each balance is a product of constellation of forces with values that will probably change, and with those changes, there will be major shifts in the ambience of interactions at each level of psychological and sociological analysis. At a sociological level, Barnes (1994) implies a current drift toward more and more lying in western societies. If clever lies are difficult to detect and if, when they are detected, their originators avoid or escape any costs and losses, then in an individualistic competitive society that has no countervailing collective morality, achieving the ends will be primary, the means unimportant. In the current spate of financial scandals, criminal convictions are rare, and when they do occur, those convicted are not required to relinquish their gains anymore than are those who have made fortunes out of insider trading, drug dealing, or bank robberies in the past. Taking "commissions" for contracts signed, licenses granted, and cases won for businesses appears to be increasingly endemic in regional and national politics in so-called advanced societies.

At the moment, the countervailing forces against exposed lying and deceit appear to be weak relative to the gains from both successful and failed lies. Both cost-benefit analyses and reinforcement theories of learning would predict a continuing rise until other forces are brought to bear. How these and other changes will act to change the significance of features of the model has to be uncertain at this juncture, but one general presumption of the model could become more problematic. There is a presumption that, generally speaking, people who lie are concerned with hiding some aspect of reality and avoiding exposure of their lying as well. If societies care less and less about "offenses" that need to be covered up, then lies about such matters should decrease.

The Model's Frame of Reference

Buller and Burgoon's (in press) apposite criticism of work that has focused too strongly on Person (P) might be directed against their own emphasis on Situation (S). As with so much social behavior, the correct answer has to be f(P, S), where the relative strengths of the two sets of influences and their form of interrelation can be estimated only in particular combinations of circumstances. Buller and Burgoon help to redress the balance. The f(P, S) combination is generally implicit in their account, but there is no harm in drawing attention to its importance here.

Likewise, attention can be drawn to the role of prior experience of situations and persons and to how these are likely to influence assumptions of truthfulness. In real life, such influences may loom very large as determinants of set. It is not, however, just the stereotypical vendors who lack credibility—for example, secondhand car salespeople, street corner watch sellers, and insurance peddlers. Authorities of various kinds, and perhaps especially the media, are viewed with suspicion and perhaps this is beginning to permeate interpersonal relations. In the fictional offerings of the media, it is not just sex and violence that are ascendant qualities of soap operas and thrillers. Lying and deception are portrayed as endemic components of families and close relationships. Comedies revolve around lies about marital infidelities and betrayals of trust. It may be that these fantasy worlds are dissociated from personal lives by viewers, but this is unlikely. Fantasy can expand people's ideas of what is possible, as can real-life stories. If the normative structure retains its taboos against challenging liars at the same time as it exemplifies the advantages to be gained by lying in fiction and faction, what constrains individuals from dishonesty may be no stronger than the inertia of habit.

The truth bias in the model, and in Western societies, may need to be abandoned as one of the parameters. This issue is elaborated in the final chapter.

Buller and Burgoon (in press) include more than the concealment and exposure of cues to arousal in their purview and they point out that liars risk overloading their cognitive capacities with inventions whose characteristics may be forgotten. They do not pursue in any detail several features that may become increasingly relevant to the general field. The first to be mentioned is the context in which inquiries are made. In what ambience are guilty persons most likely to reveal the truth? What ambience will be most conducive to accurate assessments of the plausibility of accounts given by persons who claim to be victims of crimes? This question has been investigated most thoroughly in alleged sex abuse crimes in Germany, and one development of that work has been the production of a technique known as criteria-based statement analysis, an attempt to generate discriminating criteria at linguistic levels of analysis. That leads naturally to questions of the possibilities of checking out statements against external criteria and whether there are general criteria. A certain kind of crime story specializes in the detective painstakingly checking minutiae and finding discrepancies between the suspect's account and reality—on the day in question the 4:30 train was canceled. Sherlock Holmes wondered why the dog did not bark.

Which questions are to be asked of suspected liars or possible relevant witnesses? Implausible as it may seem, no social psychologist had defined a frame of reference for interrogation strategies and tactics until 1994.

Lying About Events

Procedures for Truth Elicitation

The dominant focus of the detective approach has been on degrees of arousal evoked by verbal references and the ability or inability of respondents to suppress cues that might be indicative of lying. The polygraph relies entirely on physiological indicators related to a well-structured interrogation. Given the history of the field, this direction of development is understandable. The person charged has information stored in the brain, and if this information can be extracted, it will define guilt or innocence. Confessions have been held up as an ideal solution.

The extraction of confessions has been closely linked to intimidation for most of its history. Cross-examinations in courts are attempts to discredit the testimony of witnesses. Powerful competent professionals with the right to control the questions set out to show that ordinary people have unreliable memories or that one is lying. Very often, the destruction of their credibility is the object and not the elucidation of the truth—likewise for police security and parental interviewing. The induction of fear seems to have been the dominant component of interrogation situations throughout history. Why terrifying people should be assumed to increase the probability of finding out the truth is extraordinary. (The question of finding out the truth should not be confused with the functions of torture.) Prima facie, it seems most unlikely that intimidated victims will confess in the presence of very angry interrogators who may be bent on executing cathartic punishment.

If the problem is to uncover the facts about an action and a suspect is in hand, a relaxed and permissive approach that evokes a full account of the suspect's version of the relevant events or the alibi might be a more useful basis for uncovering inconsistencies. To date, there appears to be no empirical evidence on the role of context and interview conduct in the elucidation of the facts in criminal or other inquiries with adults. A start has been made with children.

Just a few years ago, child sex abuse cases in England were tried as any other case. The child was required to give evidence in open court in the presence of the accused and was subject to cross-examination. In the case of an adult male sexually abusing a young girl in the family, it is common for the male to have issued repeated threats of extreme violence if the girl tries to expose his behavior. Often the circumstances of the abuse will have been known only to him and her. Defense counsels can be quite ruthless in their cross-examinations. In the United Kingdom, there were probably several cultural myths against the child's story. Children fantasize. They cannot be relied on to tell the truth. Incest is a strong taboo, and fathers do not rape their daughters. Taboos do not have to be invented for actions that do not occur, and presumably, most adults have known that incest may be uncommon, but it is certainly practiced. Whether children are more prone to lie or fantasize than adults has not been investigated, so far as I know.

Only very recently, as a result of the judicial authorities commissioning and taking notice of research findings, has court practice begun to change. The procedures eventually adopted will subscribe to the following assumptions:

1. To optimize the chances of children telling the truth, they should be interviewed as soon as possible after the authorities have been alerted and before ideas have been suggested to them by authorities.
2. The interviewers should not be seen as powerful authority figures who may be prone either to believe or to disbelieve what the child says.
3. The interview context should be neutral.
4. The interview format should be event focused but firm and friendly. The script should be semistructured and probing should be neutral.
5. A second or third interview should be used when necessary for checking questions.
6. Any defense counsel questioning should be reserved for a final session and should be strictly controlled for harassment and intimidation.
7. The whole proceedings should be videotaped and should be shown in court only to these participants in the legal process.

In brief, the protocol will leave the jury and judge(s) to decide on whether the child's volunteered version of events is true or false.

Linguistic Analysis

Interestingly, it is the same context that is introducing the idea that the language used may be indicative of truth and falsity. Over the years, a succession of German psychologists have accumulated cases and subjected them to content analysis based on criteria said to be indicative of veracity (Arntzen, 1970; Szewyck, 1973; Undeutsch 1967, 1982, 1984; all cited in Steller & Koehnken, 1989). The basic premise of this statement analysis approach is that the qualities of the report of a self-experienced real event will differ from those of an invented story (Undeutsch, 1967, cited in Steller & Koehnken, 1989). Statement analysis requires that attention be directed to the specific account and not to the general credibility of the child. It is not based on absolute scores but on a comparative analysis of this statement with accounts of other firsthand experiences, both being assessed in the light of other background information about the psychology of the child and the familial and social context (for further information, see Steller & Koehnken, 1989; for a manual, see Steller, Raskin, Esplin, & Boychuk, 1989). Table 4.4 summarizes Koehnken's integration of 19 indices in their five categories (Steller & Koehnken, 1989).

These indices have been devised and developed in a boot-strapping manner by examining differences between testimonies judged to be truthful or fallacious by the courts (but where verdicts have been influenced by expert comments on the testimonies).

It is necessary to add that the number of cases is high; Arntzen's (1970, cited in Steller & Koehnken, 1989) work is based on approximately 24,000 cases and Undeutsch's (1984, cited in Steller & Koehnken, 1989) is based on 1,500. The testimony was not always the only evidence available. Arntzen classified 60% to 70% of statements as truthful, relying in part on poststatement confusions and in part on corroborative evidence for these judgments. Undeutsch accepts the difficulty of establishing independent criteria, notes that 95% of expert judgments of truthfulness were followed by convictions, and rests his case on the potentially disturbing observation that in no case has a verdict of guilty been subsequently rescinded.

To date, there appears to be only one field study of ecological validity with stricter controls on independence of statements and verdicts. According to Steller and Koehnken (1989), Boychuk, Esplin, and Raskin (1989) analyzed statements from 40 child witnesses alleging sexual abuse. Of these, 20 were deemed truthful by reason of

Table 4.4 Content Criteria for Statement Analysis

General characteristics
    Logical structure
    Unstructured production
    Quantity of details

Specific contents
    Contextual embedding
    Descriptions of interactions
    Reproduction of conversation
    Unexpected complications during the incident

Peculiarities of content
    Unusual details
    Superfluous details
    Accurately reported details misunderstood
    Related external associations
    Accounts of subjective mental state
    Attribution of perpetrator's mental state

Motivation-related contents
    Spontaneous corrections
    Admitting lack of memory
    Raising doubts about one's own testimony
    Self-deprecation
    Pardoning the perpetrator

Offense-specific elements
    Details characteristic of the offense

strong corroborative physical evidence of abuse (16) or confessions or both (18) of no known benefit to the accused. The 20 dubious statements relied on a combination of psychologists' judgments of no evidence of abuse, the absence of physical symptoms, denials by the accused, and an absence of physiological indicators from polygraphed interviews (13). The statements were examined for the 19 indicators, scoring 0 for *absence*, 1 for *presence*, and 2 for *strong presence*. Unaware of the origins of the statements, scorers achieved a mean total of 23.7 for "truthful" statements and 3.6 for the "untruthful" ones, with 100% discrimination between the two groups.

This result has to be seen as most encouraging in several respects. First, unlike those studies of lying in general that have been able to increase lie detection only by increasing false positives, the pronounced categorical discrimination seems to be unusually powerful. Whether this is because the 40 cases are extreme examples, or odd for some other reason, is not known. Whether or not the result is replicable is not known but is knowable.

Second, the technique and its scoring criteria have the potential for corrective, improving feedback. Given that it has a reasonable degree of validity, refinements are possible as data are accumulated. Refinements could be in changes as to what is scored. As texts become stored on discs and increasingly sophisticated programs of linguistic analysis are developed, it should be possible to elaborate on and modify the scoring system. Improvements may also be achieved by refinements of the conditions of statement collection through adapting the context of situation or the interviewer's behavior.

Third, and consistent with the ethical and empirical presuppositions of the chapter, the publication of relevant results is unlikely to undermine the value of the work done. Malicious children are not likely to read about, understand, or learn to simulate truthful scripts. In an inquisitorial system, corrupt advisers are less likely to interfere with the elucidation of the facts. This contrasts with the adversarial system where a major hazard for child witnesses has been the unscrupulous cross-examining defense lawyer seeking to expose the unreliability of the child—an all too easy task.

As Steller and Koehnken (1989) conclude, it would be premature to claim near infallibility for criterion based statement analysis. Within its main domain of application, the questions of biased sampling, doubtfulness of correctness of verdicts, and the difficulties of deciding on cutoff points from true to false on the 19 criteria generally militate against excessive claims of reliability and validity. Given the procedural rules of courts such linguistic analyses are more likely to be of use for analysis of the transcripts of witnesses than those of accused persons, particularly those of participant witnesses. Linguistic checks on ordinary witnesses is another matter, and so is analysis of guilty and innocent accused persons.

Outside the courts, little has been attempted, in part, no doubt, because of the difficulties of collecting texts whose truthfulness is known and that can be contrasted with texts that differ only in their truthfulness.

Liars do take on increased loads. First, they may have to provide alternative accounts. Second, they may have to sustain these. They run the risk that other people who have no vested interest may give different accounts. If they rely on invented memories, these may have deficiencies similar to those listed in Stellar and Koehnken's (1989) criteria; they may lack detail, especially odd detail, they forget what they have already said, and they have only their own previous verbal account as their database, unless they have transplanted a real set of events to another time or place.

In many courts, the presumption of innocence and the right to silence, which may be available to an accused, can save them from generating an alternative account of their whereabouts and activities. Parents, spouses, or peers may not be so constrained. Schools and employers, in particular, may have to tolerate a succession of notes about headaches and other undetectable pains. Children can learn which lies are the easiest to defend; simplicity, consistency, and the lack of bases for refutation being three such principles.

It will not just be linguistic criteria that are indicative. Contextual refutations are potentially clearer discriminanda.

Empirical Refutations of Accounts

Younger children are particularly prone to exposure by default. Leaving footprints on garden soil, having chocolate wrappers in their pockets, writing sick notes to school but doing so in their own handwriting are all lies that may be easy to detect. Headaches and earaches are another matter, and false claims to such pains can serve a lifelong purpose. How many psychosomatic symptoms are self-fulfilled promises kept consciously or unconsciously alive remains unknown, but the number is probably high. The epidemiology and demographics of absences from work through illness show too many correlations with other phenomena to leave doubt that many are based on lies. The patterns by days of the week, weather conditions, and days of sporting or other recreational events give some indication of the extent of lies, as do the numbers of people whose absences due to illness coincide with the highest number permitted without official inquiry or loss of earnings. Identifying which are genuine and which are fraudulent is the difficult next step, as it is with any fraudulent claims that are embedded within any pattern.

As will be discussed later, proactive fraud is strategic behavior directed toward a profitable end. It would be strange for would-be fraudsters not to find out what is likely to be plausible and what the limits of plausibility are, whether the efforts be directed toward evading tax or securing false insurance claims. Whether there are general criteria even within domains that will discriminate between the true and the false has yet to be investigated; it is possible that there are not and that each case has to be investigated individually. That leads to the question of which kinds of interrogation are likely to be most successful.

There is an extensive biographical and autobiographical literature on how to unmask spies and criminals and an accompanying array of anecdotes to support the claims made. Kalbfleisch (1994) has examined many of these confessional and advisory writings and extracted an impressive taxonomy of 15 main interactive strategies, subdivided into 38 tactics (see Table 4.5). To date, she is the only person to follow up this framework. With 356 students who were asked to check out which statements were lies in a 15-minute conversation held with a primed partner, she found that 326 used combinations of tactics to wrinkle out the truth. With these, they achieved a 60% success rate, but baseline expectancies and false-positive rates were not reported. Although this is certainly more impressive than the estimates from one-shot judgments in the simplest of detection situations, it is not that high. Moreover, the crucial summary statement by Kalbfleisch is that the individual and combined general efficacy of the strategies is unknown. After several thousand years in which interrogation has been a permanent feature of conflict situations, the professional experts have not been able to develop methods for extracting and evaluating the truth. From the painful and mortal techniques of physical and mental torture to the friendly innocent and casual question, the lie detection expertise remains unreliable in its efficacy. Apart from one study with legal experts, by Moston and Stephenson (1993), no substantiated empirical claims could be reported by Kalbfleisch.

Then how are all the claims to competence of individuals to be accounted for, and why are these treated as acceptable? At both a psychological and a sociological level, it is tempting to invoke a combination of Merton's (1957) analysis of anomie and a human yearning for a just world in which truth will be found out. If the end is to expose lies and other forms of deception, and if there are no assured means, then Merton would argue that social groups will "ritualise the means." The history of trials and the accredited techniques for exposing the truth are certainly consistent with the Mertonian analysis. Even if it is argued that torture is no longer a means

Table 4.5 Kalbfleisch's (1994) Typology of Interrogation Strategies and Tactics: Typology of Overarching Strategies Together With Interaction Tactics

Intimidation	Contradiction
No nonsense	Buildup of lies
Criticism	No explanations allowed
Indifference	Repetition
Hammering	Compare and contrast
	Provocation
Situational futility	Question inconsistencies as they appear
Unkept secret	
Fait accompli	Altered information
Wages of sin	Exaggeration
All alone	Embedded discovery
Discomfort and relief	A chink in the defense
Discomfort and relief	A chink in the defense
Bluff	Self-disclosure
Evidence bluff	Self-disclosure
Imminent discovery	
Mum's the word	Point out deception cues
Gentle prods	Concern
Encouragement	You are important to me
Elaboration	Empathy
Diffusion responsibility	
Just having fun	Keeping the status quo
You are important to me	What will people think?
Praise	Appeal to pride
	Direct approach
Minimization	Direct approach
Excuses	
It's not so bad	Silence
	Silence

for gaining information or confessions but simply a cruel sport ending in the death of the victim, in its earlier days it was presumably, in part, an aggressive expression of frustration at not being able to extract the truth from prisoners, The cross-examinations in adversarial systems of justice look far more like rain ceremonies and other ritualistic performances than serious attempts to arrive at the facts of the matter. The ritual elements are supreme and are presumably tolerated only because there are no demonstrably efficient alternatives, and there are fundamental vested interests in societies pretending that their judicial systems find the innocent innocent and the guilty guilty. What is true of courts will be true of individuals. Interrogations, whether explicit or masquerading as conversations, are much less likely to expose lies than are inconsistencies from other sources.

This is not to gainsay the potential of Kalbfleisch's (1994) taxonomy. Just as Buller and Burgoon (in press) have shifted the snapshot framework of many earlier experiments into an extended interactive video in real time, so the repertoire of strategies deployed in repeated encounters may well prove to be more successful instruments for detecting falsifications than earlier work has led us to believe, especially if interrogators desist from crueler forms of attempts at detection. Given the promising lead from Kalbfleisch, perhaps we can look forward to a more organized use of experience gained in applied situations as a basis for the construction of a scientifically sound technology of verbal strategies and contextual aids for the detection.

CHAPTER FIVE

The Polygraph

In Chapter 4, references were made to various techniques devised to facilitate the accuracy of assessments of the truthfulness of statements. Linguistic analysis is a relative newcomer to the field. Interrogation and the collection of the testimony of others is much older, although it should be noted that weighing the facts has not always been an agreed form of testing. Rhetorical competence has had a long history of relevance to settling disputes, and so has armed combat and other tests. That God did not always intervene on the side of the person whom others believed to be the victim of lies and that the better fighter won too often must have been two of the reasons for societies abandoning physical in favor of verbal dueling.

To date, the endeavors of psychologists have confirmed what history teaches; at the least, it is very difficult to unmask good liars. Only a few psychologists, however, have been working on the topic for only a few years. There is progress, and it is possible to see in which directions further progress is likely to be made.

First, combinations of approaches will be more powerful than those that rely on one technique. In the popular mind, the simplest stereotype of the polygraph is of a machine that records a blip if the respondent answers untruthfully to the question, "Did you kill Cock Robin?" At present, up to five channels of physiological activity and reactivity are used and the interviewing interrogatory that parallels this is worked out in great detail to optimize the chances of accurate diagnosis. The psychology of interrogation has to be articulated with the physiologically based technology. It is likely that microanalytic scrutiny of visible personal reactivity will be incorporated at a later stage.

Second, more channels will be included—for example, microanalysis of visual activity and linguistic behavior. Fingerprinting is not that ancient. Now there can be voice prints, analyses of handwriting, and DNA traces to facilitate identification of persons.

Third, actuarial calculations may begin to be substituted for intuitive judgments (see Sutherland, 1992). Assessors are not as efficient as machines are at calculating the conclusions of the premises of their own arguments.

Fourth, there may be a reduction in the technical complexities of procedural justice that will mark a return to a concern for truth rather than winning cases and securing employment for the legal profession and its functionaries.

These considerations are not, of course, immediately relevant to much of the criminal lying in the public domain or the deceit practiced in face-to-face encounters in domestic situations. It is difficult to imagine parents buying polygraphs to facilitate lie detection in their children, if only because children would quickly suggest that parents be subject to the same checks.

Meanwhile, the polygraph is selected as the piece of technology most commonly used in the course of detection. Its history is a strange story. Enthusiastically used in some parts of the world, it is disdainfully rejected in others. Where it is used, the slender research base and caveats of the academic experts cannot be ignored, especially as its use is being extended into personnel selection. In contrast, its detractors reject its use without inquiring into the inefficiency or injustice of their current practices. In short, it provides a typical example of diverse social reactions to new ideas. Indeed, Thurber might have written an elegantly convoluted story based on the dilemmas of polygraph, complete with one of his logically bizarre conclusions. As the use of the polygraph approaches its first centenary, there are over 25,000 practitioners in the United States, there is a professional association and a journal devoted to its study, the results of its employment constitute evidence in criminal courts in a majority of the states, and it is used to select and reselect employees among a significant minority of U.S. employers. Meanwhile, its detractors question the ethics of its mode of use, the physiological and psychological bases of its measurement, the quality and quantity of empirical evidence about its validity, and the efficiency gains allegedly achieved from its employment.

Among its protagonists, there will be those with vested interests that may obscure the impartiality of their appraisal, those who have too much faith in the validity arising from the objectivity of technology, those who think that on balance there are gains in efficiency that can supplement other evidence, and those who hope that continued research will crack the complex puzzles still defying solutions. Among the antagonists are some who wish to conserve the rights of individuals regardless of whether truth might be better served by improved means of assessing it, some who raise powerful arguments against the ethics of the procedure, some who point out the uncertainties of the physiological and psychological assumptions made by supporters, and some who offer heavy criticisms of the paucity and weakness of empirical evidence for its validity.

Some would see the whole enterprise itself as a mixture of delusion and deceit—hence its similarity to Thurber's *Container for the Thing Contained*. Perhaps there should be a mass trial of the prosecutors and defenders concerning the status of their own beliefs, each side being polygraphed and their records and other evidence assessed by the opposition. The early Christian Church used to hold councils at which articles of faith were debated and resolved, and it is strange that the practice has been abandoned. Committees of inquiry collect evidence, write reports, and make recommendations but seem to be reluctant to point to the reasons why protagonists and antagonists might not seek to examine evidence dispassionately. The review here will attempt to pose such questions, just as it does for the analysis of selectivity, bias, and falsification in other institutional publications.

A Brief History

The original idea arose in central Europe at the turn of the century. Lombroso's search for the essential physical, physiological, and psychological features of criminals led him to chart changes in the amount of blood in the arms of suspected criminals during interrogation. His colleague Moss noted the possible significance of breathing. When Wertheimer and Klein (1904, cited in Herbold-Wooten, 1982) proposed formally that criminal acts would leave traces in the brain that could be reevoked and therefore detected, the pursuit for the details was launched. Two or three persistent evangelical émigrés to the United States took up the challenge under the leadership of Munsterberg. Larson added a measure of cardiovascular change to that of respiration, and after several dramatic and apparently successful convictions aided by the combination of polygraphy and appropriate questioning, formal training schools in its use were established. Only in the past 25 years, however, has the polygraph been introduced into the world of employment as a screening and an investigatory instrument. There are now several hundred experts serving in major U.S. government departments. The greatest concentration of activity is in the business world. The judicial uses, however, have remained the major focus of research and critical evaluation. Compared with something of the order of 10,000 trained users in the United States, only Canada, Israel, Korea, and Turkey have begun to follow the United States's lead. Germany outlawed the use of the polygraph as being illegal on ethical grounds. Britain has used polygraph testing in its security services, its introduction being a mini spy thriller in itself. Lax British security checks had allowed a Soviet agent to function at Britain's main communication monitoring establishment (GCHQ) at Cheltenham. It is likely that the United States subscribes financially to GCHQ and that American as well as NATO and British secrets had been leaked to the Soviets. It is possible that the United States demanded polygraph tests on the British security services and that the Thatcher government felt obliged to accede to the request. That no one was detected as being of homosexual disposition by the polygraphic procedures makes one wonder how the authorities served the validity of the mass testing. (Blackmail of homosexuals in the British security services was supposed to have been a common basis for recruitment by the Soviets.)

Hence, the disputes about ethics and efficiency divide countries. They differentiate between states in the United States, and they certainly divide psychologists. Lawyers are accumulating a case law on the judgments in trials where the polygraph has been used either as part of a trial or as a basis for selection or dismissal at work.

The Polygraph in Use

The basic polygraph is a measurement device that charts various components of the body's physiological activity: respiration, heart rate, blood pressure and skin conductance. It is no different from instruments used in medical health checks. In criminal investigations, as a lie detection device, its recordings are set in the context of an interview. Various formats have been adopted, possibly in combination. In the guilty knowledge test (GKT), the interviewer has access to information about the details of the crime that only the criminal would know, for example, was the cat shot too? In the control question test (CQT), reactions to two kinds of question are compared: *relevant* questions (e.g., Did you steal the money?) and *control* questions (e.g., Have you ever lied to your best friend?). Innocent people are supposed to react more strongly to control than relevant, and guilty persons vice versa. The interrogatory also includes buffer and neutral items. (An older contrast between reactions to relevant and irrelevant questions has now been dropped from criminal investigations.) All questions are posed so that the interviewee answers yes or no. The schedule of questions is devised on the basis of a preliminary interview in which the interviewer attempts to establish a best set of informative contrasts between control and relevant questions. The preliminary phase also includes a softening up conversation in which the interviewer attempts to persuade the interviewee of the accuracy of the procedure. As will be seen later, criticisms focus on false positives arising when innocent people react more strongly to relevant than control questions and when guilty persons control their reactivity or do not have emotional reactions to the relevant questions. Masking by interviewees is also a problem with the guilty knowledge test, an alternative that seems to have more prima facie validity than the CQT.

For personnel selection, neither is normally appropriate, and the relevant control test (RCT) is substituted. Here, relevant questions are defined as queries about thefts or other dishonest practices with previous employers and inaccurate counterfactual verbal statements (CVSs), for example. In this case, the focus is on individual differential reactivity among the relevant questions, any question-answer that is particularly provoking when answered "No" is treated with suspicion.

What the Polygraph Measures

Polygraphs can record electrical activity of the brain (EEG), electrical signals from muscles (EMG), electrical signals from the heart (ECG), eye movements (electroculogram or EOG), respiration, sweating, and any other physiological states for which the technology exists. Typically, the machines used for lie detection record three channels (heart rate, respiration rate, and skin conductance—GSR), but they can record more.

The measuring processes for these features are reliable and valid, but their significance remains mysterious. Two hopes dominated early research. One was that raised levels of activity would signify general emotional arousal. The second was that distinct patterns would link to distinct emotional states. Neither hope was realized. Worse still, changes in physiological indices do not correlate or coordinate with each other in clearly identifiable ways.

At the psychological level of emotion, basic mysteries remain. How many and which emotions should be entered into a taxonomy is still undecided. Plutchik (1980) has argued for eight, linking each to specific functions and typical behavioral reactions; Tomkins (1982) has used nine. Ekman and Friesen (1975) have generated detailed descriptions for the recognition of Tomkins's categories, demonstrated their cross-cultural realizations, and shown how they can be masked, modulated, and simulated and how these attempts are not always successful. Neither list contains anxiety or stress, both of which are sometimes claimed to be what is measured by the lie-detecting polygraph. Of those on the lists, fear would be the single-most cited emotion associated with lie detection, along with anger and others possible. As Ekman (1985/1992) has pointed out, it was naive to assume that emotions occur singly and discretely.

How emotional states interact with motivation and thinking has also to be resolved. Directions of causation remain disputed. It is easy to devise a sequence for a polygraph victim: horror at the realization that they are suspected, terror at the idea of being falsely "convicted" by a machine, exhaustion by oscillations from horror and terror to an optimistic faith in the justice system, and the prospect of escaping to a stiff martini, shaken and stirred. Complexities abound.

There are further issues. The polygraph measures taken are based on differences in reactivity to different questions. Certain questions are expected to evoke stronger responses from guilty than from nonguilty persons; the contrasts, however, are between questions within an individual and not between individuals. Hence, the polygraph cannot be better than the question-participant interrelation. Which scores on which channels are supposed to be responsive is omitted from most reports.

At the present time, the state of knowledge about the physiological, the psychological, and the relations between the two is unsatisfactory, despite the technological efficiency of the recordings and the best efforts of capable professionals. If it were possible to predict how the research will make progress, then this would have been achieved. The interplay of the physiological with the emotion, motivational, and the cognitive in human adults has to be composed of systems of great complexity. The ethics of experimentation will probably restrict critical research to colleagues and selves. If there are basic patterns at the physiological level that get overlaid by the mix- ture of emotions and the effects of thoughts, then powerful enough programs and number-crunching capacities should highlight what these are, and once components can be analyzed, then interactive results can be charted. Work with other mammals reduces the complexities of some of the ideational components but also eliminates the capacity for self-reports.

Notwithstanding the massive ignorance about the underlying psychology and physiology, a case could still be made for the pragmatic utility of polygraphy in lie detection. Technological efficiency frequently precedes explanations for the underlying reasons. Farmers bred animals long before Darwin, Mendel, and their successors began to understand the bases of evolution and genetics. Engineers invented mechanisms and structures before their workings could be explained. If polygraph recordings can be demonstrated to be reliable and valid discriminators of truth from falsity, there is no reason not to employ them. It should also be observed that their efficacy ought to be evaluated comparatively and within the context of current practice. Societies assume that miscarriages of justice are very rare in their legal systems, but rates of false convictions and acquittals of guilty persons remain unknown. Innocent in law is treated as innocent in fact and guilty in law as guilty in fact. Elsewhere (Chapter 8), it is suggested that the adversarial contest in courts has structural disadvantages as a system that could establish who has or has not done what, especially when it is associated with cross-examinations of ordinary people by professionals bent on winning their case. Until there are valid figures for the error rate with such practices, the error rate with polygraphic evidence is pragmatically uninformative. Perhaps it is already far more efficient than what happens without its use.

Maths and Polygraphs

Kircher and Raskin (1988) provide a succinct account of an experimentally based validation trial intended to compare computer-generated discriminating power with that of an expert working with the same recordings. After simulating a theft of a ring from an office drawer, guilty participants experienced an interview with 9 control and 9 relevant questions. Innocent participants were told to wander around the building for the same time period before they were given identical interviews. Physiological data from the interviews were recorded and then edited. Initially, over 15 indices of respiratory, cardiovascular and electrodermal activity were calculated for each of the 18 questions. Scores were standardized and differential reactivity across question pairs was calculated; 12 measures were retained. Regression and discriminant analyses were run against the criterion, guilty versus innocent, and following some further statistical modeling, probabilities of truthfulness were calculated for each of the participants. The authors offer a precise description of the measurements made and how they were treated mathematically.

The point of the details given here is to show that the scores used for any decision-guiding procedure are not simply read off raw recordings. The sophistication intervening between the input data and the refined indices is double edged. Transformations and standardizations are appropriate procedures in such situations, but they are in need of both physiological and statistical justifications. Refinements and weightings can be introduced to maximize discriminating capacities in known situations, but the pragmatically significant question is whether identical weightings function as efficiently for other samples. In this particular case, Kircher and Raskin (1988) found comparable results with a cross-validation, mock-crime sample. No samples of convicted criminals were used. Research reporting requires the details given by Kircher and Raskin. In individual criminal cases, the polygrapher presumably chooses his or her own basis for reading the charts.

How Accurate Is Polygraph Detection?

The reviews of empirical studies disagree less than one might expect about the quality of the evidence and its interpretations. They disagree on the pragmatic implications. Saxe, Dougherty, and Cross (1985) reviewed nine field studies and 12 laboratory simulations. Raskin (1988) includes fewer in his more general commentary. Lykken (1981) is particularly sensible to weaknesses in the quality of empirical evidence as a basis for use in courts. Carroll (1988) focused on five laboratory and three field studies. As he points out, protagonists have typically questioned how accurate judgments of truth and falsity are, given the polygraph records and all other available information, whereas its antagonists have questioned the accuracy that relies on objective measures of the polygraph on its own.

Clearly, the two need to be decoupled. Beliefs that can be justified on objective grounds that can be made explicit are separable from mysteriously arrived at judgments. The beliefs may be erroneous interpretations but at least the premises and conclusions of any argument are both available for consideration. Raskin (1988), for example, would clearly prefer to move the enterprise in such a direction, especially because reported interscorer reliabilities can be low: Kleinmuntz and Szucko (1984) report an average correlation of .43 among 6 trained scorers compared with Horvath's (1977) .89 among 10. Although .9 may be impressive in research, innocent individuals in the 20% of the variance not accounted for would not be impressed favorably by such an error rate between scorers if scores were to be used for decision making in courts.

As discussed in Chapter 4, I have a skepticism about the results of experimental studies in which the participants are acting the role of liars. Results from such work may yield information about people's beliefs about liars' practices and their skills in simulating those beliefs, but they must miss the essential fulcrum of research into lying and its detection in the real world. Others may not share this view. Carroll (1988) reports the Office of Technology Assessment of the U.S. Congress (1983) as identifying 14 experimental investigations of the use of the CQT method: 11.4% of the guilty and 17.4% of the innocent were incorrectly classified. When Carroll reduced the number of studies to 5 by weeding out those he found to be methodologically flawed, the error rate for false negatives rose slightly to 14.6%, but the false positives jumped to 23.1%. These 5 included studies using all information available to the testers. In their review, Saxe et al. (1985) report false negatives from 0 to 28.7% and false positives from 2 to 50.7%. Raskin (1988) likewise finds the false positives to be higher than the false negatives. Both the variability across the studies and the high incidence of false positives are alarming. The false-positive rate could be adjusted downward in computer-based objective scoring by changing the decision levels; the price would then be paid in higher false negatives.

Field studies face the additional hazard of doubts about the criterion of guilt. Of the 10 reviewed by Saxe et al. (1985), 8 used data from studies based on confessions and 2 from judgments of panels and files. Six of the studies were conducted by examiners from a polygraph agency. False negatives ranged from 0 to 29%, false positives from 0 to 75%, the latter of which is significantly worse than chance. Most were much lower. With his smaller sample of studies, Carroll (1988) found a 17% false-negative and a 43% false-positive rate. More weaknesses in the designs and interpretations of the empirical investigations are cataloged by the various reviewers, and those offered here are but a sample.

Saxe et al. (1985), Carroll (1988), and Lykken (1981) are more than alarmed at the amount and quality of research underpinning such a high rate of use of polygraphy. Saxe et al. note the possibilities but see them as in the future. Raskin (1988) is more enthusiastic and optimistic. He is right to emphasize that objectivity of measurement and competence at questioning may well constitute the basis of further advancement in efficient use. In his final report for the National Institute of Justice, Raskin provides a strong critique of the poor quality of much of the evaluative work. Much of the report is based on a comparative secondary analysis of the files of the U.S. Secret Service along with the original examiners' scoring. Seven new scorers added their efforts at competent discrimination between true and false comments by Secret Service interviewees. Computer-driven analysis was added to the array. The original examiners were able to achieve higher rates of accurate identification than either the computer or the fresh experts who had only the polygraph data to work on, implying that nonphysiological information was augmenting the discrimination. Given the stringent selection of the cases and restrictions on their modus operandi, the success rates were among the best reported so far. High and promising as these were, questions can still be asked as to whether the decision to allow evidence from polygraphs in forensic cases was not premature.

Personnel Screening

Saxe et al. (1985) could find no field studies relevant to screening practices and none for the RCT technique used in them. Raskin (1988) found none either. He reports that of 2,976 examinations conducted by the U.S. Department of Defense in 1988, only 16 indicated deception. In such security cases, the polygraph evidence is used only as a basis for further inquiries. What use is being made in the commercial sector appears to be based on no empirical evidence whatsoever, and yet in 30 states in the United States, employers can legally require would-be and actual staff to submit to polygraph testing.

Defeating the Polygraph

Gudjonsson (1988) mentions various ways in which interviewees can sabotage polygraph readings. Raskin (1979) had noted that the CQT is more likely to expose defensive reactions of heart rate deceleration and blood pressure increases, whereas GKT is more likely to result in orienting reflexes and that these are associated with increased skin conductance and vasoconstriction. The CQT situation is likely to be more arousing than the GKT, except for the specific guilty knowledge questions addressed to a guilty party.

One technique for evasion of detection is to lower responsivity to relevant questions, a second is to dampen reactivity overall. Biting the tongue and pressing toes against the floor have lowered detectability, and both combined are more effective than either on its own (Raskin, 1988). There is no evidence on the efficacy of mental rehearsal, either excitatory or relaxing. Distancing oneself from the questions is another unevaluated possibility. Practice and training with biofeedback prior to testing has been shown to reduce detection rates (Honts, Raskin, & Kircher, 1984). Evidence on drugs remains equivocal (Gudjonsson, 1988).

In this battle of deception and detection, it is not surprising that there are counter-countermeasures. At the present time, however, and in the immediate future, the balance of strength probably lies with the spy in the case of security screening. Human beings have hardly begun to explore the possibilities of controlling their physiology via mental activity. Those who have developed such skills, particularly through meditative activities, have exemplified the potential of agentive control over what most of us consider to be uncontrollable. A few practice sessions in front of a biofeedback screen can yield rapid progress in controlling physiological features. One suspects that spies are well trained in such exercises. Professional poker players likewise. Criminals will also avail themselves of such training if and when it becomes necessary for them.

That said, it would be premature to write off polygraphy. Most adults know when they are lying and what they are lying about, and the idea of Wertheimer and Klein (cited in Herbold-Wooten, 1982) that traces will remain and can be reactivated is plausible. Despite our current ignorance about a whole range of significant issues in the relevant areas of psychophysiology, the interrogative and physiological technology of polygraphy is undoubtedly functioning at much better than chance levels in both field and laboratory studies. Against an ideal of no false positives or false negatives in criminal cases, however, it is not surprisingly found wanting. As yet, however, its efficacy has not been compared with the current practices.

What is extraordinary to at least one outsider is the lack of in-depth published research on individuals whose careers involve repeated criminal charges with varying verdicts. Some such persons might have been prepared to tell the truth eventually about their records, which could then have been calibrated against polygraph testing at the time of the alleged offenses. Perhaps such records are being accumulated and have not been published as yet. There must be possibilities of much more conclusive research than has been done so far. Given the importance of the issues, it is surprising that societies do not spend more. The United States and the United Kingdom both spend billions annually on their security services, armed forces, and police. Being able to detect lies would save vast sums of money as well as time and energy. The development of an increased capability in lie detection would seem to be a small price to pay for the likely benefits that would result.

CHAPTER SIX

Falsifications in Societal Institutions

Frame of Reference

Just as any study of falsification and deception in interpersonal contexts is analytically parasitic on the social psychology of unde-ceptive social behavior, so any examination of falsifications to and from members of social organizations presupposes a knowledge of the sociologies of particular kinds of society. To keep the task simple, only two kinds of society will be mentioned: the totalitarian and the quasi democratic. *Totalitarian* is defined as a society where power is exercised by a dictator or small elite who control armed forces that implement their will on and exact conformity from the citizenry. Given the international conventions of modern times and the aspi-rations and ideals enshrined in the U.N. Charter, such states are very likely to use a rhetoric that reaches degrees of falsification that it is difficult for basically honest people to appreciate. Calling themselves democracies or republics, their constitutions appear to safeguard citizens' rights, they are likely to hold (single candidate) elections with (compulsory) voting, their laws look like those in other socie-ties, but in fact all these structures and processes are perverted to serve the purposes of those with the power. Typically, there is a party police apparatus that reaches down to individuals and families to check on dissent or disdain, with fear of forced-labor camps or death as the major motivators for conformity. Hence, many of the citizens also have to lead false lives, even being careful to avoid jokes or mild criticisms about the state and its apparatus. Individuals do not know who they can trust because it is common practice to have strong political education in schools that is intended to encourage children to inform on parents and peers.

It is perhaps not surprising that populations trapped in such regimes seldom attempt to stage revolutions during the lifetime of a dictator. Dissent is quite simply suicidal; conformity is the least of the unpleasant options.

When human beings boast of the progress made by their species, it is salutary to note that in 1980 over half of the world's population was living in states that were essentially totalitarian, albeit differing widely in the efficiency and cruelty of their oppression. To illustrate how lies are used by the powers in such states, Stalin's government of the Soviet Union will be used as the sole example.

There are many varieties of quasi-open societies that differ greatly among themselves in the bases of the distribution of power, wealth, and status and in the constitutional rights and responsibilities of citizens. *Quasi-democratic* is chosen as the most suitable label for those that will be mentioned most here, mainly the United Kingdom and the United States. They suffer from the same kinds of discrepancy between words and reality as totalitarian societies. The political, ethical, and judicial ideals they enshrine in their constitutions implicitly or explicitly parallel the principles of the U.N. Charter, whereas their conduct and the inequalities generated and sustained do not. Differential access to and treatment by the law is a clear illustration of a significant inequality in human rights. Legal support is horrendously expensive in both Britain and the United States, and state aid is neither universally available nor forensically as committed as the purchased services of the elite defenders. Paradoxically, too, the rich, powerful, and well connected seem to know how to obtain legal aid, while their declared poverty allows them to continue to follow a lifestyle to which they have become accustomed. In Britain, in what is now called the Guinness affair, where various prominent people were accused of fraudulent practices in organizing an industrial takeover, one of the defendants secured legal aid to the extent of over a million pounds. Similar sums of money appear to have been obtained by the Maxwell brothers, who are being tried for financial irregularities in their business practices. If found guilty, will the prison sentence be short? Poorer people seem to be sent to prison for longer terms for apparently lesser offences, having received minimal legal aid. Just as all citizens are far from equal before the law, so the freedoms of speech and association are limited, both by the state and by the state's failure to protect dissenters. The freedoms are granted for minor protest movements in times of peace. In times of war, they are very promptly withdrawn. In the United States in the 1950s, Senator McCarthy ran an unconstitutional campaign of victimization of persons who were alleged to be communist sympathizers, and it was several years before the Senate committee under Kefauver was able to bring the persecution to a halt. The leader of the civil rights movement, Martin Luther King, Jr., was assassinated for his support of an entirely constitutional cause. Robert Kennedy may well have been shot for the same commitment; Malcolm X, likewise. Britain is less prone to assassinations than the United States but has a long history of the rough handling of dissent among workers from well before the Tolpuddle Martyrs of 1834 to the Coal Miners' Strike of 1984.

The rhetoric of democratic ideals has been preached in the United Kingdom and the United States for most of the 20th century; the reality remains rather different from the claims of the leaders—those whose voices are heard. The structures and functioning of quasi democracies, however, meet at least some of the criteria associated with common definitions of democracy, roughly definable as a social system in which the adults of that society periodically choose between two or more persons or groups who have taken part in an electoral competition—the winners then govern the society under a set of properly constituted regulations. The society also has to be one in which certain liberties are guaranteed under law, and these normally include freedoms of peaceful association, of opinions, of communication, and freedom from interference (within the law). The lists and definitions of the constituents of democracy can vary, and some people would certainly like to see the incorporation of ideas of a sense of community and mutual responsibility. Rorty (1991) would endorse the inclusion of a value that encourages the reduction of cruelty and suffering. Although such values might not be distinctive of democracies, their addition would serve as reminders that the virtues claimed for democracy itself rest on higher-order principles, which can be forgotten by those whose individual ambitions are achieved to the detriment of others; voting systems are a means, not an end.

Societies that purport to function under democratic rules will encourage and discourage different kinds of political falsifications and deceptions from those societies that are totalitarian in the exercise of combinations of military, monarchic, and tyrannical power.

In 1984, some Western writers rejoiced that Orwell's (1948) prophetic *1984* had not arrived. In that society, individuals were entirely at the mercy of a self-perpetuating elite that relied on terror and punishment to control the definitions of reality of the citizens. The lies the people were fed about enemies and the threats to their well-being kept them in their slavery. It has already been implied that citizens of most of the countries in the world would have discovered that a critical editorial of their leaders would have shown very quickly that freedom of the press to publish dissent is limited. Likewise if they had had the resources to wage a sustained media campaign against corruption and certain cover-ups in the Western democracies, they might also have found that powerful agencies would have persuaded them into silence. As will be discussed later, the freedom to criticize elites and their members is limited, especially if the accused members have behaved badly.

How do quasi democracies function and what roles do falsifications and deception play in them? In her careful analysis of the contests and contestants in Western democracies, Etzioni-Halevy (1989) adopts what she calls a "demo-elite orientation." In the customary struggles within societies for power, wealth, and status, there are more social groups in contention than any single hierarchy model can accommodate and fewer than some pluralists might imagine. Given that the political elite has to be elected periodically, its contestants have to appeal to the adult public and coexist with those other major groups that also exercise influence via the bureaucracy of public services, the plutocracy of big business, the beneficiaries of accumulated inherited wealth, the judiciary, and the leadership of those other social movements or professional organizations that have become accepted as relevant power bases with the society. Etzioni-Halevy allows that different societies will generate different groupings with different degrees of independence among them; in the main, she confines her analysis to elites she calls the political (with "governing" being used for the particular group in office), the bureaucratic, and the economic (plutocratic, business). She argues that there is competition for ascendancy between elites and within elites. Also within elites, there will be subgroups and individuals competing for ascendancy. There is also cooperation among the leaders across elites, however, so that it is sensible to talk about an elite of elites. Her primary focus is on the ways the potential contradictions of principles, policies, and practices are acted out within and without the constitutional and legal frameworks—how they are resolved to maintain what is necessarily a "fragile democracy." For present purposes, at least two of her main thrusts are relevant. The first is that manipulation and corruption are inevitable components of the dynamic equilibrium of the power games. Businesses that contribute to the coffers of political parties and their influential members are more likely to be protected by legislation and to be awarded lucrative government contracts. Bureaucratic posts are likely to be expanded in number and given to loyal party members by the governing elite so that government policies are supported in their execution; oppositions can be muted by gifts of similar positions. Bureaucrats can arrange for particular businesses to be favored, and businesses can influence bureaucrats.

The second thrust is that members of other groups will have a vested interest in exposing some of the corruption that exists; the reputations of aspiring lawyers or ambitious media hawks will be greatly enhanced if they can nail corruption in high places. (Parenthetically, Etzioni-Halevy, 1989, notes that distinctions between what is legal and illegal are seldom clear, and the twilight zones are ideal for the mutual transfer of favors and containments of pressures. Her case studies of New York City also imply that those working the systems can be either careless or arrogant in the risks they take.) Of course, these twilight activities are concealed from the public, and any mention of their existence is normally diverted. The diversions customarily include covering lies as one immediate strategy of defense. Etzioni-Halevy discusses conditions that are likely to increase the incidence of corruption and lies and deceit about corruption.

The less the independence of elites is from one another, the greater the corruption. If the governing elite appoints the bureaucrats and the bureaucrats run the elections, as in the French Third Republic, corruption will flourish. Likewise, if the governing elite is dependent on the economic elite for funding its election campaigns, corruption will flourish, as has been alleged to be the case with post-1945 Japan. If bureaucrats are arranging for the placing of government contracts, members of the economic elite will have a strong interest in securing these with the highest possible profit margins and the lowest cost in bribes to bureaucrats. When governments become the largest spenders, with perhaps a third of the gross national product under their aegis, it is not surprising that business interests will exploit whatever inducements they can offer to secure their own success. Currently, in Britain the government controls the spending of nearly 50% of the gross national product.

In addition to problems of interdependence, the "rules of the game" in democracies are typically ambiguous and even mutually inconsistent, resulting in unclear distinctions between the legitimate, the semilegitimate, and the illegitimate. Legislation proliferates in relatively uncoordinated ways. Directives are drawn up that give rise not just to ambiguities but to actual contradictions or impossibilities. The less clear it is just what kinds of self-benefiting actions are forbidden, the greater the likelihood of corruptions and subsequent cover-ups.

There is no neat way in which the types of power groups can be classified. Etzioni-Halevy (1989) confines most of her analysis to the political, the economic, and the bureaucratic but includes reference to the judiciary, the mass media, and the military. She could have added the power of "old money," originally vested in land and later distributed into basic industries but subsequently diffused further, commercially and geographically. Perkin (1989) makes much of the rise to power of professional elites, for example, legal, medical, financial, managerial, scientific, technological, and educational. These groups, ostensibly meritocratic, typically originated in service to the elite of elites but have now attained considerable power in their own right as experts in their domains, particularly via the establishment of associations and societies that publicize their achievements and protect and advance their interests. Similarly, once trade unions became legal, manual and nonmanual workers formed larger and larger combines intended to influence the governing elite in comparable ways. Large numbers of other interest groups have been formed to advance particular causes of categories of people, animals, the environment, morals, and religions often via representations and petitions to governing elites.

How to group these is beyond the current brief (and competence of the author). How to classify types of interdependence among them, ranging from direct control, through family links, to networks deriving from schools, universities, and clubs is also beyond the purview. Suffice it to say that the existence of many networks adds to the interdependence and hence the probability of manipulation and corruption, which in turn leads to proactive false representations of activities and to reactive lies to defend such false representations as are challenged by other parties.

Insofar as the leaders and members of these groups are struggling for ascendancy and success in the struggle is more important than the truth, the truth will be sacrificed. Recalling that truth is the first casualty of war, it is salutary to remember that war is just one form of interindividual and intergroup conflict.

Following zoological and sociological terminology, the term *order* will be used to refer to the large groupings discussed by Etzioni-Halevy (1989). As used here, orders are career groups with ladders up which particular people progress (or not). They are not simply a reflection of the division of labor and the thousands of types of job existing in modern societies. They are associated with jobs whose occupants have come together to form associations and societies that serve to protect and promote the interests of their members. The ones to be considered here are those that reach into the hierarchies of power, wealth, and status. Only a selection is offered, and the historical perspective is neglected. For example, no mention is made of the immensely powerful trade guilds of medieval Europe, whose descendants still play a role in current affairs. In London, the Worshipful Company of Fletchers survives, but its political and economic significance declined with the lessened importance of the bow and arrow in warfare. In contrast, the heirs to the secrets of building cathedrals in the lodges of Freemasonry retain strict secrecy about their activities, while their membership extends well into the elite of elites and covers the range of other social orders. Associations are necessary for cooperation and desirable for conviviality; some are formed, structured, or can be used as vehicles that are likely to encourage lying and deceit in the pursuit of privilege, however, and it is the illustrations and demonstrations of these conditions rather than a catalog of cases that is the primary concern here.

A Totalitarian Example

Stalin can serve as a reminder of the enormities and the enormous power that a modern tyrant can achieve and maintain by way of falsification. He reconstructed history by a systematic downgrading of the significance of Trotsky and others and upgrading his own role in the Bolshevik revolution. Photographs were revised substituting Stalin for Trotsky as Lenin's closest colleague. Masses of materials in archives were reprocessed and reprinted to authenticate the new history. In the contemporary accounts of collectivization in the 1920s and 1930s, the scale of the killings and resettlement of ordinary people was never reported in the media. Instead, the papers carried photographs and stories of the successful endeavors of happy pioneers developing industry and agriculture in Siberia and the Central Asian republics. Also, in the 1930s, show trials were staged where members of the Bolshevik Old Guard confessed to murdering other loyal colleagues and plotting against the state; they were found guilty and then executed. The armed forces were purged, with many of the senior commanders being shot.

Stalin's mechanisms of control were sufficiently efficient for him to survive as undisputed leader until his natural death in 1953. The apparatus radiated fear downward and sideways reaching into the smallest social groups. No one knew who might denounce them to the secret police. As already mentioned, jokes or careless remarks were enough to lead to deportation to labor camps. All the social orders had to conform.

Soviet science had to be different from capitalist science, and the biologists Lysenko and his colleagues found themselves generating a fraudulent genetic theory along Lamarkian lines. Psychologists had to abandon ideas of general intelligence because it was alleged to be inconsistent with Leninism-Maxism; Luria and colleagues had to show that all forms of mental retardation were linked to brain injuries. Psychiatrists had to show that dissidents were psychiatrically disturbed. Musicians such as Shostakovich had to conform to unspecified Soviet standards of composition, as did painters, sculptors and architects. Workers were free to form trade unions, provided that their representatives were publicly satisfied with wages and conditions of employment.

Literally millions of people were killed or died as a direct result of the ruthless (in)efficiency with which Stalin instituted collectivization, industrialization, and periodic purges of persons he chose to eliminate. This will was executed on a population of over 200 million for over a quarter of a century. This is a long time and an unimaginable number of people. Yet the lies and deceit were invented and sustained with very large numbers of people within and beyond the Soviet Union believing what they were being told. Mao Tse-tung contained a Chinese population several times larger. Hitler achieved similar power but for a short period only. Most of the world has experienced totalitarian governments this century. All have had leaders who relied on massive lying and deceit to sustain their positions. Many such leaders survived to die naturally. Between them, the actions of the regimes of these three men alone were associated with the deaths of perhaps 100,000,000 human beings. The scale of the killing, the suffering induced, and the deception practiced defy the imagination of those who have had no experience to register such a way of living and dying.

This brief section serves as a reminder of the continuous threat to democratic forms of government. The reminder is not so much a matter of form as of substance. It is the misery and murder of ordinary people in the millions that has been associated with societies whose populations have delayed their disbelief too long that should serve as a terrible warning to the mixture of trust or political apathy or both that allow totalitarianism to develop. As the chapter goes on to illustrate, however, it is not just dictatorships that use claims to virtue, justice, and goodwill to cover vice, injustice, and cruelty.

A Year in Britain

Etzioni-Halevy (1989) discusses conditions that increase or decrease the incidence of corruption and deceit in quasi democracies. One point she might have added to illustrate the justification of her postulation of the idea of an elite of elites could have been the common course of events that follows exposures of corruption. Assuming it is a member of the governing elite that is exposed, first the media and the opposition make a great fuss, with carefully worded but strong accusations. Second, quick decisions are made by the groupings in the political elite about capitulation to demands for resignations, etc. If the accused resigns (or apologizes), then the story disappears as well. If the accused can create sufficient uncertainty and secure the backing of senior politicians and some sectors of the media, the affair fades away, especially if a committee of inquiry is established. In Britain in 1994, three MPs were accused of receiving improper favors or funds or both. One resigned from his ministerial post immediately. One lasted several days. The third stood his ground and survived. None resigned their seats as members of Parliament. Two inquiries were begun: one to investigate how the exposing newspaper had obtained a copy of a hotel bill germane to the third case (!) and the second to consider general questions of members of Parliament having undeclared interests that might conflict with parliamentary business. These will report occasionally and eventually. The issues will almost certainly fade into obscurity.

What in Britain became known as the Pergau Dam scandal was first "exposed" by an ambitious newspaper editor. Allegations were that money from Britain's aid to Malaysia budget was given for the dam, with both bribes and understandings that Malaysia would buy British arms. This allegation resulted in a period during which Malaysia forbade British companies from tendering for contracts, the editor of the *Sunday Times* was transferred to another post, the foreign minister of Britain conceded that what he had done unknowingly was in fact illegal, and then the whole affair melted away and nothing else happened. No one resigned. No one was prosecuted. Neither the media nor the opposition parties pursued the affair. One of the defenses of the actions was that the arms deals would reduce unemployment in Britain; it was good for British business, which is good for the British people. Attempts by reporters to raise the issue of British firms supplying instruments of torture to overseas countries will probably meet a similar fate (British TV Channel 4, January 11, 1995, *Dispatches*). To a viewer, the evidence about the sale of instruments of torture was quite clear, but the superordinate company denied that such weapons were manufactured and sold, despite the sight of a letter quoting charges for the supply of them.

One of the interesting features of such events, which is entirely consistent with the Etzioni-Halevy (1989) position, is that although there is sparring and jockeying for relative advantages among the leaders, truces seem to be negotiated before too much blood is shed. Elites spar, but the exposures of concealments do not lead to the principals losing their positions. Alternatively, the powers can decide to do nothing and wait for the issue to fade.

Typically the script follows a sequence. Someone breaks a story to the press or TV (radio is less likely). Allegations are made or questions asked about a cover-up or the propriety or legality of the conduct of some public figure or figures. If it is a press scoop then it is very likely that the papers will represent themselves as the voice of the people, acting in the interests of the public good. The campaign will probably make demands for full revelation of the relevant facts and suggest drastic action if it is deemed appropriate, such as bans, resignations, or prosecutions. Action may be taken, but regardless of this the story will probably die within a week.

By the time the story is dropped it is often clear what the relevant missing facts are and how evidence germane to these might be obtained. If the media had inquiry after the truth as their highest priority (see Table 8.1, p. 244), then the discovery and representation of these would form the main focus of their activity. In so far as other goals are primary it will not. What is surprising for some of us is how seldom the relevant facts do emerge.

If there is a scare about a threat of human disease, or debility from radiation, or other forms of pollution, or from infected animals, or other people, then one obvious strategy would be to set down some evidence, preferably with numbers being cited. It is more likely, however, that a gladiatorial contest will be initiated with experts disagreeing, representatives of groups with vested interest offering their opinions, and the "public" having its say through chat shows (Livingstone & Lunt, 1995). In brief it will be the factors which boost audience ratings or sales that are preeminent rather than national and realistic enquiries and solutions.

Where impropriety by persons is alleged, the issue will not include chat shows. The guilty as well as the innocent are protected by laws about defamation and as Horatio Bottomley (Anonymous, 1923) demonstrated, persons in his position have to be experts in the letter of the appropriate laws and litigious in their attitudes to threats against them. This is another reason why the media may back off. However the media may be able to afford the costs of successfully conducted defenses which in itself may deter would-be litigants.

There can be a power struggle with skirmishing between the principals, until one party backs down or off, or a third party intervenes. The skirmishes can take on the character of the duels between males of certain species fought for females or territory. Male giraffes could easily deliver mortal blows but restrict their dueling to neck pushing. Rattlesnakes could kill each other with single bites, but settle their contests with wrestling.

Originally this section cited more individual cases, relying entirely on quotations from newspapers for the alleged facts. However, these were dropped, on legal advice. Pointing out that the quotations come from newspapers would be no defense. If unproven of course such citation is equivalent to malicious gossip, but there is an element of irony in a situation in which newspapers with circulations of millions can print material that names names and escape litigation, but in which that same material could be grounds for legal action if quoted in an academic text with names deleted and where their function is to serve as illustrations of issues rather than as accusations.

These few examples from the political domain in one year in one country could have been supplemented with what may have been a massive concealment-denial sequence about the sale of arms to Iraq to several sexual liaisons and scandals that were also denied initially. The Serious Fraud Office has brought fraud cases involving millions against various prominent businessmen (no women!). Over 1,000 insurance agents have apparently lied to persons to get them to change to inferior pension plans. Soccer players and managers have denied taking backhanders for transfers and match fixing. Prisoners have had to be released because the police have been shown to have forged statements allegedly made by those charged.

False insurance claims on holiday insurance are alleged to be costing companies over £50 million a year. If false house contents, car, and business claims were added, this would raise that figure considerably. In Australia, a far from thorough check on a sample of submissions from tax agents gave an error rate of 73% of which almost all were excessive. (An Italian colleague suggested that the true figure in Italy would be 100%, if not above it. See Chapter 9.) In Britain, there are several hundred hoax phone calls to the police, the fire service, and the ambulance service every week.

What all these public domain lies add up to in terms of numbers, costs, and the suffering of victims is impossible to estimate. Whatever judgments the public makes (see Chapter 9) and what demands there are for action to reduce such lying are not resulting in any observable activity.

Summary

In modern times, the governments, organizations, and institutions of most states feel obliged to give international justifications of their activities in what could be called "ethically correct" terms. The rhetoric is generally constructed to be consistent with principles similar to those given expression in the U.N. Charter. Giving accounts and justifications for public consumption within states, the rhetoric is likely to be crafted to conform with any constitution or widely held social representations of justice or propriety.

To the extent that members of elites within states are concealing corrupt practices, their proactive and reactive accounts are likely to contain misleading concealments at a minimum and straight lies at a maximum. It is simply a false myth to assert that there is not a lot of falsification in the higher reaches of quasi democracies. There may be less than there is in totalitarian states, and it is less directly vicious, but it is endemic and does appear to fool many of the people much of the time.

The extended examination of the ways in which significant social groups are organized in competitive individualistic quasi democracies has been a necessary corrective to any undue emphasis on persons as independent agents making personal decisions about when and when not to tell the truth. The tenor of the argument here for lies in the public arena is consistent with the perspective adopted by Buller and Burgoon (in press) for interpersonal contexts: The interplay is between situations and persons and both have qualities that can increase the incidence of lying and other forms of deceit.

Sociology does not seem to have invented a technical term that captures the groupings described by Etzioni-Halevy (1989). As mentioned earlier, the traditional notion of social orders fits some: the political, legal, economic, military, and religious. The political can be divided into the legislative and the executive, where the second would compose the bureaucracy. The economic could be said to include the media, but that would be awkward. Often, parts of the media are controlled by guangos (*q*uasi-*a*utonomous, *n*ongovernmental committees). Often, the push for profits is a subordinate goal of media enterprises owned by persons with political ambitions. The classification omits the rise in power of associations of workers and professionals, whose leaders can come to aspire to wealth, power, and status (Perkin, 1989). Entertainers in sports or on stage and screen are certainly among the nouveau rich, although the inheritance of old money is still the easiest way to acquire wealth and status.

Lies, deceit, and corruption become more prevalent when members of one of these groupings switch their commitment from the raison d'être of their group's existence to attempts to influence the affairs of other groupings or gain access to its rewards. Most of the illustrations offered have been centered on the pursuit of money: politicians, bureaucrats, and scientists accepting money from commerce and industry and then falsifying whatever needs to be falsified to honor the implicit or explicit understandings. Gifts of powerful and high-status positions can also be made by those empowered to do so.

It will be in times of rapid social change that wealth is "up for grabs." The massive dismantlement of publicly owned resources in Britain over the past 15 years has resulted in those few thousand in the right places with the right connections becoming very much richer—at the expense of the population as a whole.

There is a sense in which this dismemberment and the redistribution of wealth has involved massive deception on a grand scale, as forests, land, property, buses, bridges, and many other publicly owned resources are sold off quietly and secretly with none of the razzamatazz that has accompanied the selling off of shares in utilities to their employees and to the general public. (Most of the electorate clearly does not see the redistribution as theft and its beneficiaries as receivers of stolen goods, but that is certainly the interpretation of a minority.)

Within an era of such change and turbulence, it is not surprising that the proactive pursuit of power, wealth, and status should have become a high priority of those in positions to snatch at opportunities; neither is it surprising that if called to account for activities en route, concealment and lying should be a first line of defense, especially because it seems to be generally efficacious and goes unpunished. First, any campaign for an inquiry may fail. Second, if an inquiry is pursued, it is liable to produce a whitewash. Third, any punishment is likely to be minimal and temporary. The opportunities for lying and deceit and the pressures to do so will not be the same in the various social orders and groupings.

Certain orders and groups are omitted. For example, in the past two decades, workers' organizations have been in political and numerical decline, as have the politicians and political parties with which they have been associated; opportunities for advancements via corrupt and concealed practices have not come to public notice probably because their policies have had to be protective rather than expansionist. Chapters 7 and 8 document examples of some of those orders and organizations in which truth is most likely to be sacrificed to other priorities. If there are peculiarities of procedures that highlight this orientation, these are mentioned. The organizational features that particularly encourage lying and deception appear to be those that emphasize competition and winning more than they emphasize inquiries after the truth and rational solutions based on consensus. This is not so much a polemical position as the conclusion of an academic inquiry. Skill at poker is a matter of calculation, memory, and deception, and there is no implication that poker should be transformed to become a cooperative inquiry!

Unfortunately, at this level of data collection and interpretation it is not feasible to test the hypotheses of Etzioni-Halevy (1989). No comparative data are offered to show how linkages across orders correlate with corruption and cover-ups. Readers also need to be warned against overestimating the incidence of misrepresentation of facts on the basis of the examples cited. For example, the cases of demonstrated and alleged fraud in published scientific research almost certainly are very rare compared with the number of undoctored papers. Frauds do occur, however, and it is likely that the true estimate would be much higher than authorities voice. Similarly with biomedical research; most of the drugs on the market have been stringently tested and evaluated before being released. There are honest politicians and parties that are dedicated to improvement in social justice and rates of progress in their countries.

It is also worth mentioning that lying by authorities to the public is potentially interactive but at a much slower pace than everyday FtF encounters. Accused authorities may feel obliged to be interviewed on TV or radio. They may grant interviews to the press. They may eventually appear before committees or in court. The public can have its say too by writing to their political representatives, boycotting products, or withholding labor, for example. Of course, collective action is less likely to happen in individualistic competitive societies.

CHAPTER SEVEN

The Mediation of Messages

The Mass Media

Preamble

The mass media are culled for up-front examination because in modern times their title is apt: They do indeed mediate between authorities and the masses. What the public learns about their society and its workings is for the most part not direct. Few people have direct and continuing acquaintance with politicians, lawyers, scientists, generals, bishops, or media tycoons. What is made available for widespread dissemination is selected and constructed by the media, particularly by TV, radio, newspapers, and magazines. Hence, the peculiarly powerful position of those who control the media. Within limits, they can define the characteristics of other groups for the population, an example par excellence of power without corresponding responsibility or accountability.

In totalitarian regimes, control of the propaganda machinery is invariably of the highest priority. The rulers decide what will be transmitted. It is difficult to imagine a dictatorship that allows real oppositions to have access to the mass media.

In quasi democracies, there may be government controlled TV, radio, and publications, but these will function alongside commercially funded media, and there may be quasi-autonomous TV and radio, such as the British Broadcasting Corporation (BBC) (see Tunstall, 1983). The committees that run the BBC are not composed of a random sample of the population, however; they are appointed by the government from the elites of various social orders and, as such, have a commonality of vested interest and shared worldview with the higher strata of society, which is also true for senior management. Given the coincidence of worldviews the elites do not normally need to interfere to influence what perspectives are adopted. If management offends the government, it can be threatened with sanctions. The BBC tried to be factual in its reporting of British losses in the 1980s' war with Argentina. It was told to stop reporting these. Three IRA members were shot and killed by British forces in Gibraltar in the 1980s. No doubts were expressed about the mission of the IRA, but questions were raised about the circumstances of the shootings. A commercial station, Thames TV, produced a program conveying alternative accounts. The government of the day failed to secure an injunction against the transmission of the program; several years later, Thames TV lost its franchise.

To pretend that the media tell the stories as they really are would be to be deluded (Weaver, 1994). By their nature, they have to be selective and they can adopt an infinite number of perspectives. There are limits to what they can portray, and these limits are political, commercial, and ethical, as well as being systemically inevitable. Hence, the priority accorded to the media in this review of falsification by various significant social groupings in society. How some of the falsifications are achieved is described in the second section of the chapter.

Introduction

One of the very baffling conundrums is the public perception and use of the mass media. It will not be too difficult to present arguments and evidence as to why those who produce the media do what they do. What is more problematic is to explain why the public buys the products, physically and psychologically.

The focus here will be on the quality of what is introduced under the explicit or implicit heading of "news" and within that, the concern will be with outright falsification and bias, with bias having a superficial component registered as differential evaluation and a deeper component in terms of whose perspectives and what evidence is presented on controversial matters. TV and newspapers are the main vehicles examined.

One of the fascinating and mysterious features is the social psychology of differential credibility. Typically, people see and hear only what is produced in their own country. Within each country, there is differential appraisal of types of media and particular stations or papers within a medium; some are seen as more trustworthy than others. These evaluations differ from one social group to another (see Chapter 9). Within totalitarian states, there does seem to be pervasive public contempt for everything broadcast by the government-controlled organs. At the height of the Cold War from the 1940s to the 1980s, citizens of communist countries did not believe what was in their own media but relied on home-printed sheets and gossip to circulate world news, which was picked up from Western radio stations. This news they believed. Contrastively, this decision may have been rational, although absolutely it was still hazardous. The media moguls of the capitalist West are not dispassionate disciples of the truth at all costs, as the first example illustrates. William Randolph Hearst (e.g., see Swanberg, 1961) is usually cited as the first, and remains one of the most ruthless proprietors in his pursuit of the mixture of power, wealth, and whatever else he aspired to obtain. Probably no other newspaper proprietor has had more influence in creating a war through unfounded constructions of events. Of Hearst's ventures, the role of his *Journal* in the fomentation of the Spanish-American War was the most notorious, and the most notorious episode in that surrounded the sinking of the U.S.S. Maine.

Relations between Spain and the United States were not entirely positive when the Cubans revolted against Spanish rule, and Hearst had been a belligerent interventionist before the possibly apocryphal exchange of telegrams. He was alleged to have dispatched a photographer named Remington to Cuba to send back pictures of the imminent war. In September 1897, Remington cabled Hearst, "No trouble here. There will be no war. I wish to return, Remington." The reply was, "Please remain. You furnish the pictures and I'll furnish the war, W. R. Hearst." The consensus is that Hearst's conduct was by far the most influential single factor leading the United States into the eventual war.

After 3 weeks of a protective "goodwill" visit, the U.S.S. Maine blew up in Havana harbor on February 15, 1898, with the loss of many lives. The succeeding headlines of Hearst's *Journal* are shown in Table 7.1. Already on February 16, the passive voice of "blown up" emphasizes agency rather than accident. By February 17, the means are identified, and the idea of more than an individual agent is suggested. By February 20, the Spanish are indicted, and on the 21st the denigration is accelerated.

Table 7.1 Headlines from Heart's *Journal*, 1898

February 16	Cruiser **Maine** blown up in Havana Harbor
February 17	The warship **Maine** was split in two by an enemy's secret infernal machine
February 18	The whole country thrills with war fever
February 20	How the **Maine** actually looks as it lies, wrecked by Spanish treachery in Havana Bay
February 22	Havana insults memory of American dead

What really happened has never been discerned. The official U.S. inquiry invoked the idea of a mine attached by a person or persons unknown but had no evidence for this supposition. It is highly unlikely that a single device could have activated such devastation. It is highly unlikely that the Spanish would have provoked a conflict they tried and desperately needed to avoid. It is much more likely that the explosion was triggered by an electrical fault or a smoking accident in the ship's magazine. It is virtually certain that Hearst had no warrant for any of his five headlines, but his campaign culminated in the United States declaring war against Spain on April 19, even though the Spanish had by then agreed to all the U.S. demands for Cuba.

In September 1897, the circulation of the *Journal* was around 700,000. By the end of the war, it was 1,250,000. War can be good for circulation and the profits.

Hearst's use of his papers for vitriolic and unsubstantiated attacks on his opponents within the United States was sustained for the whole of his long life. He came close to the highest political office but made too many enemies among both Democrats and Republicans to succeed to the presidency. Nevertheless, he maintained a role as a would-be maker of presidents and retained access to them. He was received by leaders of European states as late as the 1930s when he was touring and talking with the fascists and their opponents. Unlike politicians, who have to be elected periodically, at least in the democracies, newspaper proprietors have a potentially more precarious power base, relying entirely on a public willing to buy their products. Zero sales mean massive losses and bankruptcies. Why do people buy papers that falsify the facts? Why do governments tolerate the falsifications? How does it come about that the slogan "freedom of speech" can be invoked when its use is an abuse of the rationale of the original intention in the U.S. Constitution?

These questions are asked in the final section of the chapter. First, however, there must be what can be no more than an elementary tour of the methods used to establish what constitutes a misrepresentation of reality.

Techniques of Analysis

Falsification of facts is a more problematic issue than it appears to be at first sight. Once events are in the past, various vested interests can act to reconstruct the evidence and their interpretation, especially, for example, where crimes of violence during periods of instability and war are involved. Records can be falsified and destroyed. Although it is a useful idea to propose that history is written by the winners, this century's winners can become the next century's minor power or nonexistent nation. Investigators of 19th or 20th century wars, however, can examine a diversity of records, visit the sites of military activity, examine artifacts, and perhaps even collect folk memories. What they can put together from their research may well be incompatible with some of the accounts offered about some of these events, but for others, no resolution of discrepancies may be possible. In recent times, the assassination of President Kennedy stands out as a testimony to the difficulties of arriving at the truth. Despite the fact that this event took place in public in the presence of TV cameras with the security team in place, who fired the shots from where, and why, remains unresolved. More than one plausible account survives, as well as a plethora of wilder hypotheses. Consistency of evidence of different kinds from a variety of sources is the most desirable outcome of a search for establishing what really happened. When there are inconsistencies, the accounts of those with vested interests are normally accorded the least weight.

For analyses of texts both verbal and visual, the longest established technique for representing such materials is some form of "content analysis." Proponents of some of the newer methods for describing content have been unnecessarily derogatory about the weaknesses of particular forms of old-style content analysis. Counting instances of categories in a text (or anything else) is as close to objectivity as it is possible to come, provided that the categories are well-defined and that the rules of procedure for what to do with uncertain instances are specified. Questions of how much of what constitutes appropriate samples are answerable within the customary statistical parameters. Of course, it is true that by counting trees what is significant about the forest may be missed. The categories selected may be inappropriate or inadequate. The size of unit (e.g., words) may be too small. Opponents of counting operations can surely point out particular examples where investigators have been misled by their own narrowness of vision or zeal for objectivity, but there is in fact no alternative to textual analysis that does not involve both qualitative and quantitative decisions. The academic disputes are actually no more than arguments about types and sizes of events and structures most appropriate for particular purposes. Apt illustrations of how effects are achieved in a text may not need to be counted to demonstrate a point may be true, but they still presuppose the existence of at least one exemplar.

The relative strengths and weaknesses of the stereotypes of content analysis, on the one hand, and the variety of other contenders, on the other, are in reality complementary, and all have potential relevance for the analysis of the meanings and significance of a text.

For present purposes, it is necessary to go two steps further. Academics approaching texts from backgrounds in media studies, semiotics, or linguistics are less likely to be concerned with counting than with illustrating how possible effects are achieved. They are more likely than experimentally trained social psychologists to go beyond surface meanings to deeper levels (e.g., Barthes, 1968, 1977; Labov & Fanshel, 1977; van Dijk, 1991; Woolacott, 1977). As they do so, and generate interpretations of possible readings of the text, they run greater risks of finding or constructing readings that others do not and perhaps could not. Whether these readings are made by others and, if so, with what consequences, may also be left unexamined. The most convincing illustration of a possibility is not the same as a demonstration of an actual consequence. For example, it is argued that the spatial arrangement of articles in newspapers creates associations in readers' minds that may lead to presumed real connections. In 1994, the Prince of Wales implied in an interview that he had engaged in a sexual liaison with some woman other than his wife. The following day, at least one national daily paper carried the story as its front page news, while including a right-hand column with a photograph of a woman and a comment about her. Did those people who were unaware of the gossip draw any inference about the identity of "the other woman" or not? This is a clear example of obvious and overt juxtaposition, but there has yet to be systematic evaluation of which people draw what inferences from spatial relations, type faces, angles of camera, backgrounds, and the many other possible contrasts and conjunctions that might create connections of various kinds. These issues are relevant to falsification and deception. Had a naive editor placed a photograph of Madonna next to the Prince of Wales article, would either have had grounds for litigation? Insofar as false rather than true inferences are deliberately encouraged and are drawn from features of textual presentations, then most of the criteria of lying can be said to be present. Here, such subtleties will not be pursued, but there is a promising future for methodologies that combine the strengths of each of the approaches that have been developed to enrich (or replace) simple content analysis (e.g., Krippendorf, 1981).

One difficulty of a detailed linguistic approach demonstrated by Fowler (1991) in his analysis of the relations between text and ideology in the British press of the 1980s is that the techniques demonstrated require not just a knowledge of how a particular language works but also how the cultural context in which it is operating is working. The analyst needs to be very well-informed about the sociohistorical situation to work out what particular texts are likely to be representing (or misrepresenting) and needs to be well-informed about all levels of linguistic analysis from phonetics and graphetics to pragmatics to make sense of the relations between the two.

The observations of Fowler (1991) and other textual analysts might be summarized as follows:

1. The mass media are owned and controlled by persons whose interests overlap with and depend on the cooperation of other elites, in particular, the political, the financial, the military, and the legal.

2. News will be selected to present selected issues in forms that encourage preferred interpretations that are consistent with the interests of elite groups.

3. Readers and viewers unaware of alternative perspectives on the issues will be under the illusion that what they are receiving is a representation of objective reality rather than a construction of particular subjective reality. In efficient totalitarian states, all official media will present just one reality, defined by the political supremos. In capitalist

societies, there are elites at the highest levels of a range of institutions. Although these orders and institutions are in some competition with each other, their leaders have common interests across the institutional boundaries in preserving the wealth, status, and power that accrues to elites (Etzioni-Halevy, 1989; Rubinstein, 1981).

4. Readers and viewers will be offered a consensual view of a unified society whose internal difficulties and problems stem from either the disruptive or otherwise deviant behavior of disaffected individuals and groups or from international factors over which the government has no control.

If these propositions are generally valid, then textual analyses need to demonstrate what other perspectives might have been presented. For example, in their analyses of TV documentation of the industrial strikes at British Leyland automobile works in 1975, the Glasgow Media Group (1976) pointed out that at no time was it mentioned that low investment in machinery or incompetent management might have had a greater relevance than the strike-prone dispositions of the manual workers. On the TV news during the period, there were 63 references to the striking workers, 16 to management, and 3 to investment levels. The authors report that in this period each British Leyland worker was operating with machinery worth £1,000, whereas each equivalent Toyota worker had £11,780 worth of machinery. The implications of these figures are that a comparative analysis of Japanese car makers and British Leyland might have shown that low investment precluded comparable productivity, an analysis of where British capital was being deployed would have shown that it was being sunk into property rather than manufacturing or into investments overseas, and an analysis of the organization of British Leyland would have revealed it to have been managerially extraordinarily inefficient. If any of these had been investigated, perhaps blame would have been redirected toward the elites of government, investors, and senior management.

The object of this illustration is not to argue for a particular political point of view but to show how the possibility of framing alternative perspectives requires detailed local knowledge. If that is so, it is impossible to devise general coding frames and difficult to offer more than general advice about ways of analyzing texts for possible misrepresentation. The best that Fowler (1991) can do, could do, and actually does is illustrate how he was able to analyze newspapers for misleading presentations, whereas the Glasgow Media Group (1976, 1980, 1982) performed a similar service for TV news. Where alternative perspectives are demonstrable, which particular interpretations are veridical will inevitably be contentious (Billig, 1987).

The only general-purpose analytic tools in such situations are questions:

1. Is the representation of events the only plausible description and explanation of what happened? Clues that other perspectives are possible and plausible will be that not all sides of any conflict are given opportunities to present their points of view.
2. Is any account apparently neutral or are evaluative terms used to discredit some of the actors? Does the differential treatment coincide with the interests and loyalties of the audience, the media employees, or the media owners?
3. Are the reports of other channels or papers all in agreement in other countries as well as within a country?

Simple Falsification in the Media

If a single topic is selected for examination, wars are probably the events for which media falsification is most evident, even in quasi-open societies. If a single source were to be cited, then Knightley's (1975) historical charting of the activities of war correspondents captures the main points through a succession of examples. From the 1850s, copies of what has been printed have been kept so that the international archive is comprehensive and complete enough for extended examination by those with the resources and opportunity to do so. In his necessarily selective history, Knightley attempts to portray the influence of the various forces at work, to note which determine what gets published, and how this in turn influences those who read and quote the accounts.

As Knightley (1975) illustrates, from the American Civil War to World War II, battles that never took place were given graphic accounts, whereas others that did escaped all mention. Defeats become victories. Casualties disappear. Winning can be held out as a prospect almost until the final defeat. In some ways, the 1914 to 1918 war reporting was perhaps the most impressive cover-up operation, with the public learning little from the newspapers about the scale of the casualties, the deaths from disease, or the mutinies. The tactics of sending men with rifles "over the top" into impassable mud and barbed wire to be machine gunned in the thousands was not reflected in the headlines of the daily press of any of the combatants. Vietnam may prove to be a significant watershed. Of Knightley's wars, it is the one whose denouement appears to have been seriously affected by honest reporting that defied the censors. The intimacy of the TV coverage of the Gulf War now poses questions about the feasibility of open societies mounting operations in which they begin to suffer heavy casualties. In that same war, the massive difference between the lowest and highest estimates of Iraqi casualties shows that information can still be suppressed by closed and open societies. Of course, what gets into the media is in part or almost totally filtered by governments and military authorities who are able to control what is officially released for reporting. The second filter is the media proprietors or directors.

Two main messages emerge from an examination of media coverage of armed conflicts: The first is that in-group/out-group differentiation reaches extreme proportions. The second is that in-group losses are minimized and out-group losses maximized to and beyond the limits of credibility. There are classic examples of both where the eventual facts are not disputed. After the Japanese attack on Pearl Harbor on December 7, 1941, the *British Daily Express* carried the headline, "Jap Plane-Carrier and 4 U-Boats Sunk." The first official U.S. communique was delayed until December 12 and then reported "one old battleship and a destroyer" as having been sunk.

The reality was more devastating: five battleships sunk and three badly damaged, three cruisers and three destroyers badly damaged, 200 planes destroyed, and 2,344 people killed. The full extent of the damage was never released officially. At various times up to 1967, occasional communiques and leaks raised the figures. Even today, the official guidebook at the memorial of the Arizona omits the data.

Somewhat earlier in Europe, mainly English skies witnessed "The Battle of Britain," with Churchill growling out, "Never in the field of human conflict has so much been owed by so many to so few." The British Air Ministry reported shooting down 2,698 German planes; the final revised figure was 1,733. Without a touch of irony, in 1945 the Ministry appeared to be boasting of British honesty when it noted that the British exaggeration was 55%, whereas the Germans overestimated British losses by 220%. More recently, the CNN network in its relayings of Iraqi television broadcasts revealed how a steady

imminent final victory of Iraqi forces was converted quite suddenly by Iraqi TV into an honorable peace settlement—on humanitarian grounds.

These facts are consistent with the apparent assumption by governments and military commanders that national morale (and internal political stability) remains higher if there is a minimization of in-group losses and out-group victories and a maximization of in-group victories and out-group losses.

Interpretations of Events: Overt Biases

Whether one adopts the more general realistic conflict theory of Sherif (1966), the powerful realization of the same issues through the social identity theory of Tajfel and Turner (1979) or Turner et al.'s (1987) recasting in the form of self categorizing theory, social psychological theory and empirical evidence agree on the notions of in-group/out-group differentiation in which distinctiveness on valued dimensions is given a crucial role. When this principle is combined with the various self-serving biases characteristic of attributions, the picture of what to expect in press or TV reports of wars is clear. The differences between the in-group of "us" and the out-group of "them" are maximized.

If God is invoked, then He (!) is on our side. If Justice is invoked, she is on our side. The answer to any question about who started any war is them. If the facts just cannot be constructed to allow this accusation, then it is possible to invent and use ideas of "preemptive counterattacks" or to make out how we were "forced" to act because "vital interests" or "security" were threatened. If it is asked why they are fighting us, then there is a reasonably high probability that their leaders are mad, bad, or both. If a list is drawn up of the major opponents of the Western alliances since the 1930s, it is difficult to recall enemy leaders who were not so categorized, from Hitler, Mussolini, Tojo, and Stalin to Khomeini, Gadahfi, and Saddam Hussein. At the least, they have been portrayed as fanatics who contrast with our moderation and reasonableness.

The armed forces of the enemy are quickly denounced for a standard list of atrocities: bombing or otherwise attacking civilian targets, especially hospitals and refugee camps; mutilating, torturing, and killing prisoners and civilians in occupied territories; raping and killing women and children; and looting. In contrast, our armed forces fight a clean war within the rules of the Geneva Convention. If any of our individual combatants are ever identified as being guilty of barbaric acts, these are cited as exceptions, the perpetrators being under enormous stress, temporarily deranged, or righteously indignant. In short, the explanations tend to locate blame in the circumstances or in the fleeting or uncontrollable states of the individual. This contrasts with the evil and cruelty of the enemy represented as general, stable, and controllable characteristics (Weiner, 1985), an expression of their normative characteristics.

Some people might suggest that this is a caricature at worst, a stereotype at best. Check the newspapers. Saddam Hussein and his armed forces have been portrayed exactly in these terms as soon as the Iraq-Iran war finished and he turned his forces onto the Kurds, the Marsh Arabs, and the Kuwaitis. At this point, when these arguments are being presented orally, two objections are raised. The first is that the description of Iraq in the Western media is a fair reflection of reality. That may be, but then why was the West previously portraying him more sympathetically and supporting Saddam Hussein against Iran, or at an earlier time, Stalin against Hitler? Why was the West (and its media) so ambivalent about Hitler and the Nazis during the 6 years of antisemitism and bellicose pretensions that preceded his Blitzkrieg? Either it has to be argued that leaders and their policies change from being good to being evil or that representations of them are contingent on whether they are part of a contemporary in-group or not. (It must be noted that for all the rhetoric about the virtues of democracy and the rights of the common people to self-determination, many of the military interventions since 1945 of the old imperial powers and the United States have been to secure the positions of unelected rulers in one-party or no-party totalitarian states.)

The simplest resolution of any dispute along these lines is to suggest that some of the accusations about the conduct of the enemy are probably well-founded in fact but to add that enemy media are probably able to cite comparable outrages by our armed forces and commanders. The misrepresentations lie in a pretense that we and our allies are better than we actually are. We suppress the evil actions of our allies when they are allies and then publicize and exaggerate them when they become enemies. We explain away our own evil.

This is not to deny that some regimes are more awful than others. There is no doubt that some armed forces are less barbarous and ruthless than others. What is being denied is that we are as virtuous and they are as evil as our media represent.

Interpretation of Events: Covert Biases

In some utopian world dreamed of by long-established news reporters, such as Alistair Cooke, news broadcasts would tell the public about significant events that have occurred in international, national, regional, and local arenas; it would seek to represent alternative rational and reasonable perspectives on the events if and when these exist. In the previous section, both overt falsifications of facts and reasons for such falsifications have been mentioned.

The covert biases have been studied more by academics in applied linguistics, communication science, and media studies than by social psychologists and sociologists. Of these, some would readily admit to political commitments to certain causes that they see as matters of truth and social justice. Most would probably insist that unbiased presentations are a chimera and settle for a more balanced offering of alternatives. Here a somewhat different value position will be taken. Insofar as analyses conducted can be shown to reveal consistent biases that favor the interests of some social groups rather than others, while at the same time the media claim to be objective and balanced, then there are inconsistencies between words and actions that invite or require psychological explanations.

News selected for TV presentation is generally accepted as that which can be treated sensationally. Bad news is better news than good news. For television, that which provides striking visual images is preferable to that which does not. Violence and its consequences rank highly as newsworthy in the United Kingdom and the United States, especially if suffering associates of the victims can be brought in front of the cameras. Accounts of the causes and progress of foreign wars are subordinated to the portrayed anguish of its victims. Conflicts are heavily personalized and particularized with much less attention to the political issues underpinning the disputes (see Galtung & Ruge, 1973).

Presumably, audience research by the media has shown what kind of news coverage attracts the largest audiences, and that is what is offered. If audiences did not prefer the anguish of victims of violence to critical analysis, then the media would not show such scenes. If speculation about the future were not preferred to accounts of the past, they would not be included.

Commentary

Within limits, the media supply what their public wants. The limits differ for publicly and privately owned media. The privately owned media are expected to maximize their profits, which depend on revenues from commercial and other advertisers. No advertisements, no media, unless individual subscriptions and purchases suffice to cover the costs, which at present they do not. Even within the law, neither public nor private media are free. Normally, they are franchised and licensed by central or local government. If particular media are too critical of government, their licenses may not be renewed. Hence, they are under political pressure not to be too hostile to governments. Because the revenue for private media will depend on the profitability of the advertisers, and the media are simultaneously part of the commercial world, their interest lies with political parties that favor big business. (Only when proprietors with political ambitions judge their chances of success to rest with populist support do they join more liberal or left-wing parties.) Editors and reporters who fail to conform to owners' wishes can be and are dismissed.

If media are publicly financed statutory bodies, they may appear to be more independent of economic and political influences. Any economic influence can only be indirect, but political influence is exerted directly, both by having such corporations run by committees made up of government appointees and by governments threatening to modify or actually modifying the charters under which they operate.

As will be seen in Chapter 9, the public at large is discriminating in its assessment of the trustworthiness of news and documentaries and is particularly incredulous of "the yellow press" or "tabloids." It does trust, however, both the quality newspapers and the TV news. Analyses conducted of news both on TV and in newspapers have shown that this trust is in fact somewhat naive (Fowler, 1991; Glasgow Media Group, 1976; van Dijk, 1991).

Both bias and falsification are normative. Both operate mainly to support governments and their institutions and to offer representations consistent with the interests of their financial sponsors and owners. Although what is selected and what is represented about the selections are a version of reality, the perspective offered is liable to be consistent with the preferences of elites. Representing objective reality or alternative interpretations of events will not be given primacy. When alternative interpretations are offered, these are likely to still be within the framework of the elites of the establishment. Controversies among members of elites may be real skirmishes as they jockey for relative gains, but they will be public performances rather than mortal combats.

The net effect is a dynamic stability in which competition for power, wealth, and status is constrained and confined to those who are already among the elite of their own order. To the extent that this is true, what is represented through the media is a charade, spectacles with the appearance of conflicts, debate, and discussion but that will lead only to minor readjustments at the margins, at the most, and in all probability to none at all. If this interpretation is valid, the public performances of elite members of the various social orders are conveying misleading impressions to the public at large.

The reconstruction of the past and the redefinition of the present can be facilitated by writing diaries and letters that misrepresent reality. This is also true for autobiographies and biographies. The British media tycoon, Robert Maxwell, commissioned one of his senior staff to write what reads more like a hagiography than a life history (Haines, 1988). The contrast between this work and the subsequent posthumous account by Bower (1991) provides as strong a discrepancy as one is likely to encounter between perspectives on the same person. Obituaries and gravestones add to the possibilities of creating heroes out of lesser mortals.

Media Presentation of
Research Methods, Statistics, and Reality

That 9 out of 10 cats might be persuaded into preferring YumYum to Brand X is as simple to arrange as it is to find 9 out of 10 film stars to wash with YumYum rather than Brand X. This is not the same as finding that 90% of a random selection of domestic cats will show the same preference. There are many ways in which surveys, observations, and experiments can be constructed to give desired answers, but properly trained physical and social scientists have been trained to know what these are and how to avoid them. The general public is not trained in these specialities, and neither are they trained to be wary of graphical displays and statistics (see Graphics, p. 203). It will be argued later in this section that there are problems of presenting risks and probabilistic information in forms that are comprehensible and translatable into guidelines for action, but these issues are separable from deliberate attempts to mislead. Governments are notorious for pretending that they are doing better than they are in achieving their aims. Crime figures can be cut much more quickly by changing what is to be counted than by preventing their occurrence. Rates of solving crimes are improved more quickly by catching someone who will agree to confess to more than he or she has committed. Waiting times for hospital treatment in the United Kingdom are going down steadily; people in need of treatment are simply not put onto the waiting lists. The bases for calculating unemployment rates in the United Kingdom have been changed on average nearly twice a year for the past 16 years. Bureaucrats can find convenient paper solutions to real problems, and some of the people are fooled some of the time.

It is with these kinds of lies and deception that this section is concerned. It differs from preceding sections in drawing more attention to means of deception: the hows and whys of misleading information in the public domain. The particular focus is on the occasions when deception is likely to be practiced and how the credibility of scientific expertise can be prostituted in the service of false claims that may exaggerate performance, profits, or underestimate losses. The involvement of government and the media is included because, as with the other issues dealt with in the chapter, it would be absurd to neglect sociological perspectives and the systemic influences that encourage or discourage falsification. How these are operating will be illustrated mainly through brief descriptions of cases, most of which are taken from Crossen (1994). In *The Tainted Truth*, Crossen catalogs the kinds of difficulties experienced with statistics and surveys, and the abuse of both, with a minor theme of faulty experimental designs. (All the American examples are taken from Crossen's text to reduce the incidence of individual citation.)

Background

Just as Etzioni-Halevy's (1989) thesis that corruption and lying will increase when elites from different sectors of society merge their interests, so Crossen (1994) notes similar dangers for academics tempted away from the search for truth into other social orders. Elsewhere (Chapter 8), the issues of fraud in science per se are mentioned; there, the motivation in the cases cited appeared to be mainly fame rather than fortune, although a modest fortune may well be linked to fame. Crossen's cases appear to be driven mainly by considerations of wealth leading status, and most of them concern selectivity in research methods and designing and reporting studies with a clear end in view of what the desired results should be.

The ends vary. Pharmaceutical companies that have developed products to the preclinical and clinical trial stages hope for positive results that will be accepted by the gatekeepers for society (e.g., Food and Drug Administration). They may employ biomedical experts in universities and research institutes to conduct such trials. In straight commercial competition, Coca-Cola and Pepsi-Cola have been chronically engaged in disputes about the relative qualities of their products for years, and each conducts experiments and surveys to claim its preeminence. The health hazards of cholesterol levels, smoking, or working with asbestos have been contentious issues for many years. Environmentally friendly products have appeared on the market in the past 15 years and questions can be asked about their status as pollutants. What kinds of policy and practice do the citizenry wish the government to follow and will polls give a government the information it needs? Crossen (1994) reviews studies in each of these areas.

Although empirical evidence is clearly critical to such problems and experts at a given time will have criteria to evaluate inadequacies of testing, some issues are easier to resolve than others. If working with a particular substance increases the probability of employees contracting a condition that is also caused by exposure to many other substances and if the effect is rare and does not show for 20 years, it is going to be very difficult to judge whether a particular individual's debility was work related. Even if it was in fact so, whether an employer should be liable for damages is contestable. All work is potentially hazardous, as is all living. Everybody dies eventually from some combination of factors. On the other hand, coal mining in bygone days was known to be a premature killer of large numbers of workers through disease and pit accidents, even though no compensation was paid for diseases contracted. In 1994, T and N Plc UK set aside £100 million to meet claims for ill health among ex-employees who had worked with asbestos. Although asbestos miners and users delayed their acceptance of the validity of the evidence linking asbestos to lung diseases, their original use of the substance was probably not in cynical disregard of human health. Its ill effects were not known, likewise for tobacco smoking. Claims for work-induced or proximity-related cancers are already on the agenda as problematic scientific issues. Some of these cases may be matters of defensive companies commissioning research with paid scientists arranging the data in their favor, whereas litigants select their scientists to cite evidence leading to opposite conclusions. The current state of knowledge can be simply inadequate to the questions posed, and where the statistical correlates are weak and long term, it may never be possible to translate them into defensible decisions in individual cases.

It should also be noted, however, that governments in the quasi democracies have acted in several ways that have reduced the stringency of public protection. First, with the exception of the United States, they have reduced funding from their inspecting and checking bodies; instead of charging companies for independent services, Western governments have cut back their own gatekeeping. Second, governments have simultaneously reduced funding to universities and encouraged them to strengthen their links with industry and commerce. Academic salaries have lagged behind those of comparable professionals in the past 15 years by perhaps 50% against peers in the public service and double that against lawyers, doctors, scientists, engineers, and architects in the private sector. As a result, more commercially funded research consultancies and projects have become available for those academics willing and able to take advantage of them. Among such projects are those that assess risks of environmental pollution, side effects of drugs, efficacy of treatments, and effects of food concoctions, additives, and preservatives. Companies have vested interests in certain outcomes, and so do the universities and their staff. Overheads accrue to university coffers. Staff will receive honoraria and other perquisites to facilitate the research and its dissemination, provided that the results are positive. If they are not, there may be contractual clauses preventing publication. There may be transfers of funding to other institutions. The objectivity and skepticism of the scientists may become modified by the blandishments. Results can be fixed, techniques can be preselected, and sampling can be optimized for positive results.

Insofar as this happens, it is another small set of examples of the increased probability of lying and deception when elites cease to be independent of each other. Government science can afford, and has an obligation, to be independent of commercial interests. Government-supported research in government-supported universities can also afford to be independent of commercial interests. Once the financial well-being of universities and their staffs become too dependent on links with industry and commerce, there is a danger of research becoming corrupted. This does not apply, of course, when there is no conflict of interest between company hopes and truth. Companies presumably have a built-in preference for honest results, especially if misleading results will lead to subsequent litigation and losses. At the margins, however, and no one knows how wide these are in particular cases, profits may take precedence over truth. Some of the whistle-blowing cases in Chapter 10 show how cynical of human suffering some economic decisions can be. Similarly, the health and safety standards currently exercised by some international companies in their African and Asian operations would not be tolerated in their home countries, implying that it is not their ethics so much as their cost-benefit analyses that maintain the standards for their home markets. The abrogation of responsibility by governments for the protection and well-being of their electorates from the profiting of business enterprises has been one of the hallmarks of the decline of the welfare state. (Governments have argued that these policies save public expenditure and increase efficiency, but because total U.K. taxation is higher now than 15 years ago, the claim that one tax, namely income tax, is at its lowest for over 50 years has to be one of the most misleading true statements claimed as an achievement by the U.K. government.)

The mass media enter the arena in three ways. First, they commission polls themselves. Second, they report the results of polls and scientific tests. Third, they allow advertising. For the first way, they may rely on instant phone-ins to gain estimates of the society's views and then pretend that their sample is representative. They can ask crudely biased forced-choice questions but publish answers without stating what the questions were. The whole range of survey errors that can be found listed in elementary textbooks are available for those who wish to obtain certain answers. Second, the media thrive on being first with the news. Discoveries of wonder drugs or health hazards make for dramatic stories. Arguments between experts about threats to health add zest to these audience participation shows that gain such high viewing figures, for example, the *Oprah Winfrey Show*. Third, the media might be expected to be theoretically responsible for scrutinizing the truthfulness of the advertisements they carry.

Again, there are conflicts of interest between the elites of sectors. If fresh evidence shows that a newly launched washing product fades the colors and rots the clothes, then reporting of this could lead to its manufacturer withdrawing its advertising from any TV, radio station, or newspaper that takes up the story too vigorously. Although many scientists will avoid appearing in chat shows that reduce issues to stark and improper clashes of uninformed opinions, others may be pleased to be famous for 15 minutes and to have their summer holidays paid for. As already suggested, the media announcements and discussions may be full of exciting sound and fury, but they fade fast. Typically, the incidents are skirmishes that keep audiences entertained but stop short of inflicting damage to either governing or commercial elites. These may, of course, be cumulative effects that build up long term into distrust and cynicism by viewers and listeners.

It may be helpful to set out the kinds of sequence where disputes and subsequent falsifications will not and may arise. Where the research and development procedures show early signs of product X being a failure, the research will be consigned to the archives. When product X continues to show promise and all investment yields uncontentious positive results, product X will be appreciated by everyone. The narrative that is problematic is one where

1. The company discovers or invents X, and X has commercial promise;
2. Further investment in evaluation yields some positive but some equivocal results;
3. a. The company or its evaluators or both develop beliefs beyond the evidence and fail to maintain appropriate controls and checks against overestimating the virtues or underestimating the negative features of X;

b. The evaluators come to see their wealth, power, and status as being contingent on the continuing sponsorship of the company and view this as more important than telling the truth;

4. The company is granted a license to market X and does so;

5. The efficacy or safety or both of X is contested by

a. Independent researchers, who may doubt and are unable to replicate the results claimed for X;

b. Rival companies;

c. Complaints by users of X;

d. Pressure groups whose ambits include X.

It is at the last stage that the shades of possible deception and delinquency are likely to emerge. Rival companies and pressure groups may be just as prone to misrepresent realities as the original company. The independence of researchers may be compromised by personal hatreds. Some of the users of X may themselves be making fraudulent claims and lying for personal profit or possibly trying to blackmail the company. None of Crossen's (1994) cases hint at hidden motives of other researchers. Each of the other three appear among her examples.

Self-Fulfilling Prophecies in
Product Evaluation Research

The main issues that arise in the evaluation of empirical investigations of the efficacy of treatments or risks of illness are in the context and design. The rules for checking credibility of claims about research with commercial consequences are very similar to those listed by Ekman (1985/1992) for estimating the likelihood of a statement being a lie in interpersonal encounters. Who paid for the work to be done is the first question, followed by whether they had a vested interest in the outcome. Who did the work and their vested interests in particular outcomes is a second. Further questions would relate to the kinds of experimental design used, the characteristics of the sample and their mode of selection, the objectivity of the measurements taken, and the size of the effects obtained.

Davidson is cited by Crossen (1994) as showing that of 107 comparisons of new and old treatments where the new treatment drug was manufactured by the company paying for the research, there was no case in which the new drug was pronounced to be inferior. This does not mean that any of these results are invalid. Journal policy customarily dictates that studies with no significant differences are not accepted. If a new drug is found to be inferior to existing ones, this will most likely be discovered in its development phase, and its manufacturer will presumably not market it until it is equal to or better or cheaper or both than its rivals. Davidson's fact needs a contrast of some kind to be indicative and interpretable.

One of the cases cited by Crossen (1994) shows the extent to which conflicts of interest can surround a controversy. In the disputes over the efficacy of Retin-A to reduce skin wrinkles, the lead researcher of the two positive studies received more than a quarter of a million dollars in grants from the manufacturer with a further $689,000 subsequently. He was a paid consultant to the company and received 13 honoraria in 1988. The person who wrote the favorable editorial comment on the first positive publication received $3,500 prior to the editorial and $9,000 subsequently. Her laboratory had received $393,000 before the editorial and $185,000 afterward. Crossen lists seven design flaws in the crucial study. Such contiguities cannot be interpreted unequivocally to imply undue temptation for researchers to produce some results rather than others, but social psychology is replete with studies that show how hopes and expectations can lead to actions that bring about consequences that would not have occurred in the absence of the motivational set (Rosenthal, 1966). Clearly, evaluation trials cost money and the sponsoring company is the only source likely to pay for the research, but the payments to academics combined with the apparent flaws in the research serve to raise questions about the credibility of the results.

The dispute between Bluestone and Cantekin over the efficacy of a treatment for otitis media has similar financial ingredients to the Retin-A case, except that Cantekin refused money, insisted on what he saw as more objective and prolonged evaluations, and came to negative conclusions. His paper was not accepted by the *New England Journal of Medicine* after his university asserted the prior rights of Bluestone. Various official inquiries as to the relative merits of the two data sets did not take sides. Cantekin's data were taken from him, and he was removed from various institutional positions and relocated. Subsequent international research is reported as vindicating Cantekin. Without further evidence, it is not possible to say whose story corresponds more closely to the facts. The versions are too different to be a matter of simple perspective; someone looks to be in error, seriously and persistently so, but refuses to admit it. Bluestone and Cantekin should know, and so may others, but there is no court ruling as yet.

In the field of nutrition, Crossen (1994) selected the continuing controversy about the role of oat bran in diets and its efficacy in reducing cholesterol levels. The Quaker Oats Company conducted research itself and then helped to sponsor university-based research into relations between the consumption of oat bran and levels of cholesterol. Publication in the *Journal of the American Diabetic Association* in 1986 was cited by the press as suggestions that people should be eating oat bran to lower their cholesterol levels and thereby reduce the risk of heart disease. Oat bran was added to 300 products before Sacks and Swain (cited in Crossen, 1994) published a study refuting the cholesterol level claims. This work was heralded by the media as a devastating rebuttal, but subsequent rebuttals of their study also began to appear in journals. The essence of the Sacks and Swain claim was that it was the bulk and not the quality of the bran that was the important factor, although there were also subsidiary questions about the significance of the actual and acute percentage changes over a period of weeks for the long-term morbidity rates of heart disease. The criticisms of their study focused on its mainly young, healthy and lean sample. The original promotion, however, did not suggest that only particular subgroups of the population would benefit from bran, and Quaker was accused of escalating what may have been "a 3.3% reduction in cholesterol into a 20 per cent reduction in the risk of heart disease" (Crossen, p. 50).

This study is quoted because of its ambiguities and uncertainties. That the addition of bran to diet did become a popular fetish is a fact. Companies with vested interests fed the propaganda on what appear to have been experimental rather than field studies. The media intervened explosively, first promoting the positive and then the no-help view.

A great variety of foodstuffs, however, come and go as life-shortening debilitating or life-extending-enhancing comestibles: coffee, tea, wine, beer, sugar, fruits, vegetables, red meat, oily fish, saturated and polyunsaturated fats, yogurt, and so on. When limes and lemons were introduced to be eaten on long sea voyages, the incidence of scurvy among sailers plummeted. The effects were dramatic, and subsequently, sound scientific explanations could be given for the results. Such identifiable deficiencies in diets still occur in many parts of the world, but the nutritional arguments in the Western world seem to turn around more complex quantitative and probabilistic issues that possibly have serious effects but only for an unpredictable minority.

Other dramatic cases discussed by Crossen (1994) include pelvic infections from contraceptive shields, silicone implants and their deterioration, and the environmental merits of disposable versus cloth diapers; in particular, this last case illustrates the complexities of the amount of information needed to analyze the issue in full and decide on the limits for the fullness. Are the pesticides on the cotton plants to be a legitimate part of the argument or not?

Across the range of such cases, it is certainly possible to ask which side is distorting reality and knowingly doing so and to ask which side is abusing statistical analyzes and the tenets of good experimental design. It has already been suggested that outsiders might be prone to adopt a perspective that is primarily suspicious that the big companies are the deceivers rather than their critics. Some disputes, however, are between companies and not between companies and a public watchdog. It is tempting to suggest that environmentalists have ethical and humanitarian concerns and will therefore be less likely to falsify evidence. The cases set out by Crossen (1994), however, tend to show serious design faults or reasoning on both sides of disputes, even when environmentalists are parties to the dispute.

Related to this is the question of the burden of proof. Risk analysis is a newly advanced technique for assessing likely frequencies of rare events. Vaccines protect great majorities, but they kill a few. Surgical operations have success and fail rates. Risks of earthquakes can be assessed. What is not predictable is which will occur, when and where. Individuals want to know if they will survive an operation— yes or no? For them, the outcome is a binding one of dead or alive. Risk analysis also requires estimates in its presuppositions, and if these are wrong, so are the answers. When this form of analysis has been used in commercial disputes, it can be the values of the presuppositions that differ. Do these differences arise, however, because there are genuine disagreements or are the presuppositions adjusted to modify the outcome? The waters are muddy and possibly murky, but on whom the mud should be stuck may be impossible to ascertain.

By its very nature, statistics is concerned with uncertainties, and many disputes concern outcomes that may not be apparent for many years to come, by which time it will be too late to reverse the consequences of the precipitating actions. It is irrational, however, that products or processes be banned because they just might have negative effects on human beings or the environment, unless there is some indication as to what those effects could be. It is logically and empirically impossible to demonstrate negative effects; all that can be shown is the absence of specified particular effects. Currently, some environmentalist objections are based on the kind of arguments (e.g., greenhouse effects, ozone layer depletion) supported by indicative but statistically based evidence that can be interpreted in other ways. In contrast, societies demand that drug companies have their products vetted, the burden of proof shifts to companies. In between are problem items such as supplements to animal feedstuffs, animals as sources of infection, and radiated foods. For each of these, in the United Kingdom new practices have been introduced without publicity and only when reports have been leaked or alert citizens have pursued matters have the issues been brought to light. Government spokespeople have then promptly denied the existence of risks to the public, but no evidence has been made available. As an example, spongiform encephalitis is now well entrenched in British cattle. They caught it because they were fed infected sheep brains as a fattening supplement. It was not expected that the disease would jump across a species. When it was discovered that infected cattle were being slaughtered for beef, questions were asked. The minister gave an assurance that the disease could not cross to human beings, but no evidence to support the case was forthcoming. Beef sales slumped, and currently, approximately 1,000 at-risk cattle are still being slaughtered each month in an effort to eradicate the disease within 5 years. Carcasses are supposed to be burned. The case is a classical one of what, from an observer's point of view, looks to have been a risky strategy to increase profits going awry but then being concealed, followed by unfounded claims about safety and drastic subsequent action to eradicate the disease. Britain's chicken flocks have a very high incidence of salmonella (70%), presumably spread through the factory conditions in which they live. The incidence of human food poisoning resulting is unknown. When this story first broke, the minister in charge denounced the concealment of relevant information and demanded that the public be better protected; shortly afterward, she resigned from her ministry. Infection remains.

Graphics

With Crossen's (1994) emphasis on concealed and biased experimental designs, loaded and inadequate sampling, and selective presentation of results as practices that enable scientists to misrepresent their data and to proceed to excessive or qualitatively wrong interpretations, it would be incomplete not to append a note on the ways graphics are used to offer visually misleading impressions.

As already mentioned, governments and their agencies publish statistics of trends in rates of unemployment, crime, and a wealth of other data about populations. Companies in the financial sector publish graphics indicating possible growth rates for investments in their products. Companies, public bodies, and charities publish annual reports in which numerical data are frequently given expression in graphics.

Graphics can misrepresent reality, just as texts can. Like language, the construction of graphics is based on conventions that have a consensus among the academics and teachers who use them in their disciplines. The conventions are intended to summarize sets of numbers in a form that renders relationships between variables more easily seen and understood.

How the breaking of these conventions can mislead is illustrated humorously by Huff (1969) and more seriously by MacDonald-Ross (1977), who includes graphs, bars, circles, pie charts, and maps among his illustrations. The conventions for graphics are these:

1. The axes should be orthogonal.
2. The units of the variables as drawn should be the visual equivalents of their numerical differences.
3. The variables should be labeled precisely.
4. Both variables should have a value of zero at the origin of the coordinates.
5. Any lines drawn to connect points on the graph should not presume linearity unless there is some justification for this presumption—for

example, if there are only two points on the X axis and the gap between them is wide, the relationship should be drawn as a straight line.

6. Any extrapolation should be clearly marked as such.

Misleading representations can arise because demands of aesthetics, humor, or attractiveness are given precedence over veridicality. Some arise for mixed reasons. If iconic representations are used so that bags are used to represent quantities of money and height is supposed to be the critical variable, then a doubling of the heights gives an eightfold increase in volume. This may or may not be intended. With graphs there are various tricks. By choosing particular cutoffs on the Y axis, quantities on the X axis can be made to look as though there is no change or great change, just by the choice of intervals on the Y axis. Large changes can be minimized and small ones maximized according to the political or economic preferences of the authors.

The extent to which people are misled by appearances has yet to be investigated. James (1995) has developed a test that is designed to find out the extent to which people are aware of and can specify the conventions being broken. Those persons who made higher scores were more likely to be able to give reasons why constructors would abuse conventions. They were also more likely to be wary of statements, claims, offers, and other lines offered by companies and authorities. The wariness inventory developed for this work has yet to be analyzed for its structural characteristics, but it has promise as an instrument for measuring alertness to the tricks played on the public in general and consumers in particular (Robinson & James, 1995).

Not that scientists are immune to the temptation to render the visual representations of their results more orderly and more consistent with their hypotheses than the individual readings warrant. Perhaps a survey of psychology journals would reveal less than perfect editorial quality control over published diagrams.

Commentary

Crossen (1994) reports a survey she commissioned from Gallup in which she obtained superficially inconsistent replies. Of the respondents, 76% agreed, at least for the most part, that you can find a scientific study that proves just about anything you want to prove, whereas 86% said that references to scientific research to back up a story increased its credibility and 82% thought statistics and 81% thought statements by well-known experts had similar effects. They had more faith in scientific claims about causes of disease (81%) than in reports of surveys about people liking products (63%) or those about how people feel about political and social issues (54%).

There is a diversity of views in the population and a combination of trust and skepticism about science, which might be seen as fair reflection of reality. Evaluations of the likely truth of claims about the efficacy and safety of products or the state of public opinion about issues can be founded rationally only on properly collected empirical evidence. Weaknesses will occur in the planning, procedures, and data processing of relevant investigations. If these happen to be unbiased in the likely resultant errors, interpretations of results become more difficult. If the weaknesses consistently favor the emergence of the preferred result for investigators and sponsors, however, let the evaluators beware.

Those scientists who do fix data do a double disservice: a specific disservice to those put at risk by any misleading representation of the particular facts and a more general disservice in that they lessen the credibility of colleagues who do not cheat for their personal benefit.

As Perkin (1989) argues more generally, the decline in the perceived trustworthiness of professional elites in the eyes of the public stems in part from their emergence as groups of people seeking enhanced power, wealth, and status in the same fashion as other groups. Their expertise is not always applied for the benefit of society but can be for the advancement of the members of their own profession. Proven incompetence and dishonesty by some members of a profession help to accentuate a general skepticism. Those scientists who have put falsification above truth for personal advantage are no exception.

Just as Ekman's (1985/1992) table of questions for lie detection (Chapter 4) provides a flowchart for checking suspicions, so the text of Crossen (1994) and its elaboration here offer suggestions as to how those who know enough about survey methods, experimental design, and data processing, presentation, and interpretation about claims made about polls, statistics, and testings can check suspicion.

If there are insufficient details in reports for evaluation or if conventions are broken, then one asks why. The answers need not imply any deliberate attempt to mislead, but if there are too many departures from the conventions of scientific presentation, it becomes sensible to ask whether or not these are in a direction that is consistent with some vested interest in obscuring or misrepresenting the true state of affairs.

CHAPTER EIGHT

Falsification in Particular
Social Orders and Institutions

In Chapter 8, a selection of social orders and institutions is offered to illustrate how and why degrees of deception and lying enter into the activities. There are several reasons for the selection presented. First, it can be noted that there is considerable variation in the extent to which lies and deception are required, normal, acceptable, or taboo. A generalization might be made: The more competitive the situation and the more serious the consequences of winning or losing, the more likely it is that deception will be normative or required. For some games, the capacity for misleading opponents is a crucial skill for success. In times of war, sophisticated powers deploy considerable resources to disinformation, as it is called.

Second, social institutions have peculiarities such that the procedural rules or norms caricature the original functions of the activities. In law courts and in the British Parliament, at least, the adversarial qualities of the regulative and procedural rules have led to a ritualization of the means to the detriment of the ends. British parliamentary debates are not rational and reality related inquiries to further the improvement of the society for its members. In the United Kingdom and the United States, courts of law are like gladiatorial contests for supremacy between prosecution and defense rather than a cooperative concern that "right be done." Both focus on a clash of persons rather than on tasks. Perhaps both would benefit from the kind of radical reform that unfortunately seems to occur only after destructive wars or revolutions.

Third, the observations imply that various orders are predisposed to generate deceptions based on different motives. Salespeople and advertisers seem to be bent on testing the limits of what will be tolerated to sell their wares; there seems to be a pleasure in outwitting the rule makers as well as a desire to maximize sales. There is a pleasure in probing the limits. This is not the same as the duping delight per se of artists and certain other academics. Arrogance is more likely to afflict scientists. It is more difficult to comment on the motives of scientists, drug evaluators, and engineers whose forged data must eventually culminate in disastrous exposure. In each of those areas, reality eventually wins out over inaccurate constructions of it! Some of the examples cited under religion and science look more like prostitution, a perversion of the essence of one's profession for personal gain of some kind.

The central message will be that there is no common theme. Motives for deception are varied, situational pressures differ, and probabilities of condemnation or commendation differ. This is not surprising, and explanations are understandable without recourse to arcane theorizing. What can be developed is a taxonomy and rationale for the classification adopted.

Peculiarities of Political Falsifications

Chapters 6 and 7 offered illustrative examples of antecedents and consequences of falsifications, and several of these were drawn from media reports about activities in the political order. Some concealments and denials arose from politicians accepting rewards for using their political positions to raise or promote interests of commercial persons or organizations. Others were essentially political, securing alliances overseas, for example, but doing so with impolitic and clandestine operations. Yet others combined the political and economic, whereby aid in an outward direction was linked to the beneficiary buying goods that would ameliorate unemployment in the donor country. Examples could have been given of government contracts being awarded to companies that also happened to have supported the party in government with generous donations to party funds.

Each of these derives from the power of politicians to make decisions that they have to and are expected to make. Some of the processes are necessarily confidential, and some of the decisions are possibly arbitrary; tenders for contracts may be indistinguishable. As Bok (1978) argues and illustrates, however, governments are prone to abuse secrecy. They can cite "in the national interest" to conceal activities that are in flagrant violation of declared policies and statements made. These affairs may well accrue benefits to politicians and their parties but would attract condemnation if brought into the open. Such issues are likely to involve the highest levels: presidents, prime ministers, and their closest colleagues. When these affairs operate on the grandest scale, they are also likely to be very well organized and, if exposed, most fervently denied and defended. Richard Nixon was reelected by a substantial majority after the *Washington Post* had broken into the Watergate story. Other presidents and premiers have survived attempted exposures of their concealments and falsifications, and the extent of their duplicity may not emerge until some years after their deaths.

The first peculiarity of politicians derives directly from Lord Acton's warning that power corrupts and absolute power corrupts absolutely. This generalization was presumably intended as a warning rather than a statement of fact, and of course, the political world has its share of honest people dedicated to their view of the good of their community, but quasi-democratic societies have structured the politician's career with hazards that render progress difficult to achieve without succumbing to some of the temptations presented. The power is temporary, and the temptations to exploit opportunities for socially and personally beneficial ends must be considerable; wealth that has been obtained dishonestly and even viciously can be settled in family and charitable trusts and in overseas accounts as well as in party coffers. In her three-way comparisons of France, the United Kingdom, and the United States, Etzioni-Halevy (1989) cites the French system as having had the least independence of the political order from the others and hence the greatest amount of corruption, concealed in the first instance and denied in the second.

The climactic denouements, however, may have had earlier beginnings. The first problem for would-be politicians is to be elected to whatever office they aspire to. Given the apparent rules of the game in modern states, opposing contestants are likely to try to undermine the character as well as the policies of their antagonists. Each contestant has therefore an interest in concealing negative features of personal autobiographical details and exaggerating or inventing positive features while trying to obtain evidence of falsifications and concealments by opponents. Such an adversarial focus encourages the likely incidence of reactive lies about previous misdemeanors and proactive lies about past achievements. Hart's candidature for the democratic nomination for the U.S. presidency appeared to fail because he was alleged to have lied about his sexual activities. President Johnson saw mileage in inventing a more heroic war record than the facts justified, and given the contemporary involvement of the United States in Vietnam, his apparent record may well have added to his presidential credibility.

There can also be proactive lies given as promises. Promises can be construed as lies when the candidate has no realistic intention of fulfilling these at the time they are uttered. In Britain, many of us believed that Prime Minister Major was lying in his 1992 reelection campaign when he promised no increase in taxation. He did renege on these undertakings within a few months, and dramatically so. The falsification was compounded by pretending that the "value-added taxes," special new taxes, and higher duties on various goods were not equivalent to 7p in the £ on income tax. President Bush incurred the same accusation as a result of his dramatized mouthing of "no new taxes." Once in office, equivocations and lies are frequent reactions to charges about mistakes made within a politician's orbit of responsibility. Denials of knowledge about the activities of more junior staff is also a frequent response. Did President Nixon know about Watergate? Did President Reagan know about Irangate? Did Prime Minister Thatcher know about sales of arms to Iraq? President Nixon vigorously denied knowledge about the Watergate until the tapes were heard. The others?

Sometimes, however, lies are told to cope with what could be seen as improper rather than fair questions. "Are there plans for devaluing sterling?" was judged to be a pernicious question when asked in the British House of Commons in 1976. If ministers are asked whether or not individuals arrested by foreign governments are spies, what is the minister to say? These questions are strong examples of what Bavelas and colleagues (1990) treat as not just no-win dilemmas but as sure losers whatever the reply. Presumably, such questions would not be asked by fellow politicians for whom the national interest was more important than party interest. Much parliamentary debate in Britain appears to be petty point scoring. What is said has no effect on the voting of members, and to view the exchanges as debates in which speeches might convince by rational appeals to evidence would be like mistaking children's accusations and counteraccusations for mature inquiries in pursuit of wise decisions. (In law courts, the contest between prosecution and defense does affect the outcome; in the British Parliament, it does not.)

In the face of pernicious questions, government spokespeople may well decide to lie. In the face of searching questions equivocations are much more likely. Successful equivocation was found by Bavelas et al. (1990) to be judged as better than telling the truth by their respondents. Bull (1994) found Major to be the party leader who gave the highest number of trouble-avoiding equivocal answers in the British 1992 general election.

If it is true that opponents and the public are liable to focus on and follow up the gaffs by politicians, it follows that successful surviving politicians will be those most adept at avoiding answers that offend sectors of the electorate. In an age of instant reception by as many of the electorate as choose to tune in to the media, any clear policy statement will have negative consequences for part of the electorate. It is the essence of political decisions that they involve redistributions of resources and opportunities. Giving more cake to A entails that the rest of the alphabet will have less. Generating more cake can ease threats, but differential distribution will still offend some more than others. How is a politician to appear to offer the hope of special rewards to every social category? Cultures vary in the extent to which lies are seen as positive and negative features in political behavior. The British world of politics has some customs that exhibit anomalous and apparently dissonant rules and practices.

Lying and accusations of lying are both forbidden in the House of Commons. The official guide on Questions of Procedure requires MPs "not to deceive or mislead Parliament and the public." In fact, MPs usually defend the importance of the need for concealment, justifying it in terms of the national or public interest, and then take a strong moralistic line about lying per se. When a recent attorney general confessed he had been "economical with the truth," this evoked laughter and was compared to Churchill's coining of "terminological inexactitude" as an acceptable synonym for a lie. Deft evasions and irrelevant but witty irrelevancies are typically received as adding to a festive argumentative atmosphere. On the other hand, any MP who goes bald on record (Brown & Levinson, 1987) and accuses a colleague of lying is given an immediate explicit opportunity to withdraw the accusation. If this is not done, the challenger is required to leave the chamber. The accused is under no obligation to do anything. It is the word *lie* that is anathema, an excellent anthropological example of a taboo that has become entirely a formal ritual. The substantive verbal exchanges carry all manner of concealments and deceptions for which speakers are not called to account or held responsible in any way that threatens their status. With one exception, no British minister in the past 20 years has resigned as an MP because he or she misled or deceived Parliament and the public, although the number of occasions when this could have been appropriate seems to have been rather high; more than one have resigned from the ministerships held.

The British Parliament is an extraordinarily polite if bizarre display of speechifying compared with many others. In some assemblies, verbal accusations of lying and deceit are endemic, and they can be accompanied by personal abuse and physical attacks. Yet the institution survives, although, of course, it must be remembered that in Europe only a minority of the countries have sustained democratically elected governments for more than the past half century.

As with the law courts, the adversarial systems of government and opposition encourage conflict rather than cooperation and the subordination of national to party interests. In turn, party interests require financial, media and bureaucratic support. Parties require elected members who need financial, media, and bureaucratic support to be elected. Electorates are more likely to return representatives who gain material benefits for their constituencies. At each stage, there are possibilities of interdependence between political and other orders. Politics is an insecure career. Given its competitive elections, for every successful candidate, there are others who are not elected. Not all political positions are pensionable. How are livings to be earned when not being paid for political services? If there is no such thing as a free lunch, it is improbable that there are enough free jobs for out-of-office periods and prudent politicians will keep options alive, and may act improperly to secure the necessary obligations.

Commentary

There are clearly formidable forces that impinge on careers in politics, most of which seem to expose politicians to potentially corrupting influences, which in turn will or may lead to concealments and lies. The need to have an independent source of income and the costs of being an elected member may well mean that politicians incur obligations and debts that their sponsors can call in if they wish to exert political influence.

The aspiring politician joins a party machine and a governmental apparatus that has long-established norms of conduct. Among these is the dilemma of being obliged to answer critical and perhaps pernicious questions for which no truthful answer would be politically positive. These used to be confined to debating chambers and town halls. Now, TV and radio have extended the audience and the immediacy of accountability, especially when interviewers adopt a hectoring and adversely critical approach to politicians. Questions can be insistent demands for specific promises about future actions or reactions to imagined situations. It is rare that a politician dares to point out that the interviewer is being malicious, foolish, or unreasonable. Hence, equivocation is often the honest and only feasible response to such questions.

The culture of political activity in quasi-democratic societies is caught up in a web of dilemmas. In part these arise because notions of accountability have changed. In part they arise because such governments have increased centralized control over the economy. They may be responsible for placing 50% of the national contracts by value. They have created many jobs that are in their gift, and they have control over the investment of national pension funds. At the same time as they are exposed to interrogation about some matters, they can be making appointments and spending money about which the public knows nothing.

For the foreseeable future, little change is likely. Periodic elections simply place others in comparable positions. Too much power is combined with too little real accountability and too great secrecy for the systems not to be vulnerable to corruption, cover-ups, and lies. Because it is the competing forces in these societies that created and sustain the political structure and culture, the societies themselves are responsible for what has resulted.

Lawyers in Courts

Some of the paradoxes about the means and ends of speech are at their most piquant in adversarially constituted courts of law. In these, juries of a random selection of ordinary citizens are expected to decide on "the facts" of any criminal and some civil cases and on the relationship between these facts and the relevant laws. One or more judges define the relevant laws for the juries and make explicit the contingency conditions for the jury's decision making. Juries have a double duty: to come to a judgment about the truth of the matter and to decide whether or not those facts constitute a breach of the relevant law(s) by the accused.

How is this achieved? One team of professional legal experts with its interrogators seeks to prove that the accused is guilty. A second team seeks to show that the evidence is consistent with reasonable doubt about the putative facts, that the facts are not covered by the law(s) cited as relevant, or that the constituted and regulative rules of legal procedure have not been properly followed. Both teams are composed of well-paid, highly qualified persons operating in an institutionalized framework with which they are familiar; they are colleagues as well as contestants.

In contrast, most lay witnesses have little or no knowledge of the procedural rules of a court. They are likely to be nervous and will be required to give accurate accounts of events that may have occurred many months earlier. They may well have been in very abnormally aroused states at the time of the events. More professional witnesses, such as the police, accused persons with criminal records, and those who have maintained a deception about any crime(s) they have committed, will not be quite so disadvantaged.

Within the context, the prosecution seeks to maximize the credibility of their witnesses and to undermine the credibility of the defense witnesses and vice versa. In theory, the primary obligation of counsel is to present their witnesses in the best possible light so that what is exposed is "the truth, the whole truth and nothing but the truth." In practice, what matters for the legal teams is winning their case.

This can be seen if the questions posed of practice are focused on the strategic and tactical activities of interrogators. Are these geared to the establishment of the truth or winning? Social and other psychologists have played a dual role in the development of forensic activities (see Danet, 1990, for a review of studies). They have conducted field studies and experiments that have indicated which factors operate to influence juries and judges, thereby illustrating the kinds of bias of judgment that can occur. The results of this work, however, have then been used by lawyers and other participants to maximize their chances of winning. It is alleged by psychologists that certain personality tests can facilitate discrimination between persons who are likely to return certain verdicts regardless of the evidence. These can be used to screen potential jurors—the prosecution selecting those disposed to find the accused guilty and the defense those biased toward innocence. Juries are open to influence by in-group/out-group factors. In the pretrial TV coverage of O. J. Simpson, the media-instigated polls showed a strong black judgment of innocence and a white one of guilt. This remained so after the verdict. This kind of result can be generalized to individual predispositions of a great variety of which particular constellations come together in particular cases. Jury members are also influenced by the appearance of the accused and the witnesses: how they dress, how they speak, what they look like, and what they say. Counsel advises these participants how to create and maintain good impressions. Juries are also influenced by the advocates themselves in the kinds of arguments they advance and the skill with which they mount these (O'Barr, 1982). Most of the strategic and tactical principles were correctly anticipated in Aristotle's (1926) first manual for rhetoricians; social psychology has confirmed the validity of and elaborated on classical analysis rather than refute or restructure it. It is not an accident that Plato (1971) chose the forensic situation to pit Gorgias and others against Socrates. Gorgias declared that his role was to win his case if he could, the means justifying the end. Socrates argued that the discourse should be seeking to expose the truth of the matters in hand so that justice might be done, and seen to be done. Socrates, portrayed in this case as a lonely disciple of the obligation to use the representational function of language in its truth-telling mode, appears to defeat the arguments of Gorgias and other arguments founded on the same premises—even his own.

What adversarial courts do is oppose two Gorgiases against each other as the preferred mechanism for exposing truths that at least one set of the professional contestants is professionally obliged to try to conceal or discredit. In the event of an innocent accused, the prosecution has to show that the defense is false when it is not. In the event of a guilty person being accused, the defense has to show that the falsehoods of the accused are true and the true statements of the prosecution are false.

In situations such as this where two teams of professionals seek to discredit the testimony of opposing witnesses by showing them to be fallible or dishonest or both, and where the professionals have asymmetric rights to define the questions and limit the answers, the jury is left to decide which set of witnesses was least confused or deceitful.

Reputations of advocates are enhanced by winning weak cases. Typically, their fees are positively correlated with their reputations. Insofar as the contesting legal professionals are concerned, their power, wealth, and status will be positively correlated with their success rates. In both the United States and the United Kingdom, even wealthy individuals find it difficult to afford the fees of legal representation. What is called a free market economy but tends toward a monopoly that controls its own entry numbers and raises the prices of its services accordingly remains a vital component of the social order while at the same time rationing the access of clients with its enormous cost. The lies and other falsifications told in court are but a part of a system that seems to have been moving away from its original societal functions for a very long time. At the heart of the problem lies the distance between increasing complex laws and the concepts of natural or social justice held by members of society, but the adversarial structure would also appear to be a criterial component of the forces encouraging deceit, as illustrated 2,000 years ago by Plato. What evidence is available about the adversarial system exposes its weaknesses. Whether systems based on inquisitorial methods reduce or eliminate the disadvantages of the adversarial structure has not been systematically explored. Certainly, asymmetries of control and familiarity remain, but some of the excesses of the dominating manipulation by the professionals appear to be somewhat muted (Adelsward, Aronsson, Jönsson, & Linell, 1987).

Commentary

From an outsider's perspective, adversarial legal systems theoretically place their professionals in a succession of chronic moral dilemmas. If what they believe or know to be the facts of the matter are inconsistent with the adversarial role they are playing, then the dilemma is inescapable. As human beings and citizens, they should be concerned with truth; as advocates, they are obliged to present the best case for their client and they should not be usurping the role of the jury or judges or both. The resolution of this, if there is to be a resolution, probably has to follow the hope of Isocrates and the claim of Cicero (1971) that rhetorical competence was defensible if the speaker was a person of virtue.

As things are in the quasi democracies, it may well be that the system has a double bias of injustice—the poor being more likely to be convicted when innocent and the rich being more likely to evade justice when guilty. Left to defend themselves, the same biases might also result, but these are currently accentuated if the cleverest lawyers can be bought to defend one's case. Witness the escape rates of those who appear to be financial swindlers on the grand scale.

Given the system and culture, lawyers are not unique in that the greater the apparent difficulty of their task the greater the reward, but they are unique in that their skills of overcoming the difficulties of their cases by creating falsifications, concealments, other misleading impressions, and exploiting technicalities pervert the purposes of the system within which they are meant to be operating.

It is psychologically and sociologically interesting that for prosecution cases that fall on technicalities or convictions that are found to be unsound after review, it seems to be very rare that other persons are subsequently charged for these offenses. In recent years in the United Kingdom, two of the most common grounds for unsound convictions have been the prosecution's concealment from the defense of material evidence in its possession and statements signed by the accused that have been shown to have been amended by the police subsequent to the signatures. Only the first implicates lawyers, but the other is an associated set of deceptive practices.

The greatest source of deceptions presumably is by perpetrators of crimes who manage to falsify their stories sufficiently to ensure a verdict of "not guilty." That so few of these people ultimately leave confessions in their wills or decide to reveal the truth before they die is a testimony to the human capacity to preserve secrets, and in this case, guilty secrets. Strangely, there do not appear to be any studies of this phenomenon. Perhaps this not so strange because inquiries would be potentially libelous, dangerous, or both. It is nevertheless odd that once a prosecution fails, the case disappears. Along a parallel line of argument, it is also noteworthy that it is very rare for subsequent charges of perjury to be brought against persons who plead not guilty but are found to be guilty by the court.

Although within their own domain, lawyers operate in ways that encourage lying by their clients and witnesses but make out witnesses for the other side to be incompetent or dishonest or both and thereby obscure rather than expose the truth, it is simultaneously legally qualified persons who are very likely to initiate and lead inquiries into political, commercial, and bureaucratic malpractice. Special commissions, offices, or committees may be established whose duties are to act as watchdogs and bring cases against possible miscreants. In these capacities, the roles of these groups have affinities with the pursuits of some investigative journalists.

The Economy and the Consumer

In Chapter 3, the susceptibilities of the consumer to persuasion were described with reference to the arts of salespeople in face-to-face situations, but they were discussed with as little reference as possible to the means used and the constraints on the messages that can be transmitted. As with the mass media, it should not be presumed that consumers are simple victims of capitalist machinations. They are active interpreters. In whatever way any communicative act is structured, it is open to misinterpretation. Language use (and nonverbal activity) is a matter of conventions, and those who are not familiar with the presuppositions of the originators will not be able to appreciate its significance. Advertisements that presume knowledge about other advertisements, famous quotations, or characters will not be responded to identically by those who do not and those who do share the allusions. Absurd claims that are not treated as jokes might be interpreted as lies. What is and is not misleading and where particular responsibilities lie have to be matters of consensus or judgment by officially constituted groups of some kind, and these would be expected to take into account the contemporary conventions of their society. One of these conventions is that what is claimed for a product should have some verisimilitude. What is claimed for a product is an integral part of the contract between the purchaser and the seller or producer or both. Quasi democracies have, however, introduced the principle of caveat emptor, which loads the contract against the purchaser.

In any purchase or exchange the onus is on the buyer or receiver to show that what has been handed over is defective in some respect. To provide protection for buyers and receivers, societies have laws about implicit or explicit contracts: Goods must serve the purposes for which they are described, for example. In theory, media through which goods and services are advertised are subject to controls about veracity of claims made or implied. Particular industries and professions have their own regulatory bodies that also, in theory, prescribe and proscribe the marketing of their goods and services. In complex capitalist systems, the edifice of relevant legislation and regulation is massive.

On the other hand, the overt economic objective of providers is expected to be the optimization of profit for the individuals and organizations selling goods and services, and if notions of "fair prices" and "reasonable returns" are abandoned in favor of maximizing returns within the letter of the law, then there will be a continuing struggle between sellers and buyers. Insofar as sellers have greater wealth and power than the ultimate individual buyers, it is the buyers who need the protection. Why should a company market a bar of Yukky soap as being capable of removing a reasonably high proportion of grime and sweat if it can sell the same product as Princess de Gauche at $10 and offer a route to eternal youth and luxurious living? Which individuals list all the actual and possible deficiencies of any car that they are selling to a prospective buyer?

Deceit in the marketplace is probably as old as the cracked flints and molting fur wraps that changed hands in the Stone Age. If it had not been a practice, then, like sin, there would have been no need to set up taboos and laws to control such activities. The extent and kinds of deception practiced in the pursuit of profit will be a function of what is possible within a culture: the informal norms of what is proper being supplemented by legislation (if enacted), the vigilance of institutional watchdogs, and in the last instance, the purchasing decisions of individuals. Individuals are not forced to buy particular newspapers or magazines. They do not have to buy a second bar of either Yukky or Princess de Gauche.

Academic research in the world of commerce inevitably suffers from handicaps. Insofar as multinational companies have vast power and wealth compared with independent researchers, and insofar as they have strong reasons for defending their products and the virtues claimed for them, examples of deceit will be hazardous to investigate (see Chapter 10 on whistle-blowing) and principles of successful and unsuccessful marketing, with or without deceit, will be valuable knowledge that interested companies will not wish to be made public. The best relevant data will be kept secret. And why not? In a competitive economy, it would be a strange and probably short-lived commercial that paid for and then published the findings about the efficacy of particular marketing strategies and tactics.

Researchers will also suffer from the excess of variability: What kind of lies (deceit) increase the rate of success and failure of sales will vary with who is selling what to whom under what conditions—in what cultural context. Selling goods and services involves a transaction between persons and is subject to the general social psychological principles applicable to any interpersonal encounter. Given a willing and trusting buyer and a willing and trustworthy seller at an agreed price, features peculiar to selling and buying may be minimal, but once considerations of willingness, trust, or price become problematic, peculiar features can come into play.

What follows refers to some studies conducted concerning the various issues. As with other topics, questions about lying are foregrounded against a backdrop of deceit. As also with other topics, a focus on lying per se misses the lengths to which sellers go (and sometimes buyers too) to deceive without actually lying. Actually lying about the qualities of goods or services seems to constitute a taboo, although it is one that is frequently broken. Anything short of a lie may be evaluated positively by envious competitors and amused consumers alike, and the greater the de facto deception the greater the admiration. The immediate questions to be asked are whether sellers deceive and lie and, if so, how and for which products? What purchasers believe is deferred until Chapter 9.

One final difficulty in systematizing work in this field is that, unlike criminal law, commercial law concerned with deception takes no cognizance of intention. Whether portrayals of products are misleading is the question in both the United Kingdom and the United States. Intentions are not significant. "False statements" rather than the word lie will be used where necessary. Any further inference is at the discretion of the reader, as some typical disclaimers on advertisements might be required to append in the future!

Advertising and Marketing

Deception and Lying: De Facto and Perceived. Some advertising has been raised to a degree of subtlety that is more than Gricean in its implicature. Currently, a British TV advertisement for Carling Black Label beer requires for its understanding an acquaintance with (a) the James Bond image, (b) the stereotype of Germans that portrays them as people who "book" places poolside by setting down towels early in the morning, and (c) the kind of bomb used to breech the Moehne dam in World War II! It is unlikely that anyone watching imagines that drinking this lager will enable him or her to become more like James Bond, but independent researchers have not actually studied and published who believes that about particular advertisements, so far as I know. How many teenagers think that the various creams and pastes will soften skin, remove spots, and make teeth white, hard, and free from plaque remains unknown.

Gossip and observation would offer two hypotheses: (a) Most of the people are not fooled most of the time, and (b) many people buy such products optimistically. P. DePaulo (1988) quotes a number of studies. Calfee and Ford (1988) concluded that easy-to-verify claims are treated as more credible than those that rely on extended subjective experience of a product. Ford, Smith, and Swasy (1988) found that people were indeed less likely to believe experiential subjective claims. Likewise, the more extreme the claims the less the credibility (Beltramini & Evans, 1985). The other factors that might be listed are similar to those relevant to the credibility of any message.

Somewhat ironically, the single study of Haefner (1975) quoted by B. DePaulo (1988) relating to actual TV commercials casts doubt on the ease with which consensus might be achieved. Advertisements judged by four Federal Trades Commission lawyers as being legally "actionable" were no more likely to be judged as misleading by a lay panel than was a control set of advertisements. The lack of consensus is not surprising. If real advertisements were blatantly in contravention of the law, presumably companies would not risk using them. If they were clearly within the law, no questions would be asked.

Just as it would be odd to list all the known faults of a product to be sold, it would also be odd to package it repulsively or inappropriately. If a mild blue packet creates an impression of soothing cleanliness, products that are intended to soothe and clean are likely to be advertised and marketed with such shades. If green packaging conjures up environmental friendliness, then manufacturers aiming at conservationists will use green in their packaging. Difficulties arise only when there is a clear discrepancy between advertisement and reality, a clash that will mislead consumers.

The Tricks

Creating Impressions: The Product. Visual and other illusions are well-studied phenomena in psychology, and packagers of goods have long worked out ways of maximizing desirable properties of products through these. The perceptual constancies and the dominance of the immediately seen over the analytically calculated are old friends to those who shape sweets, cookies, and other goodies. Clearly, companies would be foolish to minimize the attractions of the quantities on offer, and this is certainly not the context to do anything more than note that what looks like more may not be more.

At some arbitrary point on the scale of deceptive appearances, questions of legality can arise. There must not be too much air at the top of granular detergent packets or boxes of cereals. There may be legal limits to how much red coloring can be injected into meat displayed in misleadingly lit cabinets. There are disputes about holiday brochures that put in photographs that omit the contiguous airport and fail to mention it in the text. Whether these conventions are acceptable is a matter for each society to decide.

Clearly, quasi democracies are not puritanical in their requirements. Shelves in pharmacies are stacked with patent medicines whose written claims exceed their prophylactic powers. One of the most famous money-spinners at the turn of the century was Beecham's Pills. These were claimed to be efficacious for the relief of the symptoms of nearly 30 ailments. Their initial unit cost was .15p, whereas their sale price was 15p. Chemical analysis showed soap to be a major constituent, with aloes and ginger the other discernible active ingredients. Other shelves are stacked with cosmetic products. The offers of a physical paradise on earth are not judged to be false promises.

On the other hand, most machines and instruments on sale to the general public have specifications that are consistent with their advertisements. Hardware stores have their shelves stacked with building and decorating products that do what they claim to do. The differences between products marketed honestly and dishonestly do not correspond directly to objectively measurable and subjectively experienced criteria of discrimination; pharmaceutical and cosmetic products make objective claims, some of which are demonstrably true, and others of which are not.

Advancing Knowledge: Overcreative Creativity

Fraud in the Arts and Humanities

Forgeries and Their Authentication. Forging objets d'art is no doubt as ancient as the first exchanges of valued pieces, and of course, the most successful forgers are by definition yet to be discovered. In the European context, there are notorious examples of forged paintings, sculptures, writings, and music. New plays by Shakespeare are discovered periodically, as are missing symphonies and concertos. Van Meegeren painted too many Vermeers to remain credible. At a milder level, Fritz Kreisler's arrangements were so skilled, prolific, and popular that it became unclear which were original compositions and which were arrangements. Posthumously, Vivaldi, Couperin, and other cited composers have had some of their works reassigned to Kreisler. Chaucer's *Troilus and Cressida* is too close to being a translation of Boccaccio to be accidental. There are now more fake Corots on the market than real ones. El Greco and Van Gogh are also popular models.

The motivations vary: demands for recognition or demonstrations of talent (postexposure), delight in fooling the world in general and experts in particular, or aspirations to make large sums of money. Long ago, it became necessary to have certificates of provenance or other forms of accreditation for the public sales of major works of art, but this has not precluded scandals arising. Many more scandals have not arisen because they involve articles of lesser value whose authenticity remains untested. The number of unannounced replica pieces of antique furniture extant must now be very high.

Historians have a dual role to play. The direct role is as forgers of history. The first European historian Herodotus was christened "the father of lies" by the second, Thucydides. To become eminent, young ambitious historians have to either discover and work on significant previously unknown manuscripts or reinterpret significant events and challenge the contemporary consensus successfully. There will be temptations to squeeze the evidence into novel schemes, and given that multiple interpretations of historical events are inevitable and that decisive discriminating evidence may be unrecoverable, reputations for brilliance may be founded on a capacity to induce beliefs in others that the historian creator actually believes to be false. The subsidiary role is as an authenticator of manuscripts and other artifacts. A contemporary embarrassment was Trevor Roper's initial erroneous authentication of the forged diaries of Hitler.

Some forgers display clear signs of dupers' delight. They can be cheerfully proud to have the mastery of their art recognized; they have enjoyed fooling the experts and critics. The world of aesthetic criticism, however, has its peculiarities, and it is worth airing the issue of a wider variant of deception and lying that goes beyond forgery and imitation. This includes creators but focuses on the judgments of critics as determiners of taste. The suggestion is that one of the social functions of having good aesthetic taste is to facilitate social differentiation. Good taste is one criterion that can mark off members of the intelligentsia, the educated upper middle class, and some of the upper class from the rest of society. At least some of this good taste, however, may be of a phony and deceitful construction, and some is arbitrary.

Aesthetic Myths in the High Culture. Reasons for the existence of forgeries and lies about them do not require any addition of motives to the list, but when artistic appreciation comes to serve dividing the function of cultures into elites and the rest, it is of interest to explore the sociology and social psychology of the situation. It is not just European and North American societies that have elites. They are an international phenomenon. The extent to which assigned aesthetic sensitivity and taste enter into the discriminating variables around the world has not been examined.

The phenomenon at issue is best illustrated with avant garde activities in the arts. Once aspiring artists break with contemporary convention in dramatic ways, it is common for the society to divide into a large majority that treats innovations as confidence tricks or jokes and a tiny minority of critics who applaud the ideas. In recent years, piles of arranged bricks have been offered as sculpture, paint thrown at canvases as paintings, and silent sitting at pianos for 3½ minutes as music. Each has had art critics who have defended the value and status of the enterprise. By definition, all development implies change, and although a conservative majority may complain about any elaboration of or modification to contemporary conventions, if they always succeeded in acting as a force precluding change, there would be no developments. When change is progress and when it is gimmickry is usually decided retrospectively in the light of the outcome! It is clear that revolutionary and gradual changes in all art forms can become accepted as part of the high-art canon. Although Greek statues, Sung flasks, and Egyptian cats may have remained in the canon as masterpieces, Henry Moore figures, Cezanne cypresses, and Shostakovitch symphonies can come to achieve comparable status; they may lose status again, of course. Other ventures fail to survive beyond their initial controversial launching, and some of these are presumably exercises in salesmanship rather than art.

More generally in the Western capitalist countries, however, appreciation of the high culture has been the prerogative of a small minority at most and sometimes of a small elite. Why does this appreciation not extend to the petit bourgeoisie or the lumpen proletariat? One argument is that the development of the powers of appreciation requires experiences and education that are not open to the majority of children and adults. Strictly speaking, this is not true in that exemplars or performances of the contemporary canon are available at no greater cost than access to facilities that the majority do pay to experience. On the other hand, neither schools nor primary caretakers of the majority necessarily socialize them into appreciation of the qualities of the high culture.

Is the high culture in part simply pretentious and phony and supported by a rhetoric, and if so, why should it be so? Access to that culture can give its in-group a sense of superiority over their out-group philistines. The in-group is more sensible to the great cultural achievements of human beings and has greater knowledge of and concern for them. It is from its members that contemporary artists are most likely to be drawn. If the out-groups accept their inferiority, then "lack" of aesthetic sensitivity is added to the list of reasons that justify their lower status in the society. Just as wealth, income, and occupational prestige help to sustain social differentials, so can art and its appreciation (Bourdieu, 1977; Veblen, 1925). This will be especially true if members of the elite conspire to see virtue and virtuosity in nonsense. The blindness of the out-groups may derive from there being nothing to see. Although one might expect that such conspiracies have but brief durability, it may last long enough to help to confine one or two generations to their lowly positions.

Some of us may have spent our undergraduate years at strategically located vantage points for observing the operation of individual pretentiousness and more. At one time, such people were known as *pseuds*, the insincere talkers about their exaggerated responsiveness and sensitivity to what appeared to the majority as nonsense. Members of the majority were duly labeled *peasants, clods,* or *yobs.* If it is true that those elite collections of individuals can promote and sustain conspiracies of superiority, often in association with some philosopher-originated ideology (Nietzsche, Sartre, postmodernism), then this is one of the bases that can be cited as grounds for perpetuating the hierarchical stratification that marks modern societies. This is not to suggest the whole operation is a fraud, but only that within its activities, there are strands of deception that are serving individual and social functions: The elites and their adherents have posers and are in part sustained by support from members of the higher strata, some of whom collect objects they do not appreciate and attend performances they do not enjoy. This pretentious superiority in knowledge and sensitivity can be used to put down both individuals and whole social strata. It can be used to justify other differentials of status and power.

Lies in Science

In what amounts to both a sociological and a psychological analysis of lies in scientific reporting, Broad and Wade (1982) document a variety of cases of unknowns, the famous, and the infamous. They illustrate ways of misrepresenting results in themselves and of misrepresenting the purported author's role in generating the ideas or the data. They cite factors that encourage such behavior and act to prevent or obscure its exposure and investigation if and when it happens. They show how myths created by philosophers, sociologists, and historians of science are prone to present scientists as creatures dedicated to the pursuit of truth through objective, checked observations whose possible explanations are subjected to strict critical evaluation.

Initially, it may be alarming to see the names of Ptolemy, Galileo, Newton, Dalton, and Mendel cited as fabricators or at least selectors of data. It is surprising to read of laboratory chiefs taking the credit for discoveries made by research students and assistants. It is worrying that in a system that rewards those who publish papers, clever operators can arrange to lie undetected with 200 copied papers to their credit, all copied from other published articles.

More distressing is the fact that one reason why frauds may remain undetected is that so much of what is published remains unread or uncited by colleagues. Certainly, any obsession with numbers of publications or citations or both as indices of productivity and accountability of researchers has led to an escalation in the number of journals, along with advice as to how to maximize one's marketability with a minimum of effort. There is no doubt that academics generally are being tempted and pushed into activities that are most unlikely to be of benefit to society generally. It is also likely that frauds of various kinds are on the increase. If gossip among undergraduates, postgraduates, and research assistants is reliable and valid, the incidence of invented, selected, and modified data among themselves is now a significant percentage of what appears in published articles. Some have obviously never contemplated the idea; others readily admit to personal data fixing and see it as normative behavior.

Broad and Wade (1982) are streetwise. They point to the idealistic myths of scientific endeavors:

1. Science is a vocation rather than a career.
2. The search for the truth will take precedence over personal ambition for recognition or other rewards.
3. The checks within science ensure "the virtual absence of fraud in the annals of science." The rigorous policing is through peer review for job and grant applications, peer refereeing of journal articles, and finally and most crucially, the testability of claims via replication.

Given human variability, it is not surprising that neither of the first two can stand as universal generalizations. In science, there is no prize for coming in second, even when discoveries are independent and contiguous. Only one Nobel prize is awarded for any single discovery. This can tempt ambitious scientists to fail to acknowledge the role of their predecessors. Broad and Wade (1982) present a case that Ptolemy may have gained 1,500 years of credit for his astronomical system on the strength of using the unacknowledged observations of Hipparchus as his own.

In part, scientists are victims of systems that act to credit discoveries to individuals. All advances in science, indeed all advances in knowledge, are dependent on what has preceded them. Ideas arise from conversations and experiences; their pursuit depends on resources and opportunities. Who really contributed to what is deemed to be the crucial publication is probably not recoverable and to believe it can be isolated to its author as solely responsible is an idealization. Marketing becomes important. As mentioned elsewhere, Brecht lamented the consequences of a country with a need for heroes, but science now plays this game very assiduously by marking out individuals for honors, prizes, and other awards.

The controversy about the invention of the differential calculus led to the Royal Society setting up a committee of inquiry. The committee was required to report on the status of the rival claims of Newton and Leibniz and found in favor of Newton. The committee was English not Swiss, Newton was president of the Royal Society at the time, and he did help with the investigation. The report was said to be independent, but its contents appear to have been carefully orchestrated by one of the disputants.

Tidying up the data is another form of deception of which Newton stands accused, as do Galileo and Dalton. Each had theories that predicted certain results. Each reported results consistent with their theories. Subsequent developments of theory point to the data being too good, and the implication is that the results were cleaned up. Galileo may have simply invented some of his results. Mendel's experiments on genetic inheritance report data that are too exact to be probable, but in his case, gossip credits the gardeners with fixing the figures. Each had the advantage of having a theory that was basically correct.

Others have reported data that have subsequently been shown to have been wrong and invented. Other examples are cited under whistle-blowing (Chapter 10). Able research students, too anxious for fame, seem to be prone to this kind of activity (see discussion of Spector on p. 230), although the very mature psychologist, Burt, was placed in the same category by Kamin (1974).

One of the most extraordinary cases reported by Broad and Wade (1982) is Noguchi, who reported isolating the organisms causing syphilis, yellow fever, polio, rabies, and trachoma. He enjoyed a distinguished career and died with 200 publications to his name. After his death, none of his discoveries were confirmed, and virtually nothing of his work has stood the tests of replication. More comprehensive was the enterprise of Alsabti. Inventing an autobiography of achievements and connections as he rose through the ranks, he did not stop at inventing data. He is reported as stealing papers submitted for publication to the journal of which his professor was editor, reorganizing the titles and abstracts, and sending them on elsewhere as his own research. He seems to have conned two Arab governments and six American universities before he was dismissed from a position.

The short answer to any question about the variety of lies and frauds committed by scientists is that if a fraud can be imagined it has almost certainly been perpetrated at some time by somebody. All have to be explained by recourse to the truth being subordinated to other priorities, with perhaps the one exception of lucky arrogance. Some of the frauds seem to derive from hubris, the presumption that one's theory is correct and therefore the facts must agree with the triumph of rationalism over empiricism. In the examples, the arrogance proved to be well-founded within the contemporary limits of measurement, and only much later have the doubts been raised about the authenticity of data.

That scientists are fallible beings is to be expected; that the exposure of the forgers can be resisted so strongly might not be expected to occur.

Broad and Wade's (1982) third myth about the internal policing of scientists is quickly weakened by a consideration of the realities. With respect to the prevention of fraudulent publications, it is not true that all peer review and refereeing is a result of the conscientious judgments of disinterested equals. The judgments are made by members of the establishment within the discipline, by friends and therefore rivals, and by persons who may be prone to hasty negative or positive judgments. Assessments are subject to all the sources of unreliability and bias that social psychologists and others have demonstrated. Old boy networks, the reputations of applicants, and susceptibility to confidence tricksters add to the variability arising from genuine diversity of opinion and affect judgments about what will and will not be accepted. Articles replicating results will probably not be acceptable for publication, even though replicability is held up as a crucial criterion of scientific disciplines. Failed replications are even less likely to appear, unless they are supplemented with positive results via an amended procedure or analysis. The system may be the best that can be made to work, it may be generally efficient, and it may be as fair as can be devised, but essentially, it relies on the integrity of those participating. Too many checks and the system collapses. Given the scale of research extant, heavy policing could quickly become counterproductive. Too many frauds and the enterprise itself will fall into disrepute.

The institutional response to allegations of fraud by one of its practicing scientists is similar to the sequence reported for allegations of other forms of malpractice. High on the list of probable initial reactions is a denial and an appeal to the good character, eminence, and sound reputation of the accused. In the event of allegations persisting, it may be suggested that the dispute is simply a professional squabble that has gotten out of hand. If judgments about character or competence are made, the bias is likely to be against the junior colleague or the outsider. Eventually, a committee of inquiry may be established—its members selected by the institution of the accused. In the event of any senior member of the institution being found to be at fault, attributions of blame are likely to be moderated by pointing to the chief having been too trusting or too busy. A classic case illustrating this kind of process was a new theory of cancer causation known as the kinase-cascade theory, a brilliant synthesis of biochemistry and molecular biology. The young researcher Spector convinced the laboratory chief Racker that the empirical evidence was consistent with the theory. Although both research evidence and detective work began to undermine the story, Racker and the university continued to back the authenticity of the data. Not until the means of deception were finally exposed did anyone check the details of Spector's curriculum vitae. He had neither a B.A. nor an M.A. and he had been convicted previously of passing forged checks.

In such cases, the senior scientist, the laboratory, and the university stand to gain prizes, grants, and prestige from the achievement of a brilliant research student. The student can exploit the trust and credibility of the senior scientist, who is likely to be a friend and a colleague of the elite of the university. Loyalty can take precedence over commitments to the truth, as can the wish of institutions and authorities to appear to be more righteous than they really are.

National pride seems to have been a factor in the British reactions to the discovery of Piltdown man in the same epoch (1912). The search for the missing link between apes and human beings had been a prestigious project since the publication of Darwin's (1859) *Origin of Species*. Discoveries of Peking man, as he was named, and various African skulls were succeeded by the discovery of Heidelberg man. When Dawson displayed and reported his finding of parts of a skull of a more primitive creature in England, national pride was fed by this symbol of superiority over the Germans. Some British geologists were not persuaded and one (Hinton) laced the place of discovery with a forged ape tooth matching the skull reconstructed from Dawson's bones. Duly discovered by Dawson, its forged status was not detected. Hinton then played an absurdly English hoax. He fashioned an elephant's leg bone to simulate what might have been a Pleistocene cricket bat. Its discovery was duly reported in the *Quarterly Journal of the Geological Society*, but its function was not specified beyond the label "implement." It was another 10 years before the skull bones were accepted as being a hoax.

Commentary. It is not difficult to find examples of falsifications in the academic and artistic communities. Names can be named, as can kinds and means of falsification, but they are few in number. Ultimately, reasons are not recoverable, although strong inferences can be drawn in particular cases. The pursuit of wealth and power do not emerge as strongly as they will in the commercial world. Status does—but not so much status as a superior being with social pretensions as status among colleagues as a superior artist or academic. The pretensions to genius may be an artifact of what attracts attention. Persons who copy second-division artists or academics who forge data of little significance may simply be more likely to escape detection. They are less likely to have biographers with suspicious dispositions. Given the fact that most academic articles are cited by fewer than two people, many lying data will be left to lie.

Three reasons that stand out somewhat in the cases cited are duping delight, chronic frustration, and hubris. An exuberant pleasure in fooling the world does seem to be a factor in art forgeries; being talented enough to produce works that can pass as products of genius may be a massively satisfying experience in its own right. The same could be true in history, archaeology, or biology, but that does not emerge from the accounts recorded. A more prominent reason seems to be that the deception is a reaction to the frustrations of chronic failure to discover something that would bring wide recognition of a significant achievement. Twenty years of digging on a site that yields nothing must feel like a life wasted. Salting a site with artifacts in such circumstances contrasts with what appears to be the occasional, arrogant impatience of great theorists whose ideas stand in need of data. Collecting and processing data can be a dreary and lonely mechanical task. The temptation to clean up or invent data that exaggerate what may be observable trends may be seen as a relatively risk-free enterprise; it will require justification only if the hypotheses are in error. (There is a parallel with the police accentuating or adding evidence to secure the conviction of those they believe to be guilty.) Unlike the police, academic psychologists do not have to generate diagnoses of any particular cases, and explanations here can be confined to the general phenomena.

Once scientific claims are being translated into potentially profitable applications, there will necessarily be replications and checks. If these approach a manufacturing and sales stage, countries have official bodies to withhold or grant licenses. Minor frauds in published papers may waste the time and energy of colleagues and bring undue rewards to the deceiver, but the consequences are not matters of life or death, exploitation, or suffering. More serious frauds raise the stakes, but serious claims that cannot be replicated will be ignored. Although it may not be possible to publish failed replications, on significant topics the informal networks of colleagues working in the same area will not be fooled for long.

The sanctions for demonstrated frauds seem to be mild. For untenured staff or those on renewable contracts, appointments will probably be left to lapse. For tenured staff, institutions risk litigation in those countries amply endowed with lawyers seeking business. Doubtless calculations are made about the costs of sacking those who are exposed informally as deceivers. Gossip does not have the same status as legally acceptable evidence. Furthermore, if any dismissal were to be contested, even a successful action could be a heavy and unrecoverable cost to the institution, given the way in which laws are framed and applied. The legal conditions surrounding contracts of employment must discourage universities and similar organizations from adopting a moral rather than a cost-benefit perspective on staff who plagiarize or fix their research. When funding from outside bodies is involved, the cost-benefit perspective will weigh even more strongly against punitive action. The operating characteristics of the legal system help to protect artists and academics who seek to induce false beliefs in others about their work. Creative artists and academics as a collectivity may be comparatively free of fraudsters. There is a sense in which their commitment to truth and excellence is integral to their activities; it would be strange to choose such careers if power, wealth, or social status were among the major motivating forces influencing such decisions. This does not mean that they cannot be corrupted, however, especially if and when they become integrated with the economic and political orders.

The idea that some of the elite in the humanities sector are in unholy alliance with social elites is not original. There is no implication that those committed to the virtues of the high culture are consciously condescending to their less sensitive and sensible citizenry. Neither is there an implication that the artistic products enjoyed by the high culture may not have aesthetic virtue.

What is being noted is that access to these experiences is rationed, and social mechanisms are in place to discourage most of the population from acquiring the knowledge and experience that may be prerequisites of appreciating these artifacts. Insofar as those excluded are induced into a false belief that they are socially inferior, deception is operative. Insofar as there are phony artists and phony critics who deliberately set out to assert the existence of aesthetic qualities in objects d'art from which such qualities are absent, and members of the educated elite pretend to agree with them, there is evidence that games of claimed social superiority are being played. One social psychological problem is to find ways of discriminating between the phony and the sincere. One sociological task is to explore how aesthetic experience is articulated with social differentiation (e.g., Bourdieu, 1977). The moral and social issues are whether anything should be done about false myths that maintain illusions and delusions of bases of intergroup conflicts.

The Religious Order

In the past 20 years, churches have been relatively quiescent, with one or two dramatic exceptions in the United States. The evangelical Jimmy Swaggert was convicted of financial offenses and accused of sexual improprieties. Initial denials were followed by public confessions and a defense of weaknesses of the flesh in response to excessive temptations by the devil. His is not the first Christian sect to divert part of its wealth into worldly possessions.

Historically, leaders of the Christian churches were key figures in attempts to specify the ethics of truth telling and falsification. St. Augustine took an absolutist line on the wrongness of lies but also classified them into eight kinds of increasing wickedness. Although agreeing with this position, St. Thomas Aquinas reduced the status of two of his three kinds of lie to venial as opposed to mortal sins. By the time of the Spanish Inquisition and the intergroup persecutions that became endemic to Europe, however, the Catholic church had drawn up a rule book for when false statements would not be sinful and what formulae had to be followed to avoid sin. The fundamental argument was that it could be in the higher interests of a particular religious order to have captured believers lie than to have them tortured and killed or reveal where other believers were. The rule book has parallels with the customs of 9- and 10-year-old children. Formulae for canceling lies were to say silently to oneself that what was said was not really true, crossing fingers hidden from view while the lie was told, promising to confess—later (see Chapter 11 for further discussion).

Military Deception

Warfare has periodically adopted some of the qualities of competitive games where the contestants are expected to fight within a code of conduct, but even when this has happened, it has applied mainly to the elite among combatants; medieval knights in Europe were not killed if they were worth significant ransoms. In less chivalrous wars, it is also the case that the antagonistic elites appear to be less likely to be maltreated by their enemies than are the lower ranks or conquered peoples. Most wars are not chivalrous, especially for ordinary people.

The great lies of conquering forces are those that have promised to spare the lives of surrendering people and have then murdered them. The list of such occasions would be long and international: Chaka and the Boer leaders, the Nana Sahib and the British colonists at Cawnpore, and the Turks and the population of Famagusta.

In human history, the Nazi resettlement programs from 1939 to 1945 probably rank as the greatest and foulest set of deceptions through which 3½ million Jews and comparable numbers of Slavs were "resettled," only to be murdered. For each of the Western countries occupied, the Nazi propaganda promised a continuation of normality that subsequently turned into exploitation, oppression, and slaughter. Hitler and his team managed to sustain a great discrepancy between rhetoric and reality. Probably no other leaders have used such effective lies to facilitate the killing of so many people in a war. Whether such activities should be located in the politics section along with Stalin's exploitation of lies is arguable. Much of Stalin's activity, however, was designed to ensure his political supremacy, whereas Hitler's was to demonstrate and achieve Aryan supremacy of a particular kind.

The propaganda machines of both sides reached new levels of sophistication in the 1939 to 1945 war in their exploitation of modern technology. "Black" radio programs were designed to undermine the credibility of political and military leaders. False and true plans were planted on bodies left for the enemy to discover. Espionage and counterespionage proliferated to the extent of sacrificing own agents so that the enemy would not know that codes had been deciphered.

Strategically and tactically, inferior forces can defeat superior forces only by guile and deception and acting unexpectedly, and from time immemorial, subterfuge, false plants, and feints have been marks of victors. One particular variant of this has been to break with conventional wisdom. Battles are often suitable activities for the application of chaos theory: Chaos at one level is replaced by order at another level. At any one level, order can change to chaos and back again. Within this complexity there will be conventions guiding conduct. (The Geneva Convention is one such guideline intended to limit what is done to the enemy.) There will also be conventions about the strategies and tactics to be deployed. Breaking this with new orders of battle and the exploitation of improved technology need not involve deception, but some can. Mythically, the Greeks gained entry to Troy with the aid of soldiers hidden in the wooden horse. Rome's disbelief in the possibility of any army crossing the Alps gave Hannibal a victory. One version of the Battle of Hastings includes William's forces fleeing in retreat to turn and ambush Harold's too exuberant soldiers. Wolfe's army climbed the unscalable Heights of Abraham to dislodge Montcalm. In 1944, the anti-Nazi alliance went to enormous lengths to lead Hitler to believe that the D-Day landings would be on the Pas d'Calais and not in Normandy. Previously, of course, Hitler had made a succession of "final" demands from the reoccupation of the Ruhr to the right to have a German corridor to Danzig, each of which had been believed in some measure by some other European leaders. (Insofar as other European leaders were not really deceived, they deceived their own peoples with their reassurances about the peaceful intentions of the Third Reich.) In more recent times, the conflicts in former Yugoslavia have been marked by proclamations of cease-fires and negotiations during which regroupings and fresh offensives are prepared. Knowing when to believe what an enemy says is an impossible epistemological exercise with potentially disastrous consequences for errors.

It is not only the enemy who is to be deceived. Commanders mislead their own forces about the strength of the enemy they face, the role they are playing in some grander strategy, and perhaps even who and where they are fighting. Trapped garrisons are promised imminent relief. Pilots are given false instructions about the nature of their targets.

In brief, the primacy of winning or at least not being defeated takes precedence over all else. It is very rare for victorious armed forces to be called to account for lies and deceptions told to their own or enemy forces. The ends are used to justify the means.

Leaders, military and political, may well lie about the reasons for going to war, they will lie to deceive the enemy, their own forces, and their civilian populations, and if they win, they will sponsor the histories written within their own countries.

Games and Sports

Wittgenstein (1951/1967) found the concept of "game" a useful one for demonstrating that there were no criterial attributes shared by all games but only overlapping "family resemblances." He might have noted that it is possible to cheat and then lie about the cheating, but that is not a discriminating characteristic of games.

A few children's games are actually based on cheating. There are card games where the object is to dispose of all your cards or accumulate as many as possible by whatever means you can but without being successfully challenged as "cheat" by a fellow player who can expose where you have hidden the cards. In the disposal version, the winner is the first person to have no cards left. Cheating variants can be invented to supplement standard games. Button-

button requires a small object to pass around a circle in such a way that the guesser is misled as to how far it has traveled and with whom it resides. Someone takes the risk of retaining it and its subsequent passage is simulated.

The extent and value of deception vary greatly with the activity. In games of chance, such as roulette or bingo, it is irrelevant. In athletics, there are tactical moves that may involve lulling opponents into beliefs that may reduce their chances of winning. These deceptions may be important at the margins, but in javelin throwing or long-distance running, the competence itself will carry most of the variance between the successful and the unsuccessful.

Among indoor games, two card games illustrate different problems in deception. Contract bridge requires partners to bid in such a way that maximizes understanding about the cards held by each other while concealing or misleading their opponents about their holdings. On occasions, they may deliberately bid falsely to trap their opponents into overbidding or underbidding. Likewise in the playing during which no communication is permitted, particular cards may be played to mislead the opposition. (This second component is common to many games in which tricks are made.) The contrasting game is poker, which is a combination of luck, memory, and deception. Can you deceive your opponents into believing that your hand is inferior to theirs when it is in fact superior? Rumors exist of at least one pair of eminent academics being warned off or bought off the tables at Las Vegas; one was a statistician with a formidable memory, and his partner was a social scientist with skills in deception and detection of deception. This probably apocryphal story makes the point. No lies are told, and concealment may be a more common strategy than the emission of false cues. The costs of not being a successful deceiver are high.

In field games, both strategic and sensorimotor deceptions are significant determinants of team success. In soccer, skills of ball control and shooting are primary, but individual players need to be able to deceive those about to wrest the ball from them and can best do so by giving misleading signals as to their intentions. Likewise, shots at goal that the keeper misreads are more likely to score. The converse holds for the defense. At the next level, the effectiveness of movements of sets of players will depend on within-team understanding and the ability to mislead the opposition. There are set pieces of actions. The same is true of American football, rugby, hockey, and other such team games. The outcomes of supposedly gentlemanly games of cricket are heavily influenced by the competence of bowlers to disguise how the ball will move as it approaches the batsman. The word *googly* may be relatively unknown to non-cricket players, but a capacity for bowling them is highly prized.

These forms of deception are within the spirit of the games as well as being within the rules. Other forms are within the rules but not the spirit. In World Cup class soccer, certain players and teams are notorious for feigning injuries in attempts to gain time or free kicks. There is a whole swathe of ambiguous dirty tricks that are practiced and may be within the rules but not the spirit of the games. There are also multitudes of fouls, many of which are intended to escape the notice of referees and linesmen. An inspection of the statistics shows that fouls are very frequent in matches. Whether there are positive associations between the sums of money involved and the number of fouls or attempts to deceive would be difficult to ascertain. Folk wisdom reports that with the increase in the salaries of top players and their associates, the profits of successful clubs and the amount of gambled money have escalated as have the attempts to win by whatever means are possible.

Supplementary forms of deception (and lying when challenged) have emerged with the human competence to improve performance with drugs. Olympic athletes of the former Soviet bloc countries seemed to be developed beyond what is possible without pharmacological assistance; this was especially true of some of the women. Attempts to facilitate performances with drugs used chronically as part of training and acutely for particular performances are regularly exposed at international athletic meetings. Once tests are declared positive, the standard response is denial. A frequent excuse refers to medicines taken for recent illnesses. So far, no appeal at international events has been successful so that every set of appeals has been held to have been dishonest. Again, substantial sums of money are likely to be involved indirectly. Although, unlike scientific discoveries, there are prizes for coming second and third, one of the top three positions is probably necessary to cash in on payments for subsequent advertising or other promotions.

Although lying may be a minor player in the deception game in this area, the generalizations that may be advanced are similar to those in the other domains reviewed. Once competitive games and sports cease to be activities confined to the kinds of principles and pleasures invoked in the Olympic oath, and winning becomes linked to the economic order or the prestige of social groups from clubs to states, lying, cheating, and deception will increase.

Summary and Provisional Conclusions

Virtue in Deception

Perhaps the first point to make is that it would be feasible to try to rank order social institutions and orders in terms of deceptions of certain kinds being required, expected, tolerated, and condemned. It would not be possible, however, to write out a simple list for several reasons. First, there would appear to be a hazy but palpable factor of cleverness that can rescue some deceptions from condemnation and raise others to the status of admirable achievements. (Odysseus has to be the prototype of both.) Second, and rather mysteriously, there seems to be a wish to draw a firm boundary between lies as a reprehensible category of activity and any form of concealment, evasion, or deception that stops short of being a lie. Lies per se are taboo.

With these qualifications, it might be claimed that deception within the rules in competitive games is a greatly prized strategic and tactical skill; some might say it is the set of skills that makes the difference between competence and genius, be it displayed at the poker tables of Las Vegas or on the football pitches of São Paulo. At a professional level, such games are supposed to be free of verbal falsifications per se, but at amateur levels, lies may well enter into the game, and some children's games have skilled lying and deception as their essence.

Lies also enter into military deceptions and, with the development of radio and telecommunications, are a major component of strategies to mislead enemies about intentions, competence, and strength. Whatever ethical principles and rules can be cited as having some regulative significance, telling the truth is not one of them. The greater the extent to which the enemy is deceived, the greater the genius of the deceiving commander.

The financial sector of the business world applauds the cunning of an Odysseus, be this displayed against fellow financiers or a gullible public. Astute deals are the epitome of success. Swindling shareholders, selling worthless bonds, or borrowing money without an intention to repay appear to be less admired activities although if the deceptions are clever, even these can be excusable. Horatio Bottomley has already been referred to as a great exponent of the art in the early 1900s (Anonymous, 1923); he set up several hundred companies, ran various bond schemes, and was frequently in court as defendant and as suer for libel. His schemes bankrupted many. Simultaneously, he wined and dined with the elite, ran a string of racehorses, was twice returned to Parliament, and came to grief only through being a little too greedy at the expense of his conspirators. The same successful tricksters appear on the stage in each age. Creating and predicting climates of opinion in which others will buy what you are selling at a higher price than you paid for the same is the mark of success. To spread false rumors to win the game is part of the competence of the "big players." Precisely which kinds of lies and deceptions are required, expected, and tolerated cannot be specified, but the limits are broad and likely to be exploited by the ambitious.

Perhaps science lies toward the other extreme of the distribution, but then its essence is the generation of descriptions and explanations that are constrained by the rationality of various logics and the empirical data generated by pretension to objective observations. It must be a safe generalization to suggest that scientific journals are relatively free of deliberate bias and falsifications in comparison with the reporting of events in the mass media. The charming rogue and the poker face do not occasion admiration in the world of science.

The relevance of crossed boundaries to lying and deceit emerges most clearly in politics in its most sacred activities: formal debates in state legislatures. States differ in what they permit, but the example of Britain's House of Commons may be instructive, because its longevity and stability have led to a degree of ossification into rituals that caricature the principles originally intended to be served by the constitutive and regulative rules. Anything short of a lie is acceptable, and the wittier the evasion, equivocation, or falsification that can escape the label lie, the more it is applauded. The protracted, expensive, and ultimately inconsequential official inquiry into the

"Matrix Churchill/Arms to Iraq" affair is a case of treading the boundaries par excellence (Norton-Taylor, 1995). Form, not substance, has taken over precedence, as tends to happen with human institutions, with art, and which happened to rhetoric itself in the middle ages: Vigorous functional development becomes an optimal balance of manifest function and structure that gives way to structure without the original function.

Law courts have followed a similar principle. The immediate consequences are that equivocation and concealment are likely to be judged as indicative of deception and reduces credibility. If practiced by a defendant rather than a politician, they increase the chances of a guilty verdict rather than the alternative. It will be celebrated only in rare circumstances and only if successful. (Hence, the change in the Criminal Justice Act of England and Wales 1995, which no longer accords a charged person a right to silence. A refusal to answer questions by the police, even without a solicitor present, will be usable in court as evidence. It is assumed that charged persons are more likely to incriminate themselves before the court hearings.)

In the first draft of this chapter, a third factor of seriousness of consequences was included. In Chapter 9, this is shown to be the factor attracting the greatest severity of condemnation by the public, but this severity seems to operate independently of actual sanctions. Financiers who swindle the poor typically escape everything but a court case. They have arranged their assets and income into mechanisms that escape sequestration prior to detection. They obtain "legal aid" from the public purse to pay for their expensive legal defense. If found guilty, they receive light sentences. They are not rejected by relatives, friends, and colleagues. They show no remorse for their victims. It would appear to be the case that such schemes are evaluated very differently by different social groups. Perhaps the elites form an in-group of indifference to frauds and lies of which only lesser members of the wider community are the victims. (This would be consistent with the privileged status claimed with respect to very high incomes of top people, where great rewards are treated as encouraging productivity, as opposed to low wages and threats of unemployment that are cited as the efficient motivators for those lower in the pyramid.) Perhaps seriousness of consequences for in-group members only has to be the guiding principle for condemnation.

Power Protects

Another theme across the social orders is that organizations act to protect their own. Those at the top of organizations enjoy the double advantage of protection from their own organization and from the elites of other orders. This has just been illustrated in the preceding paragraphs. Financial swindlers know how to exploit the legal system, and they receive lenient sentences for fraud. The judiciary and the law adopt a quite different stance to small-time thieves and petty frauds. Politicians affirm the good character of such people, who have sometimes given generously to party funds. The media restrict their indignation to a few days' coverage. The significance of the lies fades rapidly.

Similar processes operate with malpractice in science. Authority and institutions act to prevent and deflect the investigation of possible frauds. The experience of whistle-blowers (Chapter 10) reveals the extent to which power is used to minimize trouble and discredit those who try to promote the cause of truth.

Myths Preserve the Establishment

It is possible to ask why what is morally unacceptable is in fact tolerated, but another way of posing the issue is to ask what kinds of arguments are invoked to dampen down objections to lies by authorities.

The kinds of defenses offered are typical of those already encountered with the in-group/out-group differentiation in terms of attributions. Public figures caught in lies will be defended by appeals to special circumstances, concatenations of bad luck, stress, illness, complexity of affairs or, expressed more succinctly, unstable, uncontrollable, external causes will be invoked to explain (away) their deceptions.

The myth of noblesse oblige may be of less cashable value in the United States than in Britain, where it can still be invoked to protect the indiscretions of the elite. Notions of lives of public service and a sense of duty can be (and may be realistically) invoked to applaud the activities of what came to be known as "the great and the good," but if it simultaneously emerges that they may have been handsomely paid for their services, their credibility becomes contendable. The endorsement of virtue by peers is a most useful if irrational and irrelevant weapon to use in rebuttals or excuses for what appear to be lies used to protect the self from exposure for delinquent or criminal acts.

Even more generally, arguments can trade as collective representations of the basic honesty, decency, and niceness of top people. Are the protests about the increased differentials of wealth and income in Britain the "politics of envy" as suggested by the prime minister, or are they simply an affront to principles to social justice, as argued by the Labour Party? Durkheim's (1898/1974) "collective representations" are enjoying a revitalized second coming as elaborated in Moscovici's (1976) "social representations." How these work differentially to exculpate or condemn individuals suspected of fraud and lying would repay investigation. What the media have to say about individuals charged with petty and grand fraud and lying to justify their actions might well uncover the in-group/out-group differentiations shown for friends and enemies in times of intergroup conflict.

Endpiece

In Chapter 4, several diagrams were used to summarize clues for the detection of deception in interpersonal contexts. Both the nonverbal and verbal schemes for facilitating the chances of a successful diagnosis of deception will no doubt be developed further, but in both cases, foundations have been laid. For the detection of deception in the public domain the same foundations exist, but insofar as the activities described in the last three chapters are proactive and chronic rather than reactive and acute, it may be helpful to note criteria that should signal a need to be wary.

A constant theme has been that wariness should come into play when arguments and explanations appear to lead to conclusions that bring differential benefits to their protagonists. Self-serving asymmetries in attributions have been a prominent feature to set alongside self-serving falsifications, but no attempt has been made to delve further into styles of thinking, their linguistic realizations, or attitudes. At the risk of being justifiably accused of oversimplification, the contrasts in Table 8.1 are offered as some possible introductory pointers.

Table 8.1 The Binary Opposition of an Emphasis on Truth Seeking and Action Orientation in Human Affairs

Socrates	Versus The Rest
Dominating Mental Activities	
Reflecting (planning, analyzing, synthesizing, evaluating, checking)	Deciding
Explaining	Justifying
Quality of Arguments	
Coherent, consistent, comprehensive, reason-conclusion	38+ Logical fallacies[a]
Linguistic Realizations	
Interrogatives (questions)	Imperatives (commands)
Qualified declaratives in relation to speaker's	Strong declaratives
Certainty	Definite
Probabilistic	All-none
Circumscribed	Always-never
Attitude to Truth	
Respect	
Indifference	Contempt
Attitude to Winning-Survival	
Secondary	Primary

a. See Thouless (1974).

The opposition of Socratic-human-being-concerned-with-truth as a basis for action and action-person-determined-to-win may be a useful analytic fiction. It certainly poses a host of questions for social psychologists.

The contrasts are too simple for at least two reasons. The first is that clever demagogues can simulate the rhetoric of the humble rational realistic servant to the community. They can offer a public face that is in many respects the opposite of what is going on inside their heads.

The second is that there are times in human affairs when too much reflection and planning will be disastrous. When delayed decisions mean disaster or death, groups need leaders who are action persons to inspire them to act in certain ways. Ancient Rome switched from a republican mode to an elected dictatorial one in times of crisis; dictators were elected for a year. It is when leaders prefer election for life that societies find it is too late to prevent the switch to totalitarianism. Because societies (and individuals) can also be too slow to anticipate their needs for decisive action, any given situation poses dilemmas.

With these two reservations, it could be informative to check examples of the sales pitches of the media, politicians, and any groups advancing their own cause or wares and examine similarities and differences in the linguistic realizations and qualities of their arguments.

What the public believes about its authorities and how it feels about their behavior is examined in Chapter 9.

CHAPTER NINE

Beliefs and Moral Judgments

Face-to-Face Lies

In Chapters 3 and 4, distinctions were drawn between what people believe to be true about lies and the real cues to their detectability. Some popular beliefs about cues indicative of lying have been shown to be false, although because people act in the light of their beliefs, people displaying such cues are likely to be seen as lying. Accused children who avoid eye contact are more likely to be judged as lying than deferential, at least in the United Kingdom and the United States. Children who smile when accused of lying are more likely to be judged as guilty than embarrassed. What these beliefs are and how they relate to behavior is one set of questions not yet addressed.

What do people believe about who lies to whom how often was examined in Chapter 3 with respect to persons within one's social network. Here it will be extended to beliefs about other members of society and, in particular, those in positions of power and authority.

At various points, the relevance of the morality of lying and deception to empirical studies has been raised, particularly how the notion of lies being seen as wrong has complicated investigations of their characteristics and the ways in which they function in social experience and behavior. The separation of the interpersonal and the public is made in the consideration of which kinds of lies are seen as wrong and why, with some attempt at an articulation.

Moral Judgments About Interpersonal Lies

St. Augustine's thinking led him to define eight kinds of lies, all judged to be wrong but some more wrong than others. Blasphemic lies headed his list, with lies bringing different degrees of harm to others occupying second and third place. Fourth came lies told for the pleasure of deceiving (Ekman's, 1985/1992, duping delight). For the fifth, the maintenance of smooth discourse was the paramount reason. In the last three, the prevention of harm to others was criterial: in the sixth, material loss; in the seventh, physical loss; and in the eighth, physical defilement. Even lies in the service of conversion of the heathen were wrong, partly on the grounds that they would be the thin end of a growing wedge. St. Thomas Aquinas agreed with Augustine about the wrongness of lies but changed the classification, first in terms of their motivation and then in terms of wrongness: The worst involves the intent to injure another, the second is intended to give pleasure to others, and the third is to help another or to protect from injury. Any lie injurious to God or one's neighbor is a mortal sin regardless of its motivation; those of no consequence or beneficial to another—venial.

These pronouncements set the scene for subsequent debate within the Christian church of the West. There are various instances of deceit or concealment in the Bible that do not appear to have provoked the wrath of God, and some seem to have been blessed by God. Particular interpretations of these various incidents were used throughout the Middle Ages to justify different forms of ways of deceiving authorities (but not God) mainly in the face of persecution by civil authorities and other Christian groups (Zagorin, 1990).

Doubtless, the religious and philosophical arguments have proceeded in some social worlds; for most of the people most of the time, however, lying and deceit will have been practiced without special concern for the distinction between venal and mortal sins. A component that does seem to be endemic to everyday life and institutions is the insistence that some forms of deceit are acceptable and others wrong, and this boundary is clearly drawn, with the label *lie* functioning to mark off the side of wrong. As *Roget's Thesaurus* lists, there are fewer than five verb phrases in English for speaking the truth, and these could be reconceived as one with several variants. There are 60 words for varieties of departures from the truth, but the word *lie* is the clearly preferred unit for condemnation. None of the others would be used to say, "And not just a lie but an X." In contrast, "And not just a falsehood but a downright lie" would be judged as more than a tautology. Hence, the maneuvering exercised to avoid the appellation "liar." Why society adopts what could be viewed as a hypocritical stand on the relation between word usage and reality is somewhat mysterious, just as is the scholasticism and casuistry that led to ritual formulae being authorized for individuals of persecuted sects to escape divine condemnation for denying one's beliefs. If God knows all, there is no need to make "mental reservation" in one's head about a lie one has just uttered!

The puzzle remains alive, however, that the acceptance of an admission of anything short of lying will be less condemned than an admission of lying. To escape a negative judgment, a counterfactual has to be reduced to just a fib, an understatement, or an exaggeration. Another defense is an appeal to being polite and considerate.

Given that lies were being classified in terms of degrees of wrongness, it is strange that even in the second half of the 20th century there is very little empirical work and less theory about differential judgments. Augustine and Thomas Aquinas both focused on motivation and consequence as variables relevant to moral evaluations, and those have been the main interest in the study of the development of children's bases of evaluation. These began with Piaget's (1932) use of a lie as one example of an action that might be judged wrong. From his data, he generalized to a contrast between an earlier consequence-based stage of objective responsibility to a later intention-based stage, an idea elaborated extensively by Kohlberg (1984) and others. Evaluation of the wrongness of lies per se was not pursued. In Chapter 3, the emphasis was on what children define as lies and how this changes with age. Two studies included data on ratings of degrees of wrongness. The two Australian studies on this topic were based on large data sets (Bussey, 1992; Peterson, Peterson, & Seeto, 1983). Abbreviating their report into six pages means that Peterson et al. either chose or were required to cram their results into very dense writing and too few tables for it to be possible to extract sufficient information about moral evaluations. With samples of 5-, 8-, 9-, and 11-year-old children and an adult sample, it is not clear to what extent the adult group was mainly responsible for age differences in trends. Because only the significance levels are reported for a number of analyses of variance, the general directions of any trends have to be inferred. The details specified in the succeeding paragraph imply that there were no discernible patterns, and because no enlightening comments are offered in the discussion, any synthesis would be premature; the comments are confined to an overall tendency for the adults to be more lenient than the children.

Likewise, the comparative status of the 10 categories of statement is not tabulated. Generally, protective lies were rated as worse than the white lie, the altruistic lie, and the practical joke. Whether it is the compression of the reporting, the excessive load on the children imposed by the procedure, or something else, what might have been a definitive study of the increasing differentiation of lying from other statements and an informative picture of the trends in moral evaluations finally raises more questions than it answers.

Bussey (1992) compared children's ratings of wrongness for lies and truthful statements: Preschool, second grade, and fifth grade were agreed that lies were worse than truthful statements. If the lie was punished it was judged worse only by the preschoolers, who were also distinguished from the older children in not attributing pride to truth tellers.

Other studies have questioned whether the age status of the teller or the recipient of a lie (Dituri, 1977) affects judgments, and of course, it is possible to proliferate other variations of teller, recipient, context, and qualities of the lie ad infinitum. For the present, however, the situation has not been greatly advanced since Piaget's (1932) original claims about moral evaluations of lies. What kind of statement is a lie and the differentiation between lies and how other kinds of speech act to lies remain in need of thorough developmental descriptions and explanations. When there is a developmental chart of the category lie and that chart can be elaborated to specify the qualities of lies that are relevant to variation in moral evaluations, it should become possible to link particular evaluations to particular qualities.

Such a program of research would be a massive venture in mapping and perhaps the immensity is a reason why no one has attempted a comprehensive attack. The situation with adults is also weak.

Two studies have set off in other directions. Maier and Lavrakas (1976) examined the relevance of the target of a lie and concluded that undergraduates believed it worse to lie to a friend than to a stranger. Across the sexes, males thought females lying to males was the most reprehensible of the four possibilities, with the females being equally self-serving. High-status liars were more condemned than low-status ones. The greater the cost or harm to the victim the worse the lie. Students who claimed to be moral thought lying more wrong than those who did not make such claims. Students overall thought they lied less than other people and that they were more suspicious of others than others were of them.

Lindskold and Walters (1983) followed a two-stage procedure focusing on categories. They used the philosophical literature to arrive at six categories of lies along with an a priori cline of increasing wrongness: saving others from shame, protecting self from punishment, influencing officials, protecting a gain or enhancing appearances, exploitative persuasion, and direct harm to others with gain for self. Equivalent forms of relevant vignettes for the six categories were constructed, and the ratings of two samples of undergraduates on permissibility of lying supported the a priori cline. A final study in which permissibility was rated for abstract descriptions of the six kinds yielded the same order. A small study by Mitchell (1994) found that the judged likelihood of people lying in the Lindskold and Walters situations was inversely related to the judged wrongness.

The derivation of any sets of stories would require comprehensive sampling along whatever the underlying dimensions of lies are. The particular set used was a strange mixture of motives, processes, and consequences. What happens to others as a result of a lie can vary independently of what happens to self, and "others" could have many different values; the suffering of innocent others would not be seen as equivalent to the suffering of fellow members of one's criminal gang.

As with children's development so with adults' evaluations—very little is known. In this chapter, it will be suggested that for lies by authorities the public differentiate among varieties: Some are seen as amusing, some as trivial, and some as acceptable, but in each case, only a minority of the sample did not say that the lies were wrong. The majority condemned all the instantiated lies. Those that had the worst consequences for the weakest members of society were most strongly condemned. Deliberate proactive lies in the pursuit of fraud were also strongly condemned. Proactive lies about one's past in the pursuit of ambition escaped majority condemnation.

These results are mentioned because they probably point to the parameters that will affect adult judgments at an interpersonal level. Statements that are defined as lies will be evaluated in terms of consequences and intentions, but as is proposed later in this chapter, the judgments are likely to have few consequences beyond the verbal if the judge is not a victim or the liar. Whether there is a loss of trust may be relatively irrelevant if the judge is an observer only. The number of people who comment on the truthfulness of acquaintances to their faces is probably small. The number who use proneness to tell lies as a criterion for selecting or deselecting acquaintances is probably small too.

As a participant, however, the rules may change. Studies of the rules people expect close friends and partners to follow place trust at the top end of any list (Argyle & Henderson, 1985) and a crucial aspect of this trust is being able to believe what they say. For marriage, Fitzpatrick (1990) has requirements of openness and positive attitudes to the other at the head of her necessary conditions of happy marriages. In both courtship and marriage, the dominant topic among writers about deception would appear to be sexual infidelity. It could be that covering up emotional indifference or boredom with each other is a more frequent reason for lying, or even fear of disapproval of personal habits. As suggested in Chapter 3, however, it will be difficult to obtain valid answers to questions about serious lies in close relationships. Lies covered and uncovered can go to the grave. Many family skeletons remain in their cupboards, as do secrets of friends. Those who meet each other later in life are unlikely to treat such meetings as opportunities for full confessionals and what is disclosed is likely to suffer from reconstructions that suffer from the self-serving biases reported in attribution theory. Parents' accounts of their child-rearing experiences change with time in the directions one would expect, just as historical accounts of unhappily married couples differ. It would not be surprising if research was to show that the memories have really changed and that there are not parallel sets of actual and cleaned-up versions. Motivation affects the processes of perception and thinking in self-serving ways, and memories will be similarly distorted, and the distortions are most likely to reduce the discrepancies between what one did and what one ought to have done. Reinterpretation, attenuation, and selectivity will be active most often to reduce residual guilt but occasionally to revive it.

That moral evaluations are affected by participant-observer roles in the same way that attributions are affected was demonstrated by Robinson (1994) who had two groups of students evaluate stories of the kind used by Lindskold and Walters (1983) but with two versions; one with named third parties as the liars and one with "you" as the liar. Kintz (1977) found that undergraduates believed that they were more against lying than were their peers.

Self-serving biases are a common feature of negatively evaluated behaviors (Weiner, 1985), and lying is unlikely to be an exception. This is what Maier and Lavrakas (1976) and Robinson (1994) have found. Students were given questionnaires that specified either themselves or a third party of the same sex and were asked how wrong it would be to lie in eight situations that would be easy to imagine experiencing. Even though this manipulation actually distinguished between being an imagined participant and observer rather than a real actor, the judgments were less condemnatory for the imagined self in all eight situations. Furthermore, the interitem correlations for self were lower and less likely to be significant, suggesting more discrimination as a function of situation and less stereotype. The mean rankings of wrongness were identical for the two roles. These findings are consistent with the biases in reasoning illustrated and demonstrated in the media (Chapter 7).

Beliefs About the Truthfulness of Authorities

It is perhaps not surprising that people believe false statements that they read in books, journals, or newspapers if the events to which these refer are beyond their personal experience in time or space. Human beings would have had to be designed differently if the default condition of our intelligence was to disbelieve what we are told by significant others.

It is the arrival of distrust that has to be explained, and as the chapter on child development shows, the distinction between telling the truth and lying emerges in early childhood. A view of the family and even of their political systems as benevolent generally lasts well into adolescence in the United States (Greenstein, 1965). Explanations for the emergence of wariness probably do not have to be profound in many cases. Children learn who lies about what and in what circumstances from both direct and indirect experience, but for the most part, the bias will remain tilted to acceptance of what one is told.

Why should anyone doubt what is reported in the history books? Why does it matter anyway? What Julius Caesar really did and why has little mediated consequences for those living today. Likewise, it matters little to most of the world whether or not some politicians on the Island of Dreams did lie about the election bribes offered.

It does matter, however, if it is your own politicians who are suspected of lying and if you find that their policies or taxes render you bankrupt or jobless or both. Worse still if they reduce medical services so that you or your loved ones begin to suffer chronic pain or premature death, for example. Any severe reductions in the quality of individual lives arising apparently from incompetent government actions and then lied about by the government should lead to a rejection of the credibility of that government. This will be particularly so if the sociological outcomes are seen in terms of relative deprivation. Runciman (1966) argued for the power of this hypothesis to explain dissatisfaction and frustration. If all are suffering, so be it. If others are prospering, and blatantly so, the relative deprivation is intensified. That appears to be what has been happening in the United Kingdom and the United States over the past 15 years for the middle and lower socioeconomic strata.

Although there are no hard longitudinal data to support the proposition that there has been an increase in the extent of deceit and lying per se in the public arenas of the capitalist West over the past 15 years, surveys and gossip are certainly consistent with such a conviction in the minds of the general public. Politicians in particular have dropped substantially in perceived credibility. Over the period of 1973 through 1993, University of Michigan surveys show almost all U.S. institutions suffering substantial losses of public confidence: Congress down by 43%, the press by 36%, financial institutions by 32%, the executive by 31%, and TV by 22%. These trends are elaborated by Lipsett and Schneider (1983) and Dionne (1991). Over the past decade, the Michigan surveys showed that by 1993 those who believe that hardly any government persons are not crooked had fallen to 9%, only 20% believed that government is not dominated by big interests, and only 23% believed that public officials care about what happens to people. An ICM quota sample survey of adults in Britain reported in the *Observer* (December 26, 1994) registered trust-distrust in institutions at the following percentage levels: the Church, 54% versus 23%; the police, 44% versus 28%; the monarchy, 32% versus 31%; the judiciary, 23% versus 42%; the civil service, 21% versus 33%; Parliament, 13% versus 47%; and the present government, 11% versus 60%.

Gallup (1993, Social Trends Report 397) has monitored the perceived honesty and ethical standards of people in different fields of employment in the United Kingdom. Their figures show slight declines for certain fields: doctors, university teachers, psychiatrists, engineers, trade union leaders, building contractors, and advertising executives. The last three mustered judgments of high or very high standards from only 11%, 12%, and 8%, respectively, but these had stayed at these levels since 1982. Lawyers had dropped from 48% to 37%, civil servants from 20% to 15%, police officers from 56% to 38%, government ministers from 22% to 9%, and members of Parliament from 15% to 7%. Only 9% of the national sample rated journalists as having high or very high ethical standards.

If the population really does hold such beliefs about those who mediate news, then presumably its members must think they can find out very little about the events affecting their society. That 9% think government ministers have very high ethical standards could be seen as surprising given the numbers who have resigned from their ministerial posts in the past 3 years.

In the United States, the beginnings of this apparent decline precede the arrival of Ronald Reagan in the White House, but in the United Kingdom, they do coincide with the incumbency of Margaret Thatcher in Downing Street and the political shift to appeals to slogans of deregulation of the economy, the virtues of competition, the need to reduce taxation of top earners, and the erosion of wasteful public welfare. From those inaugurations, the individual pursuit of power, wealth, and status as desirable ends was given a boost in the United States and a strong stimulus in the rest of the capitalist West, especially via lotteries such as the scramble for shares in the wealth previously locked into public enterprises. As has been argued elsewhere, once winning and success become more important than truth and situations open and competitive, then lying and deceit in pursuit of profit and pleasure should be expected to increase (Robinson, 1993). This can happen, however, only if the general public permits and endorses such values and conduct. Politicians can be thrown out of office at elections. They would find it more difficult to avoid medical and legal services, or resist monopoly prices, but people can set up pressure groups to reform institutions of any kind, however.

To date, there is no evidence about public beliefs about lies in the public domain. As a preliminary check on presumed frequencies of falsification by others, however, two small studies with British undergraduates in two institutions were conducted that gave very similar results, one set of which is reported (Robinson, 1994). As Table 9.1 shows, the results can be summarized as follows:

1. Families and friends were rated as relatively and absolutely infrequent lie tellers.
2. Politicians of all parties received very high ratings as lie tellers.
3. The media differed considerably. Although the *Sun* newspaper achieved the highest ranking, the *Times* and the *Guardian* were ranked 18th and 19th. TV was rated as directly comparable to the quality newspapers.
4. Professionals appeared in the bottom quartile and business people in the second highest.

One interesting further analysis yielded no interactions between personal political allegiance and judgments about politicians. Regardless of allegiance, all politicians were seen as equally frequent liars. The faith in the quality newspapers and the TV news stations might be seen as naive, but lies per se may be relatively rare in those media. The TV news is, in fact, necessarily highly selective, and the criteria of selection may lead to serious misrepresentations of reality without there being lies per se. The judged honesty of intimates corresponds more closely to the results of Lippard (1988) than to those of Turner, Edgley, and Olmstead (1975). Consistent with the University of Michigan surveys referred to in the general introduction, politicians, big business, and the example of the tabloid press, all appeared in the top quartile, with a heavy incidence of maximal scores.

These studies indicate several authorities are believed to lie frequently. To find out how the public reacts to these was the next step. Pilot studies showed a variety of reactions, subsequently used as categories of response about reactions to a set of false statements. The categories included the following:

1. Amusing—A bit of a laugh
2. Unimportant or indifferent—So what? or who cares?
3. Acceptable or expedient—It happens or they have to
4. Wrong
5. Seriously wrong

Table 9.1 Percentage Frequency of Judged Lying for Highest and Lowest
             32 Possible Sources of Lies ($N = 35$)

Source	Frequency[a]			Mean
	Never	Occasionally	Often	
The *Sun*	0	6	94	2.94
Advertisers	0	17	83	2.83
Governments	0	20	80	2.80
Conservative politicians	0	29	71	2.71
Labor politicians	0	31	69	2.69
Scots nationalists	0	46	54	2.54
Liberal politicians	0	49	51	2.51
Chief executives (industrial)	0	49	51	2.51
British Rail	9	37	54	2.40
Trade union leaders	3	54	43	2.40
Chief executives (pharm)	9	54	37	2.29
Animal liberationists	6	60	34	2.28
Vice chancellors	3	74	23	2.20
Bankers	9	69	23	2.14
Police commissioners	9	69	23	2.14
Police inspectors	14	66	20	2.06
Headteachers	14	71	14	2.00
The *Times*	14	74	11	1.97
The *Guardian*	14	80	6	1.91
ITV News	14	80	6	1.91
BBC 1 News	20	71	9	1.89
Friends of the Earth	29	71	0	1.83
Historians	31	60	9	1.77
Opposite-sex friends	34	60	6	1.71
Professors	40	54	6	1.66
Scientists	40	60	0	1.60
Archbishops	60	31	9	1.48
Archeologists	54	43	3	1.48
Family	60	40	0	1.40
Good friends	69	29	3	1.34
Your best friend	77	23	0	1.23

a. Never scored = 1; occasionally scored = 2; often scored = 3.

Given the cost of commercial surveys, the number of items for a
national study was contained at 13, and Gallup Poll (1993) interviewed 994 people across Great Britain to yield a representative
sample of the post-16 population with respect to gender, age, class,
employment, and region (see Table 9.2). Traditional procedures were

Table 9.2 Percentages of Persons From National Sample Giving Six Reactions to 13 Lie Events ($N = 994$)

	Reaction[a]						Wrongness[b]	
	Amu	Triv	Exp	Wrong	Wrong+	DK	Σ	Rank
Police forging evidence to get "guilty" verdicts on innocent people	1	1	2	18	78	1	174	3
Financiers defrauding banks	1	1	1	29	67	1	163	5
Government lying about the state of the economy	2	3	7	36	52	1	140	7
Advertisements falsely claiming cures for illnesses and ailments	1	6	3	38	52	1	140	7
The police forging evidence to get guilty verdicts on actual criminals	0	2	9	33	55	1	143	6
Newspapers publishing untrue stories about the sexual activities of famous people	8	18	4	38	30	1	98	12
Government "fixing" statistics on unemployment and crime	0	3	9	47	40	1	127	10
Newspapers falsely attributing unpopular policies to political opponents	2	12	10	50	25	2	100	11
Ministers lying to cover up hazards to public health	0	1	2	28	68	0	164	4
Advertisements greatly exaggerating what washing products can do	12	32	8	35	11	2	57	13
Ministers lying to hide personal profit	1	6	3	43	46	1	135	9
Financiers defrauding the elderly of their savings or pensions	0	0	0	11	88	0	187	1
People posing as collectors of money for charities	0	1	1	27	76	0	179	2

a. Amu = amusing; Triv = trivial; Exp = expedient; Wrong+ = seriously wrong; DK = don't know.
b. Σ is based on 2 for wrong+, 1 for wrong, and 0 for other.

followed by Gallup's team of interviewers, each of whom was given quotas of categories for sex, age, social class, and employment. Over 100 sampling points were used. The 13 statements were expressed in a general form, but each had been exemplified by recent cases widely reported in the media. For example, for Question 12, Barlow-Clowes had been convicted of defrauding old people of their savings, and the Mirror Pension Fund had been raided.

1. Main trends
   a. The categories of "wrong" and "seriously wrong" collected the great majority of the judgments. Only washing powder advertisements attracted less than 50% condemnation. The two libelous newspaper items were not condemned by 32% and 25%. By contrast, the falsehoods of five items were judged wrong by 95% or more.
   b. Of the five most condemned actions, four had very serious consequences for the victims: poverty, ill health, and imprisonment. With one exception, the victims were people, not institutions.
   c. Amusement was recorded by 12% for undangerous advertisements and 8% for newspaper sex stories; these were also seen as trivial falsehoods by 32% and 18%, respectively. False attributions of policies to political opponents of newspapers were judged as trivial by 12% and expedient by 10%.
   d. Falsehoods in pursuit of gain attracted the same measure of condemnation as those designed to save face.
2. Demographic variations
   a. *Gender.* Of the 13 items, the seriously wrong percentages were equal for 4, higher in males for 4, and higher for females in 5. It was not possible to identify which features might be underlying the differentiations.
   b. *Social class.* Although the C1, C2, and DE groups did not differ among themselves, the ABs were strongly condemnatory on more items than each of the other groups (AB vs. C1, 13/0, sign test, $p = .001$; AB vs. C2, 11/0, sign test, $p = .01$; AB vs. DE, 11/1, sign test, $p = .05$).
   c. *Region.* A clear pattern emerged with southern England being similar to the Midlands and Wales, but the north and Scotland had a higher percentage of seriously wrong judgments across more items (north and Scotland vs. south, 11/2, sign test, $p = .02$).
   d. *Age.* No general monotonic effects appeared, but two patterns did. For seven items, the 35 to 44 age group had the highest percentage of seriously wrong judgments, with a decline for both younger and older persons. For ministers lying about private profits, the two

newspaper items, and the washing powder advertisements, the percentage of seriously wrong looked to be increasing with age without any statistical analysis.

e. *Voting intention.* A detailed statistical treatment of the political data might have hidden more than it would have revealed. There were no significant differences in the percentages of the main political parties endorsing the seriously wrong category, although further data might have shown that labor and liberal voters were particularly condemning of deception by government organs.

Comments

There was sufficient patterning among the results that was consistent with current beliefs to suggest that the data themselves are reliable and valid: the positivity of the inter-item correlation matrix and the higher correlations between items sharing a common seriousness of consequence. The statements attracting the highest percentages of amusement, triviality, and indifference were not surprising. The washing powder advertisements were the least condemned, whereas lies resulting in poverty, ill health, or imprisonment were most condemned. Taking the results at their face value as being valid reflections of attitudes, any selection of highlights in an area not yet defined by theoretical frameworks is necessarily subjective. It has been mentioned that it was somewhat arbitrary to decide what size of percentage difference merits comment because an individual 2% difference is but a small effect, even though conventionally significant. Likewise, the choice of cutoffs would affect the conclusions.

For gender, attempts to identify common features within and contrasting features across the differentiating items failed. The most reasonable conclusion would seem to be that there is prima facie evidence for some gender differences but that to find out more would require more, preferably open-ended, interviewing to begin to identify the true bases of differentiation.

In contrast, both social class and region yielded patterns that might have been expected. Historically, Scotland and northern England have been the centers of nonconformist puritanism, the sects most vocal in their condemnation of sins of any kind. That they remain more condemnatory of lies would be most simply explained as a cultural heritage. That social class category AB exceeded each of the others might stem from their closer social association with the establishment figures implicated in the false statements and a rejecting reaction against the dishonesty of the few who are seen as letting down the group. Alternatively, ABs are likely to be better informed about the incidence or nature of the relevant events. What are known as the quality newspapers are read predominantly by ABs, and these have been steadily consistent in their exposure and condemnation of corruption and deceit by authorities.

The selection of items was not arbitrary, but the sampling of false statements was very restricted. An examination of the organization and structure of the underlying determinants of correlation in reactions to false statements in the public domain would require an analysis of a much larger number of items in which the content, sources, and the seriousness and kind of consequences are differentiated. The selection was deliberately geared toward false statements presumed to refer to serious events, and it might be that judgments of amusement, indifference, and triviality would be more frequent for other false statements. It is noteworthy, however, that the false statements in newspapers escaped rates of condemnation above 75% although neither of the statements referred to any established convention of permitted fiction in the service of humor or mockery, for example. What remains as the massive finding is that most false statements were condemned as wrong and seriously wrong by the great majority of the adult population.

Having obtained a broad brush portrait, the next step was to interview a small sample of shopping mall visitors, first to establish whether they also thought most of the lies were seriously wrong, then to ask them why such lies were so wrong, and finally to ask them what should be done about these situations. Neither of the last two questions evoked what might be called crystallized accounts. None of the replies were coherent, consistent, set pieces. Most answers were confined to a single comment and many could be reformulated and reduced to "it's wrong because it's wrong." There were no hints that such answers were derived from the principles of Kant (1785/ 1964) or Kohlberg's Stage 6 (1984). Generally, however, the answers carried a tone of conviction and concern. For the steps that society should take to deal with the lies, the same tone prevailed. No one invoked slogans about the freedom of the press to print what they liked. On the contrary, it was common to propose that persistently lying newspapers should be shut down. Legal controls with positive court actions were the most common responses. Dismissal from office for lying was also common. Although these sentiments might be construed as punitive, the spirit appeared to be more of a concern and sympathy for the victims. In view of this, it was not strange that some answers referred explicitly to possible restitution of losses for victims from those whose lies had defrauded them. A number of people were resigned to the existence of such events as being matters about which governments would not take the trouble to act and they believed further that lying would always be part of life in the public domain anyway. This pessimism was occasionally combined with a contempt for the indifference of governments to such events. There are several lines of inquiry that need to be pursued before it is possible to comment on how many people of what kind are likely to do what as a result of their beliefs.

Interpretations

Impotence and Apathy. No one interviewed had, in fact, done anything about any of the lying in the public domain. Of those asked, none had decided to write to their local member of Parliament about any of the scandals. None had protested to anyone in authority. Governments may be free to ignore phone calls and letters of which they become aware, but they just may feel obliged to react. Given the context of millions of persons in a single society, individuals can make their opinions heard only through the ballot box and direct communications up through the political hierarchy or indirectly through the media. At present, there is no evidence to indicate why people do not phone or write more. In the end, if a sufficient amount of people disapprove of policies and practices, they have the periodic power to evict governments. Although each individual has but little he or she can do alone, it is no more or less than the sum of their collective actions that is significant for their society and culture. The answers obtained about possible actions were pessimistic rather than apathetic. It is clear that people were sincerely disgusted that big lies were tolerated by those in authority, but of course, until this disgust is translated into action, it is unlikely that authorities will act legislatively. Switzerland is willing to pay for referenda on particular issues. State and county legislatures in the United States put out various community proposals for decisions by popular votes. In any seriously concerned social democracy, such activities would need to be extended very considerably, and they would include taking notice

Discussion

Before any attempt is made to articulate the various results reported in this chapter and earlier about the frequency and judged morality of lying, it is worth pausing to ask how lying may differ from acts such as stealing or assaulting. First, it may be noted that lying is a criminal offense only in very limited circumstances. Lying under oath in court is an offense, although accused people found to be guilty are very rarely charged with perjury. Neither do judges comment on lies offered by the accused. There seems to be a general expectation that, regardless of reality, people have a right to plead not guilty and to remain silent or lie under oath. It is as though the accused can be expected and is permitted to try to escape justice. Whether the abolition of the 5th Amendment in the United States would raise the frequency of innocent people being convicted has not been investigated. Proactive lying to defraud others can be an offense, as are slander and libel. Financiers getting people to part with money with fraudulent investment opportunities is criminal, but government ministers proclaiming that there will be no currency devaluation when this has already been planned cannot be sued successfully by victims who believe them. Lying about who is doing what in a social network is not an offense; gossipmongering and rumor spreading are not illegal, although considerable harm to others can be achieved by such means.

Although stealing is stealing, lying is an attempt to conceal some other actions, and judgments about its seriousness do not seem to be independent of the moral qualities of the actions being concealed. The extent of condemnation is considerably reduced if no harm is caused to anyone by the lie and especially if it is told as an act of consideration for others. Toward this extreme, any lie that remains defined as a lie will be seen simultaneously as wrong and yet the correct thing to do; more likely, it will be relabeled as a white lie or perhaps a fib.

As also remarked earlier, being able to have an utterance labeled as a lie rather than a fib, an exaggeration, or an equivocation increases the chances of having its author condemned although for public figures this does not normally have any consequences. Lying is far more frequent than stealing, and people lie to those from whom they would not steal. What might be concluded? One line would argue that cultures and societies appreciate the truth of the assertion made in Chapter 1 that whereas a society in which all statements were true is conceivable, one in which there are too many lies could not function. The essence of the representational function of language is that statements uttered are believed to correspond to reality, and if this relationship becomes too unpredictable, the system ceases to be a system of communication.

On the other hand, because they can be hard to detect and can therefore be very efficient means of harming others or protecting and enhancing one's own position, there is a societal pressure to minimize their unjust and destructive potential.

Both considerations together help to explain why the rhetoric about the wrongness of lying is so strong at the same time as the incidence of its occurrences is so high. They help to explain why it is the intended consequences that seem to be the basis of the strength of their condemnation as wrongful acts.

Biases in Judged Frequency and Seriousness

Given that as a category lying is condemned as wrong, it is not surprising that the biases endemic to social judgments apply. The premises of social identity theory (Tajfel & Turner, 1979) and attribution theory (see Hewstone, 1983) appear to explain the biases reported—for example, others lie more than self, others lie more to self than self does to others, and out-groups tell more and more vicious lies about in-groups than vice versa (and are more likely to attribute these to stable controllable characteristics of personality). The participant-observer distinction is relevant (Jones & Nisbett, 1972); respondents cast in the role of observer will condemn lies more severely and more generally than those cast in the role of participant liar. Unfortunately, no one has looked at the other possibility of the predictably worst lies being those told to a participant victim.

These objectively irrational (but subjectively rationalized) biases can be very strong, especially as the stakes of conflicts rise in the dissolution of close relationships, in the persecution of other groups, and in wars. The only result that did not follow this pattern was that the political affiliations of British students did not affect their judgments of the frequency of lying by politicians. The judged frequencies of lying by politicians of all parties were close to ceiling and the Scottish Nationalists attracted similar ratings, even though this group is confined to Scotland and was almost wholly unknown to the predominantly English group of respondents. Politicians have become so discredited that judgments about them have taken on the characteristics of a negatively evaluated stereotype.

Judgments of Frequency

The American and British data are consistent with each other in the assumption that friends and family lie the least. In the British data, opposite-sex friends came significantly higher, and it would be interesting to establish whether this arises from potential jealousy, fear, or validated experience. Politicians and others with political positions are in the same league as the yellow press on both sides of the Atlantic. It is perhaps surprising that by contrast, professionals are seen as lying much less frequently, but more surprising is the trusted position of the quality newspapers and news broadcasts. Any objective analyses (see Chapter 7) show up not just selectivity and bias in the presentation of events but misrepresentation as well. Even in disputes that are not internal societal conflicts in which the media have direct vested interests, the selectivity and partisanship are clearly demonstrable. On British TV, the portrayal of the conflict in Bosnia has been consistently anti-Serbian in both direct and indirect representations. It may be true that the Serbians are responsible for more attacks and atrocities than their opponents, but their opponents have performed similarly ruthless acts. To the extent that the true frequencies are misrepresented, British TV viewers are being provided with biased information.

Given the statistical biases in the thinking of ordinary human beings and the selective over- and underestimations and the self-serving components of these, the social facts are likely to remain as they are until rational realism becomes a more highly prized value and education equips people to understand statistically based information. It could be argued that one of the most glaring gaps in the curricula of schools and colleges is in the field of statistics. As Chapter 8 illustrated, the misrepresentation of statistical information in the service of its authors is a major feature of modern societies.

Judgments of Morality

The judged wrongness of lies appears to vary with the intentions of the liar and the outcomes. Deliberate lies having tragic and unjust outcomes for the victims are the most strongly condemned. At the other pole, the overtone of wrongness remains—a lie is a lie. Not all the citizens of the world have read and accepted Grice's (1989) maxims, their implications, and implicatures. They do not all see that deliberate offense against the maxim of "Be truthful" can be a clever means of uttering a more profound truth, amusing others, or displaying wit.

TV advertisements are one genre in which many false statements are not intended to mislead either superficially or more profoundly: no one is expected to believe that squirrels drink Carling Black Label Lager or that if they themselves drink they will be able to display athletic prowess in their pursuit of nuts. St. Augustine is correct, of course, that being amused by such displays may be the thin end of the wedge of being unduly influenced by other advertisements that are hidden or overt persuaders. A substantial minority of the U.K. population was not condemnatory of this kind of misrepresentation, and that was also true for certain other lies. There seemed to be an ambivalence about "shocking" disclosures of the private lives of public figures. On the one hand, these revelations were seen as a vicious intrusion on privacy, but simultaneously, they were enjoyable gossip; good luck to them having some naughty fun, but they should be setting a better example for society. In the United Kingdom, it is the sex stories and pictures that seem to command sales that reach perhaps half the population, with their combined daily and Sunday sales being in excess of 10 million. Moral fervor about such peccadillos is confined to a minority, as is a relaxed endorsement. Again, it would be possible to demonstrate internal logical inconsistency in the views held, but logical inconsistency does not entail psychological incompatibility.

This phenomenon was most clearly pronounced in the interviews of those who were strongly condemnatory of various deliberate lies that had resulted in tragic and unjust outcomes for the victims. The genuine moral fervor was inconsequential for action; the rhetoric was assertive rather than explanatory, emotional rather than intellectual, and condemnatory rather than analytic. Hence, the suggestion of its utility in conversations with like-minded others and its irrelevance beyond. The message to offenders is clear. If they can lie successfully for long enough, there will be no follow-up or follow-through. They may keep their ill-gotten gains. They may retain their jobs as elected representatives or company employees. A cost-benefit analysis yields a clear advantage for cheating and then lying about it. The figures in both the United States and the United Kingdom show the low level of public faith in the elites of politics, the media, commerce and industry, the law, and the unions, but the voting figures and action indicate apathetic acceptance of the state of affairs that has developed. Of course, the public can also lie to authorities.

Peoples' Lies to Social Organizations

It proved to be difficult to obtain estimates or even guesstimates of the extent to which members of the public lie to authorities of various kinds. This is presumably not because such lies are rare.

How many people make hoax telephone calls to the emergency services lying about fires, injuries, and crimes? (Certainly when the IRA was active in England, schools, factories, and transport services were chronically disrupted by false warnings.) After the bomb explosion at London's Victoria station, British Telecom said that it was receiving over 100 false calls per day.

Insurance companies have always been at a threefold risk: true claims, exaggerated claims, and false claims. The ultimate victims of fraudulent claims are the honest customers, and this is perhaps one reason why companies tolerate so many claims; too many claims would just be too expensive to contest. Sunken ships with forged manifests merit inquiry, as do warehouses and factories, but claims for damage to cars are notorious for exaggerated sums of money. Car owners may connive at excessive charges, but it is the garages that benefit most. Houseowners can replace old carpets and lavatory pans for new ones following accidents with cigarette burns and dropped hammers. Thefts can include more expensive stereos and videos than those present, if indeed any were. As one example, the Association of British Insurers believes it is facing an escalation of bogus claims from travelers. Home and overseas insurance put a figure of £50 million a year on the bill, virtually one third of the total paid out. The suggestion was that 40% of claims were inflated and 20% invented. (Having had three genuine accidental damage claims rejected, however, I can begin to see why some people will prefer just to drop a broken camera overboard!)

Injuries and health problems arising at work or in public amenities are a growing area for false as well as legitimate claims. Psychologists report people recovering substantial damages from companies for ill health caused by toxic substances, where the cognitive losses simply do not correspond to the symptoms that should have occurred for the particular poisoning that is alleged to have affected them. "Permanent" damage can rectify itself after claims have been met and pensions obtained. What proportion of such claims are fraudulent is unknown. As soon as affairs become matters of legal contention, lies seem to proliferate, as witnessed, for example, by the large number of not guilty pleas that are subsequently followed by convictions.

Health problems as a reason for absence from work are another context for lies. The temporal statistics point to fluctuations with days of the week, times of the year, and events in personal and public calendars that imply fabrication as well as real illness. Rates of absence vary between employers so that the more generous allowances offered are taken up more than the less generous. Again, checking up and challenging seem to be too expensive and too likely to fail so employers do no more than tolerate the losses.

Phony claims from the welfare state have been a component in the rhetoric for tougher checks and the dismantling of some benefits. The rhetoric has a measure of validity. Unemployment and housing benefits, as well as income support payments, are paid to individuals who are knowingly deceiving the community. Hessing, Elffers, Robben, and Webley (1993) report estimates of $235 million as the fraudulent unemployment benefit claimed in the United States for 1986. Two Dutch estimates gave figures of 17% and 28% of claimants earning money on the side. In their empirical study of a carefully selected sample of confessed fraudsters and presumed entitled beneficiaries, Hessing et al. found themselves with a participation rate of only 26%. Of the 96 people, 16 denied receiving any unemployment benefit, 8 from each group! Of the 43 "genuine" claimants, 5 reported having made additional income. Of the 37 fraudsters, only 26 admitted this at interview. The authors report the Kendall tau of .60 as "a good correspondence" between self-report and reality, but with nearly a third of the fraud group denying their actions, the analysis is rendered more complicated than optimism might have preferred. They compared honest with fraudulent respondents separately for the official and self-reported groups. In the comparisons there is an ambiguity about the official groups. It is not clear whether the "honest" group is those who have denied or admitted to fraudulent claims. A number of individual differences measures discriminated between the honest and the fraudulent: perceived fairness of social security rules, personal orientations of not being a free rider, not being a risk taker, not being alienated or disinhibited, believing in the Protestant work ethic, and denying horizontal equity. The honest group was opposed to three kinds of fraud against society. Situational pressures did not discriminate. Situations constraints did so only for the officially defined group. Overall, individual differences in perceived instigators and constraints accounted for more variance than situational factors.

Perhaps the most widespread lies are those that appear, or fail to appear, on tax returns. Within Europe, Britain is seen as one of the few countries in which taxation is not a form of voluntary gift to the state. Those powerful and influential enough arrange for the tax laws to be written in their favor. For example, in Britain most of the middle classes pay a 40% inheritance tax on assets over £150,000, whereas the upper classes either leave tax exempt properties such as farms or private companies or have their assets secured in family trusts and other legal modes of tax avoidance. Those who can, inflate expenses. The Australian Tax Office conducted a 5% sample survey of tax agents for 1993 returns and found a 73% error rate of which almost all were in the clients' favor; $100 million was subsequently removed from the claims (the *Australian*, July 14, 1994, p. 2). Those who are paid salaries from which deductions are made at source are probably the category least prone to defraud the tax authorities, but then they have no option.

According to estimates made by Taylor Nelson AGB (*Financial Times*, June 10, 1995), people in the United Kingdom failed to disclose an average of £1140 each to the tax authorities in 1994. The poorest fifth derived 33% of their spending and surplus without declaring it, the wealthiest fifth, 5%. This is estimated to be between 6% and 8% of the gross national product. The corresponding evasion rates for some other countries were estimated at 15% for Belgium, 25% for Italy, and 100% for Russia.

Hessing, Elffers, and Weigel (1988) reviewed earlier work on tax evasion and set up their own Dutch study examining the utility of the Fishbein and Ajzen (1975) theory of reasoned action as a basis for the prediction of tax evasion. Unfortunately, their careful sampling of officially defined tax evaders and presumed honest taxpayers showed no significant association between self-reports and official definitions: 49 of 71 officially defined evaders claimed innocence and 21 of 84 officially defined nonevaders admitted to evasions. (Just as

Table 9.3 Farm Fraud Subsidy Cases in European Community, 1993

Country	No.	Value(£)	Repaid	Country	No.	Value(£)	Repaid
Italy	47	107.8	15.9	Ireland	16	0.9	0.24
Britain	180	3.4	1.0	Belgium	21	4.9	0.08
Denmark	75	3.4	0.8	Luxembourg	—	—	—
France	118	27.5	6.5	Netherlands	61	2.8	0.48
Germany	176	15.9	2.1	Portugal	141	6.0	0.64
Greece	211	19.9	1.0	Spain	251	6.2	0.16

with the social security study, it would have been interesting to challenge those who appeared to be lying about their demonstrated dishonesty. There is, of course, nothing odd about self-reports of evasion not having been detected by the authorities; skilled fraudsters should know how to cover their tracks.) The results found were clear and dramatic. Three attitudes toward tax evasion and three subjective norm indices all correlated with self-reported tax evasion but not with officially defined evasion. In complementary contrast, measures of alienation, tolerance toward illegal behavior, competitiveness, and a self-serving orientation index all correlated both with documented status as a tax evader and with the amount of tax evaded. Hessing et al. suggest that the Fishbein and Ajzen model predicts coherence within the interview but no more. Respondents go for consistency within a session. In contrast, it is the more general attitudes toward society that predict what people will actually do.

Research of the kind pursued by Hessing and his colleagues (1988) is clearly very time consuming and difficult to set up, but both of the studies have yielded results of practical and theoretical relevance. Both sets offer challenges to resolve the puzzles the results provide.

Fraudulent claims can transcend national boundaries, and because of its foundation, the European Community seems to have been treated as a cornucopia for predators on a grand scale. Its lack of financial controls and failures to monitor and check its expenditure are becoming legendary.

As costs grow, it simply raises its bills to member states. How much money disappears through lying claims each year is unknown. Conservative estimates run up to $600 million per annum (see Table 9.3). Perhaps the true figure is £1 billion per annum. Nobody seems to know or care enough to find out. The relevant committee documented £200 million of identified false claims in 1993; just 15% was recovered. Italy accounted for 50% of the total and France and Greece accounted for over 10% each.

Just as the earlier chapters noted that lying seems to be endemic to interpersonal encounters in everyday life and later chapters will illustrate its omnipresence among the public pronouncements of elites, so this final section serves as a reminder that individuals also lie to organizations and perhaps especially to the state.

CHAPTER TEN

Whistle-Blowing

Rationale for Inclusion

In the unfolding of events involving whistle-blowing, the action can easily assume the qualities of a melodrama as ordinary people are recast as heroes, and organizations with benevolent mission statements risk transformation into immoral monsters. Lonely Virtue confronts the multiheaded Vice, whose great power presages the triumph of Evil. In old-style American Westerns, the final scene allowed Shane or Destry to ride off into the sunset leaving a better world behind him, the hero secure in his heroism. In Ibsen's *The Enemy of the People*, the noble whistle-blowing doctor is destroyed. Descriptions of some recent examples of whistle-blowing (Glazer & Glazer, 1989) read more like an Ibsen tragedy than *High Noon*, with Evil avoiding most of the comeuppance that would be obligatory in a traditional Western, and with Virtue just about surviving, albeit in a minor key. As these authors point out, however, the flowchart of actions and reactions has variety. Once an employee has gone public with a revelation of a cover-up, the organization may react with sharp disclaimers and vicious attempts at denigration and degradation, followed by demotion or dismissal. The whistle-blower may or may not choose to persevere at each phase of the action. In extremis, homicide or suicide may be his or her fate. The authorities in the organization may welcome the revelation at the outset, however. At any subsequent point in the saga, the organization can switch from being negative to positive toward the whistle-blower. Historically, however, persecution seems to be more common than rehabilitation, and it must be remembered that the cases emerging into public gaze are likely to be a biased sample. They are those where quietly blown internal whistles were not heeded. Organizations may facilitate and handle internal whistle-blowing in ways that save employees from the dilemma of whether or not to go public. To the extent that this is true, organizations that are receptive to criticism will not be setting up conditions where employees have cause to go public. It is therefore not surprising if unreceptive organizations are also likely to persist in evasion by attacking revelations.

Whistle-blowing, as defined by those concerned with it, has taken on a scope wider than the frame of reference to be adopted here: It has come to include the exposure of illegal or unfair discrimination at work, sexual harassment, and a variety of other secret practices, in addition to those that involve deliberate deception of the public. This last is the focus of concern here: cases in which organizations are exposing their customers or employees to illegal or unpublished risks to their health and safety and cases in which people in organizations are behaving corruptly for personal or company profit and against the public interest. Individual employees can discover or otherwise become acquainted with information about these dangers or corruption and "blow the whistle" by reporting what they think they have found out to the media, the police, or some other outsiders, who in turn may publicize or otherwise act on the intelligence provided. The potential range of misdemeanors in organizations is high, and their incidence is of such a frequency in many societies in which the media are not overtly under state control for there to be at least one major scandal per country at any particular time.

To date, social psychologists have not become seriously involved in studying the phenomena. Philosophers and lawyers have taken up the issues, particularly in the United States (e.g., Bok, 1984; Callahan, 1988). Through their work, a helpful clarification of the conceptual and moral issues is emerging that will greatly assist social psychologists once "whistle-blowing" comes onto their agenda.

There are at least five features of whistle-blowing directed against the cover-ups of scandals, such as Watergate or the DC-10's safety, that dramatize issues about the psychology of truth telling and lying. First, the ethical issue is transparent. Superficially, the primary obligation of people must be to the greater good; the public interest must transcend the personal and organizational advantages of silence. Once particular cases are used to inform the arguments, however, the difficulties of erecting and sustaining such a paramount principle emerge. Second, the lies involved in the original secrecy and any subsequent attempts to cover-up what has happened typically have very extensive and profound negative consequences for the potential victims in extremis death or debility. Third, the whistle-blower may well be subjected to extremes of attack that can escalate to go beyond attempts to discredit and deter; they can proceed to psychological or physical destruction. Fourth, once the whistle is blown, the drama is at least in part in the public domain and provides insight into public reactions to lying. Finally, there is the denouement. It can be observed that what is done with whoever emerge as miscreants and what societies do to prevent repetitions of such affairs. How does society value the actions of exposers of deception?

What can be written at this time has to be speculative and exploratory given the recency of scholarly interest in the phenomenon. To the best of my knowledge, the United States is the only country with a Whistle-Blowers Protection Act, and work there has been initiated mainly by philosophers, lawyers, and social scientists other than social psychologists. There are no experiments to report. There is a wealth of case study material—with more being generated on a daily basis.

Obvious examples of products and activities provoking whistle-blowing are unsafe designs, materials, or procedures in engineering ventures, ineffectual or dangerous medical products or practices, improper and undisclosed expenditure, and abuses of power for personal wealth beyond the clichéd dreams of avarice. Much occurs in countries where the concept of blowing the whistle has yet to arrive and where any form of criticism in public is likely to be met with great and decisive speed. Even where and when general public criticism is allowed, because the highest authorities are prone to be implicated in cover-ups of scandals, their vulnerability helps to explain why they move so slowly to protect and facilitate whistle-blowing. In the United States, there was no immediate decisive and efficient political action following Schroeder's statement in the opening congressional hearings on whistle-blower protection:

> The goal of good clean, clean government has been brought to center-stage by the ethical problems of so many Reagan administration officials. What better way to achieve these goals [than] by encouraging insiders, those who really know, to disclose waste, mismanagement and wrong-doing, illegalities, and dangers to public health and safety.

Does it not make eminent good sense to encourage whistleblowing and to protect, even honor whistleblowers?

As this chapter is being composed, the U.K. population continues to listen to a succession of government ministers defending their actions in the "Arms to Iraq" affair. This now-christened Scott inquiry is trying to establish, at great public expense, how it came to be that export certificates were being granted to send weaponry to Iraq while an export arms ban was in force and that the certificates were classified as secret. With the accusations and counteraccusations of lying, it is difficult to avoid the weakest prediction that one or more U.K. government ministers will be found guilty of deception and suppression of wrongdoing. This is only the latest in what seems to be more than an annual political scandal and cover-up following the whistle being blown. The United States seems to have been similarly beset. It is therefore perhaps not surprising that the United Kingdom has no directly relevant legislation and that the progress in the United States has been much slower than the reformers would have wished. A brief account of the developing American situation can be used to illustrate the progress and delays.

A Brief History of U.S. Legislation on Whistle-Blowing

Parker (1988) charts a brief instructive history of whistle-blowing legislation in the United States and the subsequent activities of the bodies responsible for investigating allegations and monitoring the fate of whistle-blowers within the civil service. In 1958, Congress established a Code of Ethics in which civil servants were to put their "loyalty to the highest moral principles above loyalty to persons, party or government department." A relevant case is that of Fitzgerald's defense for disclosing that $2 million excess costs on a government contract had been deleted from the official records; his defense rested on his citation of the primacy of telling the truth as a moral principle. He became known as the official "fired for telling the truth." He was eventually reinstated after a succession of court hearings.

Following Senate hearings in 1978 that revealed that, although Congress had encouraged whistle-blowing verbally, it had not provided either efficient channels for it to occur or subsequent protection for those who blew the whistles, legislation was passed to establish agencies within the orbit of the Inspector General and the General Accounting Agency. These were to facilitate and encourage genuine whistle-blowing. Reprisals against whistle-blowers became prohibited. Subsequent muddles about which agency was responsible for which parts of the procedural flowchart of decisions and actions were not sufficiently clarified for the writers of the reports or the activities of the Office of Special Counsel to encourage Congress to believe that its problems had been solved, and further legislation was enacted in the form of a Whistle-Blower Protection Bill.

Pragmatically, of course, what some might see as moral absolutes can give rise to nonsense. In purchasing, value for money does not always entail selection of the lowest tender. In selecting personnel for appointment or promotion, there cannot always be someone guaranteed to be the unanimously agreed ideal candidate. Even in a much more moral world than the current one, the principle of telling the truth may well come into conflict in particular cases with other equally important principles; in real-life decisions, one of the superordinate burdens is deciding which moral principles to prioritize. Neither are all whistle-blowers necessarily concerned with the public good. Any of a variety of sinister motives can stimulate false or debatable accusations.

It is quite clear, however, that in the fairly recent past there has been a clear disjunction between the official rhetoric and the realized practice to an extent that has discouraged well-founded whistle-blowing. Outside the federal service, those alert to cover-ups and deception have found themselves even less protected. They can be subject to doublespeak from their own professional codes of ethics and find that employment law favors organizations against individuals who blow whistles.

Professional Codes of Ethics

At the lower level of professional societies and their guidelines for self-regulation of the conduct of their members, many codes comment on the moral principles to be followed by members, but not all are internally consistent in their statements and those that do prioritize obligations in some way can still leave the whistle-blower exposed to charges of failure of some kind.

Callahan (1988) offers extracts from the codes of ethics of several professions, all of which cite more than one principal locus of responsibility and obligation (e.g., American Bar Association, 1983; American Psychological Association, 1981; American Society for Public Administrators, 1982; National Society of Professional Engineers, 1987). The codes differ in the extent to which they prioritize principles. Those for lawyers and social workers emphasize obligations to clients. Those for engineers and public administrators appear to stress obligations to the public at large. Some just list principles, and that for public administrators recognizes that as soon as there is more than one principle and more than one group to which one has obligations, conflicts of decision making are inevitable. It follows then that there are no unique solutions to the moral dilemmas professionals face if they try to enact their own codes of ethics. They are operating in a no-win situation and can be accused of failing to observe one principle or more at the expense of others. They are not trapped in the simple double bind but in a multiple bind. In any real world, moral dilemmas of decision making would still arise, but in a fair and just one, professionals would not be subjected to accusations that failed to consider the total set of principles and values involved and were not accompanied by a clearly prioritized alternative. Whistle-blowers appear to be prototypical victims of these dilemmas.

Of Callahan's (1988) examples of codes of ethics, that of the American Society for Public Administration (1982) is most agonized in its discussion of the inevitable conflicts of values and principles that will arise in real decisions. Individual public administrators have "two primary imperatives—satisfying their individual standards of professional performance, conduct, and ethics, and adhering to those imposed upon them by their agencies, public policies and a critical public." It is not obvious that these imperatives can be reduced to two, and it is easier to see four and also to think of yet further ones, such as the Constitution itself. The advice recognizes that "a long list" of dos and don'ts might be constructed but prefers to set a frame of reference from which individuals arrive at their own decisions.

Under the headings of both "responsibility" and "accountability," the original two primary objectives are changed: "administrators must deal with defining their ultimate responsibility to the public" and "the public administrator is answerable first to the public and second to his or her organization" These statements place duty to the community at the apex, a difference from the earlier injunctions that cannot reduce the difficulties for administrators. Helpful as other aspects of the analysis are at defining the issues, the administrators are left relatively unprotected.

The code devotes a section to whistle-blowing and endorses the disclosure of covered-up violations and argues that organizations should protect responsible whistle-blowers.

The National Society of Professional Engineers (1987) is unequivocal. The first fundamental canon is to "hold paramount the safety, health and welfare of the public." Unfortunately, the fourth canon requires them to "act in professional matters for each employer or client as faithful agents or trustees." As Kultgen (1988) illustrates, however, these words do not necessarily guide the actions of engineering societies. In the Bay Area Rapid Transit whistle-blowing case, the California branch could not agree to support the whistle-blowing engineers.

Whistle-Blowing in the United States and the United Kingdom: Examples

Callahan (1988) includes a number of specific, dramatic, and tragic cases in her collection. The three chosen for presentation here are engineering problems in which whistle-blowing failed to prevent subsequent fatalities. Others could have been chosen. Dangerous side effects or directly consequential ill effects have been spotted in advance of the production and marketing of various drugs. Health hazards from toxic effluents running into water supplies and health hazards from insecticides, fertilizers, and animal foodstuffs have been brought to the notice of the public and ministries long before any action is taken.

The injurious consequences of smoking tobacco is perhaps the most publicized battle between those who have generated the evidence for its ill effects and those who have persisted in maximizing profits or taxes regardless of the human consequences. The human species has been duly worried about the consequences of ignoring the greenhouse effect, ozone depletion, acid rain, and nuclear waste disposal, to name but four. Although as Crossen (1994) has shown, enthusiasts for the environment can forge figures as well as their opponents, the short-term economic benefits to companies and governments appear to be accorded higher priority than the longer-term benefit of the populations of their own and affected countries. Grandiose government schemes, particularly with secret defense projects, provide a continuing series of failures subsequently shown to have been anticipated long before they have been canceled. Likewise, with too many sinkings of ships, crashing of planes, and explosions and leakages at industrial plants, the inquiries bring to the surface repeated internal warnings that have been ignored.

In addition to the global issues, current tragedies waiting for further examples to happen are sinkings of roll-on-roll-off ferries, radioactive leakages from nuclear power stations, and crashes of over-engineered and improperly serviced passenger aircraft.

The three cases to be illustrated here have similarities and differences: One was based on a rare but predictable coincidence of circumstances that the company hoped would never happen, one was a known risk in which estimates were made of the comparative costs of likely litigation and modifying the design, and the third was a complex involving loss of face and status.

In July 1970, the first McDonnell Douglas DC-10 blew its cargo door, and the floor collapsed under pressurization tests. In March 1974, a Turkish Airlines plane did the same but in the air with over 350 passengers and crew, all of whom perished. The subsequent inquiry revealed evidence of a number of failures in safety procedures, but as early as 1969 the subcontractor, Convair, had prepared a report that showed that the cargo door latching system had at least nine possible sequences that were hazardous, four of which would produce sudden loss of pressurization in flight. This report was not submitted to the Federal Aviation Authority (FAA). The Director of Product Engineering at Convair wrote to the vice president of the corporation that it was "inevitable that, in twenty years ahead of us, DC-10 cargo doors will come open and I would expect this to usually result in the loss of the aeroplane" (Martin, 1992, p. 23). He was told nothing could be done because of the likely costs to Convair. The quiet whistle was not blown outside (see French, 1988, for an analysis of the ethics).

To regain lost market share, Ford launched a new subcompact in 1970, the Pinto. Testing and development time had been much less than the customary 2 years. During these, crash tests showed that an impact at over 25 mph could result in a ruptured fuel tank. An internal study showed a financial cost-benefit analysis of the consequences of modifying the tank at a projected cost of $11 per vehicle. On 12.5 million cars, the cost would be $137 million. Unit costs at $1,100 per vehicle, $67,000 per injury, and $200,000 per death came to an estimated $49.15 million. By 1978, 53 people had died in accidents resulting from Pinto fires. In 1973, a principal design engineer began to write memos to top management pointing out the hazards of the fuel tank (and windshields). It appears that none of his memos were acted on. Following his memos, his performance indicators were lowered. He was demoted several times. In 1978, he resigned.

The 1986 space shuttle Challenger was launched against a firm recommendation by senior engineers based on the fact that the temperature was well below the safety range for the seals in rocket boosters. One of them testified against senior management, became more and more isolated, took extended sick leave, and found it very difficult to obtain another job.

Glazer and Glazer (1989) estimate that two thirds of whistle-blowers suffer a succession of losses: harassments by management, including accusations of disloyalty and malice, demotions and lower performance appraisals, unpleasant transfers, firing, and blacklisting. Colleagues and professional associations seem to do little or nothing to help. What seems to keep them going is both a horror of whatever malpractice is the focus of their whistle-blowing and a conviction of higher loyalties than to their immediate employees. In an earlier article, M. Glazer (1989) noted that external allies from legal firms or the media can be important facilitators of persistence. He also observed that of the 10 cases he reviewed, all managed to reestablish themselves subsequently in alternative careers and to that extent won through in the end. The gap between the first whistle and resumed careers, however, could be a grueling 10 years. Any exercise of the imagination that re-creates the daily lives of the 10 persons involved has to lead to the conclusion that each of them was exceptional in their willpower and capacity for endurance.

Paradoxically, the industrial examples typically show from the final balance sheet that listening to the whistle would have saved the company or organization far more money than the expenditure originally required to eliminate the risks. Reputations would not have been blackened. Victims would have been spared death and injuries.

Recent examples in Britain are no different. The Association of University Teachers (AUT) acted to protect the interests of whistle-blowers in three universities. When in 1990 three philosophers at University College, Swansea, asked for an official inquiry into academic standards at the College's Centre for Philosophy and Health Care and no inquiry eventuated, one of the three made statements to the press. She was suspended and eventually persuaded into accepting severance. The other two persisted and also suffered suspension. The case was not resolved until 1993. The staff were vindicated and reinstated. The principal left. It is not clear why 3 years were taken to resolve what at first sight could have been achieved in a week. Why colleagues at Swansea and elsewhere did not help more effectively is not known. Why a sympathetic AUT was unable to expedite the case in not known.

Also in 1990, a lecturer at Bournemouth complained about a bogus claim that had been made to Brussels for ERASMUS funding. In 1991, he was removed from the program. In 1992, "the director of personnel suggested that the lecturer had 'a major health problem' and he was forced to resign" (Machon, 1993, p. 6). A case at Leeds in which a biochemist alerted the University to "financial irregularities and an alleged scientific fraud," which were subsequently authenticated was also followed by his being made redundant. These are indicative of the possible fates of those brave enough to initiate exposures. What is a topic for a journal article by an academic can be a devastated life for the whistle-blower concerned.

With that in mind, the field is being opened up with vigor and efficiency, especially in the United States, through a succession of penetrating and precise articles that set down the moral dilemmas and pragmatic considerations that confront would-be whistle-blowers and the arguments in favor of restraint (Bok, 1978; Callahan, 1988; James, 1988; Martin, 1992).

Empirical evidence about the progress and fate of whistle-blowers is beginning to accumulate (Glazer & Glazer, 1989), and there are now sufficient documented examples for the beginnings of taxonomies of types and sequences. As already mentioned, Glazer and Glazer show that the long-term fates of their cases may involve neither despair nor regrets about their personal decisions, but the biographies point to persons suffering as they survive through conviction of the rightness of their causes.

Some of the debate remains naive, apparently missing the extent to which those in positions of power are endemically subject to opportunities for corruption. To gain and retain high office in many of the 180 member states of the United Nations requires a ruthlessness either among one's ancestors or oneself that may well involve the accumulation of dispersible wealth, that in turn entails diversions of funds on a grand scale, to secure one's own power base and to weaken that of rivals or critics. In Westerns, an assumption that the sheriff is not in the pay of the "bad guys" is a standard tension-raising prelude to the naive reporting dirt farmer being the next victim of the rustlers. Population surveys do not report that national leaders are seen as self-sacrificing servants of their societies by their populations. Cover-ups of corruption with attendant lying have become a running feature of media news in the "Western democracies." Most people in the West must have seen senior politicians lying through their teeth on television and have heard what they have to say about their accusers. We have seen that whistle-blowers may well be persecuted by the superiors in their employing organizations. They can be subject to accusations of lying out of spite and of being unbelievable because they are mad. They can be told they are traitors and threats made to the jobs of their colleagues. They can be demoted, transferred, or fired. They can be prevented from getting another job.

Who cares about this kind of treatment? One might expect colleagues at work to rally around and form a protective group. One might expect professional associations to act vigorously and firmly on behalf of their members and for the public good. One might expect the media or political representatives to help. One might expect the general public to protest. One might expect prosecutions and punishments for those who were guilty of covering up the matters over which the whistle was blown and for those who subsequently slandered, libeled, and otherwise persecuted the whistle-blower.

There is scant evidence of any of these being general reactions. Ibsen's cynicism of *The Enemy of the People*, in which he charts the destruction of the doctor who warns his town that its spa water is contaminated, seems to be closer to the most defensible empirical generalization than any other. To cite the other parallel, the sheriff in *High Noon* is deserted by all but his pacifist girlfriend.

The United States has institutionalized laws and agencies designed to improve the life chances of sincere and well-founded whistle-blowing, and recent changes are in the direction of the protagonists of change. (In contrast, in the United Kingdom, the Official Secrets Act is still used to prevent whistle-blowing among public sector employees, and recently reformulated contracts for National Health Service medical personnel include clauses making whistle-blowing a breach of contract.)

This brief analysis is descriptive and not evaluative. It is an attempt to say what happens, not what ought to happen. Insofar as populations choose their preferred kind of society, and politicians legislate accordingly, the current evidence would suggest that public concern about whistle-blowing and the fate of whistle-blowers is not high enough to provoke action, even for the most dramatic cases of multiple deaths arising from preventable disasters (see French, 1982; Velasquez, 1981).

Speculative Conclusions

Public Reactions to Whistle-Blowing

Although opinion polls might yield results that would suggest that individuals in organizations should have a primary obligation to the well-being of society in general, and only a secondary responsibility to their employer or professional organizations, and should therefore blow whistles when necessary, members of the public at large clearly do not commit themselves to any actions either to support whistle-blowers or to require that those exposed of lying to defend malpractices should be fired or brought to justice for their misdeeds.

This exemplifies the bystander effect in extreme form (Latané & Darley, 1970). Piliavin, Rodin, and Piliavin (1969) had classified the rewards and costs of helping and of not helping others into six rewards for helping and six for not doing so and with six costs for helping and six for not doing so. In the context of social exchange theory (Thibaut & Kelley, 1959), a bystander would calculate a cost-benefit analysis and act accordingly. Latané and Darley developed a particular complementary hypothesis: the greater the number of bystanders, the less likely is any of them to help a victim. Their five-stage decision-making flowchart predicts not helping in an emergency: If the bystander fails to notice the event, treats it as a nonemergency, takes no personal responsibility for helping, lacks the knowledge or competence to help, or works out that the situation may be too costly to the self in some material or psychological way.

In the case of whistle-blowing, immediate colleagues might expect professional societies or unions to take the responsibility or judge the likely personal costs to be too high; more distant colleagues or friends likewise. The general public is even more distant. Most will be unaware. Most would not see what they might do to help. More generally, each person is confined in space and time and can adopt only a limited number of causes, if any.

It may also be that the general public thinks it is powerless to affect what powerful organizations do, and apart from boycotting goods or demonstrating, it is probably correct. Boycotts could be very costly, however, and therefore potentially powerful ways of helping whistle-blowers in commercial enterprises. More likely in the present cultural climates of societies, whistle-blowers might expect sympathetic general moral judgments about their conduct, but no more.

Whistle-Blowing: Professional Societies and Colleagues

Professional societies that have codes of ethics may prioritize obligations to humanity in their statement of principles, but others simply present a list of potentially conflicting principles. When members blow whistles on management, professional societies may fail to support members or provide minimal support or do so in ways that do not yield decisive and speedy deliverance for whistle-blowers. They do not enjoin or require colleagues to support any whistle-blowing colleagues. Such half-hearted support is compatible with the kind of analysis of professional societies offered by Kultgen (1988), namely that their actions are more likely to be directed toward maximizing the power, status, and wealth of their members within the contemporary power structure. Their stated moral principles of service may bear logically negative relationships to their actions.

Immediate colleagues per se do not emerge as significant in the whistle-blowing literature. Whether their obscurity implies the conclusions of a well-calculated personal cost-benefit analysis or something more moral remains unknown.

The Fates of Exposed Fraudsters:
Immediate and Superior

Although there may be understandable reasons for colleagues not to be referred to in the literature, it is extraordinary that no mention is made of the fates of those subsequently proved to have been guilty of malpractice and deception. The Watergate affair did lead to convictions, Irangate did not. The revelations about ex-President Nixon might have been expected to provoke a dash to repentance and anonymity. In what was interpreted as referring to would-be whistle-blowers among others, the unofficial Nixon handbook advised that "undesirables" be reassigned to places so remote that they would resign or be given too much work beyond their capacity or be downgraded. These last two could be preludes to required psychiatric tests that were likely to indicate unfitness for duty. Such diagnoses required the collaboration of medical professionals; lawyers constituted a high proportion of the Watergate conspirators. Until his death, Nixon remained a freelance, unofficial diplomat with international stature and could command high fees for speeches and lectures.

It seems that unsuccessfully resisting whistle-blowers can still be followed by avoiding what might be considered the just consequences of being exposed as someone who has maintained cover-ups and deceptions about malpractice, especially in the case of top management in both the private and the public sector. Power protects itself very effectively and is not molested by the judiciary or rejected by the public.

At this point, it might be instructive to set up two ideal types and examine their relative plausibility. One can imagine a society in which subsequently exposed deception about malpractice is seen as criminally wrong. In such a society, putative whistle-blowers would be given a sympathetic hearing through appropriately constituted agencies and if vindicated would be rewarded in some way. They would be honored by the public. The guilty would be doubly condemned, both for their offenses and for any lying about these. Their punishment would involve loss of power, prestige, and wealth in some combination.

The antithesis would set up would-be whistle-blowers as dishonorable traitors whose temptations to expose malpractice should have no obvious avenues of procedure. They should be left to solve their own problems arising from their actions, demotion or dismissal being legitimate reactions by their organizations. Their organizations should be free to regulate their conduct as they see fit.

A variant on the second would follow the practice described and also develop a rhetoric reflecting a highly moral, even altruistic, ideology condemning malpractice and deception in statements of principle and codes of conduct. The public would talk in similar terms. The words would define an ideal toward which literally lip service would be played.

Commentary

It has been suggested already that there are a number of predictable disasters waiting to happen. There are doubtless many more on which the whistles might be blown. Reason's (1990) analyses of several recent large-scale "accidents" point to a succession of opportunities that might have been taken to have prevented the accidents from happening. They offer a catalog of warnings not heeded and after the tragedy has occurred a succession of denials of responsibility by senior management. Workers proximal to the events are the most likely prime targets for suspicion; even design faults appear to be obvious to an outsider after the event and to insiders before the event.

The cases described in this chapter are not related to the Etzioni-Halevy (1989) theses in that the cover-ups and falsifications are within single organizations. There is a parallel with the treatment accorded enemies in the mass media. The whistle-blower is defined as out-group, and attributions are likely to be directed against the person's character. It is the accuser rather than the accused who is more likely to be deserted by colleagues and professional associations, which is consistent with the reactions described in Figure 12.1.

It was suggested that the whistle-blowers of Glazer and Glazer (1989) who resurrected successful alternative careers for themselves appear to have strong wills and a strong moral commitment to truthfulness. Their fates illustrate the hazards of confronting authorities, especially if the authorities are being deceitful.

CHAPTER ELEVEN

Truth and Truthfulness: From Then Till Now

As Chapter 1 set down from a philosophical perspective and Chapter 2 illustrated with respect to children coming to master the use of language, representation of reality is but one function of language and one that emerges late as a propositional activity. Questions, commands, and expressive exclamations are not attempts to represent reality. Only statements can function in this way, and not all statements make such claims. When they are used to tell jokes or to entertain or inspire with fictional stories, it can be inappropriate to ask whether they are true or false. When they function to express the comfort of being with like-minded others or close, their informative value is unimportant. More generally, it is mistaken to ask about their truthfulness when statements are attempts to regulate the states or the behavior of self or others. They can also be used to mark states, personal and social identity, and role relationships. These and other functions will have been present in the language mediated activities of early peoples.

The representational function will have had its role to play to inform others of facts that they did not previously know. No doubt the value of transmitting false information was also discovered and exploited. What the history is of interpersonal falsification and concealment is not the focus here. It may well be that the ways in which lies function at social gatherings or in families today are not that different from what they achieved 6,000 years ago, except that the complexities of cultural development will have elaborated the rules and rituals, a topic to be returned to later (Chapter 12).

The immediate focus is with the history of the intellectual concern with the distinction between truth and falsity at the cultural level within a frame of reference confined mainly to the European tradition derived from ancient Greece. The argument will be that the validity of appeals to rationality and empirical evidence as crucial for discovering the truth are late arrivals on the human scene. Initially, at a cultural and societal level they may have been irrelevant. Increasingly, their relevance has been recognized but only in certain arenas by certain subgroups of people. The climax of the argument will be the contentious conclusion that those members of societies who are now best placed to promote the relevance of rationality and empirical evidence to social and political issues tend to be assimilated to the elites of power, wealth, and status rather than to remain independent of these lures and advance the cause of truth! The impertinence of this position will not be as well-founded in empirical evidence as it ought to be, but the ideas are sufficiently important to merit consideration. If certain truths crucial to community and individual living have been known for several thousands of years, how is it to be explained that millions of the human species continue to be killed, oppressed, and degraded by their fellows?

First, comments will be made about some creation myths and heroic epics circulated in early societies. For these, it will be suggested that perhaps de Saussure's (1916/1959) insight into the contrastive qualities of the units and structures of language does not apply: The stories may have been accepted as true but without any implication that this truth contrasted with alternatives.

Second, it will be suggested that although by the time of the Socratic dialogues the formal distinction between truth and falsity was clearly recognized, and means were proposed for the advancement of knowledge, along with the beginnings of a specification of criteria to evaluate claims to knowledge, these were initially confined to limited arenas of inquiry (e.g., mathematics) and to very limited sections of populations.

Third, it is not until the Renaissance and the diffusion of printed works that access to intellectual inquiry based on the accumulated wisdom of the past became possible for any but the elite of the elites.

Fourth, it was not until the early period of the enlightenment that scientific methods of inquiry came to be seen as heralding a systematic if not assured basis for discovering truths about the physical and biological. Simultaneously, questions were posed about *liberté*, *égalité*, and *fraternité*.

Fifth, as alternative forms of organizing complex societies were explored, questions about the objective bases of morality and social justice have remained contentious issues. On the one hand, the societies founded by revolutions based on communist ideologies were quickly transformed into totalitarian dictatorships. On the other hand, capitalistic societies have continued to reproduce themselves and absorb threats to their social structure by assimilating their critics and by limiting access to information about their characteristics through the means set down in Chapters 7 and 8. Hence, the lure to lies, concealment, and equivocation as a means for sustaining the distribution of power, wealth, and status that is associated with a range of lifestyles whose extremes of luxury and destitution could not be judged objectively as a reflection of any rational principles of morality and justice. The scenario is a far cry from *1984* (Orwell, 1948), but its results may be seen as awful by those in the lowest strata. Whether they see themselves as suffering victims of untrue myths has yet to be investigated. The rest of society are either victims or beneficiaries.

Creation Myths

Societies constructed myths about the creation of the world and their place in it. The stories range from the mysteriously mathematical "Big Bang" formulations of today's scientific elite to the personalized gods who have laid down clear prescriptions about the purposes of and codes of conduct for human existence. Although some members of today's scientific elite avoid comments on the validity of religious beliefs, others link the achievements of science to the redundancy of needs to posit any agentive creator of the universe and are happy to relegate all claims to transcendental truths as false. They are apt also to point to the ways in which religious and political elites have authenticated and legitimated their materialist privileges by appeals to the will of the gods. The most extreme form of this syncretism is where the monarch is the personification of god on earth and has absolute power to dispose of everyone and everything in society. The claimed divine right of rulers to rule as they wished, along with a priesthood and army to justify and enforce the wishes, remains vigorous in various parts of today's world and appears in attenuated form in very many countries. This linkage of the governing with the religious elite reached its zenith of distrust in the writings of Marx in which he makes explicit the position that the promulgation of religious beliefs has kept the poor quiescently in their appointed place. Instead of rulers being the servants of God, gods and their commandments have been used to mediate the power of secular rulers.

The creation myths of early peoples were much less likely to have been devices for the cynical exploitation of the ruled initially, and it has already been suggested that the truths of the myths will not have been contrastive. Linguistically and logically, de Saussure (1916/1959) is right. The term *cup* functions contrastively as a phonological, grammatical, lexical, semantic, and pragmatic unit; it achieves its meaning and significance from its differences from all other units in the English language. Likewise, declarative sentences functioning as statements (or propositions) derive their semantic status contrastively. Although children grasp the contrastive significance for single lexical units very early, the contrastive semantics of grammatical structures such as sentences is a later development. Enabling people to understand versions of the Sapir-Whorf hypothesis (Sapir, 1921; Whorf, 1956) that the categories of a language can facilitate or inhibit the frame of reference within which people view their physical and social worlds is difficult. Monolingual undergraduates require patient and careful exposition to apprehend that it is not just a question of different languages having more or fewer words for snow and camels. It is at the level of the parameters of thinking that meanings can cease to be contrastive; they are givens. That was probably the status of creation myths. They were not contestable accounts. They described and explained origins and ends. Alternatives were simply not available. When they became available, they would have been seen as wrong.

It is not until the times of the ancient Greeks that there was an explosion of ideas about various possible origins and qualities of the world. A diversity of hypotheses was generated, and these were extended into reflective considerations of aesthetics, truth, justice, and their realizations in different forms of society. It is noteworthy that these events occurred in a cluster of city-states in which such religious beliefs as there were remained apolitical. Although political and military leaders consulted the oracles and performed religious rites, the religious beliefs were not used to justify the organization of the states. The priesthood retained its independent status but did not exercise power through its wealth. It can be argued that the absence of a religious orthodoxy in the form of a state religion was the crucial feature that freed human minds to think imaginatively and analytically and to begin to develop criteria that could be used to distinguish what might be true from what was false. The classical Greek language developed different words for beliefs relating to their sources of justification and hence to different spheres of human endeavor.

That people with aspirations for achieving or sustaining their power would attach themselves to creation myths and other religious stories is not surprising. Historians will continue to debate particular cases from primeval times to modern times. It would be strange if the relationships between the two did not have examples of the various contingencies. Religious convictions have spurred demands for social justice and limitations of power. Some powerful rulers, however, have prostituted religious authority for their own ends. Since the idea was born, it has surely been exploited as suggested earlier. As a further paradox, it can be noted that "the noble lie" of Plato (1955) can be an end rather than a beginning and secular rather than religious. Marx may have written to enable the proletariat to escape from political and economic oppression and to save them from the redemptive prospects of religion, but Stalin was able to exploit Marxist ideology to govern through one of the cruelest totalitarian regimes yet experienced by human beings.

The received truths of the multitude of creation myths and their latter-day descendants have been potent frameworks that ordinary people have found it difficult to contest. Historically, peoples have been "protected" from any temptations to ask questions by the authority of the governing elites and those who have insisted or protested otherwise have been destroyed rather than converted. Creation myths and their associated religions have typically not confined themselves to truths about transcendental matters. Historically, they have incorporated science, aesthetics, and morals within their orbit and have frequently prevented inquiries within these fields. Logic and mathematics have been least afflicted and discov-

fields. Logic and mathematics have been least afflicted and discoveries within their domains have not been treated as blasphemous or heretical, presumably because they have not constituted threats to the established order. Even their prosecution, however, can be defined as evil if the local religious beliefs condemn all exercise of curiosity.

It should be noted in contrast that different interpretations of religious truths have simultaneously been a major impetus to the development of knowledge in other fields. The promotion of social justice and the elimination of human suffering have been heavily influenced by religious believers. Particular sects of the major religions have encouraged the advancement of all forms of knowledge, including the scientific and have seen no incompatibilities between truths of beliefs to their own ends. Such sects have seldom been attached to government and are more likely to have been persecuted than supported in their endeavors.

Some conjunctions will have been coincidental. It does not require cynicism to note how often the interests coincide even in one person. The Church of England was established by Henry VIII. The relative roles of his political commitment to the need for a male heir, his passionate commitment to Anne Boleyn, his political-military commitment to the building of a great navy, and his religious commitment to the beliefs of the reformists will remain uncertain. He broke the power of the Catholic Church, stole their wealth to build his navy and to buy loyalties, married Anne Boleyn and changed the established religious commitment of the country with consequences that are still observable. It does not require more than a quick scan through world history to note how seldom rulers have held religious beliefs that encouraged them to strive for and grant all their subjects the freedoms from hunger, thirst, cold, and other physiological bases of suffering that they themselves enjoyed.

In 1995, these generalizations retain more than a kernel of truth around the countries of the world. Massive differentials in privileges and rights of rulers and ruled remain grounded in claims of a religious nature, and frequently, these are glaringly and incontestably inconsistent with the apparent truths of the religious faiths proclaimed. It is difficult to resist the conclusion that historically many rulers and their priestly acolytes must have been lying to the ruled to justify their privileged status. The discrepancies between their practices and what they have claimed to believe to be true are just too great to escape dissonance. As already observed, there is an instructive paradox in Plato's (1955) prescriptions for his ideal republic. On the one hand, he advocated the abolition of all fictional poetry and prose, plays, and stories. On the other hand, he recommended the adoption of an entirely fictional creation myth to be unquestioningly accepted by members of the republic; he believed it to be imperative to have a higher-order justification for the constitution of the republic founded on what he christened "the noble lie." Creation myths may well have achieved the status of received and incontrovertible truths, but by the time of Plato, the idea had been contemplated that a noble lie could constitute the basis of political, religious, and other kinds of knowledge.

The most that can be concluded from this brief consideration is that although ancient creation myths and their associated religions may well have begun as received truths, from Plato forward all the transcendental stories could have been contested as possible noble lies. One might have expected that this would have been particularly so with respect to those components of the beliefs that accorded too closely with the secular vested interests of the governing elite and simultaneously caused so much suffering to the governed. One might have expected that the reluctance of the governing elite to consider "alternative" interpretations of their beliefs that would have reduced their privileges and brought their behavior into line with their religious beliefs would have occasioned sufficient incredulity and distrust among their subjects to have provoked more revolutions before 1789. It may be added that the noble lies of different groups are empirically incompatible with each other of course; they cannot all be true.

Perhaps the oddest feature psychologically is that so few ruling elites in Christian Europe appear to have been concerned to be holy. The messages of the Sermon on the Mount (Matthew 5, 6) and the other preachings of Jesus are unequivocal in their condemnation of the rich and powerful oppressing the poor, avarice, greed, arrogance, killing, stealing, cruelty, and untruthfulness. Some Christian rulers have aspired to saintliness, but many more have not. As an erstwhile colleague once remarked, such people must have been totally convinced in the truth of atheism to have lived how they did. Whatever the situation, their lives were a massive lie; either their beliefs were sincere and they were tremendously inadequate, or their beliefs were insincere and their lives were vicious.

Heroic Legends

Ancient and medieval European societies also sponsored heroic tales: *Gilgamesh*, the *Iliad*, the *Odyssey*, the *Aenead*, *Beowulf*, King Arthur and his knights, the Song of Roland, and *El Cid*. Are these historically true? Archaeologists and historians have pursued their inquiries about these legends and that is their right and duty. For the storytellers and their communities, however, the more recent consensus has been that the tales were not attempts to record history but were designed to provide role models for youths and others. They helped to define aspirations and codes of conduct as well as providing pleasure. They were an early form of exhortation and infotainment. Strangely, the English language does not have an equivalent of the Ancient Greek *arete* or *philotemu* or even Latin *virtu*. Neither do the Spanish and Portuguese *brio* have an equivalent in English. John Wayne's line, "a man has to do what a man has to do," or Maslow's (1954) self-actualization are potentially misleading attempts to express the same ideas and in far less inspiring ways. The epics are stories of heroes: men and women who exhibit the virtues of bravery, fearlessness, loyalty, competence at arms, patience, and love. If they fail in some way, their downfalls arise from their weaknesses of arrogance, hard heartiness, or trust beyond what is realistic. The villains, if they exist, are likewise driven by their exaggerated characters.

The evaluative questions that present-day observers are likely to ask of these characters are not issues of truth or falsity but of effectiveness as inspirational tales that would serve to recruit youths to the service of the society. Their function was to inspire and to entertain. The stories were designed to encourage virtue and strength and to discourage vice and weakness. Their social significance as potential regulators of values and behavior had priority over their representational function.

Ancient classical Greek did not distinguish linguistically between saying and meaning, between sensation and perception, and perhaps between truth and falsity. Saying and meaning were synonymous. Perception was veridical. Heroes did not have the option of lying; they followed their destiny. That the promotion of virtue took priority over the recitation of facts is evident in ancient histories, funeral ovations, and plays. Thucydides and Tacitus were exceptional historians in their expressed concern to tell the story as it was, warts and all. Subsequent formal instruction in the classics through to medieval Europe was much more likely to rely on Homer and Virgil or on Demosthenes and Cicero as their exemplars for training in rhetoric than they were to invoke Thucydides or Socrates.

In a work that any scholar would have to be pleased to have written, Morse (1991) demonstrates the dangers of applying the truth-value logic of latter-day Aristotelians to statements in the works of both ancient and medieval European writers. She shows how ovations and writings were intended to be instructional, inspirational, and artistic. At funerals and in biographies, lives of those who might serve as models significantly became more heroic and virtuous than they were; their halos were extended to everything about them. Those who were cast as villains would have their vices and bad endings dramatized; they would carry physical stigmata to match their deformed characters. What was true for individuals was also true for the histories of peoples and societies. This was not because the representational function of language was being abused but because it was not accorded preeminence. The deviance of Thucydides (1971) has already been mentioned, but in his endeavor to collect evidence and describe the Peloponnesian war as it was, he too was happy to construct the speeches of participants as he imagined that they might have spoken. It would be strange to label these inventions as lying, because the reader should know that Thucydides and his tape recorder could not have been so ubiquitous. (Grice, 1975/1989, would have no difficult in interpreting Thucydides.)

Morse (1991) develops her theme through an account of the kinds of education and training in rhetoric that medieval students would experience. They would learn to recite Homer, Virgil, and the Bible. They would be instructed how to analyze texts rhetorically and to see how effects were achieved. They would practice elaboration and embellishment with the catalog of rhetorical devices to hand. They would study the advice of the scholarly masters: Aristotle, Isocrates, Cicero, Quintilian, the Rhetorica ad Herennium, and Erasmus, as well as the texts of the practitioners. The moral and social functions of the results of these activities would be endemic to their own constructions as recommended by the scholars. Through time, however, the embellishments and elaborations degenerated eventually into stylistic additions that lacked substantive sincerity, much as most artistic movements finally lose their vitality in a proliferation of empty detail. Rhetoric developed into an evolutionary dysfunctional dead end of style without substance at the same time as a concern for truth in scientific statements was growing.

Heroes and the stories of their great deeds, however, did not die out with the demise of rhetoric. They have continued to emerge down through the ages as models for citizens. As with the legendary figures, their virtues are accentuated and exaggerated and their vices suppressed. By the time later heroes are within the reach of historians, however, the cleaning-up processes do become dishonest and what is reported can be highly selective and false. The reported analysis of history texts and newspapers showed this to be true (Chapter 7), and some of the examples were of out-group villains. These villains may well have been heroes to their own people. Likewise, our heroes can be their villains.

In history texts, false reporting is lying, but it might be argued that when biographies are intended to serve as inspirations to youth, the omitted vices or misreported good deeds and virtues are not lies. The position is defensible but only weakly so. It does, however, point to the paradox. Fictional heroes can be entirely virtuous. Legendary heroes can be entirely virtuous. Real heroes cannot have their faults or vices glossed over. This could be taken to imply that it is better to use fictional and legendary heroes as role models in the socialization and education of the young and for the continuing edification of the adults of a society.

Particularly in the times of the British Empire, the other course was adopted and biographies of real people were written with their misdeeds and weakness omitted or falsified. The same practice continues to operate in funeral ovations, in obituaries, and on tombstones.

The historical change is analogous to the fate of creation myths. For so long as the facticity cannot be or is not contested, all virtuous heroes can serve as inspirational models, just as creation stories can include prescriptions for living. Once issues of truth or falsity can be invoked, societies collectively or their individual members decide which functions of languages should be subservient. In the case of heroes, it is suggested that although scholarly tomes may well lean toward inquiries after truth, the mass media, school texts, and popular biographies tend to give precedence to inspirational functions. Historical records may show that French-speaking Richard I put all the surrendering inhabitants of Acre to the sword; the story of Robin Hood renders Richard into a friend of the oppressed Anglo-Saxons determined to uphold justice for the English. In popular British history texts, Drake saved England from the Spanish Armada and prevented Spain from being an even more powerful colonist in America than she was. In other texts, the weather defeated the Armada, and Drake was an adventurous pirate whose treatment of Spanish prisoners gave rise to the phrase "skinning alive."

Lies in the Service of the Status Quo

Creation myths and heroic legends are but two examples of major cultural institutions where truth was initially received truth and unproblematic. Questions about alternatives were at first inconceivable and subsequently irrelevant. The choices remain today as to whether truth should be given priority over other functions, and much of this text shows that it is not accorded that priority. When it is not, lies have great potential for preserving the status quo.

In Europe, the structures of societies have undergone a succession of revolutionary changes since the Romans retreated and the settling invasions from the East ceased. Tribal chieftains gave way to successively higher levels of rulers controlling larger areas, eventually consolidating into what became known as feudal societies. These were stratified into groupings with defined rights and obligations that remained relatively constant from generation to generation. The pyramid had a single ruler at its apex whose powers were limited only by the constraints of the military power that he (or rarely she) could command. In Europe, the ascribed status of the citizenry was legitimized by the leaders of the Catholic Christian Church in the west and the Orthodox churches in the east. With the Renaissance and its revived interest in the Ancient Greeks, ideas about and a serious questioning of the legitimacy and credibility of authorities spread, and the seeds of the Reformation were sown in the west and the center of Europe. The power of the churches began to decline relative to that of an aristocracy whose wealth came from the land and whose power lay in their right (and obligation) to mobilize their tenants for military service. The pillaging of wealth from conquered territories overseas added to the wealth of monarchs, aristocrats, entrepreneurs, and the churches.

In turn, the position of the landed gentry was threatened by the emerging bourgeoisie, whose fortunes were founded on the new technologies applied to agriculture and to industrial production. The rise of the bourgeoisie was accompanied by the rise of the professionals whose material discoveries and inventions underpinned the wealth and whose legal and financial competence secured that wealth. Subsequently, the most successful bourgeoisie turned themselves into limited companies that are the second of the two major structures of wealth and power today. Just as the capitalist system of resource exploitation, manufacturing, and distribution spawned a variety of accompanying professional services to facilitate its functioning, so the increasing power of elected central and regional governments spawned a substantial bureaucracy to execute its legislation.

Each of these changes and developments was resisted by the contemporary power structure, but by mixtures of force of arms, purchasing power, and constitutional authority, changes were achieved by the succeeding waves of protagonists. Constitutions were written and transformed into legal frameworks. Laws were passed changing rights and obligations; taxes were changed; what was criminal and what was not were redefined; punishments for particular offenses were changed; ownership of land was registered and codified; working conditions became regulated. Changes were almost invariably contested. Arguments were won or lost mainly by voting along party lines or group interest lines rather than by the plausibility of the cases advanced. How truthfulness and lying were and are relevant to these changes is the focus of what follows.

Generally, truth through rationality and empirical evidence were claimed by the progressives; rhetorical appeals were more common among those who wished to preserve the status quo. The seeds of the duality of the heritage are, in fact, evident in both Plato (1971) and Aristotle (1926). Plato contrasted the arguments of Gorgias with those of Socrates, where Socrates was represented as the defender of careful rationality, critical consistency, and questioning uncertainty. Gorgias defended the virtues of winning arguments by whatever means are most efficacious; language should be used to persuade. Aristotle played both roles. First, he invented formal logic and set out the rules of valid and invalid deductive arguments. In setting truth values for inferences of different syllogisms, he established criteria for rationality that retain their force today. He also helped to establish facts as the basis of science. Second, he wrote about the art of rhetoric with insights that more than anticipated some 20th century social psychological findings about persuasiveness. The dual possibility of inducing belief in others by appeals to rational arguments based on sound empirical evidence or inducing conviction by inspirational rhetoric subsumes *lying* in the second component. The first strategy has to rely on what the speaker believes to be true. The second subordinates issues of truth and falsity to the importance of persuading the audience. If lies help, use lies.

The two traditions continue to maintain a degree of independence, but at various times in history they have clashed with each other. It would be foolish to try to cite a beginning to such clashes. They were evident in Plato's writing, and Aristotle was not apparently a continuing victim of personal cognitive dissonance. In medieval Europe, church leaders had devised formulae that exculpated tortured members of a sect from telling the truth (Zagorin, 1990), but it is with Machiavelli that lies were specifically cited as devices necessary for princes to maintain their supremacy. Authorities had been using lies and deceit to maintain their positions long before Machiavelli (1961) wrote his advice to the prince, but he was the first person whose pragmatism gave explicit expression to the benefits of deceit. He has, of course, been condemned to the extent of having a psychological construct named after him. A kinder argument would say that he was simply expressing a well-known truth of *realpolitik*. (It may be noted that politicians whose lives exemplify the "advice" of Machiavelli continue to protest their abhorrence of lying and deceit, while demonstrating its utility for their survival and supremacy.)

It is from the times of Machiavelli that the myths of the rights of rulers and the aristocrats began to crumble in Europe. Social mobility by force of arms remained the surest claim to hegemony, but individual mobility through flattery and sycophancy were also feasible options for enhancing power, wealth, and status. Revolutions that dispossessed and executed rulers were prosecuted on the basis of revised creation myths and denials of the justifications of the privileges of inheritable elite status. The political revolutions that undermined the status quo in a succession of European monarchies were succeeded by revolutionary changes in agriculture and industrialization, both of which created new elites of wealth that could eventually expand to embrace power and subsequently status. These events succeeded and coincided with the Enlightenment, the period during which science emerged as a systematic body of knowledge whose development was supposedly guaranteed by the collection of supposedly objective observations of the relevant constituents of the world under appropriate experimental or field conditions. The rational powers of logical reasoning in combination with these observations would advance the truth. The same strategy was presumed to be appropriate for elucidating the concepts of liberty, justice, and equality, along with other ideas central for the evaluation and creation of social progress.

On the one hand, European societies were developing a basis for the creation of societies founded on truth, rationality, and justice. On the other hand, they had opened up opportunities for those fortunate enough in their selection of inventions or discoveries and ruthless enough to exploit these to push their way to great fortunes. The white settlers in the United States had no entrenched vested interests blocking their social mobility, and each of the great industrial and commercial sectors gave birth to immensely rich dynasties (e.g., railways, Stanford, Hartington; steel, Harriman; oil, Rockefeller; banking, Morgan; news media, Hearst). By 1890, the spirit of capitalism was vigorously alive in the United States and has remained so for a further 100 years. In Europe, it has always been in contention with socialist ideologies that have included a concern for those who have been trapped in poverty while the few have accumulated great excess.

What has this to do with truth and lies? It would be insultingly inaccurate to link the elites of the bourgeoisie and the upper classes too closely to a lack of concern for the truth. It would be accurate, however, to point out that for many of them their successful accumulation of wealth, power, and status means that their ancestors accorded retaining and winning personal wealth as a high priority. Their dominant subsequent conduct has been in the tradition of Gorgias rather than the idealized Socrates. The justifications mounted for the rights to inherit whatever is left to them and the right to control the legislation and political decisions that entrench their own high positions display all the characteristics of in-group favoritism and out-group denigration described in attribution theory. The arguments from the lower strata might well contain the corresponding biases, but given the differential access to the media, their voices are not heard.

What seems to happen is that if a new social group mounts a successful challenge to the hegemony of the contemporary power elites, then its leaders are assimilated to the establishment, at least in some measure, after they have tasted the benefits of elevation. Their opposition is then muted by the potential loss of their individual power, wealth, and status. In Britain, in the political sphere this has happened to successful liberal and then labor politicians. It happened to the leadership of some trade unions. It happened to senior bureaucrats and successful industrialists. In brief, it gave rise to the family of elites referred to by Etzioni-Halevy (1989).

Most serious, perhaps, has been the assimilation of the leaders of the professions to this family. More of those who have studied law and its underpinnings in principles of morality and social justice might have been expected to remain dominated by those principles, concerned to ensure both that laws were as simple and transparent as possible in their linkage to their ethical principles and that they were enacted with a concern that the innocent were not convicted and the guilty were. More of those who have studied law might have been expected to practice restraint in the charges exacted for their services so that the principle of equality before the law might not have become a matter of who can afford to pay for legal services. Medicine has suffered similarly; in the 20th century, its ethic of service has become heavily mixed with many of its practitioners coming to form an elite pursuing personal and occupational power, wealth, and status to the exclusion of the relief of unnecessary suffering.

The interest here is not in the facts about professional social groups maximizing their power, wealth, and status but in their justifications for their rewards; some seem to feel obliged to preserve a rhetoric of moral principles that is increasingly distant from their current practice.

Given the churlishness of some earlier comments about the characteristics of some history textbooks, it is salutary to acknowledge a debt to the historian Perkin (1989) for his account of this century's ascent of the professionals as a potential major brake on the abuses of power by elites. He then documents how their leaders have joined the status quo rather than challenge it, as the legal and medical examples imply.

Etzioni-Halevy's (1989) point that there are competing elites that go some way to hold each other in check and that in a partly meritocratic society aspirants to leadership within elites will exercise restraints on those currently in commanding positions is effective, however, only while that new potential leadership focuses on its expert role and its potential implications.

The professions rose to influential positions because their knowledge was the foundation of the generation of the technology that has created the additional wealth of the 20th century. This has improved the quality of life by eliminating or reducing the suffering inflicted by disease and injury and for part of the world has reduced the physical slavery of so much productive and domestic drudgery. The same qualities of reasoning and observation transferred from technology to a study of the organization of social life would point to the false bases of so many of the arguments for the current institutional framework.

What has been written about biases in attributions and, in particular, the self-serving justifications for discrimination against outgroups applies within as well as between societies. As an illustration, it is argued that the chief executives of large companies have to be provided with high salaries and large additional benefits so that the best people are attracted to these positions. The same authorities argue that wages further down their companies should be kept low and that countries need a pool of unemployment at these levels to ensure profitability and low inflation. But why not try to control inflation by keeping prices down, profits lower, and all staff payments low? Why not create a pool of unemployed executives whose much lower salaries could be linked to the cost effectiveness of their companies and who would become threatened with impoverished unemployment if their companies became moribund?

Social comparisons are made by British senior management with America and Germany. Two features of these comparisons merit comment. First, comparisons are not made with Japan. Top management in Japan receives roughly 4 or 5 times the national average wage compared with the 20 or 30 times figure in the United States, Germany, and now Britain. Second, there is no suggestion that normal workers' pay in Britain should be raised to be comparable with their peers in Germany or America. British Ford is not offering its production line workers anything approaching the $50,000 currently claimed to be a feasible achievement in Cleveland, Ohio. The asymmetries of the arguments are transparent. The reality is of small networks of senior management having the power to maximize their wealth and doing so. They are doing so within the law, and doubtless many others would be delighted to gain similar privileges. The exercise of legitimated power is not what is interesting from a social psychological perspective. What is interesting is the self-serving reasoning used to justify the salaries; it is the rationality of this reasoning that is at issue.

Leaders of the professions might have been expected to contest the logic, but they have not gone beyond the ritualized skirmishes that have been cited earlier. These seem to wax and wane in approximately half-lunar cycles. What is true is not really a significant component of the arguments of the powerful for exercising their power to their own benefit. The rhetorical tradition of Gorgias takes precedence among the participants—and for the observers.

What is true rather than false in the fields of moral and political philosophy remains problematic, and de facto it appears that it will remain defined by those with the power to define it as that other opponent of Socrates, Thrasymachus, observed.

It might be argued that when Thrasymachus (Plato, 1971) claimed that "might was right," he was denying the existence of right and wrong. An alternative position would be that he was an early social constructionist who recognized that the powerful define what is right and wrong; insofar as the laws of societies are formulated by and executed by the powerful, he is correct. They define the frame of reference not just for what is criminal but what the principles of taxation and redistribution will be. Adversarial party political systems encourage revisions and redistributions to the benefit of the supporters of parties in government. In the quasi democracies, the dominating principle of voting would appear to be mainly subjective cost-benefit analyses of an economic nature; this is particularly so in individualistic, high power-distance societies such as the United Kingdom and the United States (Hofstede, 1980). The concepts of social justice and community are not vote winners. Given that governments are voted in and that whatever their rhetoric, their real intentions can be discerned, populations are only victims of policies for which they have voted. Protesting minorities using arguments about principles of social justice have to wait until they command majorities.

If Socrates's arguments were the valid ones, however, then it might be argued that states are being run on ignoble rather than noble lies. Historically, these lies were often based on religious justifications,

communism being a secular ideology that was substituted and sub-
verted into totalitarian dictatorships in many countries in the 20th
century.

Traditionally and typically, the justifications for any particular
kind of society have been offered by those who gain the greatest
secure power, wealth, and status from that form of society. Here it is
noted their arguments are characterized by the qualities listed as
"dishonest tricks" by Thouless (1974); they are properly labeled as
dishonest rather than mistaken because the errors are self-serving or
based on highly selected parities, and the suggestion that the irrationality was not dishonest would be difficult to defend. Just as at
the interpersonal level, deception and lying are most frequently
practiced for the benefit of the liar, so at the societal level, elites of
social orders have vested group interests in promoting the significance of their social order and vested personal interests in their own
ascendancy within their orders.

Although considerations of rationality and morality might have
been expected to exercise constraints on thinking about what is true
and what is false, by themselves they cannot be used to decide what
is likely to be empirically true or false. For that, evidence has to be
obtained, and there have to be criteria against which to evaluate the
likely truth or falsity of this evidence.

For particular informal events, people have strategies and tactics
for evaluating the truthfulness of statements made. Historians have
their rules of evidence, as do courts of law. For more general descriptions and explanations of the world's physical qualities, the rise of
science has replaced myth and legend.

The Sciences

The methods of modern sciences are not infallible. They do, however, provide criteria for the collection, processing, and evaluation of
empirical evidence that are qualitatively appropriate for assessing
the kinds of claims made. They do not rely on ex cathedra pronouncements from religious or ideological doctrines. They do not rely on
opinions of the ill informed or misinformed. That advances in science
are neither timeless nor assured is irrelevant to the fact that at

particular points in time, the consensually agreed on descriptions and explanations are the best estimates available.

The history of science charts its gradual emancipation from religious and political conservative elites. The heliocentric view of the universe of Galileo and Copernicus was contested by the Papal authorities of their day, but subsequent astronomy was not. Darwin's (1859) theory of evolution was contested and ridiculed by church authorities, but Mendel's genetic mechanisms were not. The temporary truths of these sciences have been the basis of the technological advances that have subsequently accrued so much wealth to those who have exploited the discoveries and inventions in a mixture of benefits and costs to others.

At the cutting edge of problems, scientists may disagree, but about much of their work there is a consensus, and only someone unfamiliar with the extent of this consensus and its foundations might raise logical and hypothetical objections to its achievements. The sciences that focus on human beings as other than individual biological organisms are in a much greater state of flux and uncertainty.

Psychology has joint roots in philosophy and physiology, with the latter providing the criteria for evaluating the evidence of claims made from empirical studies and the former providing many of the processes and products of interest: attention, sensation, perception, thinking, action, learning, motivation, and emotion. The study of these components of human experience and behavior remained somewhat esoteric interests compared with other sciences until they were given a strong impetus from applied problems in the world beyond the laboratory.

It has been suggested that one major impetus arose from the 1914 to 1918 European war (Rose, 1990). When the United States joined the conflict, how was it to prevent the inclusion of unsuitable recruits in its armed forces? Psychological tests were used to facilitate these decisions. Psychologists were also able to conduct examinations that enabled the armed forces to deselect those whose experiences in battle had rendered them unfit for service. Subsequently, psychology widened its presumed competence by fitting and or training persons for tasks. This strand of its value has grown greatly so that consultancy, testing, and training in industrial and commercial settings are now major occupational niches for psychologists and are now perceived necessary components of organizations.

The writings of the early psychologists read as sincere efforts to devise reliable and valid tests. The margins of error were recognized. Critical evaluations were made. By the 1980s, however, the situation had changed. Personality tests that had been shown not to be valid earlier were being used to select and deselect employees. Expensive selection training schemes and programs were introduced and run without any checks on their efficacy. Psychologists running such enterprises successfully have become wealthy.

Likewise in the clinical world, the small world of Freud's psychoanalytic therapy in bourgeois Vienna expanded so that by the 1990s a wide variety of psychological therapies exist. Their differential efficacy remains untested. The exhaustive trials to which pharmaceutical products are subjected are not required for psychological interventions. Sociologists of Marxist persuasion have long viewed psychologists as collaborators in the myths of capitalism (Rose, 1985). The argument has been that psychology pathologizes individuals rather than social systems. Explanations for failure or deviance in education are to be sought in individual characteristics —likewise for delinquency and crime. Being unable to cope with jobs can be attributed to inadequacies in the person. Although they are correct that blaming the victims has been a continuing theme of governing elites of the past two decades, the same characteristics were evident in Soviet society. In that society, failures and critics were also pathologized. Welfare psychologists have been placed in a no-win dilemma by their circumstances. For practicing psychologists to have demanded changes in social systems and simultaneously neglected those individuals who were failing to cope would have left their jobs undone and themselves open to charges of professional misconduct. Helping the individuals leaves psychologists open to the charge of propping up cruel systems.

The increasing value of psychologists to the economy is paralleled by the expansion of psychology in tertiary education. This contrasts with the contraction of philosophy and the relatively static position of sociology. It is the conjunction of questions in moral and political philosophy with social facts of the kind published in official statistical records and their explanations that give rise to the issues mentioned here. Correlations of crime and other indices of relative deprivation with business cycles (Henry, 1954) are robust findings of some longevity. It is their implications for government policies that are not addressed. Hence, the unpopularity of sociologists with governments of various hues. Mao Tse-tung saw them as "the running dogs of capitalism." The elites of the United Kingdom and the United States are more prone to see them as "Reds under the bed." In their descriptive role as collectors and publishers of social facts that are inconsistent with the claims of governments, sociologists are threats to propaganda machines. They are not enemies of the truth, but they are enemies to lies. Furthermore, their explanations for malfunctions are likely to draw attention to the operation of social systems set up and maintained but not scientifically evaluated by governments. The very posing of the sociological questions is a threat to governments concealing or misrepresenting social (and physical) realities. The likely answers to the questions are a threat to credibility of government as being "of the people, by the people and for the people."

That the people are increasingly wary of governments is shown by the loss of credibility in recent years (Gallup, 1993), although as yet little has happened to change even the direction of public distrust. Indifference and apathy to political affairs appear to be the dominant reactions in both the United Kingdom and the United States.

The Vested Interests
of the Human Sciences

The argument in this section might be seen as leading to an inevitable climax in a special plea for social psychology to be adopted as the subject most likely to reveal the advantages of truthfulness in a deceitful world. Is it a subject whose time has come, and will that lead to clever and ambitious social psychologists clambering up the social ladder and acting as the chief advisers to governing elites? A frightening prospect, but not so frightening if it is seen as one component necessary for human progress—in the creation of less irrational, unrealistic, and unjust societies than those that currently make up the United Nations.

What will be suggested is that philosophy, psychology, and sociology make up a trinity of disciplines that between them can, at the worst, show up some of the ignorance, errors, and lies currently promulgated about the characteristics of human beings and their groupings into societies and that leave many of them much more impotent and miserable than they need be. Plato's (1955) vision of a republic governed by philosopher rulers can be seen as the first draft of a set of ideas that might be resurrected, moderated, and adapted as providing some principles on which societal developments for the 21st century might be founded.

In fact, the specialists in the three disciplines have no vested interests in the diffusion of the appreciation of what their disciplines have to offer because they are just as subject to the conclusions and implications as anybody else. In this and earlier chapters, it has been suggested that as leaders of successive social groupings have become recruited to the upper echelons of the elites of power, wealth, and status in society, they have forgotten the force of the arguments that was used to promote the increase of the influence and have connived at the subsequent maintenance of any new status quo that is willing to assimilate them. This assimilating process has secured a conservative pattern of distribution of both material and cultural capital (Bourdieu, 1990) that has maintained the stratification of societies that it currently obtains. Restricting visions of what could be better to educated elites ensures that any general will of the population is unlikely to be exercised in the direction of rationally and empirically evaluated change.

Access to knowledge has always been rationed by rulers and their governments. In particular, the people have been protected from seditious literature. It was less than 200 years ago that a number of British men were sentenced to transportation to Australia simply for having read Thomas Paine's *The Rights of Man*. The crowned heads of Europe spent much of the 19th century concerned that the ideas that had inspired the French Revolution would stimulate similar insurrections elsewhere. Control of access to literature was instituted much earlier than the 18th century and in particular the Vatican was a burner of forbidden books; those seen as heretical and threatening the status quo. The books banned have typically been those concerned with visions of alternative forms of social organization and government and the arguments that might be advanced to justify such changes.

In totalitarian states, school education normally has a strong political component that justifies the regime in power. In quasi democracies, policies differ, ranging from having explicit courses in civics to the squeezing out of political or moral philosophy by not having these in national curricula or examinations. Such decisions can be supported by the maxim that education should not have political components—thus ensuring that students remain politically ignorant and naive. What is not taught may well not be learned.

A major reason for people not being more enlightened about possible universally applicable principles of logical reasoning, principles of morality and justice, and criteria for evaluating evidence about social facts is that they are not taught about such matters. Only those few who choose relevant subjects in tertiary education will come across ideas about principles of social organization.

To begin with logical reasoning, Garnham and Oakhill (1995) provide a succinct summary of the state of current psychological beliefs about thinking and reasoning. They demonstrate the shortcuts, heuristics, and commonly occurring biases and errors in current human reasoning. The accounts offered, however, are described and founded on a framework of an ideal of logical consistency and validity. The experiments show what particular people in a particular society do in particular situations. They do not show what other people might be able to achieve given a different cultural milieu and education. The frameworks of analysis themselves testify to the fact that the psychologists designing them are able to conceive of more than their experimental participants manage to display! This is not to claim that there is one ideal system of rationality where the concept of rationality is restricted to the logical consistency and validity of arguments defined within sets of defining axioms; it is to claim that already existing criteria of description and evaluation are of the current performances of participants in experiments and therefore display a gap between contingent performance and possible competence.

Interestingly, Garnham and Oakhill (1995) make no reference to Thouless (1974) and his 38 varieties of crooked thinking. Their text adopts a perspective that does not consider how people exploit pseudologic to mislead others. There is no reason why they should have done so, but an exploration of the tricks that work best in particular contexts would also throw some light on the clines of departures from consistency and validity. If inconsistencies are noted in arguments, it will be when they are consistent with the vested interests of the protagonists that questions of deliberate falsification arise. All human beings in all contexts are accountable against the same criteria, and neither social scientists nor philosophers have special rights.

The same kind of argument can be developed about morality and justice. Kant's (1785/1964) principles of universifiability and goodwill are two synthetic a priori propositions that many people would find impossible to contest. Rorty's (1991) principle of avoiding cruelty to others may also be definable in an untautological way. Rawls's (1971) notions of justice and Popper's (1966) defense of open societies, along with his pragmatic maxims for making progress, are candidates for evaluating answers to questions about morals and justice. Interestingly, these criteria are not dissimilar from the psychological contributions of Piaget (1932) and Kohlberg (1969). None of these criteria or principles give rise to special privileges or rights for rulers or associated elites. Neither do they grant immunity from responsibilities to any social groupings.

What is realistic and sensible must also take into account what is believed to be true (contingently) in the psychology and sociology of contemporary societies. The chapters of this volume are replete with examples of the kinds of bias and falsifications likely to arise in interpersonal and intergroup encounters and communications, and it has not been difficult to diagnose the kinds of motives people have for displaying bias and falsifying facts. That concealment of the truth and lies arise out of dilemmas posed by requirements to answer questions for which a truthful answer may cause more harm than good and that in turn these situations arise out of the peculiarities of the social systems human beings have created or allowed others to create simply means that the systems, rather than individuals, also stand in need of reform. The interdependence of psychology and sociology in subordinating truthfulness of representation to other functions of language is illustrated by the continuation of the voluntary purchasing of newspapers that their own readers see as frequently untruthful and simultaneously condemn as wrong for being so.

The analyses reported here show something of the nature and extent of the concealment and falsification of the truth in the United Kingdom and the United States. Whatever is said about the wrongness of lying in particular contexts, what is done about that lying does not seem to be seriously directed toward its reduction or elimination. In addition to the face-to-face and mediated communication where falsifications seem to be required, for many other situations it is normative. For yet others it is tolerated. It seems that only children are punished for lying per se. If other people are punished for lying, it is the topic about which they have lied rather than their untruthfulness per se that is the focus of moral judgment. Given such conditions, it might be said that societies deserve the institutionalized lying that they experience. The key empirical thesis and generalization advanced here is probably the suggestion that truthfulness is the first casualty of vested interest, provided that the concealment or lies can be sustained for long enough. When a cost-benefit analysis gives a greater advantage to a feasible successful concealment or lie, this seems to be the preferred course of action.

If this is indeed a reflection of the spirit of the culture, it is not surprising that the currently demonstrable truths of social psychology and sociology are matters of indifference to society as a whole. At this point, it is tempting to note that Plato prophesied that democracies decline into anarchies and then tyrannies because their citizens become more concerned with personal pleasure than with civic responsibilities. It is also tempting to ask whether such a state of affairs is particularly likely to arise in particular kinds of quasi democracies, namely those that are individualistic rather than collectivistic and have high power-distance differentials (Hofstede, 1980).

Collectivism emphasizes responsibilities to the social groups of which one is a member and the values of cooperation and harmony. In such a culture, lies will be told to preserve harmony in relationships rather than to give an individual competitive advantage or the possibility of avoiding punishment, but they will not be tolerated as a means of excusing one's own misdemeanors. Trust is essential for the preservation of harmony and lies are a betrayal of trust. By contrast, in a competitive individualistic society trust is a hazardous relationship. In Chapter 8, it was clear that skill at deception is a strong component in the profile necessary for success in competitive games, be these genuine games, serious sports, business deals, or armed conflicts. Where winning is what is important, openness about intentions would be a recipe for losing. It is not surprising in an individualistic and competitive society that skill at deceit becomes a valued competence across the whole range of relationships and behavior. The secret of maximizing success is to be a trusted liar who is not found out, at least not until after one is dead. Of recent American presidents, Kennedy, Johnson, Nixon, and Reagan all had skeletons in their spacious cupboards. A steadily increasing number of Major's 3-year-old government have so far resigned over failed concealments, some of which have been accompanied by falsifications.

To extend the idea of people deserving the governments they have, it might be suggested that if people subscribe to the values of economic success and individualism, they should not be surprised if truthfulness ceases to be a priority in communication, and if Plato's understanding of social systems is as insightful as it appears to be, they should not be surprised if their society drifts toward a mixture of anarchy and tyranny.

CHAPTER TWELVE

Loose Ends, Strands, and Progress

The contrast of telling the truth versus telling lies has not been as clear and simple as might have been hoped. It has involved many contrasts rather than one, even within the frame of reference adopted here. The inclusion of work from psychopathology would have added greatly to some of the comparisons made, as would cross-cultural data and social category differences within societies. Simply tracing the strands of analyses arising from the Ancient Greek philosophers and historians, and seeing how their contributions have been developed and elaborated with special reference to the English-speaking descendants of those traditions, has yielded a wide range of issues of relevance to social scientists.

Social psychologists interested in the antecedents, correlates, dynamics, and consequences of telling the truth and telling lies can and must focus on particular narrow issues for individual empirical and explanatory studies, but such work can benefit only from being located in a more ecologically comprehensive manifold. That a reader may judge that this text has not done very well in trying to achieve such an aim does not undermine the validity of an argument that progress is built on improving on the contributions of others and that the next volume directed to this end may be more successful in articulating the diverse strands considered here. In the final chapter, an attempt is made to assess to what extent the strands are loose ends and to what extent they can be woven together.

There are methodological difficulties peculiar to the field, and it may be helpful to summarize some of these. The issues of detecting and challenging lies without making false accusations has been, is, and will continue to be a dynamic struggle, with shifting advantages to deceivers and detectives, which merits comment. If, in their wisdom, societies decide that they are allowing too many lies in too many fields of activity, what might they do to reduce their number? That is a socially significant issue as well as a theoretically interesting problem. At several points, it has been necessary to think in terms of layers of reality, and it may be useful to try to consider how many such layers are necessary.

Finally, the crucial contrast from Chapter 1 has to be reviewed in the light of what has been reported. Is the human species to continue to engage in its self-debilitating, intraspecies, intergroup, and inter-individual competitions on a basis that gives priority to winning out over others, or are its members going to accord greater priority to confronting discoverable truths that may increase individual virtue and cooperation within and among communities? Is the design of the human being consistent with the second option?

Methodological Hazards in the Study of Lies

Quality of Materials. At the outset it is important to distinguish between those difficulties inherent in the field and those that have been created by investigators. In many areas of study, it is necessary for the investigators to go to the objects of study, be these ice floes in Antarctica, archaeological remains in Turkey, tigers in India, or Torres Straits Islanders in the Torres Straits. Neither inconvenience nor the expense are reasons for absurd substitutions. The time taken to collect data cannot be defined independently of the problem.

Social psychologists seem to have been particularly hasty to design experiments for captive undergraduates seeking course credits. The length of a procedure seems to be liable to be defined by slots on the timetable. Role playing is used too readily to replace reality. Studies of lying and deception have been bedeviled by these shortcuts. If the objectives of a study are to find out what Year 1 Introductory Psychology students at the University of X believe are the nonverbal and verbal indexical markers of lying, then appropriate investigations may be designed to be administratively convenient as well. If the objectives are to find out how good such students are at lying in certain ways about certain topics, then again designs might be devised that are administratively convenient. The design, the materials, the procedure, the participants, and the treatment of the data should relate to the hypotheses or questions posed. If these criteria are applied to the conclusions drawn from the studies of lie enactment and detection of lies, too many fail.

Beliefs about indexical markers of lies and role-playing competence are relevant subtopics in the field, but their centrality can be contested. James (1902) can be quoted to the effect that studies of psychological phenomena should begin with real people seriously engaging in a clear form of the act or experience in focus.

It is not until the 1990s that advisory writing began to render this principle explicit (Buller & Burgoon, in press; Miller & Stiff, 1993). Previously, much energy was wasted asking whether a set of primed students could discriminate between truthful answers and simulated lies told by fellow students. (Of course, if the answer had been that they could discriminate with 95% accuracy, then research could have benefited, but their near-chance performances vitiated this shortcut.)

If real lies are to be used, where are they to come from? Laboratories, clinics, and TV companies must now have video libraries with many statements made in front of the cameras that the authors have subsequently admitted and the world has judged to have been lies. Many of these will have occurred in monologs, but there must also be examples where they have been offered by interviewers who have challenged the veracity of the speakers in extended conversations. Such sources do not appear to have been exploited either for microanalyses of the presentations or for judgments by panels of different categories of persons other than by Ekman (1985/1992) and Buller and Burgoon (in press). There are biases and complications in that liars caught on recordings are a limited subsample of the population, likely to be relatively proficient in the relevant skills, but at least the data would have ecological validity. Experimental manipulations remain possible, although these are increasingly at risk for definition as unethical. Permitting or encouraging people to cheat and then lie, as in the Exline procedure (Exline et al., 1970), is one variant. Ekman's (1985/1992) nurses trying to pretend that the film they had witnessed had not been upsetting is another. As Ekman notes, this plausible and possibly defensible manipulation gave the nurses good reasons for trying to disguise their true feelings and to find words that were inconsistent with what they had witnessed. (It should also be noted, however, that the initial instructions that look as though they should have worked, did not in fact do so.) Miller and Stiff (1993) list other methods but each involves role playing in various circumstances. Of course, it would be possible to video job interviews and other situations in which naturally occurring lies could be collected. Confidence tricksters would seem to be ideal characters to demonstrate their competence as liars. Actors have been used, and DePaulo and DePaulo's (1984) judges seem to have found their lying performances undetectable. That being so, simulated lying, especially by professional actors, could be calibrated against real lying, and microanalytic techniques could be exploited to demonstrate whether or not these two are discriminable from each other. If it were to be shown that they were not, this would help to authenticate the use of simulations. Microanalysis may be time consuming and tedious, but as has been argued, validity cannot be compromised. The suggestions made here would not permit penetration of interactions in close interpersonal relationships, although these too might be filmed from counseling sessions. Partners could be asked subsequently about the truthfulness of particular remarks, and speakers could subsequently be asked to comment. Accounts given by partners of marriages and their breakdown differ. Both descriptions of events and attributions exhibit self-serving biases or more (Jones & Nisbett, 1972). There must be lies as well. Properly checked, these could become usable materials.

It would appear to be the case that social psychologists have been somewhat slow to exploit opportunities to record real lies that happen to have been recorded. Neither does there appear to have been a systematic examination of the relations between real lies and various simulated ones. If the two do not differ, even in the studies using students, then the validity of much of the data, half discounted in this and other texts, should be seen as useful for revealing what people can achieve by way of concealing what they believe to be the indexical markers of lies. At present, this is unknown. Recordings of court proceedings are another naturally occurring possibility, and it is particularly surprising that what has been manifested in court has not been cross-checked against the polygraph records discussed in Chapter 5.

Correlatively, there are possibilities of using more skilled detectors and finding out how they succeed, if they do. Raskin (1988) lists the categories of experts who have failed to demonstrate their competence. But are there individuals within categories who are greatly superior, and can the basis of their expertise be rendered public? No study seems to have used conjurers and magicians as assessors. These archdeceivers have trained themselves to deceive audiences in three main ways. One is by subtlety of movement in combination with their apparatus. They do things that escape the attention of even the most attentive audience, including those who know that they should not focus anywhere the magician is luring their eyes. With the variants of finding the "correct" playing card, there appear to be two techniques. One is to know the location or identity of the card all the way through the trick but have a ritual entertaining patter. The other is not to know but to have an audience stooge reveal when the card is shown. Certainly, with some practice, it is possible to catch eye movements and widening pupils, but real magicians must be doing more in their sensitivity to the nonverbal signals of others and their competence at misleading other people with their own. Magicians have been called in to expose frauds of various kinds. Whether they would be willing to share their secrets for the advancement of the study of deception and lie detection remains to be seen. It is also reasonable to hope that training in microanalytic techniques and the art of interrogation might also begin to raise valid discrimination between truthful and lying statements and provide the basis for bootstrapping improvements.

Against this optimism must be stacked the lessons of the past. With a long (in)human history of interrogating prisoners, suspected criminals, heretics, and other categories of possible liars, an accumulating wisdom about detection is sadly absent. The use of modern technology and clever interrogation strategies by the security and law enforcement officers of the most psychologically sophisticated states cannot boast of scientific breakthroughs. In intelligence, the layers of tactics become so complex that university psychologists are unlikely to find out what intelligence experts do and do not know about deception and detection. There will be times when security forces would wish outsiders, either friendly or hostile, to believe that they know more than they do and others when they would prefer people to underestimate their capacities. There is scant evidence to suggest that intelligence services are ahead of academics, but would there be any if they were?

To date, perhaps because the polygraph exists, more effort has been focused on the detection of emotional states than on the development of interrogation strategies. Kalbfleisch (1994; see also Chapter 3) has offered a list and a review that implies that progress has been minimal, and it may be that the use of these components should be pursued with greater vigor. Ethical issues will probably surface, but perhaps volunteers might offer themselves as challenges to interrogators.

Linguistic analyses are not quite as neglected as interrogation strategies, but they seem to be confined to German and Scandinavian evaluations of children's testimony in abuse cases. Although these are important and ecologically valid in origins, it is strange that such work is so confined in terms of kind of putative offense, kind of possible liar, and Nordic investigators. As with polygraphic analysis, criteria-based statement analysis is probabilistic in its discriminating capacity, but its premises are psychologically promising. Memories may be reconstructions of the past rather than veridical reflections, but the technique brings into focus that lies are based on a discrepancy between what happened and what the liar says happened. Until such time as a liar has repeated the alternative false version sufficiently to have come to believe its veracity, there will be two sets of incompatible memories in mind—the real and the fabricated. Logically, it should be possible to drive a wedge between the two. Psychologically, it seems that people are extraordinarily competent at persisting with the false version.

For lies in the public domain, there have yet to be any linguistic analyses. Often, these can be checked against alternative sources of information, especially if objective data are in dispute between antagonists. Linguistically, the only offering is Robinson's (1993) (see Table 8.1) contrast based on presumptions about truth-seeking and crowd-rousing speech.

What a combination of linguistic, nonverbal, and physiological data combined with suitable interrogation might reveal has yet to be systematically studied. Expensive as this might be, so far as customary levels of funding are, the issues would seem to merit expenditure; expenditures on military weaponry and on legal fees in courts are so much higher than any prospective project along multidimensional lines would need to be.

Table 12.1 Probable Outcomes if A Accuses B of Lying

If A is superior to B	If A is inferior to B
Acceptable (if no alibi and offense suspected)	*Not acceptable* especially in public
Law enforcement officials → citizen	B denies lies, seeks retribution
Police → suspect	
Barrister → witness	
Tax/license/inspectors → suspected fraudster	Other authorities will cover B whether right or wrong
	B and allies will tell A
If no lie, counter is unnecessary	1. Disloyal
	2. Troublemaker
	3. Should have seen B et al. in private and used proper channels
Acceptable in certain circumstances	
Parent-child if error or omission	
or if offense suspected or known but identity of offender not	A will be deserted by colleagues, friends, etc.
Teacher-pupil	
Boss-employee	
If no lie, perhaps an apology	
Counters: lack of trust or confidence/always pick on me	

That lies are seen as morally wrong is another hazard researchers face, especially because their use is most likely disguising a more serious offense. The course of helping research pales as a benefit against the possible costs of disclosure. In the world of action, especially for public figures, being exposed as a liar about some concealed activity carries risks. Even if the activity is not illegal, the concealment may well be grounds for resignations or part-resignations from public office. The final procedures surrounding U.S. appointments to high office are not recounted across the Atlantic, but many people might have seen employing a Filipino maid without a work permit as a weak reason for debarring a prospective attorney general from office.

These considerations make it particularly problematic for ethological studies aimed at finding out how many lies of which kinds are told to whom by whom. One tactic is to try to obtain estimates of lies told to individuals rather than by them, but the validity of these judgments would be unknown. Given the frequency with which respondents in field studies have reported lies and given the incidence of easily detectable misrepresentations in the media, it is clear that lying is the immediate default reaction to many accusations and the preferred option for proactive presentation of self-serving information.

The Variability of the Definitions of Lying and Cognate Activities. As Chapters 1 and 2 showed, there is no consensus among speakers of English as to when a statement is a lie. In the first place, in part, this stems from the fact that the intellectual appreciation of what it is to lie requires a mastery of several constituent concepts however it is defined. Children develop their understanding and presumably some do not attain a mature knowledge of what most people mean by a lie. In the second place, however, there is no perfect consensus among adults. In part, it looks as though this stems from the moral condemnation of statements judged to be lies. One means used to avoid this is to redefine lies into white lies, fibs, and not really a lie. A third source probably stems from the absence of simple, single words for many of the 11 ways in which statements can deviate from being truthful, complete, relevant, and not misleading (Bradac, Friedman, & Giles, 1986). For example, although Burgoon (1994) found a distinction between equivocation-concealment and lies, some people might treat either equivocal or concealing answers as lies even though nothing false was stated. This third source could be seen as a component of an absence of understanding rather than as a misuse of words.

Each of these sources of variability means that tasks set to respondents will suffer from error variance arising from differential interpretations of any instructions that ask about lies unless a defining gloss is given that is understood and followed by respondents.

It also means that there is a particular difficulty with the distinctions between lies and unintended falsehoods. The requirement to diagnose the intentions of tellers of falsehoods presents any investigation with epistemological dilemmas that can achieve no more than probabilistic resolutions. This may well remain indefinitely problematic.

Challenging Liars

At various points in the text, questions have been posed about someone "going bald on record" and making explicit the belief that someone is lying. Indications have been given that in the United Kingdom and the United States this can be a hazardous act for the challenger and that denials and counteraccusations may well reverse the prima facie obligation to justify what has been said and done.

In certain formal situations, however, very bald and harassing accusations about lying are allowed: suspected shoplifter-security services, accused-police, or court witness-cross-examiner. These situations are those of role relationships in which there are substantial power differences. Harassing tactics are commonly excused by the ends; the accused may give up lying and confess to the truth and perhaps to a criminal act. An innocent person is presumed to have nothing to fear. It is not unknown, of course, for the accused to confess just to escape from the unbearable unpleasantness and either go through with a punishment or make a subsequent retraction. There is no evidence that such tactics are efficacious (see Kalbfleisch, 1994, or p. 149), but they are probably the customary practice in criminal inquiries and trials (see Moston & Stephenson, 1993, for an account of their relevance in the courts of England and Wales).

The polar opposite scenario arises in many cases of whistle-blowing. Commonly, successive attempts by a challenger to obtain action within the organization are discounted and deflected, until finally the accusations about the organization are made public. Whether the case is one of scientific fraud, life-threatening designs, or dangerous drugs, the modal response for organizations is to set up procedures for covering up liabilities and accusing the whistle-blower of as many insane or evil intentions as possible. The parallels with personal and media attributions about enemies are clear. So also for the parallels with disasters; pilot or driver error is more often offered as an immediate explanation than faults in designs and procedures (Reason, 1990). In these cases, denial of, and therefore avoidance of, responsibility is probably the most common motive, and attributions are likely to presume insanity or malice of those onto whom the burden of responsibility is directed. In these cases, the documented evidence (Callahan, 1988) can provide confirmatory evidence of cover-ups and falsification, but associated legal actions are often defended and contested for as long as possible. The truth may be transparently obvious to outsiders, but "not losing," by whatever means are possible, is commonly assigned a higher priority. (One of the examples cited by Broad & Wade, 1982, was the case of the Dow-Corning silicone breast implants, whose characteristics have led to billions of dollars of claims against the company. In 1995, the company went into liquidation, and presumably, the laws about company structure will protect the shareholding companies from meeting further claims.)

These extremes are informative because they are complementary with respect to differences in power. In both cases, the more powerful party controls events; in the first case, risking false confessions by oppressive techniques and, in the second, by acting to hide the truth by whatever means it can muster and, if necessary, by illegal ones (see Table 12.1).

In familiar relationships involving unequal power, similar tactics might be used, particularly by some parents interrogating younger children. In familiar and intimate relations between equals, initial sequences are likely to be more tentative. In more equal seriously dating or married couples, the sequence of events will be even more problematic. Because "being able to trust" is one of the most serious rules of intimacy (Argyle & Henderson, 1985), any accusation of lying carries a double risk. If it turns out to be ill founded, there is a risk of "How could you not trust me?" from the accused. If exposed, the accuser has demonstrated that a key relational rule has been broken by one partner. Repairing broken trust can be difficult. The value placed on the relationship will be one factor militating against accusations being made. A further component of this can be the preference to be careful not to check out suspicions about a partner possibly concealing or lying about some behavior or feeling; what is not investigated or brought to explicit verbalization may be less threatening and may disappear.

The conservative advantage enjoyed by liars is neither sociologically nor psychologically surprising. This is consistent with the default conditions of human nature underpinning the theme of the text. To maintain that language is a communication system and can be used as a vehicle in which statements can be true requires that this is the normative intended use of such statements. Sociologically, society has to be presumed to be functionally coordinated for the benefit of its members. The extreme alternative is a Hobbesian state of nature. Hence, perhaps the tenacity with which organizations deny their corruption against whistle-blowers and all other individuals who validly declare that some emperor is not wearing any clothes. It may be unjust and viciously cruel on the individuals. It may be unjust that those who have committed the offenses and those who fail to make rational and realistic investigations to inquire into these events typically do not suffer the consequences their actions deserve, but if the bias were toward believing or even investigating every accusation made against institutions and organizations, the social fabric could collapse into permanently undermining inquiries. (Already, there is a developing trend for individuals to sue organizations for fictitious injuries or offenses; lies can be told by persons against organizations.)

Psychologically, for communication in interpersonal encounters, a case has been mentioned for the necessity of a default position for truth on the grounds of the impossibilities of information processing if all meanings were unpredictable in truth value or had to be assumed to be opaque, and this will be taken up in the final section.

Discouraging Lies

One reason that lying is as high as it is on the agenda for reactive defense and proactive exploitation could be that exposed lies are quickly forgiven if not forgotten. Loss of trust as a result of exposure as a liar may rank high rhetorically as a consequence to be avoided in close relationships of friendship, kinship, or marital partnership, but in fact, when lies are exposed, it may be rare for the relationship to be seriously threatened. Marriages and friendships survive adulterous affairs with best friends as one of the partners, and after a period of turbulence there may be an apparent return to the original situation. The fear of discovery may be strong, but the consequences may be slight. As with detection, it may be the offense rather than the lie that is de facto paramount despite what is actually said.

Employees caught lying at work are less likely to be laid off than those caught stealing. Those people in court whose testimony is shown to have been legally untrue by verdicts of the court are very

is the propaganda? Here is not the place to repeat the examples given. It is the place to note that the uncertainty about self-deception versus conscious deceit is common to all the (intrapersonal), interpersonal, person-group, group-person, and intergroup situations.

To the extent that it is true that repetition of lies may actually lead to their coming to be believed by the liar, the puzzles become even more difficult to unravel. Certainly, with very young children what is experienced is coterminal with the real, and the subsequent differentiations of reality from appearance, of fantasy from reality, and of remembered reality and redefined reality (lies) can each suffer from relapses, ending with lies that can come to be believed. There is no reason to assume that adults cannot suffer from (enjoy) the same confusions, especially through systematic selective and self-controlled training. Actors do occasionally become their roles, and to the extent that people behave differently across contexts that remain separate, they too can develop different and seemingly incompatible personas for these. Torturers, serial killers, security personnel, and exploitative business people can have all the positive qualities of human beings as well. One variant on this theme has not been explored at all. From their experience and knowledge, older people come to know more about the risks involved in adventurous activities. Much of their knowledge may come from the media. A typical example would be the dangers of travel: earthquakes in Japan, bandit gangs in Cambodia, tiger sharks off coral reefs, muggings in New York, or knifings in Moscow. People accumulate catalogs of specific events but with no idea of the probabilities associated with these risks and others. For example, at the height of the troubles in Belfast, Northern Ireland, being injured or killed in vehicular accidents carried a much higher probability than being a victim of paramilitaries, but no doubt people were much more frightened of the latter than the former. (As soon as one of my daughters mentions an enthusiastic prospect of an enjoyable venture overseas, my experience lists the hazards of that country with no sense of their probabilities and no offsetting countables of a positive nature.) It is likely that many of the fears of the elderly of being attacked are equally ill judged as a result of news coverage. Aristotle (1926) noted that the elderly are cautious and suspicious; this would seem to be a false perception of reality that acts to reduce pleasure and experience for no rational reason. Spreading such rumors would not be lying but would be misrepresenting for others and self-deception for oneself.

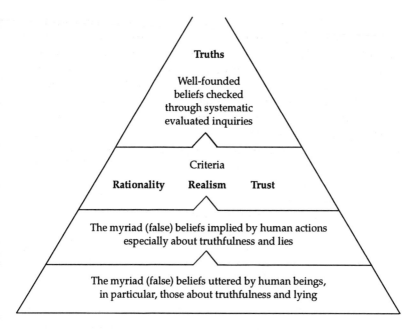

Figure 12.1. Aspirations to reduce false beliefs and lies through rationality, realism, and trust.

Such perspectives inject both an extra layer to issues of lying and deception and imply that what is functional rather than dysfunctional requires more than a binary contrast.

A Pyramid of Truths and Falsehoods

One of the problems in bringing order into the disparate topics is to find a metaphor that captures the relevant characteristics but does not carry misleading implications as well. Unfortunately, the molecular structure of truthfulness versus lying would come to resemble some camel-shaped compound with asymmetric protuberances, and it may be less misleading to adopt a too simplifying pyramid (see Figure 12.1).

If that is done, the bottom stratum has to be the collectivity of gossip about truthfulness and lies: the diverse patchwork quilt whose bits and pieces of diverse cloth, pattern, and color constitute all that ordinary human beings believe to be true, especially about truthfulness and lying. It will include what they believe and say they believe about truth within and across the branches of knowledge (logical, everyday empirical, scientific empirical, religious, moral, and aesthetic). It will include what they believe about indexes of lying, about their competence at deception and detection, and about others' competence. It will include what they believe about the frequencies of lying by everyone else and themselves. It will include their reactions to lies of various kinds. It is all the talk in which people indulge about truthfulness and lying.

Above this stratum, and interacting with it, is the action stratum—what people actually do. The possible relations with the lowest layer are complete consistency, complete independence, and a mixture of the two. (A completely predictable inconsistency is realistically impossible.) Mixed relations is the only realistically feasible choice among the three. The extent to which people feel obliged to achieve consistency and in which directions they seek to resolve inconsistencies will differ from individual to individual. Ideally, inconsistencies should be resolved in the direction of what is really the case, an issue to be mentioned after passing through the higher layer.

The third layer involves the professional scientists and other academics working on truthfulness and lies. Theoretically, at least, they have been endeavoring to find out what is true in all fields of knowledge, including the superordinate issue of the nature of truth and falsity and incorporating all that social science can sensibly say about truth telling and lies, but their activities have to be subordinated to criteria of rationality, realism, and trust if they are to reduce ignorance and false beliefs.

If progress is to be made, the two lowest layers of public action and public rhetoric should be influenced in the long run by what the professional academics find out. In turn, the professional academics are obliged to study the perceived realities and to be rational in their collection and processing of evidence.

The apex is what is true about everything there is to be known. Infinite and immensely and incomprehensible complex as this encyclopedia is, the idea itself is not beyond the grasp of the human mind. What is to be known about truth and truthfulness, lies, falsification, and other deviations from the truth is part of the apex and of special concern here. Some of what little has been proposed as true about this subsection of knowledge has been reported here, but it was deemed appropriate to go beyond issues of lying and telling the truth as currently believed to wider questions of what is true and the extent to which various groups of human beings do not accommodate to these truths.

From perception of self through perceptions of others and interpersonal relationships through to perceptions of social groups and societies, to the perceived reasons for human existence, it is possible to suggest that two opposing forces are at work in human beings. On the one hand, there is a wish to assure ourselves that all is well with us, our immediate associates and, our own social worlds. We want happy security. On the other hand, we know from what we know of our ignorance, our irrationality, and our differences from most of our fellow creatures that each of us is in a set of tiny minority groups that differ from the rest of our species. We delude ourselves that this is not the case. We delude ourselves that others are more trustworthy than they are. We delude ourselves that we are more virtuous than we are.

These delusions on the grand scale are not normally considered as part of the literature on lying and deception, but it is difficult to see on what grounds they should be excluded. Lies are lies whether they are told to parents about not having taken a biscuit from the larder or pretending to ourselves that we have unequivocal answers to the meaning and significance of human existence when we have not.

What might be hoped for in the future is that more people will have the opportunity to bring their rhetoric in line with their experience and behavior, that both may be consistent with what philosophers and scientists claim to have found out, and that all three may be consistent with what sensible rational realism affords.

The prospects of immediate progress toward the apex for most people in most communities is zero. The forces at work that are mentioned in Chapters 6 through 10 will act to prevent or reverse progress if past precedent is a guide to the future. Those forces will be aided rather than opposed by many of the ideas put forward by professional academics. Most oppressive movements claim a rationale for their hegemony on the basis of religious, philosophical, or scientific claims. Currently, for example, biologists of neo-Darwinian persuasion seem to be the gurus justifying the inevitability of "survival of the fittest" as being in the interests of all; this is then translated into the idea that competition for material success leads to efficiency, which benefits the whole community! Truth and truthfulness do not appear on this agenda.

Survival, Success, Winning, and Truth

Biologists (Dawkins, 1976) love genes as explanatory concepts. Medical scientists have pursued the genetic features relevant to the developments of particular conditions: first physical features, then deficiencies or disease risks, and now behavioral dispositions. Social scientists note the diversity of cultures and societies and consider the consequences of generations of people in communities passing on intelligence. Developmental psychologists note that interaction breeds ideas that individuals can consider and act on. Each human being is a product of biochemistry and culture. Each of these sets constraints on what each person can become, and they render some becomings more likely than others.

How these orientations impinge on truth telling and lying may be indicative of the extraordinary combinations of the characteristics of these two activities and of the beliefs about their frequency and appropriateness. Dawkins (1976) postulated that genes will be selfish and maximize their chances of reproduction. How then is moral behavior to be explained and, in particular, what could account for what appears to be altruistic self-sacrifice? Why an adult male should plunge into the sea to rescue a drowning girl of unknown genetic characteristics is one of the philosophical conundrums posed. (Not that anyone has checked out the frequency with which adult males confronted with such dilemmas do sacrifice themselves. It is not an investigation that could be recommended as a final year project in psychology for female undergraduates.)

To cope with this kind of apparent anomaly, and following calculations of computer simulations by Axelrod (1984) and others, the tit-for-tat principle has been enunciated. In the long run, doing unto others as they do unto you optimizes the chances of survival (and hence reproduction). The phrase is unfortunate in that in everyday use, it is invariably used in the negative sense of vengeance rather than reciprocity. Just as the phrase "an eye for an eye" has not been used in its Hebrew sense to indicate the prescribed upper limit of vengeance, so people will be prone not to see the positive side of tit for tat. In the case of truthfulness, the principle advises truth for truth and lie for lie, which could be more sensibly translated into truth for truth and a willingness to lie and otherwise deceive as soon as fellow interactants have abandoned the "Be truthful" maxim. Unfortunately, this requires each person to be able to detect when the other is lying. In mortal combats, he who lies first is more likely to live to tell the tale. One Armageddon scenario has Russian and American fingers on the nuclear button and an open telephone line through which professed intentions can be exchanged. To press second means the annihilation of one's own side. To mislead the other long enough after pressing might gain its survival. What is both absurd and tragic about the human condition is that the species should have got so close to such an insane binary choice and one where trusting the other wrongly is the recipe for defeat. That this particular threat is in abeyance must be a temporary respite only.

Some time in the future, some pair of leaders will confront each other and play nuclear bluff and puff, and given the historical record of leaders being willing to sacrifice the members of their own societies in suicidal gestures, there is no reason to be assured that someone will not be willing to combine societal suicide with societal mass murder. I believe that had the species followed the advice of Socrates, human beings could have avoided much of the record of misery and suffering that its members have inflicted on each other. A pursuit of the truth would have required a commitment to rational realism, which would have come to include an appreciation of the extent to which reality is socially constructed. That having been so, the genuine progress achieved in mathematics, the nonhuman sciences, and technology would have been paralleled by the development and enactment of improved solutions to problems in the human sciences, ethics, and metaphysics.

Regrettably, more straightforward Darwinian principles of physical fitness, namely military and political prowess, have continued to dominate the human enterprise. Predominantly, the ego has indeed been the servant of the irrational and imperative demands of both id and superego. The self-indulgence and self-righteousness of those with the political and military power continue to reduce the probability of social progress, and the scramble for preferment, combined with the patronage of bread and circus exercises, provides a voluntary mediated censorship over the ideas and ideals that have surfaced periodically in Athens, the Renaissance in Europe, the Enlightenment in Europe and the United States, and in thrusts for communism or socialism with a human face in other contexts.

On the one hand, the genetically deterministic stance offers a mechanical view of human beings as driven robots. It operates on the level of gene pools and populations over long periods of time. Because a single wrong judgment of assuming a foe is a friend or that a true statement is false can have immediate mortal consequences for whole populations, it is difficult to see how such a development could achieve a sufficient critical incidence for it to become "fit." On the other hand, the power elites define their societies and cultures in terms that discourage the open consideration and evaluation of better social systems for the generation of more virtuous people. The tit-for-tat principle seems to be irrelevant to either context in serious situations.

What the various interindividual choice games with their ranging outcome matrices show is that cooperation provides the best joint outcomes on average. Competition gives rise to winners and losers, and for real people in real situations, anxiety and insecurity. Cooperation has to be based on shared assumptions and on goals that are not in conflict with each other. Conflicts can best be resolved by analyses and decision making based on rational realism, which in turn requires statements made to be truthful.

Concern for the truth becomes central for any such community. Modernized and refined in the light of contemporary understanding about knowledge generation and education, dialectical and consultative reasoning applied to appropriate evidence would point to the advantages of cooperative truth telling. It would also show that in such societies, the occasional undetected liar would be able to secure personal advantages. Such tactics would have to be discouraged by ensuring that such advantages were changed into penalties if and when discovered. The community would have to be vigilant and consensual in its treatment of offenders.

At the present time, human societies are far removed from any such scenario. What the text has claimed is that in totalitarian states, every informal and formal relationship is fraught with danger for a participant who tells the truth. Conformity to the dominant ideology is the price of survival. It is, of course, noteworthy that none of the work on lying and deception in interpersonal relationships has been conducted in totalitarian states. In states that run on fear of suffering and death, serious social psychology cannot be attempted. Quasi democracies have potential for trust and truthfulness, and despite lying of all kinds being endemic, myths of truth telling are subscribed to by enough of the people enough of the time for most interpersonal, intergroup, and person-organization interactions to occur with default values of truthfulness and cooperation. Everyday activities are not pursued in an ambience of chronic distrust. Most of the products people buy are what they claim to be and do what they are claimed to do. They are bought at defined prices and shops give the right change. The exceptions are what give rise to comment and their incidence should not be overestimated. Maintenance and service prices likewise, although there may be more predators exploiting and lying in these occupations. Professional services are an interesting case. The financial services industry in Britain has slumped in public esteem as scandals have emerged. Hidden costs and charges, dishonest advice, and quite misleading accounts of prospective returns have been prominently publicized in recent years. To a much greater extent, the political social order has also come to be seen as untrustworthy in a wide variety of its activities. The media likewise have been seen as misrepresenting reality, but probably an objective analysis of the total array of stories reported would reveal misrepresentation in only a minority. To a puritanical rational realist, the text as a whole makes depressing reading. To any kind of idealist, the gap between what is and what could be better is huge. It is probably irrational to be optimistic that the future will move human beings toward a better world with any momentum. Whether or not there is social progress will depend on the attitudes subsequently adopted toward truth and truthfulness.

Socrates's allegory of the cave (Plato, 1955) remains an awful reminder of the low priority accorded to the pursuit of truth and the subsequent failure to adopt methods of inquiry that would offer the prospect of progress, individual and societal. It is worth noting the differential progress in different fields of knowledge (where *knowledge* is taken to be the best beliefs to hold in the light of the evidence currently available; see Chapter 1). By treating logic as the superordinate inclusive term for all forms of mathematical as well as logics per se, the edifice erected is impressive. Developments are progress. Rationality of derivation is a key principle. Correspondence to empirical reality does not arise as a substantive issue because the

systems are all founded on hypothetical constructs: If . . . , then . . .
Logicians and mathematicians make mistakes, experience failure,
and no doubt some of them have tried to deceive their colleagues
about the validity of their reasoning. Unexposed fraud is particularly
difficult to achieve in what is a public endeavor with no privacy.
There may be occasions for vested interests to be at work in maintaining secrets but none in maintaining false beliefs. Hence, the
tremendous progress!

In dramatic contrast is metaphysics, the questions of transcendental truths about the spiritual world. In fact, every human being is in
a small minority in believing what they believe about the meaning
and purpose of life, and it follows that most hold false beliefs. It has
always struck me as incredible that so many people fail to answer
what seems to me to be the most important questions in life. It has
also struck me as incredible what so many people have managed to
believe about the forces of good and evil. I have little enthusiasm for
Freud's interpretations of religions, but I can see why he felt obliged
to generate deeply ego-defensive stories to cope with the primitive
qualities attributed to divine beings. As argued in Chapter 8, from
very early times, religious beliefs have been used to authenticate and
legitimize differential power and privileges of small elites to the cost
of everyone else. Many faiths continue to do so. The extent to which
some of the religious elites are themselves self-deluded rather than
conscious confidence tricksters will not be revealed by them or their
successors, although the simple test of "by their fruits ye shall know
them" seems to be a useful criterion for a discriminant analysis that
allocates them into categories of sheep and wolves in sheep's cloth-
ing. History and the present world show wolves to be common. A
minimum of progress!

Much the same considerations apply to truths in the biological and
social sciences, including psychology and sociology. Wild hypotheses in each have been used as genetic imperatives to justify the unjust
and the evil doings of people. Forms of the survival of the fittest
doctrine are themselves subjected to unnatural selectivity to justify
the unevaluated dogma that opportunities for individual power,
wealth, and status are for the communal good. The characteristics
selected as basic to human nature by such apologists are those of the
carnivorous predators living either alone or in small groups. The
arguments are phony. Tigers may kill to eat, but they do not kill to

build up power, wealth, and status beyond their needs. They may defend territory but only enough for their needs. They do not rape and pillage. They do not employ large numbers of other tigers to keep themselves in luxury. The entrepreneurship of individual tigers has no benefits for other tigers.

Not surprisingly, power elites have resisted the growth of the human sciences, correctly spotting them as threats to the status quo. They have also learned, however, how the findings can be used by power elites, and for their own advantages they have allowed useful practitioners to be assimilated to the fringes of these elites (Rose, 1990). Again, the truths about the achievement and maintenance of power have themselves been around since the times of Plato. Aristotle was tutor to Alexander the Great. The leaders of the Christian churches have typically read both Plato and Aristotle, but the subsequent influence over themselves and their flocks has been limited. Here, Chapters 6 through 8 greatly underestimate the extent to which the pursuit and dissemination of defensible versions of truths about particular events and fundamental facts have been suppressed, ignored, and otherwise discounted by authorities. Some progress!

In contrast, the massive database of putative knowledge residing in the millions of published works in libraries and realized knowledge manifest in the technological transformation of the physical world testify to the success of the pursuit of truths in the physical sciences, technology, humanities, and arts. Truth has often been ignored in history. Fraud in science has a very long history and some famous perpetrators. More fraud seems to occur when power and wealth are at issue. In scientific as opposed to applied scientific (e.g., medical) frauds, individual enthusiasm for fame can take priority over the truth. With some famous figures, a premature conviction of being right seems to have taken precedence over the hard work of investigation. In the historical international context, however, doing science properly has been the dominant commitment. With the proliferation of science and the linkage of career success to publication, however, fraud and corruption should increase, in line with Etzioni-Halevy's (1989) interpretation. If n publications per annum are needed to secure salaries, then n will become more of an imperative, and the challenges of chasing an imaginative possibility that may take a decade before it can be shown to be mistaken will lose their appeal. (Sacking the idle would be a simpler and less destructive mechanism for quality assurance in nonlitigious societies.) There is a risk that the appearance of research activity will be rendered more important than the reality in the short-term future. Nevertheless, the progress of science and technology is formidable!

Aesthetic appreciation is perhaps the most controversial type of knowledge in which to defend notions of absolute standards. Diversity through time and across societies is enormous. Appreciation itself depends on a knowledge of the frame of reference within which beauty has been created. The creative imagination of the human species has repeatedly extended the possibilities of what can be produced and hence experienced. The absence of simple ideal "forms" does not, however, mean that there is not a multiplicity of possible criteria of evaluation to which human beings can become educated through informed experience. The idea that universality of standards can be tested by showing inconsistency of judgments from instant exposure to the unfamiliar is just a dotty parody of sensible science. Whether there are universal truths remains to be seen. Minimal progress!

Socrates believed that dialectical inquiry would lead to "a vision of the good," and I have no reason to doubt the intelligence of this aspiration provided that it is conducted with appropriate evidence. Perhaps the major block to moral knowledge is the confusion between moral principles, on the one hand, and their application to cases, on the other. As with aesthetics, it may be necessary to invoke the idea of an experienced and informed reflective adult as an assessor, but given that, Kant's (1785/1964) universifiability criterion or Rawls's (1971) present-day variant would quickly eliminate much of the argument about principles expressing the good, the right and the just versus the bad, the wrong, and the unjust. If widely exercised, either Kant's "good will" or Rorty's avoidance of cruelty would begin to transform societies and human relations for the better. In real decision making, however, principles necessarily come into conflict with each other and the best that can be done is to arrive at what is least wrong. Real decisions can be contested as arguments around priorities, but most of the variance in injustice in the world has always been taken up by far more obvious acts of evil. There is no way that the suffering of most of the people most of the time has been attributable to the misdirected goodwill of others. Much more has been perpetrated in the service of the pursuit of power, wealth, and status. Progress in theory—satisfactory! Progress in practice—slow!

Valedictory

Lies are so pernicious because they destroy the commitment to the pursuit of truth and truthfulness and have done so ever since the representational function of language was devised for the communication of true statements. The distraction from efforts to arrive at truths, particularly about human beings and their raison d'être lie at the heart of the continuing tragedy of the human condition. Human beings are responsible for their social constructions and the running of the institutions through which they live. How to organize and maintain justice in communities is problematic. Institutions are no better than the people who run them, and people cannot function efficiently without sensibly structured systems. At the risk of being trite, one might say that the sincere politics of the left put too much faith in institutions, whereas the sincere politics of the right put too much faith in people, both the governed and the governors. It does not require a university degree in logic to see that both sensible systems and virtuous people are necessary. Neither does it require a degree in psychology to see that socialization and education have to be for the whole person: mind and body, intellect, motivation, emotion, and willpower. The promotion of individual virtue in the ancient Greek sense of *arete* requires discipline and training as well as intellectual education. It does not require a degree in sociology to see that individuals need not be in conflict with their communities. The oppressive communist society sacrificing individuals to the community is as vicious as the anarchic libertarian society that encourages individuals to be predators and parasites in the satisfaction of their drives for personal power, wealth, and status.

An international commitment to the pursuit and maintenance of truth and truthfulness in everyday living might provoke a double shift in endeavor. First, it might reduce commitment to seeing the world as a set of continuously competitive conflicts. Second, it might shift concern away from obsessions with individual power and wealth based on the exploitation of technological competence and encourage a greater concern for the construction of societies that were designed to prevent and reduce unnecessary human suffering. To argue, as some authors have, that a truthful society is a form of hell on earth is a sad reflection on the current state of the human condition; it assumes that the human beings of tomorrow will be as unvirtuous and lacking in goodwill as today's generations. What it might be like is not the question. The immediate question is whether it would be better to have more truth and truthfulness than exists today or better to have less. It is difficult to see how more lies and deception could be seen as better, and if that is so, then perhaps the points of departure are several. The first would be personal and necessarily carefully pragmatic: Each individual could try to reduce the quantity and qualities of the lies told to self and others. The second would be interpersonal. Within personal networks, individuals could promote the cause of truth and demote the acceptability of lies within the cultural constraints extant. Although it would be dysfunctional to be so puritanical that this deviance became a reason for being rejected by others and losing influence, in the other direction individuals do not have to subscribe to or accentuate current norms of which they disapprove. At a societal level, individuals do not have to accept the untruthfulness of the authorities in their societies. People do not have to buy their products, vote for them, or watch them. In quasi democracies, the governed decide who will govern them. The watchers of TV and readers of papers decide what they will watch and what they will read. The shopper decides whether or not to buy Snake Oil and Youthskin. It is the sum of individual actions that determines societal outcomes. If the collective will requires more or less truthfulness, it can achieve either.

The Built-in Truth Bias. One of the lessons of chaos theory (Gleick, 1993) is that what is orderly at one level is indeterminate at another. It is also true that complexity can arise out of simplicity and simplicity out of complexity. Apparently very simple outcomes can require great complexity of structure.

The human baby is a complex of billions of cells, themselves complex structures with complex rules of functioning. Bounded by its skin, this immensely complex set of activities and parts matures and learns about the immensely complicated physical and social world in which it is destined to win its life span. It is preprogrammed to organize itself in various ways, and one characteristic echoes what is called a default position in computerspeak; this specifies the action to be taken when no particular choice has been registered among the array of options.

If one asks what the default positions are about a growing baby's interactions with the world, then the following hypotheses could be entertained.

1. Initially, perception through sensation is treated as direct and veridical. In brief, there is no distinction between perception and sensation; schemas for "interpretation" and action treat the world at face value.
2. Experiences will provide opportunities for learning that the initial working hypothesis can be false. Outside the child, appearances are cues to reality but are not reality itself. Things are not always what they appear to be. The same will be true for events inside the child. The child comes to learn that dreams are not real experiences and fevers can induce visions.
3. The child will develop a set of rules for working out when and why reality may be different from appearance. The default position that remains, however, is that things are what they seem to be and that appearances are normally valid cues to reality. This will remain throughout life.

This appearance-reality distinction applies to all the targets of human belief and action, and the developing child needs to learn both what the general rules about discrepancies between the two are and how to apply them to particular instances. In dealing with other human beings, the initial working hypothesis will be equivalent to trust. Caretakers take care of babies. Again, a hypothesis of the invariant trustworthiness of caretakers will require modification in the light of discrepant outcomes.

The same considerations will apply to speech in communication: Statements will be taken to be true and to mean what they appear to mean. This is what is meant by a truth bias. Any other default position would be absurd. Grice (1975/1989) has set down some useful simple maxims and supermaxims for cooperative communication. These will be learned more or less well, possibly along the lines of the three-phase model described in Chapter 3. As was seen in that chapter, young children have to come to realize that there are contrasts with the true. The true-false contrast has to be learned. There is the further distinction between unintended and intended false statements. One working hypothesis would be that it is the emergence of a succession of binary contrasts proceeding through the three-phase model that constitutes the development of categories for use in thinking and communication but with the conservative truth bias retained as a default position.

Such an account would focus on a faith in realism, trust in others, and a commitment to truth as three core components of human development. For the story being told here, rationality has to be added. The validity of the rules of inference in logic seem to be an inevitable default position; the reflective human mind with the time, power, and will to analyze arguments does so in terms of the logics developed by logicans and mathematics. That Johnson-Laird (1983) and Garnham and Oakhill (1995) show that in real time shortcuts are taken and "satisficing" solutions accepted (Simon, 1978) is true, but these findings and interpretations can best be described in terms of deviations from comprehensive logical analyses. The consequent errors made are interpreted in terms of the more comprehensive frameworks.

The quartet of an information processing system that has default positions of rationality, realism, trust, and truth bias would seem to be an ideal design specification for cooperative individuals living in communities. Insofar as other individuals use lies, abuse trust, create false worlds, and use irrational arguments, however, the ideal becomes a recipe for exploitation for those who subscribe to it. Unless wariness is developed, the truth addict is doomed. Wariness is no more than the impetus to ask a series of questions about the status of communications from other people. For example, if the speaker's advice is followed, who will be injured and who will gain? If the speaker and his or her in-groups appear to be gaining is it in the interests of more or less social justice? The Ekman (1985/1992) questions in Chapter 4 indicate some of the conditions under which people will lie, and answers to these should provide information for the wary.

Sadly, increasing maturity would seem to mean an increasing wariness about the intentions of others. In an individualistic competitive society where winning more of what is valued becomes a high priority and where what is valued most are power, wealth, and status, the situations described in Chapters 6 through 10 are intermediate ones that could move toward greater cooperativeness or greater competition. If they move toward greater competition, then there will be more predators and parasites preying on and using others to their own ends. Life for the majority will become more Hobbesian in that it will be nastier and more brutal (Hobbes, 1651/1914). If it moves toward greater cooperativeness, then rationality, realism, trust, and truth will rise in priority, and survival will be more likely to be based on these foundations rather than the capacity for attacking others and defending oneself. It is a question of whether human beings decide to allow the current kind of competition to continue to yield a pyramidal distribution so that, at the peak of power, wealth, and status, small elites of each society arrange for their privileges to be maintained against the poverty of the base. One alternative would be to focus on achieving a better than a struggle for survival existence for much greater numbers by eroding the lies and deception that regulate and justify the current inequalities. To move toward the latter would require a profound shift in aims for societies.

References

Adelsward, V., Aronsson, K., Jönsson, L., & Linell, P. (1987). The unequal distribution of interactional space. *Text, 7,* 313-346.

Adorno, T. W., Frenkel-Brunswik, E., Levinson, S. J., & Sanford, R. N. (1950). *The authoritarian personality.* New York: Harper & Row.

American Bar Association. (1983). *Model rules of professional conduct.* New York: Author.

American Psychological Association. (1981). *Ethical principles of psychologists.* Washington, DC: Author.

American Society for Public Administration. (1982). *Workbook and study guide for public administrators.* Washington, DC: Author.

Anonymous. (1923). *The gentle art of exploiting gullibility.* London: D. Weir.

Ardrey, R. (1969). *The territorial imperative.* London: Fontana.

Argyle, M., & Henderson, M. (1985). *The anatomy of relationships.* Hamondsworth, UK: Pelican.

Aristotle. (1926). *The art of rhetoric.* London: Loeb Classical Library.

Austin, J. L. (1962). *How to do things with words.* Oxford, UK: Oxford University Press.

Axelrod, R. (1984). *The evolution of cooperation.* New York: Basic Books.

Ayer, F. J. (1936). *Language, truth and logic.* London: Gollanz.

Barnes, J. A. (1994). *A pack of lies.* Cambridge, UK: Cambridge University Press.

Barthes, R. (1968). *Elements of semiology.* London: Cape.

Barthes, R. (1977). *Image-music-text.* London: Fontana.

Baumeister, R. F. (1993). Lying to yourself. In M. Lewis & C. Saarni (Eds.), *Lying and deception in everyday life* (pp. 166-183). New York: Guilford.

Bavelas, J. B., Black, A., Chovill, N., & Mullet, J. (1990). *Equivocal communication.* Newbury Park, CA: Sage.

Berger, P., & Luckmann, T. (1967). *The social construction of reality.* Harmondsworth, UK: Penguin.

Berlin, B., & Kay, T. (1969). *Universality and the evolution of basic color terms.* Los Angeles: University of California Press.

Billig, M. (1987). *Arguing and thinking. A rhetorical approach to social psychology.* Cambridge, UK: Cambridge University Press.

Bok, S. (1978). *Lying.* Sussex, UK: Harvester.

Bok, S. (1984). *Secrets.* Oxford, UK: Oxford University Press.

Bourdieu, P. (1977). *Distinctions.* London: Routledge.

Bourdieu, P. (1990). *Reproduction in education, society and culture.* London: Sage.

Bower, T. (1991). *Maxwell: The outsider* (Rev. ed.). London: Mandarin.

Bradac, J., Friedman, E., & Giles, H. (1986). A social approach to propositional communication: Speakers lie to hearers. In G. McGregor (Ed.), *Language for hearers* (pp. 27-151). Oxford, UK: Pergamon.

Brandt, D. R., Miller, G. R., & Hocking, J. E. (1980). The truth-deception attribution. *Human Communication Research, 6,* 99-110.

Broad, W., & Wade, N. (1982). *Betrayers of the truth.* New York: Simon & Schuster.

Brown, P., & Levinson, S. (1987). *Universals in language usage: Politeness phenomena.* Cambridge, UK: Cambridge University Press.

Brown, R. (1965). *Social psychology.* Glencoe, IL: Free Press.

Bruner, J. S. (1966). On cognitive growth. In J. S. Bruner, R. Olver, & P. M. Greenfield (Eds.), *Studies in cognitive growth* (pp. 1-67). New York: John Wiley.

Bruner, J. S. (1983). *Child's talk.* New York: Norton.

Bull, P. (1994). On identifying questions, replies and non-replies in political interviews. *Journal of Language and Social Psychology, 13,* 91-114.

Buller, D. B., & Burgoon, J. K. (in press). Interpersonal deception theory. *Communication Theory.*

Burgoon, J. K. (1994). Nonverbal signals. In M. L. Knapp & G. R. Miller (Eds.), *Handbook of interpersonal communication* (pp. 229-285). Thousand Oaks, CA: Sage.

Burgoon, M., Callister, M., & Hunsaker, F. G. (1994). Patients who deceive. *Journal of Language and Social Psychology, 13,* 443-468.

Burgoon, M., & Miller, G. R. (1985). An expectancy interpretation of language and persuasion. In H. Giles & R. St. Clair (Eds.), *Recent advances in language, communication and social psychology* (pp. 199-229). London: Lawrence Erlbaum.

Burton, R. A., & Stricharz, A. F. (1992). Liar, liar, pants afire! In S. J. Ceci, D. Simone, & M. E. Putnick (Eds.), *Cognitive and social factors in early deception* (pp. 11-28). New York: Lawrence Erlbaum.

Bussey, K. (1992). Lying and truthfulness. Children's definitions, standards, and evaluative reactions. *Child Development, 63,* 129-137.

Callahan, J. (Ed.). (1988). *Ethical issues in professional life.* New York: Oxford University Press.

Camden, C., Mothey, M. T., & Wilson, A. (1984). White lies in interpersonal communication. *Western Journal of Speech Communication, 48,* 309-325.

Carroll, D. (1988). How accurate is polygraph lie detection? In A. Gale (Ed.), *The polygraph test* (pp. 19-28). London: British Psychological Society.

Chandler, M. (1988). Doubt and developing theories of mind. In J. W. Astington, P. L. Harris, & D. R. Olson (Eds.), *Developing theories of mind* (pp. 387-413). Cambridge, UK: Cambridge University Press.

Chandler, M., Fritz, A. S., & Hala, S. (1989). Small scale deceit: Description as a marker of two-, three-, and four-year-olds' early theories of mind. *Child Development, 60,* 1263-1277.

Chomsky, N. (1965). *Aspects of a theory of syntax.* Cambridge: MIT Press.

Christie, R., & Geis, F. L. (1970). *Studies in Machiavellianism.* New York: Academic Press.

Cialdini, R. B. (1985). *Influence: Science and practice.* Glenview, IL: Scott, Foresman.

Cicero (1971). *De Oratore: On the good life.* Harmondsworth, UK: Penguin Classics.

Clements, W., & Perner, J. (1993). *Implicit understanding of belief.* Unpublished manuscript. University of Sussex, UK.

Cody, M. J., & O'Hair, H. D. (1983). Non-verbal communication and deception. *Communication Monographs, 50,* 175-192.

Coleman, L., & Kay, P. (1981). Prototype semantics: The English word *lie. Language,* 57, 26-44.

Cook-Gumperz, J. (1973). *Social control and socialization.* London: Routledge.

Crossen, C. (1994). *The tainted truth.* New York: Simon & Schuster.

Danet, B. (1990). Language and law. In H. Giles & W. P. Robinson (Eds.), *Handbook of language and social psychology* (pp. 537-560). Chichester, UK: Wiley.

Dart, R., & Craig, D. (1959). *Adventures with the missing link.* New York: Harper.

Darwin, C. R. (1859). *On the origin of species by means of natural selection.* London: Murray.

Davidson, D. (1984). *Inquiries into truth and interpretation.* Oxford, UK: Oxford University Press.

Davidson, D. (1986). A coherence theory of truth and knowledge. In E. Le Pore (Ed.), *Truth and interpretation.* Oxford, UK: Blackwell.

Dawkins, R. (1976). *The selfish gene.* Oxford, UK: Oxford University Press.

Dennett, D. C. (1978). *Brainstorms: Philosophical essays on mind and psychology.* Hassocks, UK: Harvester.

DePaulo, B. M. (1992). Non-verbal behavior and self-presentation. *Psychological Bulletin, 3,* 203-243.

DePaulo, B. M., & Kirkendol, S. E. (1989). The motivational impairment effect in the communication of deception. In J. Yulle (Ed.), *Credibility assessment* (pp. 51-70). Deurne, Belgium: Kluwer.

DePaulo, P. J. (1988). Research on deception in marketing communications: Its relevance to the study of non-verbal behavior. *Journal of Non-Verbal Behavior, 12,* 253-273.

DePaulo, P. J., & DePaulo, B. M. (1989). Can deception by salespersons and customers be detected through non-verbal behavioral cues? *Journal of Applied Social Psychology, 19,* 1552-1577.

Derrida, J. (1984). *Margins of philosophy.* Chicago: Chicago University Press.

De Waal, F. (1986). Deception in the natural communication of chimpanzees. In R. W. Mitchell & N. S. Thompson (Eds.), *Deception: Perspectives on human and non-human deceit* (pp. 221-242). New York: State University of New York Press.

Dionne, E. J. (1991). *Why Americans hate politics.* New York: Simon & Schuster.

Dituri, J. (1977). Ten year olds' moral judgments of similar peer and adult behavior. *Graduate Research in Education and Related Disciplines, 9,* 5-21.

Donaldson, M. (1978). *Children's minds.* Glasgow, Scotland: Fontana.

Dunn, J. (1988). *The beginnings of social understanding.* Oxford, UK: Blackwell.

Dunn, J. (1991). Understanding others: Evidence from naturalistic studies of children. In A. Whiten (Ed.), *Natural theories of mind* (pp. 51-62). Oxford, UK: Blackwell.

Durkheim, E. (1974). Individual and collective representations. In Durkheim, E. (Ed.), *Sociology and philosophy.* New York: Free Press. (Original work published 1898)

Edwards, A. L. (1957). *The social desirability variable in personality assessment and research.* New York: Dryden.

Ekman, P. (1992). *Telling lies.* New York: Norton. (Original work published 1985)

Ekman, P., & Friesen, W. V. (1975). *Unmasking the face.* Englewood Cliffs, NJ: Prentice Hall.

Etzioni-Halevy, E. (1989). *Fragile democracy*. New Brunswick, NJ: Transaction Publishing.

Exline, R. V., Thibaut, H., Hickey, C. B., & Gumpert, P. (1970). Visual interaction in relation to Machiavellianism and an unethical act. In R. Christie & F. I. Geis (Eds.), *Studies in Machiavellianism*. New York: Academic Press.

Eysenck, H. J., & Eysenck, S. B. G. (1964). *The manual of the Eysenck personality inventory*. London: University of London Press.

Fay, P. J., & Middleton, W. C. (1941). The ability to judge truth-telling, or lying, from the voice as transmitted over a public address system. *Journal of General Psychology, 24*, 211-215.

Fenson, L., & Schnell, R. E. (1986). The origins of exploratory play. In P. K. Smith (Ed.), *Children's play: Research developments and practical applications*. Oxford, UK: Blackwell.

Fishbein, M., & Ajzen, I. (1975). *Belief, attitude, intention and behavior*. Reading, MA: Addison-Wesley.

Fitzpatrick, M. A. (1990). Models of marital interaction. In H. Giles & W. P. Robinson (Eds.), *Handbook of language and social psychology* (pp. 433-450). Chichester, UK: Wiley.

Flavell, J. H., Botkin, P. T., Fry, C. L., Wright, J. W., & Jarvis, P. E. (1968). *The development of role-taking and communication skills in children*. New York: John Wiley.

Fowler, R. (1991). *Language in the news*. London: Routledge.

Freeman, N. H. (1994). Associations and dissociations in theories of mind. In C. Lewis & P. Mitchell (Eds.), *Children's early understanding of mind* (pp. 95-111). London: Lawrence Erlbaum.

Freeman, N. H., Sinha, C. G., & Condliffe, S. G. (1981). Collaboration and confrontation with young children in language comprehension testing. In W. P. Robinson (Ed.), *Communication in development* (pp. 63-87). London: Academic Press.

French, P. A. (1982). What is Hamlet to McDonnell - Douglas or McDonnell - Douglas to Hamlet: DC10? *Business and Professional Ethics Journal, 1*, 1-13.

Friedman, H. S., & Tucker, J. S. (1990). Language and deception. In H. Giles & W. P. Robinson (Eds.), *Handbook of social psychology and language* (pp. 257-270). Chichester, UK: Wiley.

Gallup Polls. (1993). *Social trends*. London: Gallup.

Galtung, J., & Ruge, M. (1973). Structuring and selecting news. In S. Cohen & J. Young (Eds.), *The manufacture of news* (pp. 52-62). London: Constable.

Garnham, A., & Oakhill, J. (1995). *Thinking and reasoning*. Oxford, UK: Blackwell.

Geis, F. L., & Christie, R. (1970). Overview of experimental research. In R. Christie & F. L. Geis (Eds.), *Studies in Machiavellianism*. New York: Academic Press.

Gigerenzer, G. (1991). How to make cognitive illusions disappear. *European Review of Social Psychology, 2*, 83-116.

Gilbert, D. T., Krull, D. S., & Malone, P. S. (1990). Unbelieving the unbelievable. *Journal of Personality and Social Psychology, 59*, 601-613.

Glasgow Media Group. (1976). *Bad news*. London: Routledge.

Glasgow Media Group. (1980). *More bad news*. London: Routledge.

Glasgow Media Group. (1982). *Really bad news*. London: Writers and Readers Publishing Cooperative Society.

Glazer, M. (1989). Ten whistleblowers and how they fared. In J. Callahan (Ed.), *Ethical issues in professional life* (pp. 322-331). New York: Oxford University Press.

Glazer, M. P., & Glazer, P. M. (1989). *The whistleblowers*. New York: Basic Books.

Gleick, J. (1993). *Chaos: Making a new science*. London: Abacus.

Goffman, E. (1959). *The presentation of self in everyday life*. New York: Anchor, Doubleday.

Goffman, E. (1969). *Strategic interaction*. Philadelphia: University of Pennsylvania Press.

Greenstein, F. I. (1965). *Children and politics*. New Haven, CT: Yale University Press.

Grice, P. (1989). *Studies in the way of words*. Cambridge, MA: Harvard University Press. (Original work published 1975)

Gudjonsson, G. H. (1988). How to defeat the polygraph tests. In A. Gale (Ed.), *The polygraph test* (pp. 126-136). London: British Psychological Society.

Habermas, J. (1979). *Communication and the evolution of society*. London: Heinemann.

Habermas, J. (1984). *The theory of communicative action* (T. McCarthy, Trans.). Cambridge, MA: Polity.

Haines, J. (1988). *Maxwell*. London: Futura.

Hall, G. S. (1891). Children's lies. *Pedagogical Seminary, 1*, 211-218.

Halliday, M. A. K. (1975). *Learning how to mean*. London: Arnold.

Hample, D. (1980). Purposes and effects of lying. *Southern Speech Communication Journal, 46*, 33-47.

Harris, P. L. (1989). *Children and emotion*. Oxford, UK: Blackwell.

Harris, P. L. (1992). From simulation to folk psychology: The case for development. *Mind and Language, 7*, 120-144.

Hartshorne, M., & May, M. A. (1928). *Studies in the nature of character: Vol. 1. Studies in deceit*. New York: Macmillan.

Hegel, G. W. F. (1956). *The philosophy of history* (J. Sibree, Trans.). London: Constable. (Original work published 1914)

Henry, A. F. (1954). *Suicide and homicide*. Glencoe, IL: Free Press.

Herbold-Wooten, H. (1982). The German tatbestands diagnostik: A historical review of the beginnings of scientific lie detection in Germany. *Polygraph, 11*, 246-257.

Hessing, D. J., Elffers, H., Robben, H. S. J., & Webley, P. (1993). Needy or greedy? The social psychology of individuals who fraudulently claim unemployment benefits. *Journal of Applied Social Psychology, 23*, 226-243.

Hessing, D. J., Elffers, H., & Weigel, R. H. (1988). Exploring the limits of self-reports and reasoned action: An investigation of the psychology of tax evasion behavior. *Journal of Personality and Social Psychology, 54*, 405-413.

Hewstone, M. (1983). *Casual attribution*. Oxford, UK: Blackwell.

Hobbes, T. (1914). *Leviathan*. London: Dent. (Original work published 1651)

Hofstede, G. (1980). *Culture's consequences*. Beverly Hills, CA: Sage.

Hogan, R. (1983). A socio-analytic theory of personality. In M. M. Page (Ed.), *Nebraska symposium on motivation* (Vol. 29, pp. 55-89). Lincoln: University of Nebraska Press.

Honts, C. R., Raskin, D. C., & Kircher, J. C. (1984). Effects of spontaneous countermeasures on the detection of deception. *Psychophysiology, 21*, 585.

Hopper, R., & Bell, R. A. (1984). Broadening the deception construct. *Quarterly Journal of Speech, 70*, 288-302.

Horvath, F. S. (1977). The effect of selected variables on the interpretation of polygraph records. *Journal of Applied Psychology, 62*, 127-136.

Hovland, C. I., Janis, I., & Kelley, H. H. (1953). *Communication and persuasion*. New Haven, CT: Yale University Press.

Hovland, C. I., Lumsdaine, A. A., & Sheffield, F. D. (1949). *Experiments on mass communication*. Princeton, NJ: Princeton University Press.

Huff, D. (1969). *How to lie with statistics*. London: Gollancz.

James, G. (1988). In defense of whistle-blowing. In J. Callahan (Ed.), *Ethical issues in professional life* (pp. 315-322). New York: Oxford University Press.

James, S. (1995). Factors associated with competence to spot errors in graphics. *Proceedings of the Annual Conference, Social Psychology Section, British Psychological Society, 1995*. Leicester, UK: British Psychological Society.

James, W. (1902). *Varieties of religious experience*. London: Longmans.

James, W. (1907). *Pragmatism*. New York: Longmans.

Johnson-Laird, P. (1983). *Mental models*. Cambridge, UK: Cambridge University Press.

Johnson-Laird, P., & Wason, P. (1977). *Thinking*. Cambridge, UK: Cambridge University Press.

Jones, E. E., & Nisbett, R. E. (1972). The actor and the observer. In E. E. Jones, D. Kahnemann, P. Slovic, & A. Tversky (Eds.), *Judgments under uncertainty* (pp. 79-94). Cambridge, UK: Cambridge University Press.

Jones, E. E., & Pitman, T. S. (1982). Toward a general theory of strategic self-presentation. In J. Suls (Ed.), *Psychological perspectives on the self* (pp. 231-262). Hillsdale, NJ: Lawrence Erlbaum.

Kahnemann, D., Slovic, P., & Tversky, A. (Eds.). (1982). *Judgments under uncertainty*. Cambridge, UK: Cambridge University Press.

Kalbfleisch, P. J. (1994). The language of detecting deceit. *Journal of Language and Social Psychology, 13*, 469-496.

Kamin, L. (1974). *The science and politics of IQ*. New York: Lawrence Erlbaum.

Kant, I. (1934). *Critique of pure reason* (J. M. D. Meiklejohn, Trans.). London: Dent. (Original work published 1781)

Kant, I. (1964). *Groundwork of the metaphysic on morals* (H. J. Paton, Trans.). New York: Harper. (Original work published 1785)

Karmiloff-Smith, A. (1992). *Beyond modularity: A developmental perspective on cognitive science*. Cambridge: MIT Press.

Kellerman, K. (1984). The negativity effect and its implications for initial interaction. *Communication Monographs, 51*, 37-55.

Kintz, B. L. (1977). College students attitudes about telling lies. *Bulletin of the Psychonomic Society, 10*, 490-492.

Kircher J. C., & Raskin, D. S. (1988). Human versus computerized evaluations of polygraph data in a laboratory setting. *Journal of Applied Psychology, 73*, 291-302.

Kleinmuntz, B., & Szuko, J. (1984). A field study of the fallibility of polygraphic lie detection. *Nature, 308*, 449-450.

Knapp, M. L., & Comadena, M. E. (1979). Telling it like it isn't. *Human Communication Research, 5*, 270-285.

Knightley, P. (1975). *The first casualty*. New York: Harcourt Brace.

Kohlberg, L. (1969). Stage and sequence: The cognitive developmental approach to socialization. In D. A. Goslin (Ed.), *Handbook of socialization theory* (pp. 347-480). Chicago: Rand-McNally.

Kohlberg, L. (1984). *Essays on moral development* (Vol. 2). New York: Academic Press.

Körner, S. (1955) *Kant*. Harmondsworth, UK: Pelican.

Kraut, R. E. (1978). Verbal and non-verbal cues in the detection of lying. *Journal of Personality and Social Psychology, 36*, 380-391.

Krippendorf, K. (1981). *Content analysis*. Beverly Hills, CA: Sage.

Krout, M. H. (1931). The psychology of children's lies. *Journal of Abnormal and Social Psychology, 26,* 1-27.

Kultgen, J. (1988). *Ethics and professionalism*. Philadelphia: University of Pennsylvania Press.

Labov, W., & Fanshel, D. (1977). *Therapeutic discourse*. New York: Academic Press.

LaPiere, R. T. (1934). Attitudes vs. actions. *Social Forces, 13,* 230-237.

Latané, B., & Darley, J. M. (1970). *The unresponsive bystander: Why doesn't he help?* Englewood Cliffs, NJ: Prentice Hall.

Leekam, S. (1991). Jokes and lies. In A. Whiten (Ed.), *Natural theories of mind* (pp. 159-174). Oxford, UK: Blackwell.

Leonard, E. A. (1920). A parent's study of children's lies. *Pedagogical Seminary, 27,* 105-136.

Levine, T. R., & McCornack, S. A. (1992). Linking love and lies. *Journal of Personal and Social Relationships, 9,* 143-154.

Lewis, C., Freeman, N. H., Hagestadt, C., & Douglas, H. (1992). *Narrative access and production*. Unpublished manuscript, University of Bristol.

Lewis, M., Stanger, C. M., & Sullivan, M. (1989). Deception in three-year-olds. *Developmental Psychology, 25,* 439-443.

Linden, W., Paulhus, D. L., & Dobson, K. S. (1986). Effects of response styles on the report of psychological and somatic distress. *Journal of Consulting and Clinical Psychology, 49,* 773-775.

Lindskold, S., & Walters, P. S. (1983). Categories for acceptability of lies. *Journal of Social Psychology, 120,* 129-136.

Lippard, E. P. (1988). "Ask me no questions, I'll tell you no lies." *Western Journal of Speech Communication, 52,* 91-103.

Lipsett, S. M., & Schneider, W. (1983). *The confidence gap: Business labor and government in the public mind*. New York: Free Press.

Livingston, S., & Lunk, P. (1995). *Talk on television*. London: Routledge.

Lloyd-Morgan, C. (1894). *Habit and instinct*. London: Arnold.

Lockard, J. S., & Paulhus, D. L. (1988). *Self-deception: An adaptive mechanism*. Englewood Cliffs, NJ: Prentice Hall.

Lorenz, K. (1966). *On aggression*. London: Methuen.

Lykken, D. T. (1981). *A tremor in the blood*. New York: McGraw-Hill.

MacDonald-Ross, M. (1977). How numbers are shown—a review on the presentation of quantitative data in texts. *Audio-Visual Communication Review, 25,* 359-409.

Machiavelli, N. (1961). *The prince*. Harmondsworth, UK: Penguin Classics. (Original work published 1514)

Machon, M. (1993). Whistling in the dark. *AUT Bulletin, 194,* 6-7.

Maier, R. A., & Lavrakas, P. J. (1976). Lying behavior and the evaluation of lies. *Perceptual and Motor Skills, 42,* 575-581.

Malinowski, B. K. (1923). The problem of meaning in primitive societies. Republished in C. K. Ogden & I. A. Richards (Eds.), *The meaning of meaning* (10th ed., pp. 296-336). London: Routledge.

Martin, M. (1992). Whistle-blowing: Professionalism, personal life and shared responsibility for safety in engineering. *Business and Professional Ethics Journal, 11,* 21-40.

Marwell, G., & Schmitt, D. R. (1967a). Compliance gaining behavior: A synthesis and model. *Sociological Quarterly, 8,* 317-328.

Marwell, G., & Schmitt, D. R. (1967b). Dimensions of compliance-gaining behavior: An empirical analysis. *Sociometry, 30,* 350-364.

Masek, B. J. (1982). Compliance and medicine. In D. M. Doleys, R. L. Meredith, & A. R. Ciminero (Eds.), *Behavioral medicine: Assessment and treatment strategies.* New York: Plenum.

Maslow, A. M. (1954). *Motivation and personality.* New York: Harper.

McClaughlin, B. B., & Rorty, A. (Eds.). (1988). *Perspectives on self-deception.* Los Angeles: University of California Press.

McCornack, S. A., & Parks, M. R. (1986). Deception detection and relationship development. In M. L. McLaughlin (Ed.), *Communication yearbook* (Vol. 9). Beverly Hills, CA: Sage.

Meadows, S. (1986). *Understanding child development.* London: Hutchinson.

Merton, R. K. (1957). *Social theory and social structure.* Glencoe, IL: Free Press.

Metts, S. (1989). An exploratory investigation of deception in close relationships. *Journal of Social and Personal Relationships, 6,* 159-179.

Miller, G. R., Boster, F., Roloff, M., & Seibold, D. (1987). MBRS rekindled: Some thoughts on compliance gaining strategies in interpersonal settings. In M. E. Roloff & G. R. Miller (Eds.), *Interpersonal processes: New directions in communication research* (pp. 89-116). Newbury Park, CA: Sage.

Miller, G. R., Mongeau, P. A., & Sleight, C. (1986). Fudging with friends and lying to lovers. *Journal of Personal and Social Relationships, 3,* 495-512.

Miller, G. R., & Stiff, J. B. (1993). *Deceptive communication.* Newbury Park, CA: Sage.

Miller, N. E. (1959). Liberalization of basic S-R concepts. In S. Koch (Ed.), *Psychology: A study of science* (Vol. 2). New York: McGraw-Hill.

Mitchell, A. (1994). *Group serving bias with respect to gender in judgments of the likelihood of lying, equivocating and telling the truth.* Unpublished dissertation, University of Bristol.

Mitchell, P., & Lacohée, H. (1991). Children's early understanding of false belief. *Cognition, 29,* 107-127.

Mitchell, R. W. (1986). A framework for discussing deception. In R. W. Mitchell & N. S. Thompson (Eds.), *Deception: Perspectives on human and non-human deceit* (pp. 1-39). New York: State University of New York Press.

Morgan, C. L. (1984). *An introduction to comparative psychology.* London: Walter Scott.

Morse, R. (1991). *Truth and convention in the middle ages.* Cambridge, UK: Cambridge University Press.

Morton, J. (1988). When can lying start? *Issues in Criminological and Legal Psychology, 13,* 35-36.

Moscovici, S. (1976). *Social influence and social change.* London: Academic Press.

Moston, S., & Stephenson, G. M. (1993). The changing face of police interrogation. *Journal of Community and Applied Social Psychology, 3,* 101-115.

Mulkay, M. (1985). *The word and the world: Explorations in the form of sociological analysis.* London: Allen & Unwin.

Mussen, P. H. (Ed.). (1970). *Carmichael's manual of child psychology.* New York: John Wiley.

National Association of Social Workers. (1979). *Code of ethics.* Washington, DC: Author.

National Society of Professional Engineers. (1987). *Code of ethics for engineers.* Washington, DC: Author.

Newson, J., & Newson, E. (1976). *Seven years old in an urban community*. Harmondsworth, UK: Penguin.

Nietzsche, F. (1958). *Thus spake Zarathustra* (A. Tille, Trans.). London: Dent. (Original work published 1886)

Nisbett, R., & Ross, L. (1980). *Human inference: Strategies and shortcomings in social judgment*. Englewood Cliffs, NJ: Prentice Hall.

Norton-Taylor, R. (1995). *Truth is a difficult concept*. Manchester: Guardian Books, 4th Estate.

O'Barr, W. M. (1982). *Linguistic evidence: Language, power and strategy in the courtroom*. New York: Academic Press.

Office of Technology Assessment. (1983). *Scientific validity of polygraph testing*. Washington, DC: Congress of the United States.

O'Hair, H. D., & Cody, M. J. (1993). Deception. In W. R. Cupach & B. H. Spitzberg (Eds.), *The dark side of interpersonal communication* (pp. 181-205). Hillsdale, NJ: Lawrence Erlbaum.

Orwell, G. (1949). *1984*. London: Warburg.

Paine, T. (1969). *The rights of man*. Harmondsworth, UK: Penguin. (Original work published 1791)

Parker, R. A. (1988). Whistle-blowing legislation in the United States: A preliminary appraisal. *Parliamentary Affairs, 4*, 149-159.

Paulhus, D. L. (1991). Measurement and control of response bias. In J. P. Robinson, P. R. Shaver, & L. S. Wrightsman (Eds.), *Measures of personality and social psychological attitudes* (Vol. 1, pp. 17-60). New York: Academic Press.

Peill, E. (1975). *The invention and discovery of reality*. Chichester, UK: Wiley.

Perkin, H. (1989). *The rise of professional society*. London: Routledge.

Perner, J. (1991). *Understanding the representational mind*. Cambridge: MIT Press.

Peskin, J. (1992). Ruse and representations. *Developmental Psychology, 28*, 84-89.

Peterson, C. C., Peterson, J. L., & Seeto, D. (1983). Developmental changes in ideas about lying. *Child Development, 54*, 1529-1535.

Piaget, J. (1932). *The moral judgment of the child*. London: Routledge.

Piaget, J. (1951). *Play, dreams and imitation in childhood* (C. Gattegno & F. M. Hodgson, Trans.). London: Routledge.

Piaget, J. (1970). On Piaget's theory. In F. H. Mussen (Ed.), *Carmichael's manual of child psychology* (4th ed., Vol. 1, pp. 703-732). New York: John Wiley.

Piliavin, I. M., Rodin, J., & Piliavin, J. (1969). Good Samaritan: An underground phenomenon. *Journal of Personality and Social Psychology, 13*, 289-299.

Plato. (1955). *The republic* (H. D. P. Lee, Trans.). Harmondsworth, UK: Penguin Classics.

Plato. (1971). *Gorgias*. Harmondsworth, UK: Penguin Classics.

Plutchik, R. (1980). A general psychoevolutionary theory of emotion. In R. Plutchik & H. Kellerman (Eds.), *Emotion theory, research and experience* (Vol. 1, pp. 3-33). New York: Academic Press.

Popper, K. R. (1966). *The open society and its enemies* (Vols. 1 & 2). London: Routledge.

Popper, K. R. (1972). *Objective knowledge*. Oxford, UK: Oxford University Press.

Popper, K. R. (1976). *Unended quest: An intellectual biography*. Glasgow, Scotland: Fontana/Collins.

Potter, J., & Wetherell, M. (1987). *Discourse and social psychology*. London: Sage.

Rabinow, P. (Ed.). (1984). *The Foucault reader*. New York: Pantheon.

Raskin, D. C. (1979). Orienting and defensive reflexes in the detection of deception. In H. D. Kimmel, E. H. van Olst, & J. F. Orlebeke (Eds.), *The orienting reflex in humans* (pp. 587-605). Hillsdale, NJ: Lawrence Erlbaum.

Raskin, D. C. (1988). Does science support polygraph testing? In A. Gale (Ed.), *The polygraph test* (pp. 96-110). London: British Psychological Society.

Rawls, J. (1971). *A theory of justice.* Cambridge, MA: Harvard University Press.

Reason, J. (1990). *Human error.* Cambridge, UK: Cambridge University Press.

Reddy, V. (1991). Playing with others' expectations. In A. Whiten (Ed.), *Natural theories of mind* (pp. 143-158). Oxford, UK: Blackwell.

Riggio, R. E. (1993). Social interaction skills and non-verbal behavior. In R. S. Feldman (Ed.), *Applications of nonverbal behavioral theories and research* (pp. 3-30). Hillsdale, NJ: Lawrence Erlbaum.

Robinson, E. J., & Robinson, W. P. (1981). Ways of reacting to communication failure in relation to the development of the child's understanding about verbal communication. *European Journal of Social Psychology, 11,* 189-208.

Robinson, W. P. (1972). *Language and social behaviour.* Harmondsworth, UK: Penguin.

Robinson, W. P. (Ed.). (1981). *Communication in development.* London: Academic Press.

Robinson, W. P. (1984). The development of communicative competence with language by young children. In H. Tajfel (Ed.), *The social dimension* (pp. 21-50). Cambridge, UK: Cambridge University Press.

Robinson, W. P. (1993). Lying in the public domain. *American Behavioral Scientist, 36,* 359-382.

Robinson, W. P. (1994). Reactions to falsifications in public and interpersonal contexts. *Journal of Language and Social Psychology, 13,* 497-513.

Robinson, W. P., & James, S. (1995). *The measurement of wariness about the truthfulness of claims in the public domain.* Manuscript in preparation.

Rogers, C. R. (1970). *On becoming a person.* Boston: Houghton Mifflin.

Rorty, R. (1989). *Contingency, irony and solidarity.* Cambridge, UK: Cambridge University Press.

Rorty, R. (1991). *Objectivity, relativism, and truth.* Cambridge, UK: Cambridge University Press.

Rosch, E., & Mervis, C. B. (1975). Family resemblances. *Cognitive Psychology, 7,* 573-605.

Rose, N. (1985). *The psychological complex: Psychology politics and society in England, 1869-1939.* London: Routledge.

Rose, N. (1990). *Governing the soul: The shaping of the private self.* London: Routledge.

Rosenthal, R. (1966). *Experimenter effects in behavioral research.* New York: Appleton-Century-Crofts.

Rubinstein, W. D. (1981). *Wealth and inequality.* London: Faber.

Ruffman, T., Olson, D. R., Ash, T., & Keenan, T. (1993). The ABCs of deception. *Developmental Psychology, 29*(1), 74-87.

Runciman, W. G. (1966). *Relative deprivation and social justice.* London: Routledge.

Russell, J., Jarrold, C., & Potel, D. (1994). What makes strategic deception difficult for children—The deception or the strategy? *British Journal of Developmental Psychology, 12,* 301-314.

Russell, J., Mauthner, N., Sharpe, S., & Tidswell, T. (1991). The "windows task" as a measure of strategic deception in preschoolers and autistic subjects. *British Journal of Developmental Psychology, 9,* 331-349.

Russow, L. (1986). Deception: A philosophical perspective. In R. W. Mitchell & N. S. Thompson (Eds.), *Deception: Perspectives on human and non-human deceit* (pp. 41-49). New York: State University of New York Press.

Ryle, G. (1949). *The concept of mind.* London: Hutchinson.

Sapir, E. (1921). *Language.* New York: Harcourt Brace.

Saussure, F. de (1959). *Course in general linguistics* (W. Baskin, Trans.). New York: Philosophical Library. (Original work published 1925)

Saxe, L. Dougherty, D., & Cross, T. (1985). The validity of polygraph testing. *American Psychologist, 40,* 355-366.

Schlenker, B. R. (1980). *Impression management: The self-concept, social identity, and interpersonal relations.* Monterey, CA: Brooks/Cole.

Schneider, D. J. (1981). Tactical self-presentations: Toward a broader conception. In J. T. Tedeschi (Ed.), *Impression management* (pp. 23-40). New York: Academic Press.

Schwarz, C., Davidson, G., Seaton, A., & Tebbit, V. (Eds.). (1988). *Chambers English dictionary* (7th ed.). Edinburgh: W&R Chambers.

Selman, R. L. (1980). *The growth of interpersonal understanding.* New York: Academic Press.

Shepherd, A. (1995). *Truth-telling and deception in doctor-patient communication.* Unpublished dissertation, University of Bristol.

Sherif, M. (1966). *In common predicament: Social psychology of intergroup conflict and cooperation.* Boston: Houghton Mifflin.

Sherif, M., & Hovland, C. I. (1961). *Social judgment: Assimilation and contrast effects in communication and attitude change.* New Haven, CT: Yale University Press.

Simon, H. A. (1978). Rationality as a process and product of thought. *American Economic Review, 68,* 1-16.

Smith, P. K., & Cowie, H. (1991). *Understanding children's development* (2nd ed.). Oxford, UK: Blackwell.

Snyder, M. (1987). *Public appearances/private realities: The psychology of self-monitoring.* San Francisco: Freeman.

Sodian, B. (1991). The development of deception in young children. *British Journal of Developmental Psychology, 9,* 173-188.

Sodian, B., & Frith, U. (1992). Deception and sabotage in autistic, retarded and normal children. *Journal of Child Psychology and Psychiatry, 33,* 591-605.

Solomon, R. C. (1994). What a tangled web. In M. Lewis & C. Saarni (Eds.), *Lying and deception in everyday life* (pp. 30-58). New York: Guilford.

Spinoza. (1982). *The ethics and selected letters* (S. Shirley, Trans.). Indianapolis, IN: Hackett. (Original work published 1677)

Steller, M., & Koehnken, G. (1989). Criteria-based statement analysis. In D. C. Raskin (Ed.), *Psychological methods in criminal investigation and evidence* (pp. 217-245). New York: Springer.

Steller, M., Raskin, D. C., Esplin, P. W., & Boychuk, T. (1989). *Child sexual abuse: Forensic interviews and assessments.* Unpublished manuscript.

Stern, C., & Stern, W. (1909). *Errinerung, aussage, und luge in der erst kindheit [Remembering, statements, and lies in first childhood].* Lepizig: Barth.

Stich, S. P. (1990). *The fragmentation of reason.* Cambridge: MIT Press.

Stiff, J. B., & Miller, G. R. (1986). Come to think of it . . . *Human Communication Research, 12,* 339-357.

Sullivan, K., Winner, E., & Hopfield, N. (1995). How children tell a lie from a joke: The role of second-order mental state attributions. *British Journal of Developmental Psychology, 13,* 191-204.

Sutherland, S. (1992). *Irrationality.* London: Penguin.

Swanberg, W. A. (1961). *Citizen Hearst.* New York: Scribner.

Tajfel, H. (1981). *Human groups and social categories.* Cambridge, UK: Cambridge University Press.

Tajfel, H., & Turner, J. W. (1979). An integrative theory of intergroup conflict. In W. G. Austin & S. Worchel (Eds.), *The social psychology of intergroup relations* (pp. 33-46). Monterey, CA: Brooks/Cole.

Tate, C. S., Warren, A. R., & Hess, T. M. (1992). Adult liability for children's "lie-ability." In S. J. Ceci, M. D. Leichtman, & M. E. Putnick (Eds.), *Cognitive and social factors in early deception.* Hillsdale, NJ: Lawrence Erlbaum.

Taylor, S. E. (1989). *Positive illusions: Creative self-delusion and the healthy mind.* New York: Basic Books.

Taylor, S. E., & Brown, J. D. (1988). Illusion and well-being: A social psychological perspective on mental health. *Psychological Bulletin, 103,* 193-210.

Thibaut, J. W., & Kelley, H. H. (1959). *The social psychology of groups.* New York: John Wiley.

Thouless, R. H. (1974). *Straight and crooked thinking* (Rev. ed.). London: Pan.

Thucydides. (1971) *The history of the Peloponnesian war.* Harmondsworth, UK: Penguin.

Tomkins, S. S. (1982). *Affect, imagery and consciousness.* New York: Springer.

Torris, D., & DePaulo, B. M. (1984). Effects of actual deceptions and suspiciousness of deception on interpersonal perceptions. *Journal of Personality and Social Psychology, 47,* 1063-1073.

Tracy, K. (1991). The many faces of facework. In H. Giles & W. P. Robinson (Eds.), *Handbook of social psychology and language* (pp. 191-208). Chichester, UK: Wiley.

Tunstall, J. (1983). *The media in Britain.* London: Constable.

Turner, J. C., Hogg, M. A., Oakes, P. J., Reicher, S. D., & Wetherell, M. (1987). *Rediscovering the social group.* Oxford, UK: Blackwell.

Turner, R. E., Edgley, C., & Olmstead, G. (1975). Information control in conversations. *Kansas Journal of Sociology, 11,* 69-89.

van Dijk, T. (1991). *Racism and the press.* London: Routledge.

Veblen, T. (1925). *Theory of the leisure class: An economic study of institution.* London: Allen & Unwin. (Original work published 1912)

Velasquez, M. (1981). *Business ethics.* Englewood Cliffs, NJ: Prentice Hall.

Vygotsky, L. S. (1961). *Thought and language.* New York: John Wiley.

Vygotsky, L. S. (1978). *Mind in society: The development of higher psychological processes.* Cambridge, MA: Harvard University Press.

Weaver, P. H. (1994). *News and the culture of lying.* New York: Free Press.

Weiner, B. (1985). An attributional theory of achievement, motivation and emotion. *Psychological Review, 92,* 548-573.

Weir, R. (1962). *Language in the crib.* The Hague, The Netherlands: Mouton.

Whorf, B. L. (1956). *Language, thought and reality: Selected papers* (J. B. Carroll, Ed.). New York: John Wiley.

Wimmer, H., Gruber, S., & Perner, J. (1984). Young children's conceptions of lying. *Developmental Psychology, 21,* 993-995.

Wimmer, H., & Perner, J. (1983). Beliefs about beliefs: Representation and constraining function of wrong beliefs in young children's understanding of deception. *Cognition, 13*, 103-128.

Winters, K. C., & Neale, J. M. (1985). Mania and low self-esteem. *Journal of Abnormal Psychology, 94*, 282-290.

Wittgenstein, L. (1967). *Philosophical investigations* (2nd ed., G. E. M. Anscombe, Trans.). Oxford, UK: Blackwell. (Original work published 1951)

Wittgenstein, L. (1974). *Tractatus logico-philosophicus* (D. F. Pears & B. F. McGuinness, Trans.). London: Routledge. (Original work published 1922)

Woolacott, J. (1977). *Messages and meanings.* Milton Keynes, UK: Open University Press.

Wrightsman, L. S. (1991). Interpersonal trust and attitudes towards human nature. In J. P. Robinson, P. R. Shaver, & L. S. Wrightsman (Eds.), *Measures of personality and social psychological attitudes* (Vol. 1, pp. 373-412). New York: Academic Press.

Zagorin, P. (1990). *Ways of lying.* Cambridge, MA: Harvard University Press.

Zipf, G. K. (1949). *Human behavior and the principle of least effort.* Cambridge, MA: Addison-Wesley.

Author Index

Subject Index

About the Author

W. Peter Robinson is currently Professor of Social Pschology at the University of Bristol where he was previously Professor of Education. His interest in communication and language began in the era of national concerns with the development and education of those who were known then as disadvantaged children. His book *Language and Social Behaviour* was the first social psychological text in the field, and Howard Giles and he were responsible for establishing the continuing series of *International Conferences on Language and Social Psychology*. Since then, he has taken a special interest in lying in the public domain: the conditions that affect its incidence, the reasons people lie, and the reactions of others to those lies. In this volume, these issues are presented and discussed alongside the more traditional concerns with lying and its detection in interpersonal contexts.